THE LIES OF
SARAH PALIN

THE LIES OF
SARAH PALIN

The Untold Story
Behind Her Relentless
Quest for Power

Geoffrey Dunn

St. Martin's Press
New York

www.stmartins.com

ISBN 978-0-312-60186-7

First Edition: May 2011

10 9 8 7 6 5 4 3 2 1

Contents

PROLOGUE

A truthful witness does not deceive,
but a false witness pours out lies.
—Proverbs 14:5

Political Fictions: The Lies of Sarah Palin

---

*It's like a really bad Disney movie, you know? . . . It's a really
terrifying possibility. The fact that we've gotten this far—and
we're that close to this being a reality—is crazy.*
—Matt Damon, *interview with the Associated Press*

*Palin's value to those patriarchs is clear: She opposes
just about every issue that women support by a majority or
plurality. . . . She is Phyllis Schlafly, only younger.*
—Gloria Steinem, *Los Angeles Times*

*She lied. But that's what she does. She lies. Over and
over and over and over again. She is a liar.*
—Dan Fagan, *The Alaska Standard*

ON THE AFTERNOON OF FRIDAY, August 29, 2008, Sarah Palin suddenly
appeared on the horizon of American politics like a dazzling comet from
the far nether regions of the universe. Her spectacular alighting had all the
makings of a political fairy tale. Never in the history of U.S. presidential elections had a candidate come from nowhere quite like this. Named as John
McCain's running mate on the Republican national ticket at a carefully scripted
press conference in Dayton, Ohio, Palin captured successive twenty-four-hour

news cycles throughout the weekend and stole any momentum that Barack Obama may have generated in the aftermath of his historic and triumphant acceptance speech only the night before at the Democratic National Convention in Denver. "She's not from these parts, and she's not from Washington," McCain intoned in one of the campaign's great understatements, "but when you get to know her, you're going to be as impressed as I am." That McCain had spent less than a total of two full hours with his newly named running mate went unstated in Dayton, and it was kept, if only momentarily, from the rapidly spinning narrative of the 2008 presidential election.

Ever since her auspicious debut in Dayton, Sarah Louise Heath Palin—a woman of nearly infinite contradictions and a multitude of deceptions—has maintained a unique platform as both a conservative political icon and a powerful symbol of evangelical Christian values in the ever raging culture wars that engulf the United States in general, and the Republican Party in particular. With her fiery, indeed inflammatory, speech at the Republican National Convention in Minneapolis less than a week later, she not only established herself as a permanent, albeit polarizing, fixture in the American political conversation, she stopped cold the Obama machine's propulsion heading into the final two months of the hotly contested battle for the American presidency. Single-handedly, and with a political résumé so thin some argued that you could see through it, the less than half-term governor from Alaska had momentarily reinvigorated the Republican Party—and most importantly, its conservative evangelical base—and had given it a newfound hope and energy for the impending November election.

In an age of instant celebrity, Palin's had spontaneously combusted. Almost simultaneously, the national and, indeed, global media cast her as a "maverick" and "rising star" in American politics. She was the Republican Party's modern-day version of Cinderella. While the current historical memory of the moment contends that Palin was greeted with a harsh welcome, far too much of the incipient attention focused on her style—her folksy speech, her designer eyeglasses, her Tina Fey looks, her penchant for moose stew. She was portrayed as a prototypical, everyday American woman—a *hockey mom*—who had just given birth to a son with Down syndrome. And she was *glamorous*. Television producers and newspaper reporters alike latched on to her widely publicized fashion spread in *Vogue* magazine six months earlier, in which she had been uncritically depicted as the "golden girl of the Republican Party, a hardworking, pro-business politician whose friendly demeanor (that Palin smile!) made her palatable to the typical pickup-driving Alaskan man." Still other accounts centered on her celebrated categorization as "the hottest governor from the coldest state." At a time in which political equations are often calculated by the lowest common denominator, Palin's youthful vigor and girl-next-door sex appeal were viewed as vital complements to the presidential candidacy of the staid and elderly John McCain.

Indeed, the media covering the 2008 American presidential race were slow to the draw. While Palin had, in fact, been a controversial and polarizing figure in Alaska politics for sixteen years, her actual record as an elected official—as a council member and mayor of her hometown, Wasilla; as a failed candidate for lieutenant governor in 2002; as the controversial chair of the Alaska Oil and Gas Conservation Commission; and for twenty months as the contentious and once again polarizing governor of Alaska—went largely overlooked. The media bought into the Palin myth, one that she had carefully constructed and protected over the years, as a folksy, plain-speaking populist who had entered politics to take on the "good ol' boys network." Speaking from along the Glenn Highway that runs through Wasilla in the heart of Alaska's grand Matanuska Valley, MSNBC correspondent Savannah Guthrie reported that "there's no question that she was a popular mayor here and she is a popular governor here"—failing to mention a recall movement that formed against her in Wasilla and an even more freshly launched legislative investigation aimed directly at Palin for abuse of power in her governorship. And while the same media would grow harshly critical of her astonishing and seemingly endless faux pas along the campaign trail (and her family's equally endless private soap opera back in Wasilla), they never sufficiently vetted her on her well-documented and often problematic political career in Alaska, one that caromed recklessly out of control until her astonishing resignation as governor in July of 2009.

In *Political Fictions,* her brilliant analysis of the American polity, Joan Didion pointed out that the principal activity of a modern-day national presidential campaign is the construction of "narratives" both about, and around, the principal candidates and the shaping and reshaping of those narratives throughout the campaign. The primary target of these narratives is not the public at large (what the Greeks called the *demos*), but a narrow group of selected "target" voters (moderates, independents, "undecideds") who determine the outcome of each presidential election in a handful of critical "swing" states. Didion called these narratives "political fictions," being "made up of many such understandings, tacit agreements, small and large, to overlook the observable in the interests of obtaining a dramatic story line." In a fascinating account of the 2008 presidential campaign appearing in *The New York Times Magazine,* published just before Election Day, Robert Draper noted that "the selling of a presidential 'narrative'—the reigning buzz word of this election cycle—has taken on outsize significance in an age in which a rush of visuals and catch words can cripple public images overnight." A national candidate's chief political cachet in the Information Age—and this goes for both parties—is to have a "good story," which is precisely what Barack Obama said about Sarah Palin in the aftermath of her nomination.

Palin and the McCain spinmeisters constructed a narrative about her life as a dutiful mother of five, who gave of her time and energy to better her community in Alaska and cut down on taxes; that as governor of Alaska, she took on the "good ol' boys network" that had dominated the Last Frontier for the past fifty years, holding herself to a higher standard than her predecessors. The reality was and is far more complicated. "What strikes one most vividly about such a campaign," Didion lamented, "is precisely its remoteness from the real life of the country." Perhaps it should not be surprising, then, that more than two years after her entrée into national politics, after several fawning hagiographies written about her and a ghostwritten (and bestselling) personal memoir, much of Palin's political career still remains largely overlooked, along with the early, formulative details of her life in Wasilla.

Palin has added considerably to the myth in her own duplicitous memoir, *Going Rogue,* in which she presents herself as a "common sense conservative" (her latest meme and the one directed at a presidential bid in 2012) and claims the conservative mantle of Ronald Reagan, though when she had the opportunity to craft a speech about the Gipper in the summer of 2009, it was astonishingly apparent that she knew little about his life and even less about his political legacy. "Written" poolside in San Diego during a five-week tape recording session in the summer of 2009 with evangelical author Lynn Vincent, *Going Rogue,* which soared to number one on several bestseller lists immediately after its publication was announced in the fall of 2009 is riddled with lies, fabrications, omissions, misstatements, and distortions. When I spoke in the immediate aftermath of its publication with Steve Schmidt, the widely respected GOP political advisor who headed up the McCain campaign, he characterized Palin's rendition of events as "total fiction." Schmidt's colleague Nicolle Wallace, another widely respected senior advisor in the McCain camp, described *Going Rogue* as a "bizarre fixation" that was "based on fabrications." Even McCain himself was forced to acknowledge certain inaccuracies. He directly refuted Palin's claim that his campaign had charged Palin $50,000 "for legal expenses related to her vetting." McCain also defended his two senior advisers who had received the brunt of Palin's attacks in her memoirs by noting that he had "the highest regard" for Schmidt and Wallace.

Going Rogue is a modern-day Cinderella story, replete with evil stepsisters (read her political opponents), and several princes competing for her favors. Its release in the fall of 2009 unleashed a media frenzy throughout the United States and further solidified her standing as the most divisive and polarizing figure in American politics. Rushed to bookstores without benefit of an index, footnotes, bibliography, cover blurbs, or, apparently, a fact check (one of Palin's greatest gaffes was attributing a quote to basketball legend John Wooden that was actually made by Native American activist John Wooden Legs), *Going Rogue,* with all its inherent failures, nonetheless catapulted Palin once again to center stage in the baffling configuration of American political discourse. She was a central player in the 2010 midterm elections and looms as a significant GOP contender in the 2012 presidential sweepstakes.

Palin's status as the first woman in Republican Party politics to have gained co-billing on a national ticket has figured significantly into her political ascendancy. That she followed immediately on the heels of Hillary Clinton's historic quest for the Democratic Party nomination (one in which she hammered "18 million cracks" into the presidential glass ceiling) was painfully ironic. As Gloria Steinem noted in a widely circulated op-ed piece for the *Los Angeles Times* a few weeks after Palin's nomination in St. Paul, the McCain-Palin ticket carried the banner for a Republican "platform that opposes pretty much everything Clinton's candidacy stood for." The attempt by Palin and her campaign advisers to claim any part of Clinton's mantle was probably the most galling aspect of Palin's candidacy. During her debut speech in Dayton, Palin actually asserted that her election would "shatter the glass ceiling once and for all." Katha Pollitt, of *The Nation,* called such an assertion "ridiculous." The glass ceiling, she argued, is the "invisible barrier of gender prejudice" that prevents qualified women from rising to their level of abilities and accomplishments in the workplace. Palin's single qualification, Pollitt pointed out, was that "John McCain thought she'd lend his sagging campaign a shot of estrogen and some right-wing fairy dust." In the end, Pollitt later asked, "why should women who care about equality vote for a woman who wants to take their rights away?"

Rebecca Traister, who superbly covered Palin on the campaign trail for the Internet magazine *Salon,* described Palin's candidacy as "a grotesque bastardization of everything feminism has stood for." What Palin represents, Traister argued, "is a form of feminine power that is utterly digestible to those who have no intellectual or political use for actual women. It's like some dystopian future . . . feminism without any feminists." That Palin could in some way serve as a "stand in" for Hillary Clinton, Traister argued, was as repulsive as it was hypocritical.

> We began this history-making election with one kind of woman and have ended up being asked to accept her polar opposite. Clinton's brand of femininity is the kind that remains slightly unpalatable in America. It is based on competence, political confidence and an assumption of authority that upends comfortable roles for men and women. It's a kind of power that has nothing to do with the flirtatious or the girly, nothing to do with the traditionally feminine. It is authority that is threatening because it so closely and calmly resembles the kind of power that the rest of the guys on a presidential stage never question their right to wield.

Palin played on her *femininity* not her feminism. She achieved her power and her position, Traister noted, "by doing everything modern women believed they did not have to do: presenting herself as maternal and sexual, sucking up to men, evincing an absolute lack of native ambition, instead emphasizing her luck as the recipient of strong male support and approval."

In a video interview that appeared on the *Salon.com* Web site, Traister, whose book *Big Girls Don't Cry* would chronicle the role of women—and the substantive reconfiguration of feminism—during the 2008 presidential campaign, noted that there was an effort being made by McCain operatives to take the energy surrounding Hillary Clinton's candidacy and have "all of the discussion about sexism and gender bias that it generated, just sort of transfer over automatically to the candidacy of Sarah Palin." While acknowledging that many of the questions being raised about Palin were foundationally sexist in their framing, Traister stopped short of embracing the emerging GOP narrative.

> Carly Fiorina, newly minted Republican spokesperson, released a statement yesterday in which she said, "I am appalled by the Obama campaign's attempt to belittle Governor Sarah Palin's experience. The facts are that Sarah Palin has

made more executive decisions as a mayor and governor than Barack Obama has made in his life." Well, guess what? Questioning Sarah Palin's experience is not a form of sexism. In fact, it's its opposite; it's treating her the same way as you would treat any other candidate for the job of vice president, and potentially for the job of president.

Then there was the celebrated Palin flip-flop on the issue of her own "feminist" identity. In September, Katie Couric of CBS asked Palin a direct question: "Do you consider yourself a feminist?" Palin responded immediately: "I do. A feminist who believes in equal rights." Yet the following month, when NBC's Brian Williams asked Palin if she was a feminist, Palin responded with an irritated tone: "I'm not going to label myself anything, Brian. And I think that's what annoys a lot of Americans, especially in a political campaign, is to start trying to label different parts of America, different backgrounds, different—I'm not going to put a label on myself."

In the end, even conservative Republican feminists were affronted by Palin's candidacy. "Like so many women, I've been pulling for Palin," Kathleen Parker wrote for the *National Review Online,* "wishing her the best, hoping she will perform brilliantly. I've also noticed that I watch her interviews with the held breath of an anxious parent, my finger poised over the mute button in case it gets too painful. Unfortunately, it often does. My cringe reflex is exhausted." Declaring Palin "out of her league," Parker actually went so far to suggest that Palin should resign from the ticket. "Do it for your country," Parker implored.

By then, Palin's intellectual shortcomings had exhausted the cringe reflex for a significant portion of the American people, fully 55 percent of whom felt that she was not fit to serve as president. During her notorious sit-down interview with Couric, she revealed her penchant for mangling the English language and her inability to construct cohesive, meaningful sentences. This mangling of the English language came as no surprise to Palin's constituents in Alaska, where they dubbed Palin's peculiar grammatical constructions as "word salads." Her utter lack of interest in policy issues and world events also was painfully familiar. Andrew Halcro, a moderate Republican who ran as an independent against Palin in the 2006 Alaska gubernatorial race, tells the story of the time that he and Palin sat down together in an Anchorage coffee shop during the campaign. "Andrew, I watch you at these debates with no notes, no papers, and yet when asked questions, you spout off facts, figures, and policies, and I'm amazed," Palin acknowledged. "But then I look out into the audience and I ask myself, 'Does any of this really matter?'"

This was the singular lesson that Palin took from her career as a politician in Alaska—that her charisma and celebrity trumps both substance and experience in the American electoral process. As Sam Tanenhaus noted in a review of *Going Rogue* in *The New Yorker,* Palin represents the erasure of any distinction between the governing and the governed. "Her insistent ordinariness is an expression not of humility but of egotism," Tanenhaus pointed out, "the certitude that simply being herself, in whatever unfinished condition, will always be good enough." Palin herself says that "government experience really doesn't amount to much." Does any of this really matter, indeed?

T HOSE WHO PREDICTED that Palin would flame out following her fifteen minutes of fame as John McCain's running mate in 2008—and there were many who predicted precisely that—simply never understood the depth of her ambition or the power of what she represents to a narrow but fervent swath of the American body politic. Sarah Palin is a product of the New Millennium and a decidedly contemporary phenomenon. I would argue that the likes of Palin could never have emerged as a national political figure prior to the advance of the Internet and the dominance of cable television in the national political dialogue. "As our communication system speeds up," former *New York Times* editor Joseph Lelyveld has noted in *The New York Review of Books,* "news cycles take on characteristics of a tropical storm: swirling centripetal winds, sudden shifts of intensity and direction, a tendency to darken the horizon and blot out memory or awareness of anything else that might be happening." Palin was, and remains, the beneficiary of this postmodern propensity to blot out memory—to not only forget history, but in many ways to deny it. Americans never fully understood the breadth or depth of her political plunder in Alaska.

Only weeks *before* she had been selected by McCain, Palin had been the focal point of a *bipartisan* legislative investigation in Alaska (composed of ten Republicans and four Democrats) for her role in the firing of Alaska's highly regarded commissioner of public safety, Walt Monegan. But by the time of her nomination, that was already old news. And while the so-called Troopergate investigation dogged Palin throughout the remainder of the campaign (and throughout the rest of her aborted governorship), the complex details of those charges never quite managed to coagulate into a dominant narrative during the campaign. When a special prosecutor hired by the Alaska Legislative Council, Steven Branchflower (also a Republican), issued legal findings that "Governor Sarah Palin abused her power by violating Alaska Statute 39.52.110(a) of the Alaska Branch Ethics Act," Palin simply lied and said that she had been "exonerated." Palin's actions in the Troopergate scandal are distorted beyond recognition in *Going Rogue*.

The role of celebrity in contemporary American politics is as troubling as it is pernicious. In California, Arnold Schwarzenegger rode his fame as an actor in action hero movies all the way to the statehouse and made no bones about his presidential ambitions (though he wasn't born in the U.S.), even as California crumbled from his failures as its chief administrator. Jesse "The Body" Ventura, a former professional wrestler, did similarly in Minnesota. In a communications age dominated by imagery, the lines between "politics" and "entertainment" have become increasingly blurred. Both politicians and entertainers have become commodities in the communications marketplace. "Through political campaigning and image management," media critics Philip Drake and Michael Higgins have noted, "the politician—like the celebrity—aims to appeal to a mass audience." During the 2008 presidential election, John McCain's campaign strategists tried to cast Barack Obama's "celebrity" as a negative attribute, comparing him, at least with short-term success, to Paris Hilton and Britney Spears. Less than a month later, however, in a provocative exposé of the McCain campaign written by Robert Draper for *The New York Times,* McCain's take-charge strategist Steve Schmidt was quoted with enthusiasm as saying about Palin, "Arguably, at this stage? She's a bigger celebrity than Obama." Perhaps more than any other political adviser in the world, Schmidt—who managed Schwarzenegger's reelection campaign for governor in 2006—understands the intrinsic value of celebrity in contemporary American democracy. Indeed, Palin's celebrity was, and remains, the one legitimate bona fide on her national political résumé.

That it was all about style and symbol, as opposed to substance and performance, was not lost on the McCain advisers as the vaunted "Straight Talk Express" crashed into a wall during the final days of the 2008 campaign. It also led to no small amount of cynicism. Matt Taibbi, in an article on Palin's ascendancy for *Rolling Stone,* called Palin "all caricature." The single political legacy of her candidacy, he contended, "is that huge chunks of American voters no longer even demand that their candidates actually have policy positions; they simply consume them as media entertainment, rooting for or against them according to the reflective prejudices of their demographic, as they would for reality-show contestants or sitcom characters."

F OR ALL OF HER ANOMALOUS qualities and personality quirks, however, Sarah Palin taps into deep, long-standing strains in American political history. In the 1840s and 1850s, as historian Timothy M. Gay has noted, Millard Fillmore (a vice presidential selection made by General Zachary Taylor as a concession to the reactionary right in the Whig Party) headed up the so-called Know-Nothing movement that caught fire in the United States in the decades preceding the Civil War. Fillmore blamed political and economic turmoil in antebellum America on Catholics, immigrants (particularly those from Ireland), and other undesirable outsiders. His was a vicious cast of nativist xenophobia that eventually destroyed the Whig Party. Sarah Palin, who has induced deep-seated fissures in the modern-day GOP, both nationally and in Alaska, would have felt right at home with the Know-Nothings.

But Palin's brand of political fury reaches into even deeper and more sinister strains in American politics that date back to the hysteria of the Salem Witch Trials of 1692. In a provocative essay entitled "The Paranoid Style in American Politics," first published in the fall of 1964, Pulitzer Prize–winning historian Richard Hofstadter argued that our nation "has served again and again as an arena for uncommonly angry minds." Hofstadter was particularly concerned about assessing "how much political leverage can be got out of the animosities and passions of a small minority." Hofstadter branded it the "paranoid style simply because no other word adequately evokes the qualities of heated exaggeration, suspiciousness and conspiratorial fantasy that I have in mind." In many ways, Hofstadter's prescient essay remarkably anticipated— and foreshadowed—the entrance of Sarah Palin into the American political arena.

Indeed, the paranoid style often rears its ugly head during transformative moments in American history—from the advent of Jeffersonian democracy and the onset of the Civil War, on through to the New Deal presidency of Franklin D. Roosevelt and, a generation later, the election of John F. Kennedy. Enter the transformative candidacy–cum–presidency of Barack Obama, and the paranoid style has once more found fertile soil in the American political landscape. While right-wing radio hosts and cable news commentators like Rush Limbaugh, Sean Hannity, and Glenn Beck give voice to the New Millennium's paranoid impulse, Palin not only personifies the style, she has franchised it. She is the only political figure in the right-wing conservative movement with actual electoral agency and fire. The likes of Newt Gingrich and Mike Huckabee are mere wannabes. They have neither Palin's mojo nor her charisma.

That Palin seems to be profoundly obsessed with Obama only adds to the tenacity of her political paranoia. The paranoid tendency, Hofstadter contended, is "not susceptible to the normal political processes of bargain and compromise." Palin is an absolutist. Hers is a win-lose world of political Manichaeism. Everything is black and white, good and evil. When her attacks on Obama at rallies drew scattered calls of "Kill him!" from her supporters, Sarah Palin said nothing. She did nothing. And she has defended those unfounded attacks to this day.

Sarah Palin caters to the dark underbelly of the American psyche. She preys on fear and racial divisions, as she did on the campaign trail in 2008 when she accused Barack Obama of "pallin' around with terrorists" and not being "a man who sees America like you and I see America." The violent verbal eruptions to Palin's malevolent oratory along the campaign trail in the fall of 2008 startled many who witnessed them. Her silence said passels about both her intent and her integrity.

In these respects, Palin's brand of demagoguery is remarkably reminiscent of another great malcontent in American history, Huey P. Long, the legendary governor of Louisiana during the Great Depression who served as the inspiration for Robert Penn Warren's Pulitzer Prize–winning novel, *All the King's Men*. Judged solely by appearances, Palin and Long couldn't be more disparate. While Palin's carefully crafted look is part of her political brand (she famously wore bright red Naughty Monkey Double Dare pumps on the campaign trail), Long, as the late biographer Marshall Frady observed, was "a dumpy figure, as plain and pudgy as a potato." But if Palin played the swan to Long's ugly duckling, she is every bit his match in respect to both guile and ambition.

Louisiana of the 1920s and 1930s was a political and economic backwater—an oil state—rich in natural resources, much the same as modern-day Alaska. Long positioned himself as an outsider when he first ran for governor, identifying himself as one of the "common folk," just as Palin has done throughout her career. Perhaps most significantly, both positioned themselves as oppositional voices to popularly elected presidents—Long to FDR and Palin to Obama—during times of economic upheaval, and both played to the fear and anger of a body politic wary about the present and uncertain of the future. Those observing Long during his heyday noted that "the people do not merely vote for him, they worship the ground he walks on. He is part of their religion."

The same, of course, could be said of Palin. Her supporters in the Lower 48 embrace her—and her image—with a religious zeal and fervor unparalleled in recent American political discourse.

As the provocative journalist Max Blumenthal has noted in his pathbreaking work, *Republican Gomorrah: Inside the Movement That Shattered the Party,* Palin represents the personification of the extreme right-wing base of today's Republican Party, a base that is "almost exclusively white, overwhelmingly evangelical, fixated on abortion, homosexuality, and abstinence education; resentful and angry; and unable to discuss how and why it had become this way." Blumenthal cites the post-Holocaust work of psychoanalyst Erich Fromm in identifying the political implications of Palin's presence in national politics. In his definitive work, *Escape from Freedom,* written during the midst of the Holocaust, Fromm argued that "the function of an authoritarian ideology and practice can be compared to the function of neurotic symptoms. Such symptoms result from unbearable psychological conditions and at the same time offer [an authoritarian] solution that makes life possible." Perhaps most importantly, Fromm noted that *"the lust for power is not rooted in strength but in weakness."* (Emphasis added.) The modern-day Republican Party, Blumenthal argues, has found its neurotic, authoritarian voice in Palin.

Palin's supporters are vast and rabid. Blumenthal argues that they are united not primarily by shared political views, but by a shared sensibility of crisis, scandal, and private trauma. Citing Eric Hoffer's *The True Believer,* Blumenthal posits that modern-day mass movements attract their followers not because of doctrine but because they provide a refuge from the "anxieties, barrenness and meaninglessness" of modern society. Alaskans call those who support their former governor uncritically either "Palinistas" or "Palinbots"; they have been said to have "drunk the Kool-Aid." Faith in such a cause or individual, Hoffer observed, "is to a considerable extent a substitute for the lost faith in ourselves." It is something akin to a religious conversion. Indeed, Palin's attachment to American evangelical icon Billy Graham and his son Franklin (who provided Palin with a private jet during her book tour last fall) has further blurred the lines between church and state in respect to Palin's political ambitions.

I F SARAH PALIN REFLECTS DARK AND TROUBLING forces in American political history and social movements, she is also a distinct product of Alaska, the so-called Last Frontier. In his devastating profile of Palin for *Vanity Fair* in

August 2009, Todd Purdum noted, "In the same way that Lyndon Johnson could only have come from Texas, or Bill Clinton from Arkansas, Palin and all that she is could only have come from Wasilla." He is absolutely right. Purdum referred to the oft-cited passage by John McPhee from his resplendent 1977 account of the Last Frontier, *Coming into the Country,* that "Alaska is a foreign country significantly populated with Americans. Its languages extend to English. Its nature is its own. Nothing seems so unexpected as the boxes marked 'U.S. Mail.'"

I first discovered the majesty and beauty of Alaska in the summer of 1974, a year before McPhee's initial sojourn, when my father and I embarked upon a fishing expedition through the northwest wilderness of the continent, a nearly six-thousand-mile trek, beginning in northeast Oregon, up through British Columbia and the Yukon Territory, across the U.S.-Canadian border, and then down through Anchorage, all the way to Homer at the tip of the Kenai Peninsula. We then turned around and made our way back through Mount McKinley (now Denali) National Park and Fairbanks. It was a glorious journey, one that made a lifelong impression, culturally and politically. Alaska was booming with oil money then—Anchorage was filthy with it—and the Alaska rivers and streams were teeming with several varieties of salmon, grayling, and trout, making the fishing superb and equally memorable.

If McPhee's oft-cited observation seemed true enough then, it seems somewhat less so today. Contrary to perception, 70 percent of Alaska's 670,000 residents currently live in *urban* areas of the state. Anchorage is now a bustling modern city with a rising (if jagged-tooth) skyline, and the southeast has become a haven for tourists arriving on cruise liners, to the tune of more than a million annually. The Matanuska-Susitna Valley, in which young Sarah Heath was raised and came of age, has been transformed from an agricultural paradise into a sprawling, horrifying mosaic of poorly planned strip malls and suburban tract homes. Fairbanks, the so-called Golden Heart City located in Alaska's interior (young people in Alaska call it "Squarebanks"), has also swelled into a sprawling post-wilderness metropolis of nearly 100,000. Just about every coffeehouse in these urban and quasi-urban enclaves (and there seems to be one on every street corner from Anchorage to Ketchikan) has an Internet connection along with its high-octane caffeine. With the exception of the bush and rural areas (which do indeed remain something of a foreign country), Alaskans are now plugged into the grid and modernity in ways that they were not three and a half decades ago.

That said, Sarah Palin's own claim during her campaign for the vice presidency that "Alaska is a microcosm of America" is patently absurd. As we move into the second decade of the New Millennium, McPhee's less noted observation that "it is sheer foolishness to approach Alaska in terms of the patterned traditions of the Lower Forty-eight" is closer to the mark.

It was in 1867, in the immediate aftermath of the Civil War, that the United States, at the urging of Secretary of State William Seward, executed the purchase of Alaska from the Russian Empire and Czar Alexander II for $7.2 million—then viewed as an exorbitant sum of money for such a remote wilderness, leaving the unpopular transaction to become widely known as "Seward's Folly." For the next seventeen years, Alaska had no laws and no formal government; it was loosely administered by various federal departments, including the U.S. Army and Navy. In 1882, the naval cutter *Corwin* shelled and destroyed a Native Alaskan village called Angoon on Admiralty Island, south of Juneau. The incident led to the establishment of the District of Alaska in 1884 and then the Territory of Alaska in 1912, in which federal law and federally appointed courts ruled the entire region until Alaska became a state in February 1959. There is bitter resentment over federal rule and influence in Alaska to this day. Sarah Palin, even while running for vice president of the United States, derogatorily referred to federal officials as "the Feds."

During the 1890s, the Klondike Gold Rush brought approximately 100,000 would-be prospectors from around the globe to southeast Alaska and the Yukon Territory in neighboring Canada, a history that would be popularized in the fictional works of Jack London, most notably in his wildly successful novels *White Fang* and *The Call of the Wild* and in his collection of stories, *Lost Face,* which included his short masterpiece, "To Build a Fire." In 1925, Charlie Chaplin would tap into the same history for his cinematic masterpiece *The Gold Rush,* the highest-grossing silent film ever produced.

John Muir's seminal work of wilderness writing, *Travels in Alaska,* first published in 1915, chronicled his early explorations through the state and introduced a wider global audience to its vast and nearly unimaginable beauties. Three years later, the celebrated American painter and author Rockwell Kent spent the winter with his son on Fox Island, near Seward, and chronicled the experience in his elegiac *Wilderness: A Journey of Quiet Adventure in Alaska.* Much of the literature about Alaska since then has followed in Muir's and Kent's footsteps by celebrating its wilderness majesty—*A Land Gone Lonesome,* by Dan O'Neill, and *Passage to Juneau,* by Jonathan Raban, are two superb examples—or the impact on its wilderness caused by careless resource extraction. Three of the classics from this latter genre include Joe McGinniss's charming *Going to Extremes,* a rollicking character portrait of the Last Frontier during the heyday of its oil binge in the mid-1970s; Susan Kollin's *Nature's State,* which assayed the *Exxon Valdez* oil spill of 1989 and the various ways in which it threatened "the meanings and values assigned to Alaska in the popular national imagination"; and Stephen Haycox's thoughtful *Frigid Embrace,* which explores the historic intersection of Alaska's oil economy with its wilderness expanse. There is also a growing body of Alaska Native literature, such as William L. Iggiagruk Hensley's *Fifty Miles from Tomorrow* and *Blonde Indian* by Ernestine Hayes, which provide moving glimpses of the peoples and their cultures who have shaped the region for ten thousand years.

In spite of these cinematic and literary traditions, however, and even after fifty years of statehood and Sarah Palin's iconoclastic candidacy for vice president, Alaska still remains something of an unknown quantity to most Americans—distant, remote, and untamed. Far away from the glitzy communications centers of Hollywood and New York City, the Last Frontier has been largely ignored or shamelessly stereotyped by the U.S. information and entertainment industries. During the 1990s, the American television comedy *Northern Exposure* focused on the eccentricities of small-town Alaska, replete with overly drawn caricatures and racial stereotypes. In the last decade, a slew of films "set" in Alaska—most notably Christopher Nolan's *Insomnia,* starring Al Pacino—were actually filmed in British Columbia. Both the book, *Into the Wild,* written by Jon Krakauer, and its cinematic version, directed by Sean Penn, focus on an Outsider, Christopher McCandless, coming into Alaska to find himself and die. This is also the dramatic arc of Werner Herzog's troubling documentary film *Grizzly Man* (2005), the true story of the bizarre Timothy Treadwell, who traveled each summer to Kodiak Island to live among the grizzly bear, only to be devoured by one of them, along with his girlfriend, in the summer of 2003. Alaskans were generally disgusted by these troubled Outsiders who lacked the respect and experience for wilderness necessary to survive in the Alaska backcountry. Add now to that list the political narrative of Sarah Palin—and her own contribution to the genre, including her memoirs *Going Rogue: An American Life* and her "reality" television show, *Sarah Palin's Alaska.*

For better and, often, for worse, Alaska has stayed true to its nickname, the Last Frontier, situating itself intellectually beyond the parameters of the American consciousness—still perceived by most Americans in glaring stereotypes as a vast and foreboding arctic landscape inhabited by polar bears, Eskimos, and quirky misfits. Only a fractional percentage of Americans have ever set foot in Alaska and few know anything about its political landscape or its history.

This isolation, both internal and external, has been the definitive factor in Alaskan politics since it became the forty-ninth state of the union. While virtually half of the state's current population is centered in the greater metropolitan area of Anchorage, the remainder is scattered across some 586,000 square miles (twice the size of Texas) at small remote outposts connected only by rugged airstrips, frozen highways, and slow-moving ferries. That its state capital, Juneau, is accessible only by boat or plane, has further added to the isolationist qualities of Alaskan politics. This internal geopolitical isolation has led to the creation of small, yet concentrated, loci of political power at both the state and local levels, and with it, no small amount of corruption. With oil money running through the veins of the state's otherwise impoverished private sector economy, Alaskan politics have always been susceptible to its influence.

On the afternoon of March 30, 2006, while Sarah Palin was running for governor of Alaska in the Republican primary, Bill Allen, then CEO of the VECO Corporation, a powerful oil industry construction firm based in Anchorage, was videotaped in Juneau's historic Baranof Hotel handing over wads of cash to well-known Republican legislator Vic Kohring. During the course of a six-month investigation, the FBI taped Kohring assuring Allen that he would support VECO's legislative efforts in Alaska and provide the company with helpful information along the way. According to testimony later rendered by Allen, he would usually pay Kohring "six or seven" hundred dollars in cash each time they met.

There would be dozens of other meetings recorded in the Baranof between VECO officials and various legislators, and by the end of the investigation headed up by the Public Integrity Section of the U.S. Department of Justice, more than a dozen Alaska state legislators—including Kohring—and their political aides would be convicted on various graft, bribery, and racketeering charges (although on appeal a new trial was ordered for Kohring). Alaska's senior U.S. senator, Ted Stevens, would also be caught up in the investigation, and he, too, was convicted of seven felony counts for taking gifts from VECO (although his conviction was dismissed because of a U.S. Supreme Court ruling that narrowed the status under which he had been convicted). Jim Clark, who served as chief of staff to former Alaska governor Frank Murkowski, was also convicted of procuring illegal campaign funding from VECO. After more than two years of legal delays, Allen, who cooperated with federal investigators, was eventually sentenced to three years in prison and levied a $750,000 fine.

Many Alaskans (although certainly not *all*) were surprisingly nonplussed about the string of charges and convictions against their elected officials and political associates. Kohring vowed to return to the legislature once he was released from prison. Stevens was barely defeated in a reelection bid in November of 2008, even in the face of his seven felony convictions. When those convictions were overturned in April of 2009, Palin, then still governor, actually agreed with a suggestion by the head of the Alaska Republican Party, Randy Ruedrich (who, ironically, had been the subject of a Palin-led ethics investigation earlier in the decade), that newly elected Democratic senator Mark Begich should "resign" from the Senate. After backtracking on that suggestion (Palin flat-out lied about it afterward), she then supported an unprecedented "special election" for the Senate seat, conveniently forgetting that she had called for Stevens's resignation only six months earlier. No one was buying any of it, and Begich still holds his seat in the Senate. Stevens returned to Alaska, and died in a plane crash in August 2010. In fact, prior to his death, the whole affair became something of a joke throughout the state. Legislators under investigation dubbed themselves the "Corrupt Bastards Club" and had baseball caps made with the letters "CBC" proudly embroidered on them. Few were surprised by the payola; most everyone in Alaska knew what was going on in the capital. What surprised many Alaskans was how seriously "the Feds" were taking things. For several generations, bribery and pay-to-play extortion rackets had become the currency du jour of Alaska's politicians isolated during the dark days of winter and early spring in Juneau.

This corruption extends well beyond the recent convictions of Alaska's legislators. Nearly three years after several requests for government documents during Palin's tenure as governor were made by a host of national news agencies and political activists in Alaska—and nearly two years after Sarah Palin resigned her governorship—the state of Alaska has still stonewalled public access to *hundreds of thousands of pages* of public records. As of late December 2010, the Governor's Office had filed its *fourteenth* extension in responding to these requests. The process has become little more than a political charade.

The state's appointed Personnel Board, the government body charged with processing ethics violations by the executive branch in the state of Alaska (including Palin), remains a farce. While the Alaska Personnel Act requires that "not more than two members of the board may be members of the same political party," this stipulation has been sidestepped by successive Republican governors (including Palin) simply by appointing members who are partisan operatives, even though they are currently registered as "undeclared." Several requests I made to the Alaska Department of Law, the Governor's Office, and the Personnel Board for records related to this book were outright denied, delayed, or significantly redacted. Gregg Erickson, the widely respected founding editor of the *Alaska Budget Report*, who has battled Alaska governors from all parties over access to state documents, described Palin as "the most secretive governor in Alaska's history." Her successor, Sean Parnell, has followed in her footsteps. An open and transparent democracy Alaska is not.

Last summer, when I complained to my attorney in Anchorage, Jeffrey M. Feldman, about the obstructionist machinations of Alaska state government, he made a sagacious observation:

> At the time I first arrived here, in 1975, Alaska had been a state for only sixteen years. As a state, we were still in our infancy and our politics and decision making sometimes reflected the same level of maturity, discipline, focus, and patience that you'd find in a child. Alaska just celebrated its fiftieth year of statehood and, as states go, it's the equivalent of being a teenager.
>
> We're stronger, more self-sufficient, and have learned a lot over the past half-century. But, like most teenagers, we sometimes don't have the accumulated wisdom, perception, and judgment that come with age. I don't think it's a reflection of the people who have chosen to make Alaska their home—I doubt the folks in Massachusetts were doing any better when they hit fifty years of statehood in 1838. It just takes time for the politics, history, and culture of a community to evolve and mature.

Sarah Palin is the political progeny of this adolescent moment in Alaskan politics and of the two dominant components that continue to define it: isolation and corruption. During a span now of nearly two decades—beginning with her first campaign for Wasilla City Council in 1992—Palin's career has been both shaped and defined by these two symbiotic forces. She has run as both an outsider and a crusader, defining and consistently recasting herself in opposition to those she alleges to be politically corrupt. At the same time, she has found herself consistently susceptible to the same forces, changing her political positions in accordance with the wind or money flow. Palin has benefited from the isolation of her public record in Wasilla (no one outside the small community was aware of her controversial tenure) and she has moved up the political ladder to a national platform without ever having to account for the wreckage that defines her career as an elected official.

I N HIS PREVIOUSLY DISCUSSED essay addressing the "paranoid style" in American politics, Richard Hofstadter was careful to distinguish "clinical" paranoia in an individual from "paranoid modes of expression by more or less normal people." In the case of Palin, as those who have witnessed her closely over the years will attest, this distinction becomes blurred. Ever since her political debut nearly two decades ago in Wasilla, she has embraced the paranoid style as not only a form of communication but, even more importantly, as a means to power. The style has not only shaped and defined her entire political career, but both her private and public persona as well.

Perhaps the most controversial aspect of Todd Purdum's *Vanity Fair* portrait of Palin was his contention that "several people" had confided in him their belief that Palin suffered from a "narcissistic personality disorder." Purdum noted they had looked up "the definition of [it] in the *Diagnostic and Statistical Manual of Mental Disorders*—'a pervasive pattern of grandiosity (in fantasy or behavior), need for admiration, and lack of empathy' "—an assertion that several of Palin's most ardent supporters contested in print. Purdum further noted that when her son with Down syndrome, Trig, was born, Palin wrote an e-mail letter to friends and relatives, signing it as though she were God: "Trig's Creator, Your Heavenly Father." No one challenged *that*.

After spending part of the summer of 2009 in southwest Alaska, I can confirm that the vast majority of Alaskans I spoke to (albeit none of them psychologists or psychiatrists)—from across the political spectrum, both men and women—believes that Palin suffers from a "psychological disorder." Indeed I woke up one morning to find an opinion piece in the *Anchorage Daily News* headlined: "Crazy Palin Leaves Stain on Alaska's Oil Industry." The piece, much to my surprise, was written by Dan Fagan, a Palin loyalist and conservative talk show host who had staunchly supported Palin in her run for the governorship and during her first year in office:

> Between the bizarre tweets, the incoherent "good-bye Alaska"
> speech, and the ensuing and constant pleading that quitting

is fighting and fighting is quitting, it has become abundantly clear to anyone with any sense that Sarah Heath Palin has become "Crazy Governor Lady."

Yes, she has lost it and revealed herself as flaky, delusional, dishonest, slightly paranoid, and in way over her head.

Alaska's politics can be rough-and-tumble, a bit like a semipro hockey game, but even in that context, this was a high-stick attack. That same summer, in the aftermath of Palin's resignation from Alaska's governorship, Fagan wrote a piece for *The Alaska Standard*, entitled "Sarah Palin Has Become Mentally Unstable." It was equally harsh. The real question to ask about Palin, Fagan asserted, is: "Has she become so mentally unstable and delusional that Palin now believes if something comes out of her mouth it becomes true?" He described Palin as "an approval seeker on steroids. And it has driven her to lose all sense of reality."

Everyone in Alaska, it seemed, had an opinion about Palin's psychological stability. Not much of it was favorable. Interestingly enough, many of these street-corner psychiatrists were not rendering their observations out of spite or even anger, but often out of concern. They saw Palin's plight as a contemporary Alaskan tragedy. One of her former campaign aides who worked very closely with Palin on her 2006 gubernatorial campaign, Paul Fuhs, an ex-mayor of Dutch Harbor and a longtime political operative in Alaska, told me he thinks that Palin suffers from a persecution complex rooted in her Christian faith:

> She believes she's being persecuted because she is a Christian. And the persecution is affirmation of her faith. So the more she feels persecuted, the more it brings her closer to God. It becomes a circle that feeds itself, and whatever casualties pile up behind her become justified to fulfill God's will. She knows she's doing God's will because of how much she is persecuted for it.

Considerable attention has been paid to Palin's evangelical religious beliefs. Palin was originally baptized as a Catholic, when she was four-months old, at Christ the King Roman Catholic Church, in Richland, Washington, where her mother, Sally Sheeran, was raised in a staunch Irish-Catholic family. The Heath-Sheeran household remained Catholic until the late 1960s and early 1970s, when Palin's mother began her conversion away from Catholicism to the Assembly of God. During the summer of 1976, in the chilly waters of Little Beaver Lake, roughly twenty miles west of Wasilla, Palin, her mother, and her siblings were all rechristened by Pastor Paul Riley of the Assembly of God Church. Howard Bess, a Baptist minister at the Church of the Covenant, located in the Matanuska Valley, contends, "I do not believe that you can understand Sarah Palin apart from her being a devout, Fundamentalist Christian." Bess feels that it's important to comprehend Palin's political worldview as an extension of her Pentecostal faith. "She understands life as an ongoing battle between good and evil," Bess told me. "She believes in this dualism where you identify enemies, you fight the enemy. Her manner of decision-making— this black-and-white dividing line that is so much a part of her personality and belief system—springs from this dualistic Fundamentalism. It is *always* a battle for her between good and evil. She seeks to destroy her enemy, whether it's a foreign government or the Muslim world or Barack Obama."

After spending time in Palin's hometown of Wasilla, one is struck by both the power and pervasiveness of the cult of personality that has sprung up around her. That it has a Christian aura to it goes without saying, but its substance would seem to have little to do with the tenets of Christianity. In a posting on *First Things*, a Web site sponsored by the Institute on Religion and Public Life, a contributor noted that a friend had recently spoken to a member of Palin's family who proclaimed that Palin is "the most important person in the world right now" and that Christians needed to get behind her and pray for her. "It disturbs me that so many people across the country have seemingly swallowed hook, line, and sinker whatever she tells them," he observed. "It feels like her fans are more like disciples."

The Alaskan blogger AKMuckraker (Jeanne Devon), who gained international renown for her work at the blog *The Mudflats* covering Palin both during and after the presidential campaign, agreed that Palin suffered from some form of "mental disorder." Citing "memetics" theory first promulgated by the biologist Richard Dawkins in the 1960s, who argued that cultural and, sometimes, political phenomena are passed from generation to generation through choice words and catchphrases, Muckraker noted that Palin "finds a *meme* that works for her, that she can wrap her mind around, and she never ever lets go. This is why she usually gets what she wants." The instability actually works to Palin's favor.

I wrote a paper in college that examined Alexander the Great through the lens of pathological narcissism. I put Palin in the same category. If she were Queen of Somewhere 500 years ago, she'd be ordering armies and conquering countries for their own good, and mowing them down in the name of her God and her glory.

Narcissists often go far fast, and then burn out in a blaze of self-destructive glory. Nobody will dare tell her that she's off the road and heading for a cliff. If they do, they lose favor or lose their job, and she just plain scares them. Bush was an empty vessel. Sarah is not. She is full of righteous crazy, and that's her fuel.

Even those far removed from the Last Frontier zeroed in on Palin's apparent narcissism. Former Ronald Reagan speechwriter and conservative *Wall Street Journal* columnist Peggy Noonan was struck by Palin's focus at the time of her resignation in the summer of 2009.

[Palin] experienced criticism as both partisan and cruel because she could see no truth in any of it. She wasn't thoughtful enough to know she wasn't thoughtful enough. Her presentation up to the end has been scattered, illogical, manipulative and self-referential to the point of self-reverence. "I'm not wired that way," "I'm not a quitter," "I'm standing up for our values." I'm, I'm, I'm.

While the diagnoses varied, there were a pair of overwhelming consistencies in the traits that people used to describe Palin: first, she is absolutely tenacious. Her high school nickname of "Barracuda" was given not because of her treatment of her *opponents,* but because of how she treated her own *teammates.* Palin thrives on going for the jugular. In a now celebrated e-mail that went viral just after Palin's selection, Anne Kilkenny, a resident of Wasilla who voted for Palin twice in her runs for City Council, mentioned Palin's "predatory ruthlessness."

More recently Kilkenny described Palin as "a dishonest, unprincipled character whose aberrant and erratic behavior is savagely destructive and sows hate." On one occasion during her tenure as governor, Palin went on a radio show with a pair of conservative shock jocks in Anchorage who were belittling Palin's former mentor, the matriarch of Alaska's Republican Party Lyda Green, by calling her a "bitch" and a "cancer." Palin actually giggled throughout their remarks even though she knew full well that Green was a breast cancer survivor. Palin then added ever so sincerely that "we'd be honored" to be visited by the shock jocks in Juneau. "She really has no moral compass," says Green. "She uses people in a very un-Christian way. She only does what is best for Sarah." Perhaps the biggest shock to those living in the Lower 48 is how much Palin is despised by *conservatives* and *Republicans* in Alaska. "I was never called 'Barracuda,'" Green said to me rhetorically. "Were you?"

The second thing those close to Palin will tell you is that she will say anything at any time if it serves her purpose. Recall her claims about the infamous Bridge to Nowhere that she championed during her gubernatorial campaign and then denounced immediately after she was named McCain's running mate. Recall her "going rogue" on the campaign trail with her mean-spirited attacks on Barack Obama, proclaiming him a "socialist." This was nothing new to her. She has refined backtracking and scapegoating into high political art forms. More than a decade ago, in 1997, her hometown newspaper, the *Mat-Su Valley Frontiersman* (a paper at which she once worked as an aspiring journalist) declared that Palin "fails to have a firm grasp of something very simple: *the truth*." One longtime political operative in Alaska, Leslie Ridle, who ran Tony Knowles's campaign for governor against Palin in 2006, put it more succinctly: "Sarah Palin is a pathological liar." This innate duplicity has served her well. It nearly brought her to within a single breath of the American presidency and it has poised her for yet another run at national office.

Contrary to the image she has tried to project as a political reformer, Palin has engaged in a dance with the truth and an ethical expediency throughout her political career. Records filed with the Alaska Public Offices Commission (APOC) reveal that in 2002, during her failed run for lieutenant governor of Alaska, Palin accepted contributions totaling $5,000 from Bill Allen, his VECO associates, and their wives. Moreover, during the weeks leading up to her gubernatorial campaign in September of 2006, Palin was the beneficiary of a $100,000 television advertisement campaign paid for and produced by the Republican Governor's Association (RGA). Such outside advertising campaigns are common, but election law requires that there be no cooperation between the candidate and their campaign with the so-called "527 group" organizing and producing the ads. Throughout the election process, Palin maintained her innocence about knowing anything related to the RGA efforts, particularly about a negative television spot that featured her opponent, Tony Knowles, walking backward in slow motion. The RGA ad, she told Kyle Hopkins of the *Anchorage Daily News,* is "out of character for the Palin camp. It's not something that we would have produced and aired."

Previously unreleased internal e-mail communications from Palin's campaign team, however, suggest that Palin and her campaign advisors were in touch with the RGA as early as August of 2006. On August 28, Palin's friend and campaign worker Ivy Frye sent out an e-mail to Palin's campaign team, including Palin, that she "just got a call from the [RGA] inquiring about who our campaign legal council [sic] is? Hmmm." On September 6, 2006, Palin's campaign manager, Kris Perry, sent out an e-mail to the campaign's inner circle, also including Palin, indicating "it's important that we keep each other in the loop" about RGA activities and further acknowledged that she was "putting together a list of potential businesses/contacts for the RGA for the purpose of fundraising." Earlier that day Perry sent out an e-mail to Palin noting that she had spoken directly to Mitt Romney, then serving as chair of the RGA. Romney announced "that he'd like to speak with you directly and we'll [sic] try to make that happen in the next day or so." She concluded, "they are very interested in the Governor's race and are supportive of your candidacy. They want to support financially and are exploring the most effective means of doing so." Later that afternoon, Kristopher Knauss, who had worked as Frank Murkowski's policy director, e-mailed yet another Palin campaign adviser, Frank Bailey, that "the RGA will be in Anchorage next week and a poll is going into the field in the next 48 hours," and that he wanted to give "you and Sarah a heads-up" about RGA's activities.

Once the television advertisements began to air in late September, Tim Barry, a friend of Frye's and then serving as communications director for the Alaska Department of Fish and Game, sent Frye and Palin an e-mail entitled "RGA," in which he advised that Palin not engage media queries about the ad: "I strongly urge you to respond NOT by having the candidate address the issue. Someone lower down in the campaign should tell reporters that the campaign has asked the RGA to stop running the ads . . . while pointing out that Sarah has no control over them." On October 4, Palin weighed in on the ads herself via e-mail to her campaign team. She auditioned what would be her public response: " 'I would not have mentioned Tony had this been our production. And I would have spun it all more positively.' Whaddya think?" Then she relayed a discussion taking place in the Palin household about the ads: "Bristol and Willow are arguing it now—W [Willow] says it's totally negative and to 'delete it now, Mom!' and B [Bristol] says, 'Hey, it's free publicity.'"

The Alaska Democratic Party filed a complaint with the Alaska Public Offices Commission charging that Palin's campaign "solicited and accepted a prohibited contribution by coordinating with the RGA." The Palin campaign denied the allegations—the e-mail trail of contacts between the Palin campaign and the RGA had not been brought to light. In January 2007, APOC fined the RGA a total of $26,600 in fines for illegal activities during the campaign and warned that the fine could have been levied as high as $6 million. The Palin campaign escaped an APOC citation because there was never any concrete evidence presented of coordination.

Anchorage-based good government activist Andrée McLeod, whose image appeared in one of the RGA ads on behalf of Palin and who would later come to file several ethics complaints against her while governor, says that Palin's pattern of denial is predictable. "She's a liar," says McLeod, who was a close associate of Palin's and supported her in her run for governor. "She lies and lies and lies."

During the 2008 presidential campaign, Palin became irritated with published reports that her husband had been a member of the Alaskan Independence Party (AIP), the platform of which called for the secession of Alaska from the United States. It was an accurate report—he had been a member for seven years and Sarah Palin had actually produced a glowing welcome video for an AIP convention as recently as March of 2008—but she demanded, in an e-mail sent to McCain campaign manager Rick Davis, chief strategist Steve Schmidt, and senior adviser Nicolle Wallace that they:

> Pls get in front of that ridiculous issue that's cropped up all day today—two reporters, a protestor's sign, and many shout-outs all claiming Todd's involvement in an anti-American political party. It's bull, and I don't want to have to keep reacting to it. . . . Pls have statement given on this so it's put to bed.

In fact, it wasn't "bull." Moreover, Palin, according to those close to the campaign, had greatly exaggerated the response she had encountered on the road. Her request came at a time when the campaign was scrambling to prepare McCain for his final debate with Obama at Hofstra University.

Schmidt, ever the disciplinarian, and wanting his entire campaign focused on the debate, responded tersely:

> Ignore it. He was a member of the aip? My understanding is
> yes. That is part of their platform. Do not engage the protes-
> tors. If a reporter asks say it is ridiculous. Todd loves America.

But Palin could not let it go. She never can. Never one to duck a crisis, she expanded the recipient's list to those she felt would be empathetic with her demands.

> That's not part of their platform and he was only a "mem-
> ber" bc independent alaskans too often check that "Alaska
> Independent" box on voter registrations thinking it just
> means non partisan. He caught his error when changing our
> address and checked the right box. I still want it fixed.

It was a bold-faced distortion. Todd Palin's voter registration forms, provided through a Public Records Act request from the State of Alaska Department of Elections, reveal that he didn't register to vote until he was twenty-six years old, in October of 1990. Party registration was listed as "optional" at that time, and he did not check any boxes. Four years later, he re-registered as a Republican. The following year, 1995—*there was no change of address*—he switched to the Alaska Independence Party (the word "independent" is not used). Four years later, he registered again to the AIP, then the following year, in August 2000, switched again to "Undeclared," then only two months later, back to the AIP again, until he switched back to "Undeclared" in July 2002—again with *no change of address*—in time to vote for his wife, then running for lieutenant governor in the Republican primary. In sum, he had registered for the Alaska Independence Party *on three separate occasions*. Schmidt was not amused by Palin's duplicity:

> Secession. It is their entire reason for existence. A cursory
> examination of the web site shows that the party exists for
> the purpose of seceding from the union. That is the stated
> goal on the front page of the web site. Our records indicate
> that todd was a member for seven years. If this is incorrect

then we need to understand the discrepancy. The statement you are suggesting be released would be inaccurate. The inaccuracy would bring greater media attention to this matter and be a distraction. According to your staff there have been no media inquiries into this and you received no questions about it during your interviews. If you are asked about it you should smile and say many alaskans who love their country join the party because it speaks to a tradition of political independence. Todd loves his country.

We will not put out a statement and inflame this and create a situation where john has to address this.

When I had this e-mail exchange read to me by a McCain operative shortly after the election (it was later reported online by the authors of *Sarah from Alaska*, Scott Conroy and Shushannah Walshe), I was startled by how riddled with deceit it was and how openly Palin was willing to lie, even to her *allies* in the McCain campaign in the middle of a *national* election.* She was so used to getting away with it for so long in Alaska that it seemed to be second nature. "It's so easy for her, that it's almost frightening," says her former mentor Lyda Green. "I'm not sure she even realizes she does it anymore."

It is a pathology of deceit.

Perhaps the most illuminating document in the Palin archive, however, does not come from Alaska or even Palin's ill-fated run for vice president. It comes from a small county in the Idaho panhandle. It is the combined marriage license and certificate of her parents, Charles ("Chuck") Heath and Sally Sheeran. The document—which is located in the Bonner County Recorder's Office—discloses that Heath and Sheeran filed for their marriage license on June 30, 1961. They were twenty-three and twenty years old respectively. The couple was married a month later, on Saturday, July 29, at St. Joseph's Catholic Church in Sandpoint, Idaho, by a Roman Catholic priest, Albert Dulberg. Their first child, Charles Jr., was born little more than six months later, on

---

* The e-mail exchange was also published in Scott Conroy and Shushannah Walshes book, *Sarah from Alaska: The Sudden Rise and Brutal Education of a New Conservative Superstar.* New York: PublicAffairs, 2009, pages 166 to 168.

February 7, 1962. Getting married when one is pregnant, of course, is not an uncommon occurrence, but in the conservative Catholic circles of small-town Idaho and eastern Washington in the early 1960s, one can imagine that it might well have created a stigma, one that the young couple might never fully escape. There would always be whispers.

While the story would be told that it was economic opportunity in Alaska that called the Heaths to the Last Frontier, those who know the details of the story suggest that this situation is, in part, what pushed the family to Alaska. Most significant, it created a shroud of secrecy in the nuclear family that would shape them on their journey, first to the small and isolated community of Skagway, in southeast Alaska, and later to Wasilla. Not everyone in the Mat-Su Valley knew the story, of course, but some who are close to the Heaths were aware of it. "Oh sure, I knew," says a longtime Wasilla resident whose own children were classmates of the Heaths. "Sally confided in me. But this was not something that was openly discussed, not even today. There are lots of secrets in the [Mat-Su] Valley."

It was a pattern that would repeat itself in the succeeding generations of the Heath and Palin families in Alaska, incorporating more layers of secrecy and the fabrication of more fables. Many people who were raised in Wasilla during the 1970s and '80s will acknowledge that it was a similar circumstance that led to the marriage of Todd Palin and Sarah Louise Heath in the summer of 1988. "Yes, she did elope and get married because she was pregnant . . . FACT!" one of Sarah Palin's close friends and classmates wrote to me entirely unprompted. When asked how she knew, she said, "[W]e never lost touch and she told me when they were living in the townhouse," located across from Wasilla High School and where the newlywed couple moved prior to the birth of their first child. She said that Palin's brother, Chuck Jr., also told a family member of hers that Palin was pregnant when she eloped.

Sarah Heath and Todd Palin were married on August 29, 1988; their first child, Track Palin, was born on April 20, 1989, seven months and three weeks following their marriage. When he interviewed Jim Palin (Todd Palin's father), *People* magazine editor and Sarah Palin biographer Lorenzo Benet was told by Jim Palin that "he never got an explanation for the month gap" and that "Track's birth was normal and on time." On the eve of Election Day in 2008, Sarah Palin's private physician, Dr. Cathy Baldwin-Johnson, issued a letter in which she stated that Palin had "four term deliveries," including one in 1989 (Track), and "one pre-term delivery" in 2008 (Trig). Palin had gone to full term with her first child. "None of my babies had been early," Palin confirmed herself at a small press conference in Anchorage on April 21, 2008. "It's pretty simple. Sarah was pregnant when she and Todd got married," says her former brother-in-law, Mike Wooten, the Alaska state trooper with whom she would become obsessed a decade later. "The whole family knows." He further acknowledged that his former wife (Sarah Palin's sister Molly) also was several months pregnant when they were married in 2001.

Sherry Whitstine, a conservative Christian activist in the Mat-Su who was raised in nearby Chugiak and moved to Wasilla as a young adult in the early 1980s, said that Sarah Palin's pregnancy was common knowledge. "Everyone pretty much knew about it," said Whitstine, whose sister was in Sarah Heath's and Todd Palin's class at Wasilla High. "It was part of the community fabric, I guess you'd call it, and everyone talked about it when Palin began running for mayor as a conservative Christian."

J. C. McCavit was a classmate of both Sarah Heath's and Todd Palin's at Wasilla High School and a teammate of Todd's on the basketball team. He and Todd palled around in high school and for several years afterward; they even worked together on the same crew in the local gravel pits. "Everyone assumed that the reason they got married was because Sarah was pregnant," he says. "I mean, it was a bit of a rush job. And the timing [of the birth] pretty much confirms it, doesn't it?"

Indeed, the varied nuances of Sarah Palin's elopement story simply don't hold up to scrutiny. In *Going Rogue,* she says that after a summer of fishing together in Bristol Bay, she and Todd "didn't want to spend any more time apart." But they had just spent part of the summer together in Dillingham, on Bristol Bay, and they had returned to the greater Anchorage area several weeks earlier. By various accounts of the day they were married, Sarah and Todd were supposed to meet Sarah's sister Heather and some friends at the Alaska State Fair, located on the Glenn Highway on the outskirts of Palmer. Without telling anyone—not even the sister with whom she was living in Anchorage and whom she was supposed to meet at the fair—they bolted to the nearby Palmer Courthouse and were married by Kay Fyfe. "I suspect that was right around the time they found out," says a friend. They were in such a rush that they had failed to bring witnesses. Indeed, the favorite daughter and son of Wasilla High, with an extensive network of friends and family only a few miles away, were forced to go across the street and select a couple of seniors living in a retirement home to witness their marriage. One arrived in a wheelchair, the other used a walker. They went to a Wendy's drive-through for their wedding dinner and then left small bouquets with notes attached for their parents.

Even by Palin's own account, the news devastated her mother, who broke down in tears.

"Come on," said a close friend of Todd Palin's at Wasilla High. "Do you really buy the story of them being broke? Their parents weren't broke. The Heaths could have thrown a big potluck that wouldn't have cost a thing. Same with the Palins. They could have had a ceremony out in Dillingham. But it would have taken time. They needed to rush it as soon as Sarah found out. Sarah was panicked. The longer they waited, the more apparent it would have been." In fact, the Heaths held a potluck party for the newlyweds at their home approximately two weeks after their marriage, replete with salmon, wild game, fresh fruits, vegetables, and a homemade wedding cake baked by a friend. According to Benet, a neighbor sang "Sunrise, Sunset" from *Fiddler on the Roof* at the reception. It didn't cost Todd and Sarah a dime.[†]

"To tell you the truth," says Todd's friend, "none of us really gave a shit. Who cared? We knew it was a cover-up, but it was no big deal." That is, until Sarah Palin's political career blossomed and the cover-up story became reified and embellished, first in newspaper and magazine articles, and then in Palin's best-selling memoirs. By then she had also become the darling of the conservative Christian right, and, along with her daughter Bristol (who also was famously pregnant without being married), a national mouthpiece for the abstinence-until-marriage movement in the United States. "The lie is one thing," Todd's friend asserted. "The hypocrisy is really staggering." The Palin wedding story was yet another elaborate fable constructed by Palin to serve her political ambitions.

Palin's capacity to lie is so wrapped up in her very core that it became inexorably interwoven in the popular counternarrative that challenged her political legitimacy. MSNBC's then pertinacious Keith Olbermann vowed to donate $100 to charity every time Palin "lies or repeats a lie in the course of campaigning." Less than halfway through the campaign, he was forced to write a check for $3,700 to the Alaskan Special Olympics Fund (a program for which Palin cut state funding). After Palin called Obama a "socialist" during

---

[†] Palin's marriage and pregnancy is covered by Lorenzo Benet in *Trailblazer: An Intimate Biography of Sarah Palin*, New York: Threshold Editions, 2009, pages 53 to 58. Palin addresses her marriage in *Going Rogue: An American Life*. New York: HarperCollins Publishers, 2009, pages 49–51.

the campaign, an irate Olbermann dubbed her a "hypocrite, double-talker, snake-oil seller . . . and a fraud."

The Atlantic's irrepressible blogger and social commentator Andrew Sullivan had a running column at the magazine's Web site called "The Odd Lies of Sarah Palin," in which he dutifully chronicled each of her public deceits. By the end of the campaign he had reached more than thirty. "We are merely including things she has said or written that can be *definitively* proven as untrue, by *incontestable* evidence in the public record," Sullivan asserted. "After you have read these, ask yourself: what *wouldn't* Sarah Palin lie about if she felt she had to?"

In the aftermath of Palin's book release, Sullivan took his assessment of her duplicity one step further. "Palin is a delusional fantasist, existing in a world of her own imagination, asserting fact after fact that are demonstrably untrue, and unable to adjust to the actual reality after it has been demonstrated beyond any empirical doubt," he wrote. "She is a deeply disturbed individual whose grip on reality is very weak, and whose self-awareness is close to nil." Senior McCain advisers confided in me that this psychological compulsion of hers was the root source of their contentious relationship with Palin and why they were fearful of allowing her to be interviewed by members of the press in the early days of the campaign. In a televised interview following the release of *Going Rogue,* Alaska media personality Shannyn Moore asked Palin's widely respected former legislative director John Bitney, who had known Palin since junior high school and who worked closely with her on her 2006 gubernatorial campaign, if Palin were sane. "Is a sociopath sane?" Bitney responded.

Hannah Arendt, the great German political philosopher who escaped the Holocaust with her family to the United States in 1941, once observed in an article for *The New Yorker* that "no one has ever doubted that truth and politics are on rather bad terms with each other, and no one, as far as I know, has ever counted truthfulness among the political virtues." In the case of Sarah Palin, this would seem a notable understatement. Arendt went on to point out:

> Lies have always been regarded as necessary and justifiable tools not only of the politician's or the demagogue's but also of the statesman's trade. Why is that so? And what does it mean for the nature and the dignity of the political realm, on one side, and for the nature and the dignity of truth and truthfulness, on the other? Is it of the very essence of truth to

be impotent and of the very essence of power to be deceitful?
And what kind of reality does truth possess if it is powerless
in the public realm?

Forty years after Arendt wrote those prophetic questions they remain profoundly germane to this day. The lies of Sarah Palin cast a dark and ominous
shadow on the contemporary American political horizon. They have found
their way to a national platform and a national audience. Her ambition is as
unbridled as it is morally corrupt. How far will her lies take her?

PART I

ALASKA

It would lift up great mountains, the highest in North America. It would accumulate vast glaciers, none superior in the world. It would house, for some generations before the arrival of man, animals of the most majestic quality. And when it finally played host to wandering human beings coming in from Asia or elsewhere, it would provide residence for some of the most exciting people this earth has known: the Athapascans, the Tlingits and much later the Eskimos and Aleuts.
—James A. Michener, *Alaska*

CHAPTER 1

Wasilla

All I ever needed to know I learned on the basketball court.
—Sarah Palin, *Anchorage Daily News*

*Palin seems to have assumed her election was instead
a coronation. Welcome to Kingdom Palin, the land of
no accountability.*
—Editorial, *Mat-Su Valley Frontiersman*

*With Sarah, do you get the feeling that in high school she was
voted Least Likely to Write a Book and Most Likely to Burn One?*
—Robin Williams, *Late Show with David Letterman*

THE MATANUSKA AND SUSITNA valleys spread across the interior of southwest Alaska like a partially open Japanese fan, at a nearly 90 degree angle from one another. Both are formed by imposing mountain ranges along with the majestic Alaska Range the Talkeetna and Chugach, which sweeps northeast across central Alaska into the Yukon. "Young, soaring, vivid in form, tremendous in reach," the novelist James Michener would write, "these peaks stab the frosty air to heights of twelve and thirteen, nineteen and twenty thousand feet. Denali, the glory of Alaska, soars to more than twenty thousand and is one of the most compelling mountains in the Americas."

Outsiders often refer to the region as the Mat-Su Valley, but longtime Alaskans, or Sourdoughs as they are called, more commonly refer to it as simply the Mat-Su or the Valley. It could be argued that in recent years the Mat-Su has become as much a cultural reference as it is a geographic index. Indeed, there's a certain weight attached to the term that transcends place. It was to the Matanuska Valley, in the early 1970s, that Chuck and Sally Heath would bring their brood of four young children—Chuck Jr., Heather, Sarah, and Molly— to the close-knit community of Wasilla, located roughly forty-five miles down the George Parks and Glenn highways from downtown Anchorage. In the 1970s, it was a full hour's drive, even in the best of conditions. Today it is little more than a forty-minute cruise along what is largely a three-lane highway in each direction, albeit with moose crossings and vistas that still take one's breath away.

It is apparently one of American history's great secrets—it certainly finds no mention in Sarah Palin's personal memoir or in any of the varied tracts about her life—that the Matanuska Valley served as one of the great social experiments of *liberal* economic policy during the dark days of the Great Depression. In 1935, as part of Franklin Roosevelt's New Deal response to the collapse of global capitalism, the Federal Emergency Relief Administration and the Department of the Interior relocated more than two hundred families from the rural poverty of the Great Lakes region—primarily Minnesota, Wisconsin, and Michigan—to start an agricultural collective in the fertile Matanuska Valley. There, the short but intensive summer growing season produced remarkable yields of vegetables that grew to massive size during the twenty hours a day of summer sunlight. The Matanuska Colony, as it was called, established the region around Wasilla and Palmer as an agricultural stronghold in Alaska and provided the economic foundation for southwest Alaska's growth spurt following the Second World War.

Many of the region's prominent families—including that of Oscar and Elvi Kerttula, whose son Jalmar "Jay" Kerttula would serve as an Alaska legislator for three decades and whose granddaughter Elizabeth "Beth" Kerttula currently serves as minority leader in the Alaska House of Representatives— were members of the original settlement. The families were selected because of their ability to endure long winters and to farm in challenging conditions. It was a hardy lot and a select group. The New Deal guidelines suggest that they were looking for resourceful families with a multitude of skills:

> As far as possible, families should be selected first on their farming ability and secondly, those who may have secondary skills and who may adjust themselves to a diversified farming activity and can assist with carpentry on their homes and

then those who may know something about machinery and blacksmithing and who have leadership qualities.

More than 90 percent of the families had young children, and the vast majority were of Scandinavian ancestry. They spent their first summer in tent homes and forged a living from the land. It was from this collective—this bastion of federal and liberal economic orthodoxy—that Sarah Palin would receive many of her peculiar speech patterns and "Midwest" accent, though she absorbed little of the political vernacular that created it in the first place.

As a result of its New Deal roots, the Matanuska and Susitna valleys were Democratic Party strongholds well into the 1970s. But with the coming of the Trans-Alaska Pipeline System, the construction of which began in 1974 and was completed three years later, there was a new wave of immigration to Alaska from the Southern Bible Belt (Texas and Louisiana, all the way to Florida), and in a matter of a few years Alaska underwent a social, political, and economic transformation of grand proportions. By the end of the decade, historian Stephen Haycox noted with no small alarm, "Alaskans inexorably became wedded to the oil industry." This second wave of migration, as author Nick Jans observed, transformed the region "from a free-thinking, independent bastion of genuine libertarianism and individuality into a reactionary fundamentalist enclave with dollar signs in its eyes and an all-for-me mentality."

It was in this cauldron of conservative transformation that Sarah Palin came of age and in which many of the myths surrounding her life and political career were first forged—many of them half-truths and others outright lies that continue to prosper to this day. From the distance of the Lower 48, they have taken on the quality of a fairy tale. In fact, it is a dark story, often painful, with cover-up after cover-up, lie upon lie, and with a highway full of victims—stretching from Wasilla to Juneau—who have been tossed under Palin's proverbial bus.

S PEND ANY TIME IN THE MAT-SU talking to those who grew up in the proximity of the Heath family, and you will hear one thing with no small amount of consistency: Sarah Heath may have received her religious convictions and apocalyptic worldview from her mother, but she is very much her father's daughter—a product of his ego, drive, hardheadedness, and darkness.

Charles R. "Chuck" Heath was born in March of 1938, at the time the Matanuska Colony was in its infancy, though he in a more welcoming valley, the San Fernando, north of Los Angeles, when it was still an agricultural haven of citrus trees and vegetable farms. The family lived on Farmdale Avenue, near the base of Laurel Canyon, close to where Studio City is located today. Heath's mother, the former Nellie "Marie" Brandt, a descendant of a *Mayflower* family, was a devout Christian Scientist, the Christian sect founded by Mary Baker Eddy in the 1860s. She was also a schoolteacher in North Hollywood and later in Sandpoint. His father, known as Charlie, was an itinerant sports photographer in the Los Angeles and Hollywood of Nathanael West and John Fante. During the 1920s, Charlie Heath served as the "official photographer" for James Jeffries, boxing's so-called Great White Hope, who lost a celebrated championship bout to the great African American heavyweight Jack Johnson in 1910 and then retired to an alfalfa farm in Burbank, not far from Heath's studio. There is no record of Charlie Heath having served in World War II, though he was clearly of that age, and after the war, in 1948, when young Chuck was ten, he whisked his family to the Idaho panhandle.

One of Chuck Heath's claims to fame is that he was a high school teammate of legendary Green Bay Packers offensive lineman Jerry Kramer, who played for the immortal coach Vince Lombardi (after whom the Super Bowl trophy is named). Heath was a four-sport star in high school, including track, and is a member of Sandpoint High's Athletic Hall of Fame. Sports clearly provided an outlet for the teenage Heath, one that would shape and define his life, but also an escape from the drama at home. It was during his teen years that Heath essentially ran away from his family and moved into the home of Dorothy and Gordon Mooney. An obituary for Dorothy Mooney that appeared in the Spokane *Spokesman-Review* on February 11, 1992, listed her survivors as including "an adopted son, Chuck Heath of Wasilla." Palin did her best in *Going Rogue* to explain away the informal "adoption," but she did acknowledge the scars, noting that her father rarely discussed his childhood and that "his parents' acceptance of pain must have translated beyond the physical." She added that her father's childhood appeared to her as "painful and lonely."

Palin has painted an idyllic portrait of her early childhood in Wasilla in *Going Rogue* and other biographical accounts of the Heath household, but those growing up with her in the Mat-Su say that the narrative serves as a cover for what was a very overbearing hand by her father. Chuck Heath served as a science teacher at the local junior high school but also as his children's track coach at Wasilla High. Palin hints at her own scars left by Chuck Heath. Having her father as a coach, she noted, resulted in "extra scrutiny and pressure." She acknowledges experiencing "a jealous twinge" and "even hurt" when he seemed to favor some of her teammates or show them affection rather than her to counteract any sense of preferential treatment. Instead, he issued her "the proverbial slug in the arm" and urged her to "work harder."

Those who ran under Coach Heath in high school present a spectrum of views on his temperament. All considered him "tough" and "demanding," but a classmate of Sarah's who knew the family since elementary school said that while Heath was "very competitive," she "never saw anything mean in his treatment of Sarah," though her mother felt that he "treated Chuck [Jr.] horribly," and that he "pushed" Sarah to play sports. But another childhood friend, Yvonne Bashelier, from a longtime Alaska family, who also was a teammate of Sarah's at Wasilla High, described Chuck Heath as an overbearing and dysfunctional coach who heaped far too much attention on her, often bringing her to the point of tears. "He drove me nuts," she says. Her own father, she acknowledges, treated her similarly. "I never had any control over my life between my dad and Chuck," she asserts. "I imagine Sarah got it even worse than me. Sarah's dad drilled into her head from a very young age—never give up and never lose."

Bashelier, who was a star sprinter and an all-regional volleyball player, says that Chuck Heath's obsession with winning led him to prevent her from transferring to a high school in Anchorage, from which she would have been far more likely to obtain a college scholarship. "Winning meant everything to him," Bashelier recalls, to the point of Heath making her work out, even when she "was running a high fever and sick as a dog." She says he pushed his daughter mercilessly. "Sarah *can't lose*," Bashelier contends. "That is her worst fear in life, and that is what her father not only did to her, but me also. Sarah's gone to a dark hole inside herself and I think every move she makes, she hears her father in the background, yelling at her, pushing her, and pushing her. I know it, I lived with it for several years, seen it, touched it, breathed it."

Bashelier, who suffered from epilepsy in childhood and adolescence, tells a startling story about how Chuck Heath visited her once at the hospital after she had nearly died from seizures and had been in a coma for close to two weeks. "When he came to me in the hospital, he noticed that I had lost a lot of weight," she recalls, "and I remember him telling me it would be great for my performance in track if I could 'keep the weight off.'" Bashelier was shaken by the remark. "What a bizarre thing to say to a sick person who almost died."

Bashelier says that Chuck Heath's overbearing ways not only had a significant impact on her adolescent psyche—she says that Heath and her father placed so much stress on her around sports that "she became severely depressed"—but it also had a profound impact on her family. According to Bashelier, her younger sister, also a fine athlete, became so distraught by pressures from both Chuck Heath and her father to participate in sports and perform well, that at age fourteen, she began skipping practices to avoid Heath and eventually ran away from home to get away from the demands that he and others were placing on her.

For Sarah, Bashelier says, there was no such escape from Chuck Heath's overbearing personality. "I actually feel like out of all his kids he destroyed her the most," she says. "I feel as if Sarah internalized what her father did to her, made her a machine who speaks with canned language." She recalls returning home to a funeral at which Sarah, then mayor, delivered a eulogy. "It really affected me," she recalls. "She showed no emotion, not one tear. I couldn't see any emotion in her at all . . . Chuck Heath was there, too. He was also emotionless. Is that a sign of strength?"

In the early days of his daughter's brush with national celebrity, it was Chuck Heath who always provided the most critical and revealing portraits of his daughter. In an interview with Emily Smith of the British tabloid *The Sun,* Heath described his daughter as "very stubborn. I wasn't mean to her but I taught her discipline. But I could seldom bend her if she'd made her mind up on something." In several accounts, young Sarah Heath's "refusal to bend" is dated back to the time she was two years old. "Sarah was always very determined," Chuck said. "Whatever she lacked in skill she always made up in determination." There are many who say that Sarah Palin's refusal to acknowledge errors, even in the face of overriding evidence—her refusal and her inability to back down—stems from her childhood relationship with her father. As the third child, young Sarah sought her father's approval on her own terms. Heath's good friend, the late Curtis Menard, Sr., said, "When children are a way down in the pack, they often want to excel, show they can move forward and get into Dad's favor—especially girls. On reflection, I think there was some of that going on with Sarah."

Chuck Heath told Palin biographer Lorenzo Benet that Sarah actually boxed with neighborhood kids when she was young. "She was a tough little girl," he said with no small amount of pride. But once again he returned to her stubbornness. "From an early age, she thought she was always right," he observed, before adding the caveat, "and she usually was." And then he added perhaps the most revealing comment about Palin's childhood: "If I needed something done, I could bend the other kids one way or another, but Sarah was strong-willed, and it was hard to change her mind. That's still her." In between teaching her to hunt, fish, and to field dress game, Heath taught Sarah what he could about the ways of the natural world. But of his four children, his third daughter was clearly his challenge.

When another British journalist, Christine Toomey from *The Sunday Times Magazine,* showed up in Wasilla at the Heaths' doorstep, the first thing Chuck Heath asked her repeatedly was: "What are you famous for?" It was a mantra that took on something of a challenge. "Sarah got a lot of stern discipline from me," he acknowledged, "and a lot of love, devotion, and faith from her mom. I wasn't mean to her [a phrase he used a second time], but I'd push her a lot in sports and outdoor activities. I taught her to believe she could do anything in the world she wanted to do if she put her mind to it."

THE CHILDHOOD PORTRAIT of Sarah Heath has become something of a fable, a political fiction in its own right, an unchallenged gloss of nuclear family values—*Father Knows Best* meets *Lassie* in the Last Frontier. Like many such narratives, it smooths over troubling bumps in the road and completely omits darker elements and passages that don't shine a uniform white light on its protagonist. It is in one of those narrative omissions from Sarah Palin's eighth grade year at Wasilla Junior High in which she revealed many of the tendencies and psychological patterns that would manifest themselves over and over again in her lifetime and throughout her political career.

Palin has been cast as Wasilla's favorite daughter, but in fact, when the Heaths first arrived in the Mat-Su in the early 1970s, when Sarah was in second grade, they were viewed as "outsiders" to those who had been born and raised in the valley and whose lives had been carved out in the close-knit pockets of southwest Alaska. Like all her siblings, Sarah Heath had to navigate her way through the challenging web of childhood networks and friendships. By eighth grade, Sarah had established herself as a determined, if not gifted, athlete, and a good, if not outstanding, student. Her religious beliefs were solidly formed, and even at an early age she was not afraid to proselytize. One close friend says that by then if you weren't part of her religious circle, then well, you weren't part of her social circle at all. "She was very prissy," says another classmate from Wasilla. "Very uptight. She had her way of seeing the world and it was the only way. There was no give and take with Sarah. None ever."

There was a close—and closed—circle of friends with whom Sarah Heath bonded, mostly girls, but she had a special friendship with her classmate and family friend, Curtis Menard, Jr. Tall, blond, bright, and handsome, Menard was widely liked by his classmates. By most accounts of those close to her in Wasilla, Sarah had a serious emotional attachment to Menard, an adolescent crush that bordered on an obsession. In her book, Palin says she viewed him as a "brother," while another friend agreed that it was platonic but "very possessive."

As she readied for her eighth grade year, Sarah Heath's world was about to grow bleak. A new girl had arrived in Wasilla, from Hawaii no less, very much Menard's feminine counterpart, in the form of Cheryl Welch—tall, tan, bright, a solid athlete with beach-girl good looks. She came from a broken home, her family had moved around a lot, and her eighth grade move actually reflected a return to Alaska, as she had attended sixth grade at Ptarmigan Elementary School in Anchorage. She loved the outdoors and spent a lot of time on the Big Island of Hawaii in the warm ocean water, swimming, body surfing, and snorkeling. She was in great shape from her time in the ocean and her skin was a dark bronze from the tropical sun.

When Welch returned to Alaska early in the summer of 1977, she was shocked by "how white everyone seemed" in the Mat-Su, how "unnaturally pale." Although with sun-bleached blond hair no one mistook her for an Alaska Native, she was actually darker than many of the Native kids her age. Her stepfather, Bob Sowash, a successful contractor in Anchorage and also a renowned innovator in shotgun munitions, had purchased a homestead outside Wasilla on the Little Susitna River. The property had a rustic cabin on it into which the family moved for the summer—it only had an outhouse with no indoor toilet—and Sowash immediately went to work, with the help of some cousins, building a custom A-frame home. Welch took baths in the Little Su running by her house, a pristine if freezing stream fed by the Mint Glacier and snowmelt in the Talkeetna Mountains.

Eighth grade can be a tough time for girls, and Welch knew it wasn't going to be easy fitting in, but she also knew her way around being the new kid in school. "I didn't make friends real quickly," she says. "I remember that. I was used to walking into a situation where everybody knew everybody and I knew from my past that it took a while. If you were needy and wanted to break in or needed to break in, then you were really going to suffer. You were never going to make friends."

Welch says she "just did my own thing" for a few weeks, pretty much keeping to herself. Then one day in PE class, early into the school year, one of her classmates approached her while they were running laps. She had noticed him in the first two weeks of school, nothing more, but he was tall, friendly, good-looking, and confident for his age. In that awkward time of adolescence, he seemed different. He asked her "to go with him," and Welch immediately said no. "I just thought it was a little too forward, and 'how do you even know me?' kind of thing. And so I said no."

The incident had shaken Welch out of her new-kid-on-the-block nonchalance.

And as often happens in young-teen circles, the encounter did not go unnoticed by her peers. When she returned to the locker room, several girls from a particular clique confronted her about what Menard had said to her. Her locker was directly opposite that of a short intense girl with cropped brown hair and thick glasses who hadn't been the slightest bit friendly to her since she arrived. "What did Curtis Menard ask you?" they queried.

"I said, 'Oh, is that his name?'" Welch responded, trying to be dismissive. "I really didn't know who he was." But the air was riddled with drama, bordering on confrontation. Welch remained casual. "I said he wanted me to go with him." There was a gasp and then dead silence. And then the short girl with the glasses burst out sobbing. It was Sarah Heath. As a way to diffuse the situation, Welch said she made it clear: "I said no, and I kept repeating, 'I said no! I told him no!'" But her response made little difference. "I remember the whole energy of the place changing, and everybody kind of holding still. . . . And just the sob that burst out of Sarah. And she was totally distraught, slamming her locker, she was forever slamming stuff and carrying on. Everybody was, 'Oh, Sarah, Sarah'—her clique kind of huddled around her, and they just whisked her out, and I was just standing there—and everyone's looking at me, like, 'Oh, way to go. You know, she's been in love with him since second grade. She wants to marry him. Their parents want them to . . .'"

Welch suddenly felt like the outsider again. Sarah Heath stared straight at her. She was crushed. Welch threw up her hands. "I said no!" she reiterated. "I told him no. *I don't even know who he is.*" Nothing mattered. It was almost as if Welch had shattered something that was sacred.

That incident—and the social ostracism that ensued—would mark Cheryl Welch for the rest of her days in Wasilla and carry with it painful memories. She wrote about it in her diary and kept written tabs of what Sarah Heath did to her throughout the school year. From that point on, she was ostracized by Palin and her crowd. Eventually, Welch decided that if she was going to be marginalized by the "in crowd," particularly the girls in Sarah Heath's "coterie," as she called it, she might as well take the plunge with Curtis Menard. "So I think part of my rethinking Curtis was at least I'd have one friend." She used an intermediary to approach Menard—J. C. "Bones" McCavit, Menard's best friend (and who, ironically, would become a close friend and basketball teammate of Todd Palin's at Wasilla High three years later)—and told him that she was ready to go out with Curtis. For most of the rest of the school year, with one short break, they were an eighth-grade couple, hanging out when they could, holding hands, and making out when the opportunity presented itself.

A gifted student, Welch was also a star athlete, and so in addition to pairing up with Menard, Welch was a threat to Sarah Heath in the classroom and on the playing field. It was far from pleasant. There was always tension. "She didn't want to talk to me," Welch says. "She didn't want to be friends—you know, I got that right off and she made it pretty clear. And when I went out for the basketball team it was the same sort of animosity there."

On the basketball court, Sarah Heath took her aggressions out on Welch. "She was just physically so difficult to deal with, because she would just come at the ball no matter what, flying elbows and throwing herself at me," Welch says. "And they're not calling fouls in practice, so I just had to assert myself and say 'Back off!' It was clear she had it out for me." The intensity never eased up and lasted throughout the year. "Oh, God! She was just terrible. I don't know what—she was just a baby, is what I always used to think. You know, if we lost, she cried. . . . I just remember her always being just mad, just that hot, angry-tears-mad. And she would pout. She would stomp off. She was, like, smoldering."

Welch's memory of Palin on the basketball court prefigured Palin's high school career where she was known for her aggression:

> She was just scrappy as hell. You know, she'd just get in there
> and mix it up. And in games she would foul out. She didn't
> have a governor on herself. It was just, go-go-go-go—it was
> not too balanced, always in high gear. It was like she wanted
> what she wanted so badly, she didn't stop to strategize. It was
> just go for it and keep going for it, and then she'd foul out,
> you know? I'd think, "That did us a lot of good."

Welch remembered one particular incident that always stuck with her. The Wasilla Braves' opponents had to forfeit a game because they couldn't field enough players, which meant a victory for Wasilla. Welch was disappointed that they didn't play the game, but Sarah Heath, Welch remembers, was "thrilled because we won. And I just remember thinking, I would rather play. But to her it seemed like the victory was enough. And I just remember thinking, that's weird. We're here to play basketball—it's more fun to play than to just be handed a victory. But she seemed plenty happy with that."

Welch never cracked any of the other cliques at the junior high either. She made a few close friends—some of whom she's still in touch with—and learned to make her own way. "I had no interest in those people [that were close to Sarah]," she says. What Welch found odd was how loyal this small group of friends was to her, that Sarah Heath played the role of the queen bee even in adolescence. "If she was mad, then they all ran off after her. That's how they were. They just watched her for signs that she was upset or mad—and it seemed like she was always upset and she would run away. It's like, well, there goes Sarah crying again. Constant drama."

Yvonne Bashelier, who was friends with Welch but who also remained on the periphery of Palin's inner circle, recalls the tension between Welch and Palin during their eighth grade year. Sarah, said Bashelier, usually manipulated people "in a quiet way" and rarely confronted anyone directly. "She had a way of getting people to do things for her," Bashelier said. "If she didn't like you, she would never say that to your face; you would find out by the way she ignored you and her friends ignored you, by not letting you into the group." But with Welch it was another matter. Bashelier confirms that Palin went "crazy with jealousy" and made nasty remarks about Welch to her friends. In particular, she remembers a long basketball road trip during which Welch and Curtis Menard were getting affectionate on the team bus. "I thought Sarah was going to explode," Bashelier recalled. "She was pissed off and making nasty remarks about how Cheryl was a slut."

It added no small amount of insult to Sarah Heath's injury that Welch was chosen to give the commencement speech at her eighth grade graduation ceremony, a selection based on her leadership skills and academic performance. Welch has a large collection of photos she took at the graduation party held at Pizza Napoletana in Wasilla—one with Menard, McCavit, and their friend Dan Fleckenstein, hamming it up with big smiles—while another with a bespeckled Sarah Heath, off to the side, looking not so much at Welch taking the photo, as beyond her, without acknowledgment, expressionless.

Welch remembers one further incident in which Sarah Heath figured directly that year. Somehow, one of the notes between Menard and Welch was intercepted and it got back to Sarah. Menard and Welch referred to each other as "3.95," in reference to their grade point average. "Sarah was furious about that," Welch recalls. "Jealousy and anger, all right at the surface—stomping, storming, stewing, pouting. She was never, ever bold enough to do anything directly confrontational. She ran to her friends, and hid out. In the end, I felt sorry for her."

WELCH'S FAMILY LEFT WASILLA FOR CALIFORNIA THE following year, where Welch became a star athlete at Saratoga High School in Silicon Valley. Palin took her elbows-and-hustle game with her into Wasilla High, where her ambition and determination on the basketball court defined her high school persona and identity. Palin would later market herself as a "hockey mom," but her high school basketball career would become a central component of her carefully constructed political brand and narrative. "All I ever needed to know, I learned on the basketball court," she has said repeatedly, including in her memoir. "I know this sounds hokey, but basketball was a life-changing experience for me," she told Alaska writer Tom Kizzia during her 2006 gubernatorial campaign. "It's all about setting a goal, about discipline, teamwork, and then success." When he first began promoting her as a GOP vice presidential nominee early in the summer of 2008, Palin's neoconservative inamorata Bill Kristol, who had visited her in Alaska the previous year, would glowingly champion Palin's abilities on the hardwoods. "You know, she was the point guard on the Alaska state championship high school basketball team in 1982," he declared with no small amount of hyperbole. "She could take Obama one-on-one on the court."

That Palin was a direct beneficiary of Title IX, the federal legislation that outlawed gender discrimination in all institutions that received federal funding, goes without saying. She herself acknowledged as much in Going Rogue, declaring that she was "a product" of Title IX and that she was "proud" of the role Alaska Senator Ted Stevens played in facilitating the legislation. While Palin doesn't acknowledge that she would later betray Stevens on several occasions in her political career, she trumpets Stevens's role as a way of distancing herself from the "radical mantras" of feminism and the women's movement that played a definitive role in seeing the legislation through Congress. She quotes admiringly from fellow Alaskan athlete Jessica Gavora's book, Tilting the Playing Field, who declared that "Instead of reflecting, and, indeed, reveling in our expanded horizons, the feminism of the National Organization for Women (NOW) and other so-called 'women's groups' . . . depicts women as passive victims rather than makers of their own destinies, and overlooks our individuality in favor of our collective political identity that many of us find restrictive."

Title IX, now known officially as the Patsy T. Mink Equal Opportunity in Education Act (named after the Democratic Party congresswoman from Hawaii who was the principal author of the legislation), was, in fact, a direct product of both legal and political efforts advanced by not only NOW but other feminist organizations, including the Women Equity Action League— and the gender-based equal opportunity clause of the legislation has been consistently attacked by conservative Republicans in Congress over the four decades since its implementation.

If Palin would later distort the role of the progressive women's movement in establishing Title IX, she would also distort her high school basketball career as well. In *Going Rogue,* she declared in an awkwardly worded passage that she had played basketball during high school, "my name next to number 22 on the varsity roster all four years." *My name next to number 22 on the varsity roster?* Technically it was true. All Wasilla athletes who were ever listed on the varsity roster (if only once in a season) according to one of Palin's classmates, were awarded their varsity letters. In fact, the top point guard at Wasilla High during Palin's era in high school and who played ahead of Palin was her sister Heather, who is considered by those who played with both to be the far superior ball handler and playmaker of the two. "Heather was a team player," says one, "very talented and very focused. Sarah was not."

Palin claims she "rode the bench" on varsity her first three seasons, but according to several of her schoolmates, she was actually forced down to the JV squad for most of her first three years in high school, including her junior year, much to her dismay. Her former teammates claim she put considerable pressure on the assistant coach, Cordell Randall, into persuading head coach Don Teeguarden to bring her up to the varsity. "She was bitter and even angry about it," says one of her former teammates. "And she let everyone know it, including Teeguarden. She played angry all season." Her younger sister, Molly, then a freshman, also played on the JV team. "She was so upset with me," Randall told Palin biographer Kaylene Johnson. "I'm sure it was humiliating to play down."

When Heather Heath graduated in the spring of 1981, Palin finally moved up to the varsity her entire senior year. She was named one of three senior co-captains of the team, although there were many who still considered her play uneven. "I'd see her out on the court sometimes," says longtime Wasilla resident

Nick Carney, whose niece, Michelle, was a talented teammate of Palin's and who himself would figure prominently in Palin's political career in the years ahead, "and I couldn't help but wonder why she was getting so much playing time." Carney, from a well-known Catholic family in Wasilla, was a lifelong basketball aficionado. He had played on a small-school state championship team for Wasilla High in 1959 and had refereed basketball games throughout southwest Alaska for nearly two decades. "I thought there were other girls on the team who were clearly better ballplayers," says Carney. "I just didn't understand why she was in there."

One parent of a prominent Wasilla High School athlete says point-blank, "There was an Assembly of God clique on all the sports teams, but especially in basketball. If you weren't part of the church you did not get the playing time that others did, especially if you were a marginal or average player. It wasn't a balanced playing field. There was clearly a lot of favoritism, and once Heather graduated, Sarah was the recipient of that favoritism." Several parents of non–Assembly of God athletes in Wasilla spoke openly of this preferential treatment. "It was blatant," said one, "but there was little we could do about it. Our kids were afraid for us to rock the boat."

Even a top-notch athlete like Yvonne Bashelier says she was victimized by the religious ostracism in high school sports. She says she was kept on the periphery of the in group, of which Sarah was the "darling." "Before every basketball game we had to pray," Bashelier recalls. "Everyone would gather in the locker room, hold hands, and usually Sarah would lead the prayer. It was like a cult to me, but I knew if I didn't go along, I would be ousted from my community."

Bashelier says that her Assembly of God teammates encouraged her to attend a healing at the church, to which she went, in the hopes that her epileptic seizures would go away. "So they started talking in tongues and laying hands," Bashelier recalls. "I've never been so scared. People were passing out on the floor. It was a huge church, and every seat was full of everybody I knew. I felt embarrassed." When Bashelier's seizures continued, she says, "I asked the in group why, and they told me I didn't have enough faith. I felt like it was all my fault because I didn't have enough faith. After that, I felt guilty every time I had a seizure at school."

Bashelier, a member of the graduating class of 1982 like Sarah Heath, said that Sarah was at the center of the Assembly of God athletes at Wasilla High. "She had a silent but known princess attitude about herself," Bashelier asserts. "She could be very condescending and quick with the tongue, snide—behind your back, or to her friends, but rarely to your face." These qualities, according to Bashelier, manifested themselves most strongly on the basketball team. "Sarah never really had to compete for anything," Bashelier contends. "If you have your coaches who are also in the tight religious community of which she belonged, you will be favored."

As Bashelier describes it, the favoritism and ostracism were so blatant that the coaches (who were also members of the Assembly of God) would invite players over to their houses for pizza get-togethers and exclude those players who were not members of the church. "A few of my teammates and I were not invited," she relates, continuing,

> It would always hurt me when the "chosen ones" would come back to school the next day bragging about their pizza party. How was I supposed to feel? How were the few other basketball players supposed to feel to know they were not invited on purpose? It was like this all through high school—secret pizza parties with the coaches. They didn't even care how this might affect the other players to not be invited. But it raised Sarah's status even more that she was special. . . . It really was a sick dysfunctional system of who's in and who's not, perpetrated by the coaches and the staff who ran the high school.

Bashelier was injured during basketball season her senior year when Sarah Heath finally played a full season on varsity, but she says that "Sarah was hardly the star." In fact, with two big post players, Wanda Strutko (5'8") and Heyde Kohring (6'2"), starring on the team, the backcourt's job was to get the ball inside—a strategy, according to Lorenzo Benet, that Heath and the other guards "were not thrilled about." Much has been made of Heath hitting a last-minute free throw in the state championship game against Robert Service High of Anchorage, but even the significance of that particular shot has been greatly embellished. Palin biographer Joe Hilley claimed that Heath actually sank two free throws—the first a "swish"—just before the buzzer to win the game. In fact, she was playing on an injured ankle (later identified as a stress fracture) and was forced out of the game for most of the second half because she was getting beat on defense. With Heath on the bench, Strutko and Kohring took control of the contest. Never able to put the team's destiny above her own, Heath was angry again about being pulled from the game. Her coach Teeguarden kept her out until less than a minute to play, with Wasilla holding a relatively secure four-point lead, 57–53. Heath hit the front end of a one-and-one situation with a four-point lead and ten seconds to play (her shot caught the front rim, then hit the backboard and banked in), but then missed the second shot. Heath had all of one point for the game, and only nine in the entire three-game championship series. Newspaper coverage for the game in the *Anchorage Times* placed the laurels deservedly on Strutko and Kohring, who combined for forty-two points. But Sarah Heath had a state championship and her first taste of statewide acclaim.

Wasilla High alumni estimate that a little more than half of the 1982 championship team belonged to the Assembly of God. And in a small school of roughly three hundred, they contend, as many as sixty Wasilla High students participated in the Fellowship of Christian Athletes program. Sarah Heath co-captained that team as well, which met regularly on school grounds. "None of us ever questioned it at the time, the fact that this was happening at a public school," said one of her teammates. "We just accepted it." Nearly three decades after she graduated from high school, the very idea that such a practice might be problematic irked Palin to no end. In *Going Rogue*, she sarcastically mocked "ACLU activists" who believed in the separation of church and state as it related to prayer at public schools.

M UCH HAS BEEN MADE OF SARAH HEATH PALIN's erratic and scattered college education—she attended a handful of different colleges over a period of five years—and in many ways it reflects the erratic and scattered nature of her professional and political life as an adult in the years ahead. Palin has never released a formal record of her collegiate career—in *Going Rogue* she says she stressed out over a D grade being revealed during the vice presidential campaign, but gives no details of where or when—and, as with most accounts of her life, the details are vague and constantly shifting. What is even more astonishing in her memoir is that she mentions not a single book or intellectual idea or class that inspired her half-decade college odyssey. Not one.

This vacuum embraces those who encountered her during this formative period of her young adulthood. In a lengthy account of her collegiate career published during the 2008 national campaign, Robin Abcarian of the *Los Angeles Times* noted that "in the five years of her collegiate career, spanning four universities in three states Palin left behind few traces." Palin, she wrote, "is barely remembered at all."

"Few traces" was putting it mildly. In fact, Palin attended at least *five* colleges between 1982 and 1987—and at not one was there a single article of note by or about her in any of the college newspapers, not a single television newscast in video files at any of the institutions. "Looking at this dynamic personality now, it mystifies me that I wouldn't remember her," Palin's journalism instructor at the University of Idaho, who had her in a course with merely fifteen students, told the *Times*. "It's the funniest damn thing. No one can recall her." Her academic adviser, Roy Atwood, had no memory of her. Indeed, Abcarian contacted more than a dozen professors with whom Palin had taken courses, and not a single one had the slightest recollection of her.

By virtually all accounts, Palin and her former Wasilla High teammate Kim "Tilly" Ketchum selected the University of Hawaii, Hilo, as their first academic destination based on photographs of the campus in a brochure they had reviewed. After spending their adolescence cooped up in the subarctic weather of southwest Alaska, they were ready for some tropical sunshine. They arrived in Hilo in the late summer of 1982, apparently without knowing that Hilo, located on the windward side of the island of Hawaii, is one of the wettest cities in the world, ranking right behind Ketchikan in Alaska's panhandle. They reportedly attended orientation at Hilo but never formally registered for classes. It would always be cited that the perpetual rain is what drove the young coeds off the Big Island. But in *Sarah from Alaska,* reporters Scott Conroy and Shushannah Walshe elicited a far different explanation out of Heath's father:

> According to Chuck, Sarah's decision to join her high school friend in transferring out of the school had to do with being outside her comfort zone for the first time in her life in an environment dominated by Asians and Pacific Islanders. "It just wasn't exactly what they expected," he says. "They were a minority type thing and it wasn't glamorous, so she came home."

It's unclear what Hawaiian "school" Chuck Heath was referring to, as Ketchum and Heath left Hilo and departed for Honolulu, where they enrolled at Hawaii Pacific University, a private liberal arts school located downtown. Palin was registered as a full-time student in business administration for fall classes of 1982. This time they left after a semester, claiming the weather in Honolulu to be too hot. They then enrolled for two semesters at North Idaho College, a two-year community campus in Coeur d'Alene. She left there without receiving an associate's degree.

Palin dropped out of school after the fall semester of 1983 and returned home, competing in the Miss Wasilla beauty pageant, which she won, and then went to the state pageant in June of 1984, at which she placed third, or "second runner-up" (not second, as was widely reported), and at which she was named Miss Congeniality—only she wasn't, apparently, so congenial. She lost to the first African American Miss Alaska, Maryline Blackburn, a self-described Army brat from Fairbanks, who later said that Sarah Heath had been "very calculating" during the pageant. "You could tell she was always thinking, 'What's going to be my next move?'" Blackburn told the New York *Daily News*. "One look in her eyes, and you could see there was so much more going on."

Palin returned to school for the fall semester of 1984 at the University of Idaho at Moscow, her father's alma mater and where her brother, Chuck Jr., was a star running back on the Vandals football team. Heath kept her head down and plodded her way through her course work, returning home several times, taking additional classes at Matanuska-Susitna College in Palmer, before returning once again to Moscow to receive her diploma in the spring of 1987, a bachelor of science degree in broadcast journalism. "Everybody who grew up in [Wasilla] at that time was looking for a way out," her former basketball teammate and fellow UI alum Michelle Carney told Abcarian. Palin had been involved in a minimal amount of collegiate activities at UI—no sports, no college government, no extracurricular intellectual pursuits. "She wasn't out to get attention at school," Carney concluded. "She kept to herself."

M ICHELLE CARNEY'S UNCLE, DOMONIC "NICK" CARNEY, is one of those salt-of-the-earth characters one often encounters in Alaska, who just also happens to be a distinguished alumnus from the Ivy League. The son of a working-class family from eastern Ohio that made a *Grapes of Wrath* migration to the Alaskan Territory in the mid-1950s, Carney was one of five members of the graduating class of Wasilla High School in 1959 (he was valedictorian and likes to note that he "graduated at *the* top 20 percent of his class"). A Dartmouth grad, he eventually made his way back to Alaska to serve in the private and public spheres, both with distinction, before retiring with his wife, Kay, to Utah, where he's able to play golf a little longer each year than he was in the Matanuska Valley. He has also written a pair of delightful memoirs about his and his wife's respective families in the Mat-Su, *We're Going to Alaska* and *Our Home Is Wasilla*.

In the early 1990s, when community business leaders were in search of a tax base and police force, it was Carney, then president of the local Chamber of Commerce, who helped persuade Sarah Palin into the political arena for the first time. (She acknowledged as much in *Going Rogue*, writing that Carney "set me on a path" toward serving in public office, though she would mock Carney as a "self-proclaimed mover and shaker" who viewed Wasilla as "*his* town.") Community leaders had formed an organization called Watch on Wasilla (WOW) and were looking to beef up Wasilla's tax base and to form a police force in the face of a rising crime rate. They were looking for someone with a slightly different demographic to join them in their political effort.

Carney had known Palin and her parents since she was in elementary school. The Carneys' daughter, Katy, was in the same class as Palin, and he had watched Palin play basketball in high school and had watched her grow up, even if from afar. Carney insists that he saw nothing in Palin's personality or character at the time that gave even the slightest hint of the political force she was to become. "She was a warm body," he asserts. "That was it. It was simply that she was available."

Carney maintains that he and his WOW colleagues were looking for a candidate "who could carry the younger voters for our cause—a sales tax and a police force. And we were looking for someone that had a family, that wasn't working—and frankly, because she was a young woman was also an asset—because we were being accused of being the 'good ol' boys' in town, and we needed somebody as a foil to the charge of this being pushed solely by the good ol' boys."

Carney acknowledges that Palin had a certain political cachet—she had played on the championship basketball team and had been Miss Wasilla and her parents had been involved with the school district. But "Wasilla was a very small town," he observes, "everybody knew everybody. So people knew her, sure. But it wasn't like she was outstanding above anybody else."

According to Carney, Palin was then very much in support of the 2 percent tax increase and the creation of a police force. "She pledged full support for our platform," he recalls. "She never expressed the slightest doubt." Carney was a strong political ally of the mayor of Wasilla, John Stein, who had been elected to his second term in 1990. They brought Palin around to various members of the community and introduced her to key political figures. She proved to be a popular candidate, winning Seat F on the council with 530 votes. The 2 percent sales tax also passed (which also included a cap on property taxes) by a mere sixty-one votes and an advisory measure on the establishment of a police force passed by only fifty-one votes. It was small-town politics in all its glory, and Palin did exactly what Carney and the other members of WOW had hoped: she brought in young families to support both ballot measures. Three years later, in 1995, she won again, though her vote total dropped to 413. Carney was elected for a second term as well.

In fact, Palin and the WOW contingent on the Wasilla City Council sat in opposition to an older, more conservative organization in Wasilla known as Standing Against Government Excess (SAGE), that was strongly opposed to local taxation and a local police force. One of its members—Mark Chryson—a computer technician from Wasilla, served for seven years (1997–2004) as state chairman of the Alaskan Independence Party (AIP), the same party that Todd Palin had joined and which advocated for the secession of Alaska from the union. Chryson says that SAGE was composed mostly of AIP members, Libertarians, gun advocates, and various conservative political sects who viewed government at all levels with disdain. They had developed a pair of slogans in response to the proposed taxes in Wasilla—"Taxation Is a Dangerous Drug" and "Just Say No"—that Chryson characterizes as "extremely effective" in slowing down the growth of local government in the valley. They viewed the likes of Stein and Carney, both moderate, pro-business Republicans at the time, as akin to "drug dealers" when it came to expanding government services. Chryson himself, who had first moved to Anchorage in 1987 and then to the Mat-Su in 1990, had long left the Republican Party behind. He says that while he liked Palin personally and found her "an attractive figure on the council," he disdained her politics ("didn't really trust her") and viewed her as a "rubber stamp" on the "pro-government council." Chryson says that he doesn't recall Palin ever reflecting "anti-tax sentiment" or "SAGE's perspective" during her early political career. "She was pretty gung-ho on the WOW agenda," he says. And she was effective in bringing younger Wasilla residents on board. To true conservatives in Wasilla, Chryson says, Palin was in the enemy camp.

Palin's first few years on the council, Carney recalls, "were largely uneventful." He says that she voted against the majority on occasion, but for the most part, "she was in full agreement with us. There was never a hint in those early years that anything was wrong. It wasn't a rubber-stamp deal, because she certainly had some differences of opinion on certain things, but she was al-

ways in our camp where on the main issues—the budget and the sales tax or-
dinance and the police—she was solidly with us on those. Solidly." Palin
participated in an aerobics class at the local gym that included the Carneys,
Stein's wife (Karen Marie), and Wasilla's new police chief, Irl Stambaugh.
"Everyone seemed to be getting along just fine," says Carney. "There wasn't
even the slightest bit of indication of anything brewing on the horizon. Not
the slightest bit."

I N THE SPRING OF 1996, SARAH PALIN, now with three young children, was
finding herself "boxed in," according to a friend, unhappy with the landscape of her life. She had grown restless on the Wasilla City Council, and her
ambitions had thoroughly dwarfed whatever possibilities there seemed to be
on the political horizon. She felt alienated from the inner workings of Stein's
close circle—one that included Carney and Stambaugh, city engineer Bob
Gilfilian, and city attorney Dick Deuser—which, Stein acknowledged, certainly could have looked like a "good ol' boys" network from the outside
looking in. "One of the things that would happen is after a city council meeting," Stein says, "we'd often go for a debrief down at one of the local water-
ing holes. That was something, in hindsight, I think the people who were on
other sides of issues looked at that and thought, 'Yeah, here's the tight-knit
little group—the *cabal*—that's running the city and we need to break that
open."

He realizes now that Palin felt excluded, even insulted by the practice. "I
think that's why she got on my case," he says.

There's been considerable attention paid to an early news story about
Palin that appeared in the *Anchorage Daily News* in April of 1996, chronicling
the arrival of Ivana Trump in Anchorage. In an article entitled "Alaskans Line
Up for a Whiff of Ivana," *Daily News* reporter Tom Bell opened with the following paragraph:

> Sarah Palin, a commercial fisherman from Wasilla, told her
> husband on Tuesday she was driving to Anchorage to shop
> at Costco. Instead, she headed straight for Ivana. And there,
> at J.C. Penney's cosmetic department, was Ivana, the former
> Mrs. Donald Trump, sitting at a table next to a photograph
> of herself. She wore a light-colored pantsuit and pink finger-

nail polish. Her blond hair was coiffed in a bouffant French twist.

One of the many insights contained in the story about Palin's psyche at the time is that she had felt the need to lie to her husband Todd just to get out of the house. She couldn't be honest with him even about a simple trip into Anchorage to see an international celebrity. Palin was fascinated by celebrity, by its power and mystique, and she was drawn to it, so much that she executed the near hour-long drive for a glimpse of the limelight that she herself coveted and craved. The story did not mention that Palin at that time served on the Wasilla City Council, and described her, instead, as someone who "admittedly smells like salmon for a large part of the summer." More than five hundred people joined Palin that afternoon trying to catch a glimpse of the former Czech skier—who had once been married to the billionaire real estate mogul Donald Trump—promoting a new line of perfume. Her "fans" in Anchorage, Bell wrote, were mostly "middle-aged women [who] see the forty-six-year-old jet-setter as a sort of feminist hero—a woman who got dumped by a man but then found the gumption to succeed in businesses on her own."

Palin stood in line with the rest of the stargazing hoi polloi. "We want to see Ivana," she told Bell, *"because we are so desperate in Alaska for any semblance of glamour and culture."* (Emphasis added.) The comment provides a remarkable bit of insight into the thirty-two-year-old woman who would, in only a dozen years, be tapped as the vice presidential nominee of the Republican Party.

Just a few weeks earlier, Palin had submitted an application to the city of Palmer for the position of police dispatcher. It is a fascinating document. Attached to it was a one-page résumé, which included some classic Palin schmaltz and self-promotion. Under her "strengths," she declared: "Lifelong resident of Alaska. An innate ability to 'be in the right place at the right time.'"

Palin signed that everything in the document "is true or complete to the best of my knowledge" and that "any intentional misrepresentation or omission and any material negligence or innocent misrepresentation or omission" would disqualify her from employment and "may be considered for immediate discharge from employment." The document was notarized on March 12, 1996.

Rather than list her home address, Palin listed a post office box in Wasilla. She also noted that she was "unemployed" at the time of the application and curiously checked the "yes" box when asked: "If you are under 18 years of age, can you provide required proof of your eligibility to work?" She was thirty-two at the time. She checked every box in terms of her availability—full time, part time, shift work, and temporary. Under the listing of "Education," she declared that she had graduated from Wasilla High in 1982 with a "college prep" course of study. In respect to her "Undergraduate College," she listed solely the University of Idaho, where she indicated that she had completed five years, with a course of study in "Political Science/Journalism"—in that order. On her résumé accompanying the application, she says that she completed a minor in "political science" and also added "political science studies" to her list of "specialized training."

And then comes a more curious representation. Under "Graduate Professional" education, she declared "Post-Grad General Studies" for one year. Just where this graduate school education took place she did not indicate, nor has there ever been a record of such postgraduate work made public by Palin, in her memoir or elsewhere. In a sworn deposition, taken in 1998 for a case related to her performance as mayor of Wasilla, she was asked, "And did you have any further degrees or seek any further education [following your graduation from the University of Idaho]?"

PALIN: Yes, seeking a—hopefully—will be able to some day work further for a master's degree.

She was asked later in her deposition: "When you were on the city council did you attend seminars or take any courses in public administration?" Her response: "Not specifically for public administration. I don't recall any."*

When asked to state "any additional information" helpful to considering her application, Palin responded "Lifelong Valley Resident; *Willing* [underlined twice] & Able To Work Shift Hours. . . . Excellent Attitude." She also listed a trio of references, all of whom were to figure significantly in her life. One was her lifelong family friend, Dr. Curt Menard; a second was Brad

---

* Joni Kirk, associate director of media relations at the University of Idaho, could not confirm nor deny Palin's minor in political science. "Due to student privacy laws, which do extend to alumni, I am unable to provide any information about any minor she may have earned." Kirk provided an Internet link to an article about Palin appearing in the January 2008 alumni magazine, *Here We Have Idaho,* that referred to her undergraduate degree in journalism but made no mention of a minor in political science or any postgraduate work. Kirk said that minors are not recorded on UI diplomas.

Hanson, a Palmer city councilmember and business partner of the Palins, with whom the *National Enquirer* would link her romantically a decade later during the presidential campaign[†]; and the third reference, placed at the top of her list, was Wasilla mayor John Stein—the man, in just a matter of a few months, against whom Palin would run the most vicious and personal political campaign in the history of the Matanuska and Susitna valleys.

N ICK CARNEY SAYS THAT HE SENSED IT COMING, that he knew Palin had set her sights on being mayor of Wasilla as much as a year before it happened. "The first indication was about a year prior to the time she filed for mayor," Carney recalls, "when all of a sudden she started attacking John Stein." Palin began criticizing Stein for allowing the city budget to "grow by leaps and bounds," says Carney, and "of course, Palin had voted for everything. It was growing because the tax money was rolling in, and it had nothing to do with John. The council controlled the money. And Sarah never did anything to change the direction of the council. Nothing. She always voted to approve the budget." Palin had picked up on community resentment toward the 2 percent sales tax that Stein had promoted to support city services, even though she had supported it as a council candidate herself a few years earlier. At one point, Palin's ramped-up rhetoric became so intense—and its motivations so seemingly obvious—that Carney called her on it at a meeting. "I said, 'Sarah, sounds like you're running for mayor,'" recalls Carney. "And she got really upset—really huffy about it." Palin refused to respond and just glared at him.

Like many other political operatives in the Mat-Su, Laura Chase—who would become Palin's mayoral campaign manager—was also a longtime Alaskan. Born in California in 1950, Chase's family migrated to Fairbanks in 1958

[†] In a series of articles appearing in the *National Enquirer* on September 22, September 29, and October 6, 2008, reporters John South, John Blosser, Alan Butterfield, and Rick Egusquiza asserted that "Sarah Palin engaged in an extramarital affair with her husband's former business partner" whom they identified as Brad Hanson. The *Enquirer* cited three in-laws of Hanson's—including Jim Burdett, the former brother-in-law of Hanson's wife's brother—as sources for the story. According to the *Enquirer*, "Burdett passed a rigorous polygraph test regarding his claims about Palin and Hanson." Palin and Hanson denied the story at the time.

when she was in the second grade. Her father, a talented mechanic and a former minor league baseball player, had become infatuated with the promises of the Last Frontier and secured work in Fairbanks, where he soon brought his young family to join him.

They bounced around a bit, following employment opportunities, before winding up in the small outpost of King Salmon, in the far western region of the state. Chase graduated from Bristol Bay High School in 1968 and had hoped to join the Air Force, but her parents forbade her, and she was literally forced to take courses at the University of Alaska Fairbanks campus instead. She lasted a couple of years. As did the young woman for whom she was later to work, Chase also entered beauty pageants as a means of earning scholarship money and was named Miss Bristol Bay in 1968. She dropped out of college, got married, and raised two children, before finally earning a degree in 1989 (right before she turned forty) from the School of Communications from the University of Idaho—yet another parallel with Palin.

Fate brought Chase back to Alaska—one of her sons was involved in a near-fatal car crash outside Anchorage (he recovered)—and in 1991 she was named executive director of the burgeoning Wasilla Chamber of Commerce, of which Nick Carney was president. Wasilla mayor John Stein was a strong supporter and a close political ally.

Chase originally met Sarah Palin through the Chamber in late 1991 or early 1992, shortly before Carney encouraged Palin to run for City Council. Like both Stein and Carney, Chase viewed Palin as a political ally who supported the sales tax and a police force in Wasilla. And also like Carney, Chase felt that Palin didn't make much of a mark during her early years on the council, though there were two personal traits that made her take pause. One she describes as a "false innocence" that Palin possessed, "a feigned vulnerability, a shyness," that Chase now views as an "act," as some quality that was "a false thing." She likens Palin to "a very good actress" with the political arena as her stage. "She kind of projected herself as being 'just a mom' and shy," Chase recalls. "She would say things like 'Oh, I can't do that,' and people would respond 'Oh, yeah, you can.' It was her way to get people to say, 'Oh, sure you're great, you can do this.' She could turn on this particular aspect of her personality that made people feel like they needed to step in and help her or rescue her."

Her other trait, more overtly political in her early years on the council, according to Chase, was equally deceptive and also fed her desire for the spotlight. "She hid it," Chase asserts, "and only pulled it out at certain times, where she would be extremely assertive in a very weird way." Palin, she said, would fixate on a particular issue—bike paths, for instance—that were often tangential to the larger discussion at hand. "It's kind of like her focus was always off a little bit—on things that weren't as important at the time," Chase says. "But she'd ride that issue and use it as a way to get people to concentrate on her, you know. It's like she'd keep feeding it over and over. The only purpose was to bring the attention back on her. She's gifted in the sense that she has the capability to do that."

Chase, like many who have dealt with Palin throughout her career, believes that Palin suffers from a narcissistic personality disorder. The first time she went to Palin's house, she says, "she walked me straight into her bedroom to show me the picture of her as Miss Wasilla in her crown and all that, so she could tell me about being in the Miss Alaska pageant." Chase let her know that she had been a beauty queen, too. "I just said, 'Yeah, it's fun, isn't it?'" Chase recalls, but she also wondered to herself, "Why are you showing me this? I don't whip out my crown to show everybody when they come over."

Chase also ran for the council and was elected in 1994. She eventually left her job at the Chamber and went to work as a legislative aide for Lyda Green, the matriarch of the Republican Party in the Mat-Su who had been elected to the State Senate in 1994 as part of the conservative Republican tide that had taken over the valley. During the legislative session of 1996 (essentially January through May), Chase joined Green in Juneau. When she returned to Wasilla, Chase was approached by Palin in Green's legislative office. Palin told her that she was going to run against John Stein for mayor. Chase was a bit startled by Palin's boldness and by what she felt was a betrayal of an ally. Chase actually had thoughts of running for mayor of Wasilla, too—but only after Stein retired. When Chase pressed her about her motivations, Palin, she said, spoke in the vaguest of terms. "He's not thinking about what the people want," Palin declared. Then, according to Chase, she "rattled on about taxes and bike trails." Although Chase had minor issues with Stein (she thought that certain department heads were exerting too much influence over him), Chase felt he had done a good job—"you can't move the wheels of government bureaucracy at high speed all the time"—and she felt a certain amount of loyalty toward him. But Palin insisted that Chase run her campaign.

Looking back on it, Chase realizes she got caught up in the excitement of the moment. Palin was extremely enthusiastic, saying, "Well, just think, two University of Idaho graduates—we're gonna go in there and kick butt and we're gonna clean up the place." Palin also made Chase an offer she couldn't refuse. According to Chase, Palin said, "I could be the mayor and you could be my deputy mayor . . . well, city administrator was the proper term"—and it was a promise she would reiterate to Chase throughout the campaign.

Chase speculated that Green had encouraged Palin to challenge Stein. And when Chase went to Green to discuss Palin's offer, worrying about a perceived conflict of interest, she only received encouragement. "Lyda just said, 'Well, I think you should, it'd be good for you, you know, I mean you'll have that experience, and I think it'd be great.'"

A decade and a half after her decision, Chase still has regrets. She had her own political ambitions and was worried about her personal financial situation, but she is consumed by a guilt that lingers. "I should have just flat-out said no to Sarah to begin with," Chase acknowledges, "because I felt rather like I was stabbing John in the back. And in fact, in retrospect, I'm sure that's exactly what I was doing, though I didn't see it that way at the time." Her decision came with a heavy price attached. "Oh, my God, I lost friends over this, and I'll still to this day never forgive myself for it."

Before the campaign got fully underway, Palin came over to Chase's house where they had a meeting about the upcoming election and went over some of Palin's early drafts of campaign literature that were spread out on Chase's dining room table. "It was junk," Chase recalls. "All over the map. No consistency." They got to talking about various issues, one of which was term limits. Palin said she didn't believe in them, that "the voters set term limits." And then the conversation took a startling turn.

According to Chase, Palin then declared, "If I'm still here in this job after two years, then I'm quitting. I mean, I better be moved on to something bigger and better than that by then." Chase was a bit taken aback by the implied arrogance of Palin's remarks, but she also saw Palin's political potential and she could foresee Palin's career trajectory taking her beyond the confines of the Mat-Su. "Well, Sarah," Chase responded, "you could end up being governor before you're done with this, maybe in ten years." Chase watched Palin as she shuffled through the papers. Without missing a beat, and without the slightest trace of irony, Palin responded: "I don't want to be governor. I want to be president."

Palin's unbridled ambition hit Chase full force. She was uncertain what to make of it and chalked it up at the time "to the adrenaline of the campaign." Palin never bothered to look up and kept riffling through the paperwork. "Where in the hell did that comment come from?" Chase wondered at the time. "It was like right out of left field. Why would anybody with no political experience whatsoever even conceive of jumping from running for small-town mayor to president of the United States?" Palin soon shifted the conversation to another subject. "We just kept working," Chase recalls. "It was very bizarre."

P ALIN'S CAMPAIGN FOR MAYOR LEFT SCARS in Wasilla that linger until this day. More than a decade later, Nick Carney still shakes his head. "I always characterized that mayoral campaign as the moment of Wasilla losing its innocence," Carney says ruefully of his former hometown. "It was very vicious."

John Stein was also a longtime Alaskan. He had arrived as a teenager—to the southeast, in Sitka—on July 4, 1959, the day Alaska became the forty-ninth state in the union. His father was a mechanical engineer who worked for pulp mills, and so the Stein family moved around the States during his youth, from Minnesota to Georgia to Washington and, finally, to Alaska, where Stein's father took a job at the Sitka Pulp Mill, which had been financed entirely with Japanese money. (It was the first major foreign investment in the U.S. made by Japan after World War II.)

Stein graduated from Sitka High School in 1962, and then he knocked around the Pacific Northwest a bit, working in a variety of jobs from meter reader to an engineer's aide for Boeing, while earning an associate of arts degree in industrial engineering, and later, a bachelor of science degree in public management from the University of Oregon. He had hoped to find public administration work in southeast Alaska, preferably in Sitka, but when none materialized, in 1985 he relocated to Wasilla, where he took a position as a city planner. It didn't last long. In little more than a year, the city transferred Stein's position to the Mat-Su Borough (the equivalent of a county) at a time when Wasilla was in transition from a "second-class" Alaska city (with a weak-mayor system) to a home-rule municipality (with a strong-mayor system). Bright and articulate, and blessed with a comforting baritone voice, Stein, then in his early forties, decided to throw his hat into the political arena during the mayoral election of 1987. He beat the incumbent by twelve votes for his first three-year term. He won again in 1990 and 1993, both handily, and he was generally considered a popular and widely respected mayor before his face-off with Palin in the fall of 1996.

Although Palin would claim in her memoirs that the race for mayor hinged on an issue involving annexation, there was also a brutal—and definitive— religious undercurrent to the campaign. Much of it flew below the community radar, but those who saw it were shocked. Palin had the strong support of her family's Assembly of God congregation, and then there was the "whisper campaign," as Carney called it, promulgated by some Palin supporters, that Stein was not a Christian, and that he was, in fact, Jewish. He was not; his parents had been raised in the Pennsylvania heartland and were of Dutch Lutheran stock. But the rumor persisted. Moreover, there were assertions by Palin supporters that she would be the "first Christian mayor of Wasilla"—an assertion that was repeated in a letter and, according to Stein, by a local television station. "That was absurd," says Carney. "All of the other mayors were Christian—not that it should have mattered. But she lied about it while she was campaigning." Stein, who was, admittedly, not an ardent churchgoer, became a target for the devout evangelical conservatives who were taking over the political and cultural life of the Valley. Afterward he produced a list of the eight previous mayors who had been Christian—but apparently not Christian enough for Palin and her minions.

There were more personal assaults. Stein's second wife, Karen Marie, used a different last name than he, forcing Stein to produce a marriage certificate to counter the charges by the small-town whisper campaign that he and his wife were "living in sin." Stein says that Palin never said any of these things directly, but that her supporters engaged in the surreptitious tactics. "These people were looking to damage my credibility and service to the community," Stein says. "Nobody from Sarah's camp ever told them to back off."

In fact, at one point early in the campaign when Stein first caught wind of the personal attacks, he actually called Palin up to discuss the matter with her. "I said, 'Can I come and talk to you? Because I don't want to get into this personal stuff.'" There were rumors of Palin's alleged affair with Hanson and there was also considerable talk of Palin essentially leaving the care of her children to her sisters. Stein says he simply wanted a clean campaign process.

> So I went to her house, which was the house on Wasilla Lake, and sat in the living room and I said, "I just wanted you to know that even though I've heard about some things that might be awkward or embarrassing, I'm not gonna use any of that stuff in my campaign. I want to stick to the issues, and I hope you'll do the same thing."
>
> She doesn't say no, but she says, "I understand what you're asking." And that's sort of what I got out of it. I didn't get a real commitment from her. She didn't say, "Well, I will stay totally away from that." It was more like, "Uh-huh, I

understand what you're saying, and I will accept that *you* won't get personal."

Stein says that he and Palin were operating on "totally different planes." Palin was "running on guns, religious fundamentalism, anti-abortion, and an anti-tax platform." Stein was running a "fix the potholes" campaign. The evangelical conservatives, Stein argues, were seeking to transform the face of Alaska politics, and they were gaining footholds wherever they could. Palin was viewed as a vehicle for that transformation.

Sarah Palin's victory in the general election that fall, on October 1, 1996, was, at least by Wasilla standards, something of a landslide, although certainly not an avalanche. Palin beat Stein 651 to 440 votes, garnering slightly less than 60 percent of the votes cast.‡

From the very beginning, Palin's victory brought utter chaos to the City of Wasilla. Only days following her triumph, there would be a showdown between Palin and the newly seated council when Palin tried to appoint two of her supporters, Steve Stoll and Diane Keller, to vacant council positions. One of them, Stoll, who was referred to in Wasilla as "Black Helicopter Steve," was a longtime right-wing activist in the Mat-Su and an ally of Chryson's with SAGE. As mayor, Palin had embraced the political fringe that she once opposed. And it also pitted her against one-time mentor and Wasilla favorite-son Carney, who had made the mistake of obtaining an Ivy League education. Palin's deep-seated class resentments bristled in the presence of her former ally. "If you spend any time around Sarah," says her former campaign manager Chase, "you'll quickly realize that she cannot stand to be around people smarter than her. She is intimidated by them." Carney successfully blocked the appointment of Stoll, but Keller was appointed (and would eventually become mayor). Palin would claim in an interview with the *Frontiersman* that her effort to place Stoll on the council was "brilliant maneuvering I had to do to deal with the impasse" and, she would allege, to get Carney off the dime. Carney saw it simply as a bungled attempt to assert her

---

‡ A long-forgotten third candidate in the race, Cliff Silvers, a heavy machine operator running for his second time, received just thirty-six votes. The avalanche would come three years later, in 1999, during a rematch with Stein, when she beat him 909 to 292. Wasilla had turned far to the right and Palin captured the zeitgeist.

power. There "was no evidence of any maneuvering," Carney said, "brilliant or otherwise."

The *Frontiersman* also saw little brilliance in the move. In a blistering editorial entitled, "Wasilla Mayor Gets a Lesson," the paper opined that Palin "failed in a blatant attempt to confuse and circumvent the law Monday night in order to pack the city council with candidates favored by her and her supporters." The *Frontiersman* accused Palin of bringing "a couple of shiny-suited attorneys up from Anchorage, both armed with bulging attaché cases," to assist her in her power play with "hocus-pocus" legal maneuverings. What Wasilla discovered, the paper concluded, is that "it has a new mayor with either little understanding or little regard for the city's own laws."

The circus didn't end there. Palin had been outraged that several city administrators had openly supported Stein during the election, and as soon as she took office she had demanded resignation letters from all of her department heads. Many refused. By October 24, 1996, Palin sent out a second letter pressing for resignations, noting that, to date, she had only "received two." She demanded that the rest submit theirs by the following day. "It is the most common practice for any new administration to expect and receive from the exempt employees letters of resignation . . ." Palin declared. "Submit by close of business Friday, October 25, a letter of resignation along with your résumé and a brief letter of note stating why you desire to be retained." Three of them still refused: Librarian Mary Ellen Emmons, Director of Public Works John Felton, and Police Chief Irl Stambaugh.

Emmons's letter of response was not defiant, but conciliatory:

> I am in receipt of your October 24 memorandum requesting a letter of resignation. Based on our conversations of October 7 and October 14, I have continued to perform my duties as Library Director with reliance upon your assurance that you intended to retain me in this position. During the first meeting, I presented a copy of my résumé, and indicated that I look forward to continuing in my position under your administration. During the second meeting, you asked me to consider a role in the potential reorganization of the Museum Department. While we discussed that issue, you indicated that you wanted me to continue in my current position, regardless of the final decision on the reorganization. I am pleased to

offer any skills which will assist you in providing service to the community.

Meanwhile, Palin's campaign manager Laura Chase, who claims that Palin had promised her the deputy administrator job, was told by Palin that she would not be getting it or any other position in her administration. Chase was crestfallen. She had worked hard for Palin in the election and she felt burned by the news. There had been additional rumors that Palin was going to give the deputy post to one of her campaign strategists, Tuckerman Babcock, who happened to be Lyda Green's son-in-law. Concerned about what remained of her reputation, Palin felt compelled to write a letter to the *Frontiersman* squashing such rumors. The newly elected mayor asserted that:

> [A]ll those who volunteered in my campaign are valued friends. They have not asked for jobs with the city, nor have I offered jobs, therefore, there is no plan to hire any of "my cronies," including Tuckerman Babcock, Laura Chase, or anyone else. However, in my opinion, the city would be well served if persons of their qualifications would consider offering their services for our city, and I did not mean to imply anything else.

Chase found Palin's letter little more than a "convenience" and "disingenuous." According to Chase, Palin had discovered during the course of the election that her campaign manager "believed in a woman's right to choose." Early on, Palin had wanted to send out a campaign flier indicating that she had "conservative family values"—which Chase realized was a code for "being religious and that you don't believe in abortion." Chase had argued that "there's no place in politics at a local level for that kind of an issue." Palin deferred, at least momentarily. Others in her campaign would help her carry that gauntlet. But Palin, says Chase, filed it in her back pocket when it came time to hire her after the election. Chase says that when Palin thanked people publicly following her victory, she failed to include Chase among those she acknowledged. The first time it happened, Chase assumed it was simply an oversight. Then it began to happen time and time again. Chase says that she was "hurt" by the omission, but still felt that Palin would honor her commitment and name her deputy administrator.

Chase had taken a leave of absence from her job to work on Palin's campaign during the final push. But Palin had made no move to offer her the job. Finally, Palin called her to meet at the Kashim Inn, a run-down bar and restaurant located along the Parks Highway in Wasilla. Chase remembers it being dark and quiet inside, and they both ordered coffee. Chase sensed that something was up. "She was looking down at the table, you know," Chase recalls. "And she just wouldn't look at me." Finally, Palin asked sheepishly, "Well, um, who do you think I should get to be the city administrator?" Chase was taken aback. "Sarah," she responded, "you said you were going to hire *me*." Palin, according to Chase, went into a long spiel explaining how it might look bad that she was hiring her friends. Chase said, well, Sarah, all hirings are political. But Palin wouldn't budge. Chase could tell it had to do with her political perspective on hard-core conservative politics.

Under Stein, the position of mayor had been more akin to that of city manager, while the role of deputy administrator had gone unfilled. Instead, on October 21, Palin appointed John Cramer, a former state official, to fill that role—even though there was no budgetary allocation for his salary of $51,000 a year, plus benefits. With the hiring of Cramer, his position became that of the "actual city manager," said Carney, while Palin's role became more of a "figurehead."

Palin then initiated more bureaucratic bloodshed. She forced the resignation of museum director John Cooper and eliminated his position. (Six months later, a trio of longtime museum staff—Opal Toomey, Esther West, and Ann Meyers—all in their sixties and seventies, retired en masse over what they viewed as Palin's disregard for local history; planning director Duane Dvorak and Public Works director John Felton turned in their resignations, both disgusted by Palin's machinations.) Palin was also engaged in open conflict with the city attorney, Dick Deuser, who had prevented her from having her way with the council appointments, and, with the start of the new year in 1997, she was still at odds with her police chief, Stambaugh, and her librarian, Emmons, with whom she had immediately sparred over the issue of censorship.

A CLASSIC EXAMPLE OF HOW PALIN STEERS DISCUSSION OF HER RECORD AWAY FROM the truth and creates a facade of deniability is reflected in the case of her explorations, when first elected mayor, of removing or "banning" books from the Wasilla Library. In *Going Rogue*, Palin claims that she "never sought to ban any books" and denied any interest in doing so. During the 2008 election the story became a serious issue that was significantly distorted when a blogger posted a catalogue of nearly ninety books that Palin "tried to have banned." The list included such classics as *Catch-22* by Joseph Heller; *Death of a Salesman* by Arthur Miller; *The Adventures of Huckleberry Finn* by Mark Twain; even *Webster's Ninth New Collegiate Dictionary*. In fact, the posting was clearly a hoax and should have alerted any journalist pursuing the story. The inventory was comprised "of frequently challenged books" compiled by the American Library Association, including volumes in the J. K. Rowling Harry Potter series, several of which were first published *after* Palin had been mayor.

The faux list became a straw man for Palin and her supporters to slay. She attacked the national media for portraying her as "the book-burning evangelical extremist sweeping down from the north on her broomstick." She accused the press of ignoring the facts about her role in the censorship issue. She triumphantly pointed out that some books she was claimed to have censored had yet to be published by the time she was mayor—which, in her mind, put an end to any further discussion about the book banning issue. Case closed.

Palin's deputy mayor, Judy Patrick, would later claim in a press release "there were no books that were ever banned from the City"—yet another straw man argument. By pushing up against the obviously false charges, the real story got buried and dismissed.

There were several witnesses to Palin's efforts to raise the specter of censorship in Wasilla during her terms as both a councilmember and mayor along with several contemporaneous accounts from both the *Mat-Su Valley Frontiersman* and the *Anchorage Daily News*. According to a story first published on December 8, 1996, by Paul Stuart in the *Frontiersman*, Wasilla Library director Mary Ellen Emmons said that Palin "broached the subject" of censorship with her on three occasions during October of that year. Emmons said that during their first conversation, prior to Palin being sworn in as mayor, she briefly touched on the subject of censorship and did so again, two weeks later, after she was sworn into office. But on Monday, October 28, according to the *Frontiersman* story, Emmons said, "Palin asked her outright if she could live with censorship of library books." Emmons, then president of the Alaska Library Association, said that the nature of Palin's request was clearly "different than a normal book-selection procedure or a book-challenge policy. She was asking me how I would deal with her saying a book can't be in the library."

Emmons, who declared that "the free exchange of information is my main job," was adamant in her response that she would tolerate no censorship. "I'm not trying to suppress anyone's views," Emmons said. "But I told her [Palin] clearly, I will fight anyone who tries to dictate what books can go on the library shelves."

Palin would later claim that her questions were "rhetorical" or "hypothetical." But according to several witnesses at the time, Palin's intentions were focused and concrete. And that focus was on a book authored by Howard Bess entitled *Pastor, I Am Gay*.

Bess was a popular Baptist minister in the Matanuska Valley in the 1990s, at the Church of the Covenant, then located in Wasilla. Raised in rural Illinois, he had been a star football player at Wheaton College and had originally served as a minister in Goleta, California (near Santa Barbara), before arriving first in Anchorage, and then in the Mat-Su in 1988. In his early career he identified himself as a conservative and a Republican, but during his ministry in California he had his first encounter with a church member who was struggling with his homosexuality. Then in the early 1990s, there had been a rash of teenage suicides in and around Wasilla, many of whom, according to Bess, had been struggling with their homosexuality in an intensely homophobic environment. The suicides had a profound impact on Bess. He further explored his conscience and his Christianity and began working on his book. In 1995, he published *Pastor, I Am Gay* to shed light on a community that had "so long been condemned, ignored, or misunderstood by most everyone and especially Christian churches." Based on his personal observations and chronicling his own inner turmoil ministering homosexual congregants, the publication of *Pastor, I Am Gay* caused a whirlwind of controversy in Wasilla, Palmer, and the surrounding area, and a good deal of it was critical—if not downright hostile.

Since he had arrived in Wasilla, Bess had participated in a weekly ad hoc breakfast meeting with a group of two dozen or more ministers and pastors in the Valley. They met at the Trout Place & Windbreak Café, a landmark restaurant in Wasilla that pays homage to the spectacular sport fishing in southwest Alaska. For many years, Bess got on well with the regional ministry, but one day, following the publication of his book, less than a handful of ministers showed up for breakfast. Bess had been blackballed. Shortly thereafter, his Church of the Covenant was "dis-fellowshipped" by the American Baptist Churches of Alaska because of the book. Bess was not to be dissuaded by the ostracism. "In my role as a pastor, I've always seen myself as being called to be a community activist—a person who is active in the public good," Bess says. "I believe that this is the truest tradition of Jesus."

The Wasilla Assembly of God—of which Palin was still an ardent member and which had played a critical role in her election as mayor—had "a different view of the Christian tradition," according to Bess, and viewed homosexuality "as the enemy of Christianity, as evil, as the devil." Initially, no bookstore in Wasilla would carry the book; he was forced to sell it out of a pair of barbershops. Bess also gave a pair of books to the Wasilla Library, and they soon disappeared. He contributed two more, and then two more again. They, too, went missing. According to Bess, he was told directly by people who had spoken with Palin that his book was specifically mentioned as a target of hers.

Wasilla resident and community activist Anne Kilkenny was a witness to one of Palin's statements to Emmons that "there were books in the library that should not be there." It wasn't "rhetorical" at all, says Kilkenny. "She wanted to know what the procedure was for removing them. Could she just go over there and remove them herself, or send someone else to, or should she prepare a list of titles." There were two other books that were also brought up in these censorship discussions: *Daddy's Roommate,* a controversial children's book about gay parenting, written in 1991 by Michael Willhoite; and *Go Ask Alice,* an anonymously written "diary" about teenage drug use that actually has an antidrug message, originally published in the early 1970s. According to Palin's former campaign manager Laura Chase, who served for a year with Palin on the Wasilla City Council, Palin specifically raised the issue of censoring *Daddy's Roommate* at a council meeting, although Palin acknowledged that she had never read it. Chase found Palin's attitude appalling. "I brought a copy to the next council meeting and offered it to Sarah to read," Chase asserts, "and her response was: 'I don't need to read that kind of stuff.'" John Stein also confirmed the discussion.

Kilkenny says that the Assembly of God fueled a "strong sentiment supporting censorship and book banning" during this era. Kilkenny spoke to a member of the same prayer group as Palin's mother, Sally Heath, and this person expressed pride in the fact that this "prayer group was removing books from the library and not returning them to get them out of circulation, and ripping out pages and using black markers to black out passages offensive to them." According to Kilkenny, another member of Sally Heath's prayer group "proudly reported that she stole from a local secondhand store and then burned some Mormon literature as her part in the 'clean up the city' effort which targeted 'satanic' literature." Another friend of the Heath family contends that Sally attempted to burn some of her son's rock 'n' roll records when he was still living at home.

There was a strong culture of censorship and repression emanating from the evangelical movement in the Mat-Su. "I have friends who are librarians and they tell me it's a common practice with the religious right to make books just simply disappear out of libraries," says Bess. "This goes on all across the country, and this happened at the Wasilla Library. And there is no copy there of *Pastor, I Am Gay* to this day."

T HE SCRAP OVER CENSORSHIP WITH EMMONS HAD NOT PLAYED well in Wasilla. There were rumblings of a Palin recall movement. Then on January 30, Palin shocked the community by issuing termination letters to both Emmons and police chief Stambaugh. Her move created more headlines and added more fuel to the fire of the recall movement against her.

Stambaugh is a big bear of man—he carries nearly 230 pounds on his 6'2" frame—but he has an easygoing disposition that belies his quarter century in Alaska law enforcement and his stint from 1968 to 1969 in the Army's Military Police Corps, serving as a convoy runner in Vietnam. Stambaugh is also a fourth-generation Alaskan—his great-grandparents had been some of the first Outside settlers in Ketchikan—and he himself had been raised in Juneau, where he attended high school before entering the Army. In 1993, Stambaugh, then a captain of the Patrol Division in the Anchorage Police Department, was selected over several other candidates to serve as the City of Wasilla's first chief of police. Stambaugh immediately developed a sterling reputation in the close-knit community of five thousand—so much so that the city nominated him to be Alaska's Municipal Employee of the Year. One of the key components of his contract, in Stambaugh's eyes—and which he had originally negotiated with Stein—was that he could "only be terminated with cause."

Stambaugh had been on the job little more than "a day or two—certainly less than a week"—when he first met Palin, then twenty-nine and just elected to her first term on the Wasilla City Council. "Sarah was definitely someone that you noticed," Stambaugh recalls. "She wasn't like the other council members. She was very forward, very confident. You got the sense that she felt the city revolved around her."

Over the next few years, as Stambaugh established himself in Wasilla and forged the foundation for the city's embryonic police force, he developed a friendship of sorts with Palin. They even took a step-aerobics class together along with other city officials. "Sarah was a runner and was all about staying in shape," Stambaugh recalls. "She cared about the way she looked. She was very concerned with appearances." He describes their relationship as "cordial."

Stambaugh watched as Palin sometimes "used her looks to get what she wanted around City Hall," often "flirting" her way into someone's confidence. Stambaugh kept a healthy distance. Trouble and conflict seemed to follow her around. And her political aspirations were on overdrive. He noticed how behind the scenes, Palin gradually turned on Stein. "She started bad-mouthing the mayor," he recalls. "She came up with this catchy term—the 'good ol' boys network.' And she ran with it."

"You could tell she was very ambitious," Stambaugh says, "and there was talk about her running for mayor. Honestly, I didn't take it very seriously. I thought she was in over her head." By the time of the election in 1996, however, Stambaugh recognized the writing on the wall in respect to the mayor's race. "About the end of summer," he recollects, "I saw it coming. Her campaign had lots of energy. And give her credit; she worked her butt off."

Stambaugh says that while he never established "solid footing" with Palin once she was elected mayor, he felt that they had come to something of an understanding. He describes the early days of Palin's mayorship "as a circus." Somehow, they got through it. Palin also imposed what was effectively a gag order on city staff, prohibiting them from talking to the media. All communication henceforth would go through her. She also initiated changes in the manner in which department heads reported to the mayor, demanding weekly reports "full of numbers when appropriate" and "at least two positive examples of work that was started, how we helped the public, how we saved the city money, how we helped the state, how we helped Uncle Sam, how we made operations run smoother, or safer, or more efficient.

"I figured that was the price we all had to pay for betting on the wrong horse," says Stambaugh in reference to the weekly reports. "Sarah enjoyed making all of us jump through her hoops." She kept up the scrutiny. "I believe if we look for the positive," Palin declared in a memo sent out to all city staff, "that is what we will ultimately find. Conversely, look for the negative and you'll find that, too . . . I encourage you to choose the prior because the train is a 'moving forward!'"

Stambaugh had hoped that after a month or two, his relationship with Palin would be back on solid ground. But the two crossed swords on a pair of red-button law-enforcement issues. Stambaugh had opposed legislation that would have allowed the carrying of concealed weapons in public buildings, including churches, bars, and schools; Palin and the National Rifle Association (NRA) strongly supported the legislation. "It was absolutely crazy," says Stambaugh. "She was playing up to the Alaska gun lobby. We were simply applying common sense to the use of guns. Even in the Old West, you left your weapons at the door." Stambaugh also wanted to close down Wasilla's bars two hours earlier than 5 A.M. (he had noticed a sharp spike in drunk driving arrests between 3 A.M. and 5 A.M., when Wasilla's bars closed only for an hour), but Palin's political ties to the bar owners led her to oppose Stambaugh on that policy issue, too, even though, as Stambaugh noted, "it went counter to her evangelical values."

Stambaugh tried to toe Palin's line. He filed his weekly reports for Palin in detail, including "lots of numbers," and emphasized the positive. He loved his job, and he was willing to do whatever it took, "within reason," to keep it. By the beginning of the new year, Stambaugh had felt things were "starting to stabilize." He and Palin had shared a few jokes and he tried to accommodate her new policy directives. According to Stambaugh, she told him that he was doing a "wonderful job" and that his position with the city was secure.

Then on January 30, Stambaugh took an urgent call from his friend Emmons, who told him that she had just been fired from her library post by Palin for "insubordination." Stambaugh was disgusted. While he was still on the phone with Emmons, an aide of Palin's walked up to Stambaugh and handed him an envelope. Stambaugh opened it. The letter said that his tenure as police chief had been terminated.

Stambaugh wasn't surprised. Nothing Palin did surprised him. But he was ticked off. After nearly thirty years in law enforcement, he considered the letter a "slap in the face." A short time later, Stambaugh got a call from Stephanie Komarnitsky, a reporter at the *Anchorage Daily News*. She said that she had heard about the firings, and had called Palin, who denied them. "There's been no meeting," Palin told the reporter, "no actual terminations." She didn't want there to be a news story. Stambaugh was appalled by the naked dishonesty. He'd seen Palin play fast and loose with the facts for the past four years. Some people jokingly referred to her as the "Town Liar." Stambaugh pulled out the letter and read it to Komarnitsky. "Although I appreciate your service as police chief, I've decided it's time for a change," Palin wrote. "I do not feel I have your full support in my efforts to govern the city of Wasilla. Therefore I intend to terminate your employment . . . ." The letter gave a final work date of February 13. "What do you think?" Stambaugh asked Komarnitsky. "Sure as hell sounds like a firing to me." For her part, Palin told the reporter, "I'm going to get myself in trouble if I keep talking about it."

Palin later changed her mind about the Emmons firing—she claimed that

Emmons had "promised to support me with my desire to restructure and combine the library and museum departments without increasing staff"—but she held firm on Stambaugh. "You know in your heart when someone is supportive of you," Palin told the *Anchorage Daily News*. The burgeoning recall movement, however, by the Concerned Citizens for the City of Wasilla eventually fizzled out, ironically, when none other than Nick Carney argued against it at a town hall meeting.

On February 7, 1997, the *Frontiersman* ran a memorable editorial about Palin entitled "Mayor's Lost Credibility." The paper's commentary opened with a rhetorical question: "We wonder, nearly four months after the election, if Wasilla voters got what they wanted when they elected Sarah Palin as mayor?" It then went on to point out that while Palin may have been elected with 60 percent of the vote, her total reflected merely 18 percent of Wasilla's registered voters. The newspaper was not impressed with Palin's opening act as mayor. "Palin seems to have assumed that her election was instead a coronation," the editorial noted. "Welcome to Kingdom Palin, the land of no accountability."

The paper then issued observations that would sound remarkably familiar a full decade and a half later:

> Wasilla residents have been subjected to attempts to unlawfully appoint council members, statements that have been shown to be patently untrue, unrepentant backpedaling, and incessant whining that her only enemies are the press and a few disgruntled supporters of Mayor Stein. . . . Mayor Palin fails to have a firm grasp of something very simple: the truth.

The *Frontiersman* was quite clear in identifying the source of Wasilla's political chaos. "While she will blame everyone but herself," the editorial concluded, "we see mostly Sarah at the center of the problem."

A few weeks later Stambaugh sued Palin on a variety of fronts for unlawful termination, all to no avail. In February of 2000, after three years of depositions and legal maneuverings, U.S. District Judge James K. Singleton, Jr., issued a twenty-eight-page final ruling against Stambaugh. In the end, it didn't matter if Palin had dismissed Stambaugh for political reasons. Singleton found that then-Mayor Stein had overstepped his legal bounds by executing a contract with Stambaugh that appeared to protect him from the consequences of "at-will" employment that was otherwise stipulated by Wasilla statutes. "Stein lacked the authority to provide Stambaugh job security," Singleton found, "at least after such time as Stein ceased to be mayor." Once Palin defeated Stein, the contract he had executed with Stambaugh had become null and void. "He could therefore be terminated by Palin," Singleton concluded, "because she perceived him to lack a shared ideology regarding how the police department should function in Wasilla."

Stambaugh was profoundly disappointed by the court's decision, but there was also a sense of relief that his dealings with Palin had reached closure. He was appalled at what he perceived to be Palin lying at nearly every turn in the court proceedings. "She was lying about everything," he said. "Are we really to believe that she didn't know if the city budget went up or down during her tenure as mayor?"

One story that Stambaugh felt Palin fabricated particularly troubled him. When Palin was on the City Council, Stambaugh often rode his motorcycle to City Hall. One afternoon, Palin had some of her young children with her, and she asked if her kids could sit on Stambaugh's motorcycle. "Sure," he said. They got to talking about riding, and Stambaugh noted that Palin's husband was a well-known snow machine racer. He suggested that maybe Todd should get a motorcycle and that they all should all take a drive up the Parks Highway one day to Fairbanks. Several years later, when Stambaugh was being deposed for the case, Palin's attorney grilled him about the incident as though Stambaugh had been inviting Palin to go for the ride alone. Stambaugh was outraged. He wondered how low this woman would stoop. "She doesn't have any integrity," Stambaugh offered. "None. It's always based on what best suits Sarah Palin. It has nothing to do with the truth."

CHAPTER 2

Juneau

She's had D.C. in mind for a long time.
She's not interested in being on the junior varsity.
—John Bitney, former legislative director for Sarah Palin

I don't think she recognizes that she's wired somewhat
different than the rest of us.
—Walt Monegan, former Alaska Public Safety Commissioner

I'm very confident that a pregnant woman should not
and doesn't have to be prohibited from doing anything,
including running for vice president.
—Sarah Palin, *Anchorage Daily News*

A s dawn broke on the morning of Monday, June 18, 2007, the cruise ship MS *Oosterdam,* of the Holland America Line, needled its way through the northern rung of Alaska's idyllic Inland Passage, a five-hundred-mile archipelago of forested islands and glacial blue fjords that forms the state's scenic coastal panhandle. Only a fistful of passengers clutching coffee mugs braved the cold, damp air on the ship's final stretch to the port city of Juneau—Alaska's picturesque capital. A pod of a dozen or so humpback whales had been spotted feeding off the starboard bow, less than a few hundred yards away. Two of the forty-foot whales breached, rising almost simultaneously out of the water, crashing loudly on their backs and shooting twin white walls of water into the air.

Several hours later, as the state-of-the-art vessel eased its way through the narrow Gastineau Channel, passengers could view from the Lido Deck the snowcapped peaks of southeast Alaska's coastal range. Hugging the shore were occasional totem pole remnants of abandoned Tlingit villages that had been vital communities little more than a century earlier. Straight ahead loomed Juneau, nestled against the mountainous horizon and laid out along a narrow coastal shelf.

With a population today of thirty thousand, Juneau was founded by European settlers as a gold mining camp in the 1880s and the city itself was built upon the tillings from miles of mines that tunneled through nearby Mount Roberts. Geographically isolated and accessible only by air and by sea, Juneau was nonetheless named Alaska's territorial capital in 1906. By the time of Alaska statehood in 1959, the official borough of Juneau had grown larger than the state of Delaware in physical size and stretched all the way east to the Canadian border. During the past half-century, it has held on to the capital in the face of continual challenges from the more populated metropolis of Anchorage, five hundred nautical miles—and more than nine hundred ferry and highway miles—to the northwest. As the high, late-morning sun cascaded against the six-story Alaska State House, built with federal money in 1931, passengers aboard the *Oosterdam* could make out Juneau's scrappy skyline, glinting gold and silver in the distance.

The stopover in Juneau would last ten and a half hours. Holland America offered an eclectic smorgasbord of more than three dozen shore excursions in Juneau, including a helicopter flight to go dog sledding on the Norris Glacier; kayaking, whale watching, salmon fishing, or even gold panning at Last Chance Basin; strenuous hikes through the Alaska rain forest to the face of the receding but still magnificent Mendenhall Glacier; or strolls through downtown Juneau, with its trinket shops, museums, and other tourist attractions that have sprung up in recent years as the cruise ship industry has expanded to bring in more than a million visitors a year to southeast Alaska. After the long, nearly two-day pull from Seattle, most of the visitors were eager to stretch their legs on solid ground.

One group aboard the *Oosterdam*, however, had an entirely different day of activities planned. Their schedules did not include the wonders of the Alaska wilderness and waterways. Cruise ships often invite religious congregations or common-interest organizations to package group tours for their memberships. On this particular cruise, the conservative *Weekly Standard* magazine, owned by Rupert Murdoch, had invited its readers to join a gaggle of conservative writers, including Michael Gerson, George W. Bush's widely celebrated evangelical speechwriter and, by then, a columnist for

The Washington Post; Fox News talking head and *Weekly Standard* executive editor Fred Barnes; and William "Bill" Kristol, son of neoconservative icon Irving Kristol, and himself the *Weekly Standard*'s founder and editor. They—and various members of their families—had been invited to lunch that day by none other than Alaska's governor, Sarah Palin, who had just completed her first legislative session to considerable acclaim.

Palin had been elected to the Alaska governorship in what seemed, in retrospect, to have been something of a cakewalk. She had challenged an unpopular incumbent—Frank Murkowski—and defeated him easily in the Republican Party primary, winning 51 percent of the vote. Murkowski finished a distant third, with less than 20 percent. In the general election, she had cruised to a 48- to 41-percent victory over former Democratic governor Tony Knowles, with independent third-party candidate Andrew Halcro skimming off 9 percent.

Many of her idiosyncratic tendencies that would be illuminated nationally in the following years had first been exposed during her candidacy for governor. She had been given the nickname of "No-Show Palin" for her failure to turn up at scheduled campaign events—forums, debates, and meetings—and the question "Where's Sarah?" became a catchphrase during the campaign. More questions were raised about her candor in explaining some of the absences. In one instance, she skipped a meeting with the chief executive officers of Alaska Native corporations, at first saying she had been previously booked, but then her campaign acknowledged that she wasn't adequately prepared on Native matters. While she did participate in roughly two-dozen debates and forums in total, she ducked more than fifteen events in little more than two months, including several of those sponsored by Alaska Native organizations, but also including the Anchorage Chamber of Commerce Board and the State Chamber of Commerce. "Palin is generally disliked by the business community in Alaska," says her former opponent, Halcro, a political moderate who runs a statewide auto rental franchise. "Because once you talk to her, you quickly realize that she knows nothing about business."

When she did attend debates or forums, she often seemed unprepared or out of her league. Halcro, in particular, was astonished by her vacuity. He recalls that she had to read her comments and responses to questions from prepared notes or "cheat sheets" at nearly all times—her campaign handlers clearly did not trust her to "think on her feet," he says—and she seemed "absolutely overwhelmed" by policy matters. He became increasingly irked by what he called her "political gibberish." At one event he aimed a barb directly at her: "To hear candidates talk about, 'Well, we're going to prioritize,' that's like saying, 'Oh, we're going to embrace efficiencies.' I mean, it means absolutely nothing. . . ." Sometimes she refused to take questions.

Knowles was equally critical of Palin, saying that she had no understanding of the major issues in the campaign. He was startled by her inability to answer simple questions directly and by the way she "meandered all over the map" while trying to make a point. He also began raising concerns about her experience. "Even in Alaska," he says, "we were concerned that being mayor of such a small town provided inadequate preparation for the issues facing our state. She seemed woefully unprepared."

At the annual meeting of Alaska elementary and high school principals in Anchorage on October 16, 2006, Knowles and Halcro were actually prepared to issue a joint statement condemning her no-shows. It was a surprise that Palin showed up at all, but when she did, she arrived with a bizarrely composed handout, a three-year-old Palin screed written about her father entitled "Who's Your Daddy?" Palin had responded to a perceived slight in the *Anchorage Daily News* in July of 2003 by drafting an extremely defensive missive that extolled Chuck Heath's virtues as an educator and coach. "My dad gave me two of the greatest gifts in my life: an upbringing in Alaska and an appreciation for all one can gain from athletics," she declared. "He never let me quit, no matter how bad it hurt or how the odds were stacked against his athletes. He taught 'no pain, no gain . . . and you reap what you sow . . . and there ain't no such thing as a free lunch . . . and dig deep, push hard and fully rely on your ROCK!' (In our case, that ROCK would be God.)"

Knowles was aghast. "Why didn't she come with a position paper on educational issues?" he wondered. "What did this have to do with education?"

Then there were her celebrated flip-flops. During a campaign speech in Ketchikan, site of the proposed Gravina Island Bridge (which had become known by critics of congressional earmarks as the Bridge to Nowhere), Palin expressed her support. She empathized with those in Ketchikan for taking heat over "this Bridge to Nowhere proposal," particularly since those from the Mat-Su, like her, had been denigrated as "valley trash."

> So, I'm standing here today sayin' oh, okay so you've got 'valley trash,' standing here in the middle of 'nowhere,' I think we're gonna make a great team as we progress that bridge. . . .
> The money that's been appropriated for that project, it should remain available for a link, an access project as we continue to

evaluate the scope how best to just get that done. This link is
a commitment to help Ketchikan expand its access to help
this community prosper and will help surrounding communities also. It will open up land, industry, tourism, opportunity.
It's not a Bridge to Nowhere—it's a link to your future.

Palin's remarks drew huge cheers. She was playing to her crowd. She had
her picture taken holding up a T-shirt reading: "Nowhere Alaska 99901." The
following month, when asked if she would support the project, she answered,
"Yes, I would like to see Alaska's infrastructure projects built sooner rather
than later. The window is now—while our congressional delegation is in a
strong position to assist." On August 4, 2006, she sent her core campaign staff
a short e-mail on the "Ketchikan project," noting "I will NOT stop progress
on the bridges . . ." Within months, when the political winds had shifted, she
would turn against the Gravina Island Bridge, and by September of the following year, as governor, she would effectively kill the project.

I N THE END, PALIN WAS RIGHT; NONE OF IT REALLY MATTERED and she
won going away. By the time of the arrival of the *Weekly Standard* entourage
the following summer, she had already generated some buzz in the Lower 48
where the media knew nothing of the details of her gubernatorial campaign.
All that seemed to matter was the perception, the *image*.

Not only did she appeal to the conservative, right-wing base of the Republican Party with her pro-life rhetoric and evangelical Christian values, she
was also portrayed as a political maverick not afraid to take on the "good ol'
boys network" entrenched in Alaska politics, even if they were in the Republican Party. At forty-two, she was the youngest governor ever elected in the Last
Frontier and also its first woman. Moreover, as a former Miss Wasilla and second runner-up in the Miss Alaska beauty pageant, Palin also projected sex appeal, in a good-girl sort of way, and had been dubbed, apparently much to her
pleasure, "the hottest governor in the coldest state." She loved all the attention
and never seemed to pass up a photo op, anytime, anywhere. Palin had a well-
practiced beauty pageant smile, and she flashed it whenever the cameras were
pointed in her direction.

Palin also had ambition by the bucketful. Her drive was so intense that even
those closest to her felt she often crossed the line when pursuing fame and

power. "Sarah always liked to say that she was all about Alaska," says conservative journalist Paul Jenkins, never a fan of Palin. "But what I soon discovered was that she really didn't care about Alaska. She didn't care about her supporters. She certainly didn't care about energy resource development. That was all lip service. All she really cared about was Sarah."

JOHN BITNEY, WHO HAD grown up with Palin in Wasilla, was then serving as Palin's legislative director in Juneau. Bitney was bright, energetic, loyal—and Alaskan to the bone. He had an extensive range of contacts in the state capital that would benefit Palin during her "wildly successful" first legislative session in Juneau, which produced two pieces of signature Palin legislation related to energy production—the Alaska Gasline Inducement Act (AGIA) and significant amendments to the Alaska Ethics Act. He would also set the stage for legislation that would pass in a special session later that November, a taxation plan called "Alaska's Clear and Equitable Share" (ACES). Palin would trumpet AGIA as "the largest private-sector infrastructure project in North American history" and committed $500 million to a foreign-based company to help share in the cost of producing a gas line from Prudhoe Bay to a distribution point in Canada; ACES broke with Murkowski's giveaway plan to tax oil production only in profitable years to a more aggressive and transparent tax structure that taxed oil companies in nonprofitable years as well. Both acts had been steered through the Alaska legislature by Bitney, who had been named as Palin's legislative director shortly after she assumed office.

Born in Wisconsin, Bitney and his family had moved to Alaska in 1967, when he was three, to the remote bush community of Mountain Village, on the Yukon River Delta, where his father took a job teaching for the Bureau of Indian Affairs. The family moved around the remote Alaska interior—Talkeetna, near Denali; then Manokatak, near Bristol Bay—before relocating to Wasilla in time for John to attend Wasilla Junior High for his seventh grade year. Bitney loved music and played the trombone in the school band, along with an eighth grade flutist named Sarah Heath. They were friendly, if not chummy, and both were good students. During Bitney's junior year, when he was sixteen, the family moved to isolated Skwentna, where he graduated from high school in 1983. His mother likes to say he was "in a class all by himself," and he was—the lone senior in a K-12 school of seventeen students in which his father was the teacher. Bitney was initially ticked off about moving away from the social

scene of Wasilla—to a place where "most students mushed dogs to school"—
but he soon operated a sixty-mile trap line for beaver, marten, and coyote
that helped to pay for his college education. His life was straight out of a Jack
London novel.

After receiving his B.A. in 1987 from Washington State University at
Pullman (where he saw Sarah Heath, on occasion, who was at school only
ten miles or so away, across the border in Moscow, Idaho), Bitney returned
to Alaska where he served as a legislative aide for nearly a decade from 1995
to 2002, before assuming the role of legislative director for the Alaska Finance Corporation. Over his fifteen-year stint in Juneau he had built up an
extensive political network in the state capital—as well as in Anchorage—
and for the next four years he worked as a lobbyist during the administration
of Frank Murkowski. When his schoolmate Palin beat Murkowski in the
Republican primary for governor in 2006, he closed down his lobbying
business and played a central role in Palin's campaign, before being named
her legislative director. He and the newly elected governor, he says, had a
"friendly, cordial" relationship, though he was closer to her brother Chuck
Heath and her husband, Todd Palin. Although only forty-one at the time, he
was considered an old hand in Alaska politics, and was not only well liked on
both sides of the aisle but understood the various pitfalls of the state capital.
"Sarah said that she had always felt she and I would do something together in
Juneau," says Bitney. "It was a feeling that I had always sensed, too. I tended
to think she would be a legislator—but she was never happy playing minor
league ball."

By the summer of 2007, Bitney—and his assistant legislative director, former journal Christopher Clark, whom Bitney described as his "wing man"—
had just "worked our asses off" on Palin's behalf. It had been a satisfying
session. Bitney was fully cognizant of Palin's personal drive and ambition. In
2002, when many people thought that Palin was likely to run for a state legislature seat, she instead reached for the silver ring and had run for lieutenant
governor against Senate Majority Leader Loren Leman, nearly pulling off a
major upset and losing by only a 1,962-vote margin. "She had no intention of
climbing the ascension ladder one wrung at a time," says Bitney. "That's just
not Sarah." Even while losing, Palin had energized a wide swath of the Alaskan electorate who had long steered clear of the voting booth; she was a long
shot who lost by a nose at the finish line. Most important, she had used the
election to establish statewide name recognition—a difficult task in such a
vast and geographically disparate state.

Afterward, Palin aggressively pursued—but didn't get—a special appointment to the U.S. Senate by Governor Frank Murkowski. Once Palin was elected governor in 2006 (in part, as payback to Murkowski), Bitney knew that she would soon set her sights on Washington, D.C. "She had no interest in screwing around with smaller offices," Bitney observed. "That whole 'hockey mom' image was a front. It was an image that was used to advance her career and to rise in public office." Shortly before her election, in October 2006, Bitney sensed that Palin would one day be poised for the Republican vice presidential nomination. "This image, this face, this gender, this generation—it was exactly what the party needed." He told people in Palin's inner circle, even before Palin was sworn into office, to expect a national spotlight shining on Alaska. "Look at where the party is, look at what its problems are, look at the message it needs to craft to get its ass out of the doldrums," Bitney said at the time, warning fellow staffers, "Sarah is going to be on the short list of people that they will identify to help them with that message and image."

As for the impending cruise-ship visits, Bitney says that while Palin was always interested in being discovered by journalists from the Lower 48, she was never excited about being in Juneau, especially in the summer. Palin absolutely despised Juneau, with its liberal leanings and damp coastal weather, and she felt like a prisoner living in the Governor's Mansion there. She had snubbed Juneau by having her swearing-in ceremony held in Fairbanks—a bastion of conservatism—and she had supported moving legislative sessions to the Mat-Su. So the arrival of the cruise ships meant additional trips to Juneau during the long, golden days of Alaska's summer, when she preferred the familiar confines of southwest Alaska and her home in Wasilla. Indeed, the official event list for the Alaska Governor's Mansion for June 2007 reveals that the *Weekly Standard* luncheon was the *only* event scheduled there for the entire month; the *National Review* reception would be the *only* event Palin would attend there in August. Moreover, according to Bitney, Palin read neither *The Weekly Standard* nor *National Review*, and knew nothing about the conservative intellectuals on their way to Juneau. "She had never even heard of them," says Bitney. "She really had no idea. It was like 'who are these jokers?'" But she knew that they represented an opportunity for her to promote her political career, to further her driving ambition Outside.

CENTRAL TO THE PALIN BRAND IN THE SUMMER OF 2007 was that she was a political reformer, someone willing to confront the "good ol' boys network," whether it be in Wasilla or in Juneau. She loved positioning herself as a political Joan of Arc. She reveled in demonizing her opponents, wallowed in it. She loved the ink that flowed from the ensuing narrative. American journalism loves to simplify stories into morality tales. Palin was the perfect vehicle. The long grind of complex legislation is tough to condense into an eight-hundred-word story. Palin made this journalistic tendency work to her favor. "Policy doesn't interest her," said Bitney. "She can't focus on it. She's consumed by human interactions. Gossip and dirt is what she lives for. She'll touch lightly on it—but in the end it's all about bad-mouthing people. Every issue turns personal. Everything becomes personalized." And, of course, in her narrative, Sarah Palin was always wearing the white hat. In addition to her energy resource triumphs during her first legislative session, Palin also pushed through a legislative package of ethics reform that achieved widespread bipartisan support. "I believe it could be a precursor for what's to come," she told the Associated Press at the time. "This bill is a good start to getting the comprehensive ethics reform that we need here in Alaska."

But for all of her positioning as a reformer, Sarah Palin had many political skeletons in her closet, more than a few instances where she had crossed the line in respect to judgment and behavior. And in one instance, she clearly violated federal election law, though she got away with it, denied it, lied about it, and moved on. Palin learned early on in her political career that given the bifurcated nature of mainstream journalism, with its implicit acceptance of "two sides to every story," if she countered hard enough with denials or counternarratives of her own, at worst she would break even, canceling out any allegations or charges of impropriety. It was all about the pushback, the denial, the counterpunch.

During the spring of 2002, while she was still mayor of Wasilla, and launching her bid for lieutenant governor, Palin made extensive use of City of Wasilla resources. Long after the dust from the 2002 election settled—and long after she would accuse a colleague on the Alaska Oil and Gas Commission of doing the same—it was disclosed that Palin had used her mayor's office in Wasilla as, what Paul Jenkins of the *Voice of the Times* called, "command center for her lieutenant governor campaign and fundraising efforts." Records obtained in 2006 by Jenkins through a Freedom of Information Act request document a series of Palin's ethical improprieties.*

---

* The records were made available to the author by Jenkins.

The records indicate that on one occasion Palin arranged for campaign travel through her administrative assistant, Mary Bixby, for a flight to Ketchikan. On another occasion she had Bixby print out thank-you notes for Palin's campaign supporters. Bixby later told Kyle Hopkins of the *Anchorage Daily News* that she had been "directed" to execute these tasks on Palin's behalf while she was still "on the clock for the city." Palin also met with the campaign advertising firm Herold Advertising Products at her City Hall offices and then had draft artwork with her campaign logo—"Sarah Palin Lieutenant Governor"—faxed to her deputy administrator at Wasilla City Hall. The following day an invoice from the firm was faxed there as well. Palin, as was her wont, called the allegations a "smear." She claimed that the faxes were the result of a "sales woman seeking her out in the mayor's offices"—when, in fact, the nature of the faxes indicates otherwise. As for her assistant handling her campaign flight, Palin's response was, "It isn't uncommon for staff to arrange travel so that they know where their boss is at all times"—another rejoiner that bordered on absurdity.

In addition to her questionable use of municipal resources, Palin also met with Bill Allen, the controversial CEO of VECO Inc. who would later go to prison as a result of political bribery and conspiracy convictions. According to the founding editor of *Alaska Dispatch,* Tony Hopfinger, Palin met with Allen over wine at his home during her run for lieutenant governor. During a two-day period in December of 2001, VECO associates and their wives contributed a total of $5,000 to Palin's campaign, reflecting 10 percent of her entire campaign budget. "Sarah Palin has always had two sets of rules by which she holds people accountable, those for her and those for everyone else," said Andrée McLeod, Palin's former ally and a good-government activist in Anchorage who would later file a series of Ethics Act complaints against Palin during her governorship.

In the aftermath of the 2002 election, Palin was one of a handful of candidates on Governor Murkowski's "short list" to replace him in the Senate. Palin had campaigned vigorously for Murkowski—she and U.S. Senator Ted Stevens went on a two-week "whistle-stop" tour that took them to the far reaches of Alaska in the period after her primary defeat to Leman. Palin reckoned that her strong showing in the primary, along with her loyalty to Murkowski in the general election and bonding with Stevens on the campaign trail, would land her the Senate appointment. Palin wanted desperately to go to Washington, D.C., to serve in the Senate, to rub shoulders with the Kennedys and Clintons and McCains. Her political ambitions had been powerfully fueled by her statewide run. She loved the juice and the acclaim. In the end, she was barely considered at all—and she knew it. Murkowski, whom Palin would describe in *Going Rogue* as "reminiscent of a large, gruff, but relatively friendly insurance sales-man," eventually named his daughter, Lisa Murkowski, to the seat—and Palin remained bitter and disappointed about it, strongly backing Tea Party candi-date Joe Miller's losing challenge to Lisa Murkowski in 2010.

Then serving in the lower house of the Alaska Legislature, Lisa Murkowski was an accomplished attorney and a pro-choice Republican, and she got along well with elected officials across the political spectrum. Like her father, she had strong links to Big Oil in Alaska and had supported drilling in the Arctic National Wildlife Refuge. Perhaps most important, Frank Murkowski knew that he could count on his daughter to play by the rules, to make sure that he was securely in the loop regarding Alaska's extensive federal funding and ear-marks, which accounted for nearly a third of the state's economy. He knew he could *trust* her. In Palin, he knew he was dealing with a loose cannon, someone who would bolt from time-honored political traditions. She had no respect for political loyalties. She had left a trail of political wreckage behind her every-where she went, and those in-the-know in Alaska politics, those people who paid attention, had followed Palin's trail all the way back to Wasilla.

Frank Murkowski was no political greenhorn. Raised in Ketchikan, he had won his first U.S. Senate seat in 1980 and had held on to it for twenty-one years, winning by a massive 75 percent to 20 percent margin in his last race against Democrat Joe Sonneman. Some would eventually argue that Murkowski had been around the block too many times, but when he caught wind of Palin's re-sentments, he wisely adhered to that time-honored maxim first proffered by the Chinese military strategist, Sun Tzu, in *The Art of War*: "Keep your friends close and your enemies closer." In the cruder vernacular of Alaskan politics, he threw Palin a bone: he appointed her as the "public commissioner" to the three-member Alaska Oil and Gas Conservation Commission (AOGCC), which convened in Anchorage and paid a staggering $124,400 per year salary. While Murkowski assured Palin that the appointment would keep her in the game of statewide politics, it also served to make Palin beholden to him.

Murkowski knew that Palin had little understanding of the politics of oil in Alaska. During her tenure as a councilmember and mayor in Wasilla, her focus had been on building a tax-base for city programs and the development of tax-generating strip malls on the highway into town. Because Palin's hus-band, Todd, worked as a field production operator for British Petroleum on the oil-rich North Slope, Murkowski figured that Palin would fall quickly into line with his plans for expanding energy production throughout the state. Oil is the lifeblood of Alaska politics, and it flowed through Murkowski's veins. As a senator he had pushed hard, if ineffectively, for oil drilling in the Arctic National Wildlife Refuge (ANWR) and he intended to bring the battle for expanded energy production with him to the statehouse.

Murkowski also appointed Randy Ruedrich, a close political chum of his, to the AOGCC. Ruedrich, a longtime manager for British Petroleum who also doubled down as boss of the state's Republican Party, was supposed to keep on eye on Palin, and keep her from meddling in the day-to-day workings of Alaska's bountiful oil and gas production. Unfortunately for Murkowski, Ruedrich fell into Palin's good-ol'-boy demographic: he was large in stature, older, and connected. And he wielded the type of political power that Palin coveted. Palin really had no interest in the politics of gas and oil. She detested political nuance and had no facility for details. She saw the political world in a Manichaean version of black and white, good and evil. Her own brief efforts in the private sector—as a sports writer and television reporter; as a snow machine dealer with her husband Todd; and as a business consultant— had all failed or never really got off the ground. While she tried to present herself as practical and concerned about outcomes, she often got lost in the process.

Just as she had during her political career in Wasilla, Palin began to focus on the inner workings of the AOGCC, its rules and bylaws. She was named chair early on in her tenure. Murkowski thought it was perfect; it tied her up with the internal operations of the commission and gave her an elevated title. Better yet, he hoped, it would turn her focus inward instead of outward. But Palin wielded her gavel with a heavy hand. As chair, Palin was also the AOGCC ethics officer. She appeared to care more about protocol than about expanding energy production.

Soon after she arrived, Palin realized that Ruedrich was conducting Republican Party politics from his AOGCC office. Even worse, she suspected that he was fronting for the oil industry on an coal-bed methane gas project in the Matanuska Valley. As with most of the old dogs in Big Oil, he wasn't playing by the rules.

Palin would later claim that others had turned in Ruedrich for making party calls on his office phone and for his conflicts of interest, but everyone else involved said it was Palin who became obsessed with Ruedrich's activities on the AOGCC. She called Murkowski to talk to him about Ruedrich, but he dismissed her concerns. Palin then phoned Murkowski's chief of staff, Jim

Clark, and had to wait three weeks for a return call. When Clark finally called back, Palin unloaded on him. Clark tried to calm Palin down and assured her that he would have his staff corral Ruedrich and bring his behavior into conformance. "That's what a chief of staff is for," Clark said. "I'll handle it."

If Palin was obsessed, Ruedrich was cavalier. He'd been doing business the same way for decades, and a political neophyte from Wasilla wasn't going to stop him. At one point, Palin confronted Ruedrich, telling him that she had spoken with Murkowski and that he could be expecting a call from Clark to discuss his activities. "Oh yeah," Ruedrich responded. "He [Clark] called me. He calls me every Sunday. He asked me if I was doing anything wrong. I told him 'no.'"

Palin was livid. And she wasn't going to back down. She kept up the heat on Ruedrich until, after consulting with Murkowski and Clark, he finally resigned from the AOGCC. Ruedrich went into his office, gathered up his papers and personal effects into a box, pulled down some photos from the wall, and told the press he was quitting. Palin learned about it from a television newscast.

Ruedrich had stepped down but he had admitted no wrongdoing. Murkowski praised him for the job he had done at AOGCC. Palin was once again outraged. She was now out to get Murkowski and the band of Big Oil cronies who surrounded him. She decided to turn up the heat. Palin contacted Attorney General Gregg Renkes and her own ethics supervisor in the Department of Administration, Kevin Jardell—all to no avail. The Department of Law had initiated its own investigation but no one was allowed to talk about it. Shortly after the announcement, Palin and an AOGCC computer technician went into Ruedrich's office and saw that it had been cleaned out. All that was left was his state-issued computer. In an interview she gave to the *Anchorage Daily News* in November of 2004, Palin said that when she "went back to work at the AOGCC, she noticed that Ruedrich had removed his pictures from the walls and the personal effects from his desk." She asserted that when "she and an AOGCC technician worked their way around his computer password at the behest of an assistant attorney general in Fairbanks, [and] found his cleanup had not extended to his electronic files." They made their way into his account. Palin was about to find evidence that would bring Alaska's good-ol'-boys network to its knees.

Palin eventually turned over her bounty to the Department of Law. She still wasn't sure about the direction of the investigation and was taking heat from Republicans, who felt that she should protect Ruedrich, and from Democrats, who wanted Ruedrich's head delivered to them on a stake. Eventually, Ruedrich was found guilty of violating the Alaska Ethics Act and received the biggest fine in Alaska history, totaling $12,000. But provisions in the Ethics Act forbade Palin from discussing the findings. She felt caught in a bureaucratic catch-22. She finally resigned her position and gave a series of interviews to Richard Mauer of the *Anchorage Daily News*. Palin's actions made her a hero in the Alaska media—and her resignation freed her to hunt bigger game. She passed up the opportunity to take on Lisa Murkowski in the 2004 U.S. Senate election and focused her sights on Daddy Bear instead. Palin's ethics assault on Frank Murkowski had taken its toll and his approval ratings had plummeted.[†]

Meanwhile, despite her role on this commission and her later two years as governor, Palin's much ballyhooed success in Alaska resources development has essentially been nil. The gas pipeline that she touted throughout the presidential campaign as being "underway" has not begun construction and most Alaska energy experts argue that it will never be built. "Sarah Palin really doesn't know a thing about resource development," says North Slope engineer Zane Henning. "She's actually been a major impediment to developing Alaska's oil and gas resources. The idea of her being an 'energy expert' is a joke. And everyone in Alaska knows it."

B EHIND THE SCENES, UNBEKNOWNST TO THOSE WORKING IN HER ADMINISTRATION—save for the immediate handful in her inner circle— Palin was pursuing another matter from her governor's office, one that focused on her former brother-in-law, Mike Wooten. Palin was mixing a family vendetta with her political office in a volatile concoction that would ultimately threaten her governorship and her ambitions for national office.

Wooten was an Alaska state trooper, then assigned to the Mat-Su, who had met Palin's sister, Molly McCann, in the late 1990s. It seemed then like a perfect coupling. Both had young sons roughly the same age from previously broken marriages. Molly, said one longtime family friend, was considered the most "fun loving" of the Heath girls, less tightly wound, at least on the surface,

---

[†] Mauer, Richard. "Palin Explains Her Actions in Ruedrich Case." *Anchorage Daily News* (November 19, 2004). Palin provides an account of her tenure on the AOGCC and her role in the Ruedrich affair in *Going Rogue*, pp. 93–100, without mentioning entering Ruedrich's computer.

than her sister Sarah. She, too, had attended the University of Idaho, and later graduated cum laude from the University of Alaska at Anchorage dental hygiene program.

Wooten appeared to be an ideal match for Molly and the outdoorsy Heath family. A native of California whose father immigrated to the United States from Honduras, Wooten had fallen in love with Alaska and its vast wilderness. While he was six years Molly's junior, Wooten had served a decade in the Air Force and three more years in the Air National Guard Reserves, and friends of the Heath family hoped that the 6'5", 260-pound Wooten would provide stability to Molly's life in the aftermath of her divorce. Wooten had participated in a trio of U.S. military operations in the Persian Gulf War—Desert Storm, Desert Shield, and Restore Hope—before returning stateside to Alaska at Elmendorf Air Force Base, about forty-five minutes from Wasilla.

The couple eventually moved in together, and then got married when Molly became pregnant. Their daughter, McKinley, was born in 2001 and a son, Heath, two years later. Pictures of the couple taken in the early years of their marriage reveal a happy family—both with big smiles, arms around each other, their children always close by. Most significant, Wooten had won over his sister-in-law, Sarah Palin, then serving as mayor of Wasilla. Although she would castigate him brutally in her memoirs, Palin wrote a glowing letter of recommendation on Wooten's behalf, dated January 1, 2000. In the letter—written on official City of Wasilla stationery—Palin praised Wooten profusely as he was applying for a position with the Alaska state troopers. "It is my pleasure to provide character reference examples for Mr. Mike Wooten," she wrote. "Since I have become acquainted with Mike I continue to be impressed with his integrity, worthwhile community spirit, and trustworthiness." She did not mention Wooten's relationship to her sister in the letter.

Palin went on to trumpet Wooten's participation in a series of "community-oriented activities" and declared that "he is awaiting future opportunities to assist the public by joining the efforts of public safety officials in our area, including potential opportunities with the Volunteer Police Reserves activities, to assist the Mat-Su Valley." She praised "his willingness to jump right in with our youth football program and successfully coach the seven- to nine-year-old boys' team during the 1999 season" and noted that he had "gained respect for his patience and dedication to the young men in his care during the season." Then Palin turned the letter "personal."

On a personal note, I have witnessed Mike's gift of calm and kindness toward many young kids here in Wasilla. I have never seen him raise his voice, nor lose patience, nor become agitated, in the presence of any child. Instead, Mike consistently remains a fine role model for my own children and other young people in Wasilla. I wish America had more people with the grace and sincerity that mirrors the character of Mike Wooten . . . we would have a much kinder calmer trustworthy nation as a result.

I believe the United States Air Force has been fortunate to have the services of Mike the past ten years. His work ethic, his American patriotism, his obvious dedication to traditional values, and his strong faith in God and truth is witnessed in Mike's everyday living.

It is an honor to know Mike and I am confident he will continue to grow in character and internal strength as he moves through life . . .

Sincerely,

Sarah Palin, Mayor

A HALF DECADE (AND TWO CHILDREN) LATER, the Wooten marriage had gone sour and their impending divorce, like many, was by any standard ugly and bitter. But it would have stayed private and between the two parties involved, had not Sarah Palin, her husband, and her father, chosen to become enmeshed in what would ultimately become a very public process that would eventually last nearly five years.

In January 2005, the Wooten marriage had clearly disintegrated. Intimate e-mails between the two—released during the scandal known as Troopergate that would erupt in the summer of 2008—indicate while there was still a bond of love between them, for Wooten, at least, the marriage was beyond repair. In one of his e-mails to Molly made public, Wooten expressed that he and his wife were "different people" who want "different things out of life and we live two different ways." He acknowledged that while "I do love you, Molly, very much," he felt "trapped" in the marriage and the deteriorating dynamic of their relationship.

According to an interview later conducted by State Trooper investigator Sergeant Ron Wall, Chuck Heath informed Wooten that he intended to secure an attorney for his daughter in the divorce proceedings. "Mike," Heath said, "you're gonna cost me a lot of money for a lawyer." From that point on, accounts of what followed differ, but Wooten's relationship with the Palin-Heath family deteriorated into an ugly series of allegations and what can only be described as a crusade by Chuck Heath and Sarah and Todd Palin to destroy Wooten's reputation as a trooper and, he believes, "to drive me out of Alaska."

On February 17, 2005, Wooten acknowledges that he and Molly engaged in a heated argument at their home over the divorce and her father's interference in obtaining legal counsel on her behalf. He says that he wanted to minimize the impacts of the divorce on their children by filing for a "no-fault" dissolution of marriage, which is permitted in Alaska on the grounds of "incompatibility of temperament."

Instead, Molly secured a divorce attorney and filed for dissolution, while Chuck Heath and Sarah and Todd Palin initiated a series of complaints attempting to have Wooten removed from his job as a state trooper. The family also hired a private investigator, Leonard Hackett, to follow Wooten and to report on his activities, both while on duty as a trooper and off duty as well. Over the next several months, Heath, the Palins, and some of their friends filed more than a dozen complaints against Wooten.

The investigation—replete with recorded interviews of all the major participants—had the attenuated drama of a bad soap opera. It did not make for a pretty picture. On May 2, 2005, Sarah Palin was interviewed at length at her home in Wasilla by Sergeant Wall, who was placed in charge of the internal investigation of the trooper. Palin's rendition of events focused on the February 17 incident at the Wooten home, which provided the source for Palin's oft-repeated charge that Wooten had threatened to kill her father. Wall asked Palin to tell him about the incident:

PALIN: Sure. It was on, umm, I believe it was on February 17th, umm, about two and half months ago when, umm, Molly called me. I was here at home with my kids and Molly was on her cell phone driving home from work and she said, "Uh-oh, Mike's really mad, he's in a rage. I don't know what he wants but he just told me on the phone to get my F'n ass home and don't tell him F'n no and, umm, I'm gonna, umm, hurt you guys better not be F'n with me." And, I told Molly, I said, "Should I come over to your house?" Because it sounded like it was gonna get bad and she said, "I, I will call you as soon as I know Mike's coming up the driveway and I'm gonna let you listen in so you can stand by in case I do need help." Umm, just a little bit whi . . . later Molly arrived home and Mike arrived home. Molly did call me and said, "Mike's coming in the house right now, umm, you need to, ah, stand by and listen to this conversation in case I do need help."

Palin told Wall that her sister put the speakerphone on so that she could listen in. "I could hear Mike come whamming through the door, umm, screaming. F'n this, F'n that. Ah, tellin' Molly, 'if your dad helps you through the divorce, if he gets an attorney he's gonna eat a F'n lead bullet. I'm gonna shoot him.' She said she was "very fearful that Molly was gonna get hurt by Mike."

PALIN: He was in such a rage. Umm, I knew that if he had did just walk in the door he probably did have his gun on. 'Cause he wore it all the time. Umm, I was fearful of that. Umm, I was fearful that he was going to physically harm Molly or that Molly would tell him, "well Mike I, if we're," 'cause at that time Mike was telling Molly, "I want a divorce." *[sic]*

Palin said that because of Wooten's behavior, she drove over to her sister's house and had her then sixteen-year-old son, Track, listen in on the conversation. According to Palin, Wooten was also screaming that "I'm gonna make your life hell" and "I'm gonna take your sister down." According to Palin, Wooten continued his threats:

PALIN: "I"—as Molly had explained—"I know people in all the right places, in high places. I know judges. I know attorneys. I have relationships with these guys. You guys are all going down." Umm, and, "I'm gonna F'n kill your dad." So, it was so concerning to me that I had my son stay on the line. I jumped in my truck to drive over to Molly's house because I was sure Mike was gonna, he was, like a ticking time bomb and I thought he was gonna blow and physically harm Molly or the kids or my dad. Um, my son was listening in. On my way over to Molly's house I called my son on a different line from my cell phone. I said, umm, "Track you need to call Molly's neighbor and ask Molly's neighbor to keep his eyes and ears open for ahh any kind of violence next door with Molly and Mike." Ahh, then my son called me back and said, "I called the neighbor," umm, and that's about all that Track said. And I told Track, "Well I'm heading over there." I drove over to Molly's house. Um, paused going in front of her house, it was dark. But the lights were on in the house.

Palin said she could "see right into the living room." She said that Wooten and Molly had come down from the second floor and that she could "see this all so clearly on a dark night."

PALIN: Mike was obviously in a rage. Waving his arms around, pacing. I could tell he was screaming. Umm, I could see this clearly through the window and I thought, "He is gonna blow it." He, he there's no other step for him to take next except from physical violence. Umm, I went over to the neighbor's driveway then after observing through, Mike, the window, Mike's body language his physical rage. Umm, the neighbor met me out there in his driveway. The neighbor and I watched through the window.

But then Palin's narrative took an odd turn. Suddenly, in recounting Wooten's rage and watching it with her neighbor, she declared. "And then the neighbor, uh, . . . and *I had to head on into Chugiak, I had ah a meeting that I couldn't miss.* (Emphasis added.) I told the neighbor, I said, 'Could you stand by and just make sure that, umm, Molly and the kids are okay in there. 'Cause it's looking dangerous.'"

With her sister involved in an incident that she described as potentially violent, frightening, and dangerous—and with her sister, in her assessment, "still scared to death"—Palin left the scene for a meeting more than twenty miles away. She was neither an elected nor appointed official at this time.

PALIN: And, umm, after standing there watching Mike freaking out for however long probably, fifteen minutes, umm, I had to leave. I took off.

Wall then asked the obvious question, given Palin's rendition of events: "Why didn't you guys call the police?"

PALIN: We knew that Mike's job probably was on the line. If he were to, umm, I didn't know if he had been drinking or not. I know, I do know that Mike does drink a lot and, and I know well if he was drinking and he had his gun on his hip and he had just driven home in a cop car, he, his job definitely was gonna be in jeopardy. Umm, so I did have some respect for his, umm, his career, his profession. But also when I spoke with the neighbor, the neighbor reminded me also that if it does become physical and we can see from physical violence through this window, definitely we call 9-1-1. We get some help. But if it's not, if it's just gonna be verbal just ranting and raging and, and umm, horrible verbal abuse, ahh, then we don't need, we don't need law enforcement to come help. So just with those considerations.

It was an odd calculation given the situation she was describing. Wall pressed her again: "So you just felt that as long as it wasn't physical?"

PALIN: Yeah. Yup, that was gonna be the line. Had that been crossed, definitely on my cell phone I would have called 9-1-1 and said, "Your colleague is having some problems." And you know through the window too so evident of his, he's 6'5" he's 260, big stature, physically seen this difference, Molly's 5'2", 120, . . . kind of a position of, umm, especially first when I first drove by before I got to the neighbor's house, umm, Mike standing over her, umm, and doing the pointing the finger and waving the arms and screaming and yelling. I, I thought, "Man if he, I hope he doesn't hit her, I hope he doesn't push her" because, umm, that's, umm, that's the line that cannot be crossed. The verbal abuse is bad enough but, ah, if it evolves into and escalates into something physical he, that's bad bad news.

She then expressed her concern about the children in the house and the fact Wooten "does have an arsenal of weapons laying around . . . you know, depending on how bad it escalated. Ahh, I was fearful that, umm, there would be, umm, not wise decisions made." Nonetheless, Palin left the scene and did not place a call to law enforcement.

Palin's son, Track, was also interviewed by Sergeant Wall about the incident. His account disputes his mother's in two significant ways. While Track agreed that Wooten was verbally abusive of his aunt and had made a threatening remark about his grandfather ("if your dad gets an attorney he'll eat an F'n bullet"), his explanation for the purpose of listening in on the conversation was quite different from his mother's:

TRACK: Ah, well me and my mom we were talking to Molly and she was just like "Ah, he's coming through the door I gotta go." And then my mom asked her to just like hide the phone and leave it on so we could hear.

WALL: Why did she do that?

TRACK: Ah, because . . . ah, at the time is when we thought like we were assuming that he was having an affair.

WALL: Mm-hm.

TRACK: And we wanted to know what he had to say when she asked him if he was.

WALL: Did he acknowledge having an affair?

TRACK: Ah, at the time he said, ah, "No way. (Inaudible) I'm staying with my friends." Lying I guess.

WALL: Any other reason you were listening?

TRACK: No. That's the main reason. The lone reason.

Track Palin also contended that his mother went over to his aunt's house *after* Wooten had left. Whatever motivations there were for listening in on the phone conversation and whether or not Sarah Palin witnessed the dispute as she said, the Palin and Heath families were not satisfied with Wall's internal investigation of Wooten. On August 10, 2005, during the middle of the investigation, Palin wrote Colonel Julia Grimes, then the director of the Alaska State Troopers Division of the Alaska Department of Public Safety, a rambling, 2,300-word e-mail in which she chronicled the litany of accusations she and her family had made against Wooten—from Tasering his son to marital infidelity to using his wife's hunting permit to shoot a cow moose—all of which had been investigated by Wall. "It is my understanding that you are aware of problems within the Alaska State Trooper family that stem from one of your officers, Michael Wooten," Palin wrote. "My concern is that the public's faith in the Troopers will continue to diminish as more residents express concerns regarding the apparent lack of action toward a Trooper whom is described by many as being 'a ticking timebomb,' and a 'loose cannon.'" [sic] Palin attached a revelatory postscript to her missive:

> Ps. Again, Wooten happens to be my brother-in-law, and after his infidelity and physical abuse of his wife (my sister) surfaced, Mike chose to leave his family and has continued to threaten to "bring down" anyone who supports her. I would ask that you objectively consider this information, disregarding my sister's pending divorce from Wooten, as I have objectively separated the divorce and Wooten's threats against me and my family with the fact that the Troopers have a loose cannon on their hands.

Palin's letter obviously had an impact. Following her letter to Grimes, Palin was then interviewed by Wall a second time, during which time he asked her if she had any firsthand information related to the various incidents she had described in her letter. In respect to nearly every incident, Wall noted, "Palin advised that she didn't have any personal knowledge."

Then it was Todd Palin's turn to press the issue. On September 12, 2005, Palin sent Wall an e-mail containing information that Palin's private investigator had provided the family.

Palin addressed his e-mail to "Seargeant" Ronald Wall in which he referenced his private investigator, Leonard Hackett, and interviews Hackett conducted of "witness's to Trooper Michael Wooten's abusive of power." [sic] He referenced the moose killing, Wooten allegedly driving while "intoxicated," and getting involved in a situation "that was none of his business."

Finally, on October 10, 2005, Chuck Heath also wrote a letter to Grimes. "I am aware of the August 10, 2005, letter sent to you by Sarah Palin regarding Trooper Michael Wooten," he wrote. "Apparently, no action has been taken by his superiors, for whatever reason. He continues to intimidate members of the Palin family, most recently on September 30, 2005, when he confronted fourteen-year-old Bristol Palin, my granddaughter, at a Wasilla High football game. In the presence of others he called her a f—asshole. This was while he was a member of the Wasilla High coaching staff."

Two weeks later, on October 29, 2005—little more than a week after Palin formally announced her candidacy for governor—Wall sent Grimes a memorandum of his findings on Wooten. The vast majority of the thirteen charges, he asserted, were either "Unfounded" or "Not Sustained." In respect to an allegation made by Palin of Wooten driving while he was intoxicated, Wall noted that Palin had "no firsthand knowledge" and there was no "corroborating evidence." In respect to the alleged threats made by Wooten against Palin's father, Wooten, according to Wall, had denied making the comments. He also noted that "a statement or implied threat to a nonpresent third party is not a crime." Nonetheless, he sustained the charges of "unbecoming conduct" and "personal conduct" in regards to the threat and also for using a Taser device on his stepson and for shooting a moose on his wife's permit.

Two months later, after reviewing Wall's findings, Grimes interviewed a pair of witnesses a second time involving one of the incidents related to Wooten consuming alcohol. She overrode Wall's initial findings and "sustained" the allegation that Wooten had consumed an alcoholic beverage before, and while, driving a state patrol vehicle.

On March 1, 2006—while Palin's gubernatorial candidacy was in full swing—Grimes issued a lengthy suspension letter to Wooten. She chronicled in detail the serious nature of the allegations.

> The history noted above indicates a significant pattern of judgment failures, during which you have repeatedly shown yourself incapable or unwilling to maintain a demeanor demonstrating or embracing departmental expectations for your proper and appropriate conduct. The history bears out your failure to change or correct your behavior or your inability to

behave according to our canons of police ethics and rules of conduct. The findings of the administrative investigation indicate that in addition to the events addressed above, that activity sustained in the investigation was occurring concurrently. The record clearly indicates a serious and concentrated pattern of unacceptable and, at times, illegal activity occurring over a lengthy period, which establishes a course of conduct totally at odds with the ethics of our profession.

Grimes pulled no punches. She noted that "it is nearly certain that a civilian investigated under similar circumstances would have received criminal sanctions." She further asserted that "these events are unacceptable, constitute a gross deviation from our department's standards, and will not be tolerated." She issued a ten-day suspension to Wooten and demanded that he turn in his duty weapons and his credentials. Most significant, she placed him on notice that his job was on the line:

This discipline is meant to be a last chance to take corrective action. You are hereby given notice that any further occurrences of these types of behaviors or incidents will not be tolerated and will result in your termination. You must comply with the Law, the OPM and direction given you.

John Cyr, who served as executive director of Alaska's Public Safety Employees Association during the time frame of Wooten's internal investigation, acknowledged that Wooten had "made mistakes," but called the Palins' relentless attacks on Wooten "the product of an ugly divorce and custody battle." He further noted that "not one complaint has ever been made about Mike Wooten's professional performance from any member of the public other than the Palin/Heath family and their closest friends. The troopers that I've talked to that have worked with Mike tell me Mike is the kind of guy they'd go through a door with. That he does his work. He's a professional. You know, just no complaints out there about Mike's work."

The charges being brought by the Palins and Chuck Heath regarding the moose hunt were especially galling to Wooten. Wooten acknowledges that he used his wife's special cow permit, but his rendition of events provides a fascinating insight into the domineering role, he claims, that Chuck Heath played in his daughters' families long after they had become adults.

In September 2003, his wife Molly, according to Wooten, had won a lottery in which she was issued a highly coveted permit, or "tag," to shoot a cow moose in the Mat-Su region. Wooten says that contrary to the perception of the Heath sisters being "hunting fools," none of them were particularly fond of hunting. Wooten had been busy at work and with other matters so he hadn't arranged for a hunt. Shooting a moose simply wasn't high on his radar. According to Wooten, Chuck Heath had badgered Molly about the issue and he began badgering Wooten as well. If Wooten didn't take his daughter out to shoot the moose, then damn it, he was going to. According to Wooten's statement to Wall:

> Molly came home all upset crying saying, "You need to take me out. We need to get a moose because my dad won't leave me alone. And he's harassed me about it and I do not want to go hunting with him under any circumstances. It's not fun. He makes it miserable and I do not want to go . . ." So we were at Chuck and Sally's house for dinner the night before we were gonna go hunting and Chuck started razzin' Molly about filling the permit. And basically I told Chuck, I said, "You know what Chuck why don't you just, just leave her alone. It's her permit. It's not yours. If we don't go hunting we don't go hunting. It's not that big of an issue."

Wooten says there was no letup. Everything was a big deal to Chuck Heath. And even though his daughters were adults, their business remained *his* business. According to Wooten, Heath said, "Well if you don't take her out there and fill that permit, I'll fill it for you." Wooten assured him they were going out the following day. Heath still wouldn't let go. According to Wooten, Heath continued "riding him." Heath said, "Well there's only three days left. Nothing like waiting 'til the end and—" Wooten finally cut him off. "Well, we're gonna go hunting tomorrow," he told Heath. "We're gonna go up river. We'll probably see a moose."

And see a moose they did—only minutes after beginning their hunt. But when it came time to make the kill, according to Wooten, he asked his wife, "Do you want to shoot the moose?" According to Wooten she said no. So he shot it with his .300-caliber Winchester Magnum. Twice. Wooten and his wife were joined on the hunting trip by Chris Watchus, a Wasilla police officer who had a small boat to take the Wootens upriver. They gutted the moose and brought it back to Chuck Heath's house for butchering. No one made any deal about it, says Wooten, and certainly no one reported it to authorities, until Molly and his divorce two years later. In *Going Rogue*, Palin made no mention of her sister being along on the hunting expedition or of her father's role in butchering the moose.

Wooten acknowledges that he wished he had "done things differently" and that he "regretted" some of the decisions he had made "when I was younger." He says that many of the allegations against him were "outright lies" or "exaggerated beyond recognition. . . . It just didn't happen the way they said it did," he said. "And they continued to harass me."

In *Going Rogue*, Palin would claim that in the aftermath of her sister's divorce from Wooten, the "chapter for our family was closed." It was not. Far from it.

EVEN BEFORE SHE TOOK OFFICE AS GOVERNOR—during the summer of 2006—a member of Palin's family told a longtime family friend that once Palin was elected governor, she was going to see to it that Wooten would be fired. In an e-mail sent out to her campaign staff on October 3, 2006, Palin responded to the fact that she did not get the endorsement of the PSEA, headed up by Cyr. "Hmmmm," she wrote. "John Cyr is the union dude who defended my ex-brother-in-law, Trooper Mike Wooten, last year while Mike was under investigation for shooting my nephew with a tasar [sic] gun, for getting busted for drinking & driving, for drinking in his patrol car, for illegally shooting a cow moose out of season without a tag, etc. Cyr wrote us a letter telling us to knock off our questioning of Mike, basically. It's no wonder he wasn't a fan while I was being interviewed by him and the group yesterday." Palin had hardly closed the chapter on the matter. Her e-mail rant was a signal to her inner circle of campaign advisers that her brother-in-law was still very much on her radar. Indeed, almost as soon as she was sworn in, Palin and her husband, Todd, would focus considerable energy on getting Wooten removed as a trooper.

In November 2006, Palin named Walt Monegan as Alaska's Public Safety Commissioner, which placed him in charge of Alaska's State Troopers. The former chief of the Anchorage Police Department (whose career in law enforcement in south-central Alaska spanned more than three decades), Monegan had been under consideration for the job during the administration of Frank Murkowski as well. He was a former beat cop who had risen through the ranks during a distinguished thirty-two-year career in Anchorage. When his selection was announced by Palin, the Anchorage-based *Voice of the Times* said that "he has no equal anywhere in the state." Moreover, he had deep roots in Alaska—he had both Yup'ik and Tlingit blood—and he had been raised in the Alaska bush. Little did he ever imagine when he took the job that his tenure as Alaska's top cop would come to be of national significance. He soon realized, however, that his new boss and her husband had a fixation on Wooten that he sensed could be problematic for her administration. He later described the Palin family's preoccupation with Wooten as an "obsession."

Although born in Seattle, Monegan had been raised by his grandparents in the isolated community of Nyac in the Kilbuck Mountains of western Alaska, about sixty miles from Bethel. His parents had met in Seattle in the summer of 1950 and married just before his father, a nineteen-year-old Marine, was shipped overseas to Korea, where he was killed in battle less than two months later. His son Walt—whom he would not live to see—was born in May of the following year.

While Monegan's mother would remain in Seattle, young Monegan was shipped off to his grandparents who were of Yup'ik and Tlingit ancestry. He attended Nyac's one-room schoolhouse until the eighth grade, then completed his high school years in Washington State, graduating from Anacortes High in the late 1960s. He attended Alaska Methodist University for a year—he realized that college wasn't for him—and perhaps feeling pulled by his father's legacy, he joined the Marines during the hot days of the Vietnam War. He was given an honorary discharge when his battalion commander (who had known his late father) refused to send him into combat because he was the sole-surviving son of a Marine who had been killed in the line of duty.

Monegan returned to Anchorage. His Marine drill sergeant in boot camp had said that ex-Marines were "good for being either cops or Hells Angels," so when he saw an advertisement for an opening in the municipal police department in the winter of 1973, he decided to apply. "I figured, okay, I'll give it a try if they hired me," he recalls. "And they did. I thought I'd keep my eyes open for something better. And wound up spending just about thirty-three years with those folks." Monegan was known as a tough but fair beat cop and was extremely well liked and respected by his colleagues in the force. He had also gone back to school, earning a bachelor's degree in organizational administration from Alaska Pacific University. He also took advanced professional training at Harvard University's John F. Kennedy School of Government, the FBI's National Executive Institute, and the National Crime Prevention Institute. When an opening came up for the chief's job in early 2001, Monegan, then forty-nine, had strong rank-and-file support.

In the fall of 2006, Monegan—who had been nudged into retirement as chief by incoming Anchorage mayor Mark Begich—says he received a call from Frank Bailey, who was then serving on Palin's transition team and who told Monegan he was being considered for the job. Monegan had met Palin on a couple of occasions during his tenure as police chief in Anchorage, and he had been asked to support her during her run for governor, which he declined. "I think police should be apolitical," he says. "I wasn't in the habit of making political endorsements." Palin still wanted him for the job. There was a lot of support for Monegan's selection—from the Anchorage media, with whom he had enjoyed a superb working relationship, and also from the rural and Native Alaska communities, because of his family roots in the bush. Monegan decided to take the job.

In her press release announcing Monegan's selection, Palin was effusive in her praise of her new commissioner of public safety. "Starting as a patrol officer and rising steadily through the ranks," she noted, "Monegan has experience in every facet of public safety, including internal affairs, crime prevention, communications, emergency operations, training, anti-gang efforts, school/youth liaison, and Crime Stoppers." She also noted that he was "credited with enhancing police effectiveness by installing mobile computers in police vehicles; implementing advanced 911 service to Alaska's largest municipal population; writing plans to address gang and youth violence; supporting the establishment of professional standards for village public safety officers; establishing a Citizens Police Academy and resurrecting police traffic units to address drunken driving." She continued:

> Chief Monegan will bring to the Department of Public Safety the perspective of a career professional peace officer and administrator with a proven record of using resources effectively to address the changing public safety needs of Alaskans. As an Alaska Native from the Lower Kuskokwim village of Nyac, he understands the special public safety on a statewide

basis. We are fortunate to have such an experienced and well-rounded police professional heading the Department of Public Safety.

Monegan says that he and Palin had a "friendly and cordial relationship" at the beginning of her administration and that Palin and her core advisers had talked with him about refocusing state-trooper efforts toward wildlife enforcement. In late December, only weeks after he assumed the position, he and Palin traveled together to assess alcohol abuse in the Yup'ik village of New Stuyahok, located deep in the Alaska bush, upriver from Todd Palin's hometown of Dillingham. Monegan said he and the governor "got along just fine" on the trip and there were several subsequent instances during which Palin asked Monegan to accompany her to the bush.

In early January 2007, however, Monegan said that a troubling process began during which the Palins—both the governor and her husband—directly brought up the matter of Trooper Wooten. Todd Palin's official title in Alaska was that of First Gentleman, an essentially ornamental position, though the Alaska media popularly dubbed him the "First Dude." Almost from the beginning, however, it became clear that he was having far more than a peripheral role in his wife's administration. The Alaskan blogger and businessman Andrew Halcro, the Republican moderate who had run against Palin as an independent in the gubernatorial election, more accurately referred to him as the "Shadow Governor."

Those who followed Sarah Palin's career in Wasilla say that her husband generally kept a distance during her tenure as a city councilmember and mayor; once she assumed the governorship, however, Todd Palin assumed a central, albeit unofficial, role in her administration. Alaska state records later revealed that he was copied on thousands of formal state government e-mails and that he often attended high-level meetings and used his wife's offices in both Anchorage and Juneau to conduct meetings with state officials. Trooper Gary Wheeler, who served as Palin's protection detail, estimated that Todd Palin spent "50 percent of his time in the governor's office." It was a scheduler from Governor Palin's office who contacted Monegan's secretary, Cassandra Byrne, to set up a meeting with Monegan. When told that it was for a meeting with the First Gentleman, Byrne did a double take. She hadn't heard the term before.

On the afternoon of January 4, 2007, Monegan arrived at the Governor's

Office in the Robert B. Atwood Building in downtown Anchorage. The governor was not there, but Todd Palin was seated at a large conference table with three small piles of paper in front of him, all relating to Wooten. Palin pushed the paper toward Monegan and at the same time began a monologue about Wooten, his marriage to Molly, and the various incidents involving Wooten that had been chronicled during the internal Trooper investigation against him. Monegan had never met Wooten and had no idea who he was; in fact this was the first time he had heard his name. According to Monegan, Palin let him know that he felt that the suspension levied against Wooten was little more than "a slap on the wrist." Monegan says that Palin expressed further frustration that Wooten had not been prosecuted for some of the activities—most notably the moose-hunting and Taser incidents—dating back to 2003. Palin gave the paperwork to Monegan and requested that he look it over to assess the situation. Monegan agreed to do so without making any promises. But he also sensed, after years of being a beat cop, that Todd Palin was simply "venting" about what seemed to be a family issue involving a bitter divorce.

On his drive back from the meeting, Monegan reflected on his odd first encounter with Todd Palin. The sole purpose of the meeting had been to address the matter of the governor's former brother-in-law. "They wanted severe discipline, probably termination," Monegan later told investigators, "and if this was going to build, I had this kind of ominous feeling that I may not be long for this job if I didn't somehow respond accordingly."

Monegan assigned the acting director of the state troopers, Matt Levaque, the task of completing a "page-by-page review" of Wooten's file. Part of the pile of paper included the findings of Palin's private investigator, including photocopied photos that the investigator had accumulated. Levaque had been aware of the ongoing problems involving Wooten. He gave the material a careful examination, and a couple of days later told Monegan "there is nothing new that we haven't already addressed in the investigation from Mr. Palin."

Never one to hold back bad news, Monegan called Todd Palin with his findings. Wooten had already been investigated thoroughly and in great detail and reprimanded for all of the incidents. To go over the same acts again would, he felt, be subjecting Wooten to doublejeopardy. Todd Palin was not happy with the news and expressed "more frustration," according to Monegan, who was also concerned about violating Wooten's confidentiality as a trooper. Monegan had served a year as an internal affairs investigator with the Anchorage Police Department, so he knew the ropes with personnel issues. Palin pushed him about filing criminal charges around the incident with the moose; Monegan explained that Palin's sister-in-law Molly and Chuck Heath would also be considered "accessories," as they had only brought up the incident in the aftermath of Molly's divorce. Palin seemed oblivious to the legal complexities of the situation and the problematic nature of selective enforcement. He wanted only Wooten charged, Monegan recalled. He was not letting go.

A few days later, Monegan says, he received a call from the governor herself. She repeated to him the very same frustrations that her husband had. She complained about the incident involving the moose. She asserted, according to Monegan, that Wooten had only received a "slap on the wrist." Monegan says that he sensed "passion and frustration" in her comments. After this particular conversation, he told investigators, he was concerned that he "may not be long for the job."

Palin would later testify during the investigation conducted by independent counsel Tim Petumenos on behalf of the State Alaska Personnel Board that she knew nothing of her husband's initial calls to Monegan regarding Wooten. Moreover, she denied that she had called Monegan and had any conversation with him about Wooten. Yet on February 7, 2007, approximately one month after these conversations, Palin sent Monegan an extremely revelatory e-mail, ostensibly about his testifying on an impending bill in the state legislature addressing the sentencing of peace officers involved with killing civilians. In the e-mail, Palin briefly dealt with the matter of Monegan testifying in Juneau ("You are absolutely free to speak your mind on this"), and then she swerved into a lengthy discussion of Wooten. It echoed many of the previous conversations Monegan had already had with the Palins about Wooten.

> In sharing a few personal examples with you (including the trooper who used to be related to me—the one who illegally killed the cow moose out of season, without a tag—he's still bragging about it in my hometown and after another cop confessed to witnessing the kill, this trooper was "investigated" for over a year and merely given a slap on the wrist . . . though he's out there arresting people today for the same crime! This is the same trooper who shot his 11-yr-old stepson with a taser gun, was seen drinking in his patrol car, was

pulled over for drunk driving but was let off by a co-worker & brags about this incident to this day . . . he threatened to kill his estranged wife's parent, refused to be transfered to rural Alaska and continued to disparage Natives in words and tone, he continues to harass and intimidate his ex—even after being slapped with a restraining order that was lifted after his supervisors intervened . . . he threatens to always be able to come out on top because he's "got the badge", etc. etc. etc.) This trooper is still out on the street, in fact he's been promoted. It was a joke, the whole year long "investigation" of him—in fact those who passed along the serious information about him to Julia Grimes and [former Public Safety Commissioner Bill] Tandeske were threatened with legal action from the trooper's union for speaking about it. (This is the same trooper who's out there today telling people the new administration is going to destroy the trooper organization, and that he'd "never work for that "b****, Palin".) [sic]

In her e-mail, the vast majority of which dealt with her former brother-in-law, Palin attempted to link Wooten's behavior with the pending legislation and as a way to denounce the Department of Public Safety's handling of its internal affairs. "[T]his is what people in the Valley are putting up with (those many residents who know of this trooper time-bomb who's supposed to be 'protecting' them)," she wrote. "I've heard too many stories from others across this state who believe DPS has been overly protective of their own, to the detriment of DPS, to the chargin [sic] of the public, and it all leads to the erosion of faith Alaskans should have in their law enforcement officials."

But then Palin included what would seem to be a direct reference to her husband's previous conversations with Monegan about the issue. Emphasis is added:

Just my opinion—I know I've experienced a lot of frustration with this issue. *I know Todd's even expressed to you a lot of concern about our family's safety after this trooper threatened to kill a family member*—so you need to know that if I am a supporter of whatever we can do to build trust back

into DPS, then there are many other Alaskans in the same
boat we are and may look on this new cop bill as a good
thing.

Thanks for letting me share my concerns with you,

Sarah

Palin was obviously aware that her husband "expressed to [Monegan] a lot
of concern" regarding Wooten. Yet a year later she would claim to have never
known of this earlier verbal communication and to have never spoken to Monegan about the matter herself.

L ESS THAN A WEEK LATER, ON FEBRUARY 13, 2007, Monegan flew to
Juneau to testify before the legislature. His cousin, Lyman Hoffman, a
Democratic state senator from Bethel, was celebrating his birthday that afternoon, and Monegan suggested that Palin call him with a birthday greeting.
Monegan said it was part of his effort to help Palin establish working relationships with those "on the other side of the aisle." Hoffman was a moderate and
a hunting and fishing enthusiast. He and Monegan were roughly the same age
and had grown up in the same region of the bush together. Palin, however, one-
upped Monegan. She suggested they go to his office and offer the greeting in
person.

As they were making their way to Hoffman's office, according to Monegan, Palin brought up Wooten to him yet again. "She said it kind of quietly,"
Monegan recalls. "'I need to talk to you about Wooten.'" Palin's protection
detail was following them. Monegan was worried about him overhearing anything, and he headed her off quickly. He remained concerned that such a
conversation would be "discoverable information." According to Monegan,
he responded by noting, "Ma'am, if it's just the same, and if there's another
complaint, I'd just as soon deal with Todd on that." He was trying to protect
her—"keep the governor out of it." According to Monegan, Palin responded
by noting, "Oh, that's a better idea." (Palin would also deny this conversation
took place.)

That same week, again during the legislative session in Juneau, Monegan
says that he was called into the office of Palin's chief of staff, Mike Tibbles.
According to Monegan, Tibbles also brought up Wooten. Monegan was firm
with him. They shouldn't be having this discussion. The investigation was

over. Wooten had been reprimanded. To continue the discussion further violated Wooten's rights. "You don't want Wooten to own your house, do you?" Monegan asked. That ended the conversation. But it didn't put the matter to rest.

A short time later, Monegan received another call from Todd Palin, who said that he had witnessed Wooten driving a snow machine while he was out on workers' compensation; Palin said he had photos to prove it. Monegan investigated the incident. Wooten's doctor, it turned out, had given him permission to make the trip. Then Monegan received a call from Department of Administration commissioner Annette Kreitzer about the Wooten matter. She covered the same terrain; he gave her the same response. Monegan cautioned Kreitzer that their conversations were "discoverable" and that "he would handle it." Later, Monegan would discover that Kreitzer had called other administrators in the Department of Public Safety to discuss Wooten as well. Todd Palin, according to Palin's legislative director, John Bitney, also had several conversations with Bitney about Wooten. Documents reveal that Todd Palin had "ten to twenty" conversations with Tibble about it. Kim Peterson, who served as Monegan's special assistant, said that she received roughly a dozen calls about Wooten. "To all of us, it was a campaign to get rid of him as a trooper and, at the very least, to smear the guy and give him a desk job somewhere," Peterson told *The New York Times*. "It was very clear that someone from the Governor's Office wanted him watched." In the end, investigators documented some three-dozen interactions over a period of a year and half initiated by either Palin, her husband, or members of her administration relative to Wooten's status as a trooper.

For Monegan, the pressure regarding Wooten tapered down. But Palin and her minions were going around and under him. On February 29, 2008, Palin's director of commissions, Frank Bailey, who had been dubbed Palin's "hatchet man," placed a call to State Trooper Lieutenant Rodney Dial in the Troopers' Ketchikan office. Bailey, then in his late thirties with two young children, was the Palins' go-to guy, an absolute loyalist, their "fixer." It was Bailey who had set up the administration's private e-mail system, linking up only Palin's closest inner circle (including her husband), and who had set up Palin's private Yahoo account, on which she often conducted official state business. He had been responsible for more than six hundred appointments to state commissions. In calling Dial, allegedly about union matters involving Alaska's Public Safety Employee's Association (PSEA), Bailey was caught off guard: his twenty-four-minute conversation was legally taped as part of standard operating procedure. The transcript of that conversation provides a detailed and vivid account of how the Palin's inner circle had grown obsessed with the matter of her former brother-in-law.

Bailey began the conversation by noting: "Hey, I've got a question that's a little bit awkward to ask, and so I want to be real respectful. I mean, if this is something you don't feel comfortable with, that—just tell me straight up, and I respect that fully. But as you know, I mean, things are really ramping up with the contract negotiations right now." He talked about some of the general issues that the administration had with the Troopers. And then, he declared, "there's a gentleman by the name of Mike Wooten, who is a Trooper in the Valley."

BAILEY: And there is—there's a family tie with the Governor there and so I think because of that, my understanding is, you know, Walt has been very reluctant to take any action.

But there are some very clear facts out there that—and this is—these things actually happened, that he tasered his 11-year-old kid. He drove drunk in a patrol car. He shot a cow moose out of season.

DIAL: Wooten did?

BAILEY: Yes.

DIAL: Uh-huh.

BAILEY: And yet he is—you know, and then there was some really funny business about a Worker's Comp claim, I think, that came up.

Bailey was treading into dangerous waters. He was revealing information that could have come only from Wooten's confidential personnel file, which is protected by Alaska state law. He then delved into Wooten's application and his medical record, and misstated several facts about the case.

BAILEY: But you know, he lied on his application when he applied. He said that he didn't have any physical impairments and come to find out, he was rated in the military and that was discovered after he retired. But the Palins can't figure out why nothing's going on.

And here's the problem that's going to happen, is that there is a possibility, because Wooten is, you know, an ex-husband of the Governor's sister. . . . .

DIAL: Uh-huh.

BAILEY: . . . . . and there's, you know, a custody situation. There is a strong possibility that the Governor herself may get subpoenaed to talk about all this stuff on the stand. . . .

DIAL: Right.

BAILEY: . . . . . over the next coming months, which would be . . .

DIAL: That's not good.

BAILEY: It would be ugly.

DIAL: Right.

Then Bailey went directly into discussing Wooten's private affairs.

BAILEY: I mean, you know, and I don't think anybody wants that, but you know, Todd and Sarah are scratching their heads. You know, why on earth hasn't—why is this guy still representing the department? He's a horrible recruiting tool, you know.

And he's—I mean, he's declared bankruptcy and, you know, and his finances are in complete ugly—you know, declared bankruptcy and then bought a new truck, and all kinds of crazy stuff, you know, that just doesn't represent the department well. And the community knows it, but. . . .

But the general . . . the general feeling is, you know, they just can't figure out why this guy is still working for—especially—you know, I know it's difficult in a union environment, you know, you've got to work within those lines. But especially the fact about him lying on his application. [Wooten denied this.]

Dial knew they were now heading into dangerous territory as well.

DIAL: And—and where did—and, Frank, where did you get that information from? I used to be a recruiter, so I'm just—and I know how that . . .

BAILEY: Yeah.

DIAL: . . . that information a lot of times is extremely confidential. So I'm just—I'm trying to find out how it was determined by anybody that—that he had indicated something on his application that look—later found was not to be true.

BAILEY: Well, I'm a little bit reluctant to say, but in—over in Admin is where, you know, we've—we hold Workers' Comp right in there. And the situation where he declared Workers' Comp, but then was caught on an eight-mile snow machining trip days—days after, you know, that—that started coming up there. So we collected statements that we forwarded on to Workers' Comp there. And so we started seeing the . . .

DIAL: Oh, okay. I got it.

BAILEY: . . . . . the application from that point.

Then Bailey began speaking directly on behalf of the Palins.

BAILEY: Everything that has come back to Todd and the Governor is basically stay away, there's nothing we can do.

And that's very frustrating because, you know, it just—but you know, this guy is the ultimate poor recruiting model, you know, for—you know, it's people like that that make it really hard to get good folks, I think, you know, because people see that and think, man, he's heavy-handed. I don't want to be part of that.

Dial was clearly growing concerned about the direction of the discussion. He kept trying to steer the conversation away from Wooten. But Bailey always veered back toward what was obviously the intention of his call:

BAILEY: You know—I mean one thing that has been verified from the school is that—and I don't know if this is illegal or wrong, but he's using his patrol car to bring his kids to school and pick them up from their visits because they've got a joint custody situation.

Dial didn't want to sound dismissive of Bailey. Nor did he want the governor to take out her frustrations about Wooten on the Troopers' budget. "We care very deeply what she thinks about the Department," he assured Bailey, who then linked Palin's frustrations about Wooten to her general inclination toward the Troopers.

BAILEY: You know—you know, I appreciate that so much. And I'm telling you honestly, I mean, she—you know, she really likes Walt a lot. But on this issue, she feels like it's—she doesn't know why there is absolutely no action for . . . for a year on this issue. It's very, very troubling to her and the family, you know. I can . . . I can definitely relay that.

Phone records obtained through the Freedom of Information Act by Alaska good-government activist Andrée McLeod reflect a trio of phone calls between Todd Palin and Sarah Palin's special assistant, Ivy Frye, the day before Bailey's phone conversation with Dial. Bailey also sent Frye an e-mail immediately following the phone call indicating that he had made contact with Dial but needed to give Frye a "heads up" by phone. Eleven additional e-mails with the subject heading "PSEA," referencing Alaska's Public Safety Employee's Association, sent the day before, or the day of, the Bailey-Dial phone conversation were not made public by the Palin administration, which claimed "executive privilege" and "deliberative process" exemptions. The authors and recipients of those e-mails included Sarah and Todd Palin, Bailey, Frye, commissioner

Annette Kreitzer, and Palin's Anchorage office director and close personal confidante Kris Perry.

When the Bailey-Dial tape was later made public, Palin referenced it during a press conference as "most disturbing" and labeled it a "smoking gun" conversation. She also acknowledged that "the serial nature of the contacts could be perceived as some kind of pressure, presumably at my direction." Walt Monegan, in an interview long after Troopergate became a national cause célèbre, would put it more succinctly. "It was an obsession," he said. Mike Wooten had become Sarah Palin's great white whale.

I F PALIN WAS OBSESSED WITH WOOTEN, she was also equally concerned about her public image, both inside Alaska and in the Lower 48. "She liked to put out that she didn't care about that sort of thing," says her legislative liaison Bitney. "But she was always checking her BlackBerrys seeing what people wrote about her. She was hyperfocused on that type of thing." Less than a year into her governorship, Palin would hire—using $31,000 of state funds paid for through a contract with the Alaska Department of Natural Resources—a promotional consultant out of Needham, Massachusetts, MCB Communications, headed up by a woman named Marcia Brier, whose efforts were directed at garnering publicity with East Coast media—*The New York Times, The Washington Post, Fortune*—regarding Palin's efforts related to resource development in Alaska. Brier was representing the law firm of Greenberg Traurig, whose counsel Kenneth M. Minesinger provided legal representation to the state regarding oil matters and had recommended Brier to state officials. Kurt Gibson, a member of Palin's oil and gas team, later told *The Washington Post*, "We are a small state far removed from major media markets. We needed someone with expertise. The objective was to raise national awareness of the project. It benefits not just the state of Alaska, but Americans in general. We want the public to understand this." It was not lost on many legislators in Alaska that the vast majority of the stories wound up focusing on Sarah Palin. From the moment she got to Juneau, said one, "she simply craved the limelight. It became all about Sarah."

Brier's promotional activity actually began on a "trial basis" in the fall of 2007. In April of the following year, Brier wrote a letter to the Department of Natural Resources (DNR) seeking a state contract. In the letter, Brier noted that MCB had landed a story entitled "Alaska Gets Tough on Big Oil" in *Fortune* and that a colleague of hers, identified as "a Pulitzer Prize–winning journalist and former *Wall Street Journal* reporter" (no name was given), had "ghost written an op-ed piece for the Governor." The letter also indicated that MCB had organized a "press tour" on Palin's behalf and had set up interviews with "the nation's top energy reporters"—only to have Palin "cancel" on the tour. Brier promised, however, that if she were hired "she could set up this tour again and get the governor publicity in many leading publications." She knew it was all about getting Palin publicity. Brier received a contract in April and an extension in August. Her mission, as directed by DNR, was to "facilitate the governor delivering her message under the brightest national spotlights."

But if Palin was generating Outside interest at the expense of Alaska taxpayers, there was another promotional development on her behalf over which she had little control, though which was clearly having an impact on how she was being viewed by Outside media and Republican political operatives gearing up for the 2008 presidential election, then well underway. Only a few months after she had been elected to office, Palin noticed that a blogger by the name of Adam Brickley had started a movement to draft her as the Republican vice-presidential nominee in the 2008 election and that he had registered a Web site: *palinforvp .blogspot.com*. Palin, according to Bitney, followed the blog with interest.

Then a junior majoring in political science at the University of Colorado at Colorado Springs, Brickley (who went by the moniker "ElephantMan") was a self-described "obsessive" political junkie who believed that the Republican Party would need to counter Hillary Clinton's almost certain Democratic Party nomination for president with a woman of their own. He had discovered Palin on the Internet, retraced the steps of her political career, and realized she had developed something of "a cult of personality" around her in Alaska. Her approval ratings, as far as he could tell, were absolutely phenomenal. He had found the candidate he was looking for. Now he needed to make his case. Trained by both the conservative Young America's Foundation and the Heritage Foundation (where he served as an intern), Brickley was also the recipient of a $7,500 Phillips Foundation scholarship, which, according to Brickley "grants scholarships to conservative student activists and fellowships to aspiring journalists." The scholarship covered his "entire tuition, plus books." Working on the Web site at the farmhouse of his mother, in nearby Falcon, a small unincorporated community roughly twenty minutes from campus, Brickley was out to prove what one motivated Young Republican with a Web site could do.

According to Jane Mayer of *The New Yorker,* "Brickley's family, once evangelical Christians, now practice what he calls 'Messianic Judaism.'" They recognize Jesus as the Messiah, according to Mayer, "but they also observe the Jewish holidays and attend synagogue." As Brickley explained it, "Jesus was Jewish, so to be like Him you need to be Jewish, too." Brickley expressed to Mayer that "the hand of God" played a role in choosing Palin: "The longer I worked on it the less I felt I was driving it. Something else was at work."

On February 26, 2007, Brickley posted his first blog entitled "Why Sarah Palin?" On March 4, he officially launched his site, explaining that he had spent a month researching a potential Republican vice presidential candidate, based on the premise that Rudy Giuliani would win the nomination. He was unimpressed with the "second tier" of GOP presidential contenders, so he developed a profile for the "perfect VP candidate":

1) An energetic, young, fresh face who will energize the electorate
2) Not connected to the current administration
3) Pro-life
4) Pro-gun
5) A woman or minority to counter Hillary or Obama and put to rest the idea that America only elects white males

Brickley said that he stumbled upon the name of Sarah Palin, who emerged as the most "appealing" candidate in Brickley's search based on the five criteria. The longer he looked, the more attractive she became.

Palin was particularly more appealing to Brickley than the other conservative GOP warhorses, most notably Newt Gingrich. "We needed youth energy, not one of the same people who've been running the party since 1994," Brickley told the local *Colorado Springs Gazette*. "I love Newt Gingrich, but even he will tell you he's getting a little stale." Brickley wasn't sure, or even all that confident, where his efforts in cyberspace would take him, but he was willing to give it the "good college try." "The power of the blogosphere to influence events is well documented (just ask Dan Rather)," he declared in an early post, "and the proprietor plans on aggressively promoting this site throughout the conservative blog world." He dubbed Palin "the Republican Obama."

Brickley did not contact Palin, nor she him. They became locked, however, in an orbit with each other. Brickley noted her every move on the Internet. Palin maintained her distance from the Web site but monitored developments on her two BlackBerrys daily.

Under the Frequently Asked Questions posting on the site, Brickley made clear that he had neither a "personal" or "official" relationship with Palin. Nor was he promoting a "favorite daughter" candidate; he had never been to Alaska and was from the "Rocky Mountain region." He acknowledged that he supported Rudy Giuliani for president (he was the GOP favorite at the time) and vowed to "not go against Giuliani if Palin backs another candidate." In answer to the question, "Isn't it a little early to be talking about the VP nomination?" Brickley acknowledged that it was, though, he observed, there was already plenty of "angling" taking place. Brickley noted that the blogosphere was presently bristling with predictions about a potential GOP running mate. If Palin were to be seriously considered, he argued, "those who support her must start working to get her name out NOW!"

During the first year of the blog, Brickley issued some fifty-seven postings. He tracked down her views on education, gun rights, health care, and the environment. Even though Palin positioned herself as something of a moderate during her first months in office—Palin "governed from the center," said Rebecca Braun, author of *Alaska Budget Report,* a nonpartisan political newsletter published in Juneau—Brickley projected her as a strong social conservative. On the issue of "free markets," for instance, he posted her quote: "I am a conservative Republican, a firm believer in free market capitalism. A free market system allows all parties to compete, which ensures the best and most competitive project emerges, and ensures a fair, democratic process." That she was doing just the opposite with the oil companies at the time in Alaska never seemed to register with Brickley.

Almost immediately, Brickley's blog generated media attention. Just a few days after he launched his Web site, *Anchorage Daily News* reporter Kyle Hopkins noted it and posted a link to the Web site on his *Alaska Politics* blog. The idea of Palin becoming the GOP vice presidential nominee became part of the political zeitgeist in Alaska, though in an early posting Brickley conceded the notion might seem "a little off-the-wall at first." Brickley provided links to Palin appearances and speeches. He trumpeted her approval ratings. Brickley himself was going to other conservative blog sites and promoting Palin, while cross-linking to his site. He began posting a variety of pictures of Palin, particularly those that represented a conservative image—with a motorcycle club, in a tank, with Navy men, dressed in Army fatigues with an Army helicopter in the background—so that anyone going to the site had a conservative frame of reference for her. Ironically, all of the photos were taken by the state of Alaska and paid for with Alaska taxpayer money. And the *Anchorage Daily News* continued to follow Brickley's efforts, ensuring that Alaskans—and everyone working in Palin's administration—were aware of it as well.

I T WAS THROUGH PAULETTE SIMPSON, the leader of the Alaska Federation of Republican Women, that Palin learned in the summer of 2007 of an impending cruise ship visits and their precious cargo of influential conservatives. A Republican dynamo in southeast Alaska, where she lives in Douglas, just across the Gastineau Channel from Juneau, Simpson was a loyal subscriber to both *The Weekly Standard* and *National Review* and a bright, ideological conservative. As early as August 1997, when she discovered that an *NR* contingent was on its way to Juneau—one that included the magazine's legendary founder, William F. Buckley, Jr., Nobel prize–winning economist Milton Friedman, conservative columnist Robert Novak, and former national Republican Party chairman Haley Barbour—Simpson set the gears in motion to hold a gala reception for the distinguished visitors at the ballroom of Juneau's Baranof Hotel.

Simpson, who then served as chair of Juneau's Capital City Republicans and who is married to prominent Juneau attorney E. Budd Simpson, chose not to hold the affair at the statehouse at that time because the then governor of Alaska, Tony Knowles, was (heaven forbid) a Democrat. In fact, much to Simpson's chagrin, the affable Knowles crashed the party at the Baranof (he was actually invited by a Republican legislator) and monopolized much of Buckley's time. Both Knowles and Buckley had attended the same prep school in New York and both were Yale alums. (Knowles recalls that they had "a delightful time together.") When a picture of Buckley, Knowles, and Republican House speaker Gail Phillips appeared on the front page of the *Juneau Empire* the following day, it added further insult to Simpson's injury.

So when Simpson learned a decade later that *National Review* would once again be hosting a summer cruise to Alaska—this time with a Republican in the statehouse—she jumped on the ball and made the connection with the governor's chief of staff, Mike Tibbles, and explained the significance of the coming cruise ship contingent. On March 21, 2007, less than three months after Palin had been sworn in, Simpson fired off a detailed memo to the governor, copied to Tibbles, entitled "Request to Host Reception at Governor's Residence." Simpson provided concise, yet detailed, background information on *National Review* and on the 1997 visit. She then listed all of the *National*

Review lecturers scheduled to be on board the ship and offered the following advice:

> It would be an incredible opportunity to once again host these nationally known and respected writers here in Juneau. Capital City Republican Women would pay the costs associated with a reception at the Governor's Residence if you would be so kind to host such a reception for these special visitors and our invited local guests.
>
> Opportunities to showcase Alaska and our issues to friendly press are so very rare.

In her memo, Simpson noted that when she "invited *NR* to participate in this personalized sightseeing" in 1997, "I had one goal in mind: *To get Alaska issues better known and understood by people who shape public opinion in this country.*" (Next to that particular passage, in a copy of the memorandum provided through an Alaska Public Records Act request, is the word "yes," written and circled in what appears to be the hand of Governor Palin.) Simpson also indicated that she would be in New York the following week and would be "delighted to call Jack Fowler," publisher of *National Review,* to set the wheels in motion for the reception.

When Simpson learned that yet another conservative magazine, *The Weekly Standard,* would also be coming to Alaska that June, another formal get-together was coordinated through the Governor's Office, this time a luncheon scheduled for noon on June 18, three days before the summer solstice.

Silver-haired and in her mid-fifties, Simpson was a tough inside player in Alaska's often no-holds-barred political squabbles. Only a few years earlier, she had gotten tangled up with some nasty partisan politics involving one more effort to move the capital out of Juneau. She had sized up plenty of Alaska's politicians during her years as a Republican Party activist, including Palin, and she sensed that the young governor had "national talent" and that she could handle the "rough-and-tumble" nature of national politics. More than a year later, after all the hoopla and the surprise of Palin's vice presidential nomination, Simpson would say in a radio interview that Palin "was outstanding. She's a natural. She connects unbelievably with people. I've never seen a more skilled politician." In an interview with the *Juneau Empire,* she was even more effusive: "Sarah Palin for her entire political career has been underestimated. She's tough, she's tenacious. I believe that she does have what it takes to get out there. Again, her ability to connect with voters and make a case is very, very, very strong."

Later during the campaign, as the poll numbers facing the McCain-Palin ticket told a grim story, Simpson would acknowledge an interesting caveat to Palin's record in an interview with none other than *National Review*. "She ruffled a ton of feathers [in her early days as governor]," Simpson conceded. "That didn't get her off on a good footing with Republicans." Ironically, although she did not say so, one of those Republicans was Simpson herself. Palin's support for moving the capital out of Juneau put her directly at odds with Simpson and the party faithful in the Alaska panhandle, while Simpson was viewed by Palin as being aligned with the statewide Republican inner circle centered around Randy Ruedrich, with whom Palin had engaged in a long-standing, often vicious, internecine battle.

So in many ways this was a reach-out by Simpson, a way to build bridges with the young governor and to heal some old wounds. In her memorandum, Simpson encouraged Palin's office to make contact with the activities coordinator for Holland America. In turn, Palin directed her administrative staff to make the necessary arrangements for the get-togethers with the incoming pundits—even if she was not fully aware of who they were.

THE *WEEKLY STANDARD* CONTINGENT negotiated the *Oosterdam*'s gangplank down to the bustling dockside of Juneau, on South Franklin Street. Palin had a small tour bus waiting for them. They passed Juneau's landmark Red Dog Saloon, once a resplendent dive, now a bustling tourist destination, replete with sawdust floors and a favorite drink known as the Duck Fart. No mingling with the hoi polloi for them.

Located less than a half-mile northwest of the Red Dog, on Calhoun Avenue, the Governor's Mansion, built in 1912, is a lovely Greek Revival–styled building, with classical columns (albeit composed of plaster) and a large, formal reception hall. Palin and her family stayed only a small part of the year in Juneau, preferring instead their own Wasilla home on Lake Lucille, two hours away by plane. Palin went all-out for the luncheon, featuring a main course of Pacific halibut cheeks, the rarely served (but highly valued) prime cut of the fish that tastes much like tender lobster. Those who attended the event recall that Palin delivered a prolonged and vigorous grace, one of her trademarks. Not only did it make clear her evangelical Christian values and set the tone for the discussion that followed, but it also focused the center of attention on her, and kept it there, throughout the meal. It was a hallmark moment.

As Jane Mayer noted in her celebrated *New Yorker* account of the luncheon, it was a decidedly "high-spirited" affair that was to leave an impression on those who attended. The governor's five-year-old daughter, Piper, was a joyous presence in the dining room and put everyone at ease as she darted in and out of the adjoining kitchen amid much laughter. Palin apparently impressed her visitors with her seeming command of energy policies and their links to foreign affairs.

A memorandum for the luncheon, dated June 18, 2007, indicates that eighteen adults were invited, including Simpson; Lieutenant Governor Sean Parnell; Attorney General Talis Colberg; Commissioner of the Alaska Department of Administration Annette Kreitzer; and eleven members of the *Weekly Standard* contingent, including Michael Gerson (whose name is listed as "Garrison" on the official guest list), Fred Barnes, Bill Kristol, and their family members.

Given his evangelical background and his commitment to Christian values during his stint in the White House, the forty-three-year-old Gerson made the most likely match with Palin that afternoon in Juneau. A graduate of Wheaton College, the alma mater of Billy Graham, and the father of two young children, Gerson was viewed by Washington insiders as Bush's closest spiritual confidant during the dark months following the September 11 attacks in 2001. "A devout Christian known to lead fellow staffers in prayer," *The Atlanta Journal-Constitution* would write of him in a glowing profile, "Gerson is what colleagues call a writer's writer, a big-picture thinker with an instinct for the broad sweep of history with the heart of a poet." His critics, however, viewed him as egocentric and self-aggrandizing. In a critical portrait of Gerson that appeared in *The Atlantic,* written, ironically as events were to unfold, by former White House colleague Matthew Scully (who would serve as Palin's speechwriter during the 2008 campaign), Gerson was depicted as frail and fidgety, possessed by pretense, vanity, pettiness, and selfishness. With Gerson, Scully asserted, "things actually sounded a lot more heroic than they actually were."

The real bonding that afternoon, however, was not with Gerson (who would later become one of her critics), but with the fifty-four-year-old Kristol—though Jewish and urbane, he, like Palin, viewed himself as an ideological maverick. Kristol had never been afraid to break from the formal positions of the Republican Party, and at times during the tenure of George W. Bush had actually criticized the president for being too *centrist.* A staunch hawk on the Middle East, Kristol, like many of his conservative ideologues, had avoided

military service in Vietnam, and more recently had significantly underestimated both the costs and the troops necessary for the U.S. occupation of Iraq.
(Comedy Central's Jon Stewart likes to joke: "Oh, Bill Kristol, are you *ever*
right?") Betraying his prep school pedigree with virtually every sentence he
utters, Kristol nonetheless fashions himself a practitioner of realpolitik, and he
saw in Palin a kindred conservative ideologue with actual governing experience.

Not wanting her guests to miss out completely on tourist attractions, Palin
had arranged for a helicopter visit to an active gold mine in Berners Bay, forty-
five miles north of Juneau. According to state records, Alaska's taxpayers paid
$4,410 for two helicopters to sortie Palin and her staff to the gold mine. While
it would later be claimed otherwise, the state of Alaska also picked up the tab
for the lunch, according to Alaska's administrative director, Linda Perez, and
it was simply absorbed in the governor's budget. Though a self-identified "fiscal conservative," Palin was never adverse to the state of Alaska paying for
events and services that would advance her political career. Palin's *Weekly Standard* guests, however, paid their own way to the gold mine.

The Berners Bay visit allowed Palin to show off her conservative credentials firsthand. Environmentalists in Alaska, under the banner of "No Dirty
Gold," have long opposed Coeur D'Alene Mines Corporation's practice of
dumping waste from the mining operation into Lower Slate Lake, a pristine
body of water in the Tongass National Forest. Invoking the Clean Water Act,
the environmentalists had taken the operation to Federal Court. According to
them, "The bay supports local commercial and sport Coho and sockeye
salmon fisheries, and also provides commercial catches of shrimp and king,
tanner, and Dungeness crab." They also cited the bay's cultural significance
to Alaska's Native peoples. Palin would have none of it. She saw the mining
operation as a significant component of Alaska's new economy. And while
she would later lose a decision in the Ninth Circuit Court of Appeals, she
used the Berners Bay excursion to show off her leadership skills and political
charisma as she addressed nearly one hundred rough-hewn mineworkers
upon her arrival. Her new admirers took note. Palin was tough and gutsy and
could hang with the guys. And she stuck to her guns. Gerson would later describe her to *The New York Observer* as "a mix between Annie Oakley and
Joan of Arc."

Fred Barnes, the veteran journalist and co-host of Fox's *The Beltway Boys,*
was especially impressed. Almost as soon as he made his way back to the
Lower 48, he would draft an article for *The Weekly Standard* entitled "The
Most Popular Governor," which was published less than a month after the

propitious meeting with Palin. "The wipeout in the 2006 [congressional] election left Republicans in such a state of dejection that they've overlooked the one shining victory in which a Republican star was born," Barnes wrote. "The triumph came in Alaska where Sarah Palin, a politician of eye-popping integrity, was elected governor. She is now the most popular governor in America, with an approval rating in the 90s, and probably the most popular public official in any state." It was a claim that would be repeated over and over by the cruise ship contingent.

Barnes was reportedly captivated by how "exceptionally pretty" and "how smart" Palin was, how "unusually confident." His article laid out the basic biographical narrative that was to attract GOP interest a year later: Palin's evangelical upbringing in the backwoods of Alaska; her being the "star of her high school basketball team" and later Miss Wasilla and Miss Congeniality in the statewide beauty pageant; her tenure as mayor of Wasilla; her "reformer" credentials.

The article further quoted Anchorage radio talk show host Dan Fagan, then still a Palin supporter, who declared, "She's as Alaskan as you can get. She's a hockey mom, she lives on a lake, she ice fishes, she snowmobiles, she hunts, she's an NRA member, she has a float plane, and her husband works for BP [British Petroleum] on the North Slope." And while the article hinted at a few "bumps" in her recent gubernatorial race, acknowledging that "she missed enough campaign appearances to be tagged 'No Show Sarah' by her opponents" and conceding that "she was criticized for being vague on issues," Barnes emphasized that Palin "sold voters on the one product that mattered: *herself.*"

> In the roughly three years since she quit as the state's chief regulator of the oil industry, Palin has crushed the Republican hierarchy (virtually all male) and nearly every other foe or critic. Political analysts in Alaska refer to the "body count" of Palin's rivals. "The landscape is littered with the bodies of those who crossed Sarah," says pollster Dave Dittman.

The flattering portrait of Palin in *The Weekly Standard* marked her first full-scale brush with national exposure. There was no mention of Barnes's visit to Juneau in his account, no reference to the cruise or the slightest hint that he had dined at the Governor's Mansion. Palin was not yet a household name, but among the conservative elite in the Lower 48, her star was shining on the horizon. Most important, Palin had been stamped with the *Weekly Standard*'s conservative imprimatur.

If Fred Barnes had been taken with Palin, Bill Kristol was absolutely enthralled. Married to classics scholar Susan Scheinberg and the father of three children (his wife and one daughter, Anne, were present at the Governor's Mansion), Kristol nonetheless would refer to Palin as "my heartthrob." In the ensuing election cycle, he would become her biggest champion, both in the press and on television. A year later, in the summer of 2008, on the eve of the Republican convention, Kristol declared boldly, "I don't know if I can make it through the next three months without her on the ticket."

It was a decidedly odd pairing. The scion of an intellectual Jewish family based in New York City (his father had been a Trotskyite in the days before World War II), Kristol had blitzed through Harvard magna cum laude in three years. After receiving his Ph.D. in government only a few years later, he had gone to work as an assistant to William Bennett in the Reagan administration and then served as Dan Quayle's chief of staff during the president of George H. W. Bush. Palin, on the other hand, had focused on athletics in high school and went through a handful of colleges before finally graduating from Idaho State.

Urbane, if not effete, in manner, Kristol was a think tank junkie; he cofounded the neoconservative Project for the New American Century and served as chairman of the New Citizenship Project from 1997 to 2005. He is a member of the board of trustees for the free market Manhattan Institute for Policy Research and is also reportedly a regular attendee at Bilderberg Group conferences, a super-elitist confab held annually to promote U.S. and Western European unity. Kristol is married to an intellectual; Palin to an avowed anti-intellectual. Yet in Palin, Kristol clearly saw something that he found politically attractive. *Very* attractive. He would promote her rigorously throughout the following year, as her name appeared in more than four dozen *Weekly Standard* articles in the aftermath of the meeting in Juneau.

B ILL KRISTOL WAS NOT TO be Sarah Palin's only serious political suitor that summer. Merely six weeks later, on August 1, another Holland America Line cruise ship, the MS *Noordam*, sailed into Juneau with a troupe of intellectuals associated with yet another conservative publication, the *National Review*. Founded in 1955 by conservative icon William Buckley, the *NR* had managed to remain a vital voice in the American conservative movement for more than half a century. The erudite Buckley, his health fading at the time (his beloved wife, Pat, had just died in April, and he would die in February of 2008), had not made this cruise, but its guest list included a coterie of well-known conservative pundits, including the magazine's current editor, Rich Lowry; the controversial legal scholar and former federal judge Robert Bork, who had been turned down for the Supreme Court in 1987 by the Senate; the renowned classics and military scholar, syndicated columnist, and Hoover Institute historian Victor Davis Hanson; *National Review* senior editor Jay Nordlinger; and Dick Morris, a frequent figure on Fox News and a columnist for the *New York Post*.

This time it wasn't a sit-down luncheon, but a reception, lasting nearly three hours, and featuring an impressive spread of fresh Alaska salmon. There was no Palin-centric grace this afternoon, but the governor nonetheless assumed the spotlight once again, welcoming her guests to the Last Frontier and delivering a fifteen-minute speech on global energy. Just as she had with the previous cruise ship contingent, she made a lasting impression.

Victor Davis Hanson, who grew up on a farm in the small town of Selma in the middle of California's agriculturally rich Central Valley, was particularly impressed with Palin. "She was utterly and thoroughly authentic," Hanson recalls. "In many ways she's the antithesis of the Eastern elite. She comes from a different America, small-town America, blue-collar America. Roots in Idaho. Five kids. Her manner of speaking. She believes in American exceptionalism. It's a profile that points to class fault lines and separates her from the Eastern elites and Beltway insiders who viewed her with aristocratic disdain. I was very, very taken with her." Those are what Hanson would describe as his "visceral perceptions" of Palin, but what he remembered most, what he took away with him that day, was Palin's discussion of energy policy. "She asked, 'Why is it ecologically unsound for us, the most careful ecological stewards in the world, to drill out of Alaska, when we don't really care that we get oil from Kenya or Russia and they desecrate the environment to get it to us? Seemed to make perfect sense to me."

Hanson scoffed at any notion of a conservative conspiracy involved in these cruise ship voyages, as many bloggers would later claim, and, as Hanson contends, was "suggested" by the Jane Mayer *New Yorker* piece. He insisted that the *National Review*'s visit to the Governor's Mansion was a thoroughly "ad hoc affair," and that he had found out about it only a short time before it was to take place. "I think it was the night before that Jack Fowler [the *National*

Review publisher] came up to me and told me about it," Hanson recalled. "The idea that this was a Machiavellian encounter is ridiculous." While he had read of Palin, and knew that there was "a woman governor of Alaska," Hanson and others on the trip insist there wasn't an agenda on his end or among any of the other pundits regarding a Palin vice presidential candidacy. It was all serendipitous. "There wasn't a helluva lot to do in Juneau," says Hanson, "and this seemed like the most interesting possibility for us to undertake on shore."

Hanson said that Morris, Lowry, Nordlinger, Bork, and perhaps a few others, were picked up in a minivan for the five-minute ride to the Governor's Mansion. Some of the guests researched Palin on their laptops en route. Upon arrival, Hanson recalls noticing an "attractive" woman at the statehouse helping out with the hors d'oeuvres, making sure that everything was perfect. Eventually, he and the rest of the contingent realized that this woman was *the governor*. Hanson was captivated by Palin. "She was absolutely striking," he says, "walking around with high heels in this big Victorian house with rough Alaska floors, saying, 'Hi, I'm Sarah.'"

The contingent was astonished by how accessible Palin was, how informal. Hanson couldn't remember for certain, but Palin had one, perhaps two of her younger children in tow, and they were running around the room "like little spitfires." She seemed "totally at ease with everyone, no fuss, no pretense."

Secondly, they were impressed by her radiance, by what Hanson dubbed her "movie star" qualities. "She has that aura that Clinton, Reagan, and Jack Kennedy had," he recalled, "a magnetism that comes through much more strongly when you're in her presence." Palin, for her part, told Hanson that she was a student of history and a fan, in particular, of the *National Review* Web site.

Palin worked the room and worked it hard. In an online column after the event, Nordlinger affirmed:

> Alaska knocked my socks off, I must say. It's everything it is cracked up to be—not overrated at all. I had not especially wanted to go to Alaska. What I mean is, it was not on my list of dream destinations. I thought, "I go to Switzerland once or twice a year; I go to Austria once or twice a year. How impressed can I be, by natural beauty?" The answer is: Very, very impressed.

Mostly he had been impressed by Palin. He described the governor as "a former beauty-pageant contestant, and a real honey, too. Am I allowed to say that? Probably not, but too bad. She is a honey in multiple ways. It was a pleasure to be with her, and her political career will probably take her beyond Alaska. Dick Morris is only one who thinks so."

If Palin's connection with Kristol was an odd coupling, her pairing with Morris was, on the surface, even more bizarre. Morris, like Kristol, is of prep school and Ivy League pedigree (a 1964 graduate of Columbia), born with a silver spoon in his mouth, the son of a Manhattan real estate attorney with political connections in New York City. Morris was fascinated by politics at an early age. His second cousin, Roy Cohn, was a member of the legal team that had prosecuted Julius and Ethel Rosenberg, and Cohn later would serve as Joe McCarthy's chief counsel. Cohn's threats against the U.S. Army led to the Senate's Army-McCarthy hearings of 1954 and would eventually lead to McCarthy's downfall. In the 1980s, Cohn was disbarred by the state of New York for unethical and unprofessional conduct.

Most people know of Morris's ties to Bill Clinton during his presidency in the mid-1990s, but his links to the Clintons actually go back to the late 1970s, in Arkansas. After graduating from Columbia, Morris, then a Democrat, had served as a political consultant in New York, where, wanting to "connect issues with electability," he first developed a penchant for polling as a policy tool. In 1977, he decided to take his act nationwide, and he met Clinton on a run through Little Rock. They connected on a variety of levels, particularly in respect to their shared pragmatic approach to politics. The following year, Morris served as an adviser during Clinton's successful run for the governorship; four years later, he was called back to guide Clinton's bid for reelection after a near-disastrous first term.

Morris was not part of Clinton's presidential war team in 1992—which featured James Carville and George Stephanopoulos, among others—but when things went sour with Clinton during the early months of his first term, Morris was brought back into the fold. A brilliant pollster and electoral strategist, Morris developed a theory of political "triangulation," whereby Clinton would distance himself from both political parties and seek centrist positions (determined by polling numbers) appealing to swing voters. Some described him as an "evil genius"; Charles "Buddy" Roemer, the former governor of Louisiana, called Morris the "weirdest guy I ever met in politics." But by all assessments, including Clinton's, the triangulation strategy was highly effective and played a key role in Clinton's reelection campaign.

Only Morris didn't get to savor the fruits of Clinton's reelection victory. On August 29, 1996, just as Clinton was about to deliver his acceptance speech at the Democratic National Convention, Morris resigned his position in the Clinton campaign after *The Star*, a supermarket tabloid, reported that Morris had been cavorting with a prostitute named Sherry Rowlands and had allowed her to listen in on conversations with the president. Rowlands, who kept notes of their trysts for nearly a year and was paid approximately $50,000 by *The Star* for her story, alleged that Morris was fond of "toe-sucking" and singing "Popeye the Sailor Man" in his underwear. *The Star* had also taken photos of Morris and Rowlands in bathrobes, at 3 A.M., on the balcony of the Jefferson Hotel, just a few blocks from the White House. The dalliance resulted not only in a tremendous amount of public opprobrium and a great deal of notoriety, but Morris also pulled off the rare feat of winding up on the cover of *Time* magazine two weeks in a row—the first in triumph, the second in shame. From that point on, both Clintons cut him off at the knees and banished him from the court.

Morris has responded in kind—for more than a decade—by castigating them, most particularly Hillary Clinton, in several books and columns too numerous to cite. (He also served as a significant source in Carl Bernstein's biographical drubbing of Clinton, *A Woman in Charge*.) During the ensuing decade, Morris went on a spiritual quest of sorts, converting to Catholicism, but his newfound spirituality failed to shield him from further ignominy. Only a few months prior to departing for the trip to Alaska, Morris was named by alleged Washington madam Deborah Jeane Palfrey (who committed suicide in 2008) as one of her customers in a story appearing in *The New York Times*; as he had a decade earlier during the Rowlands scandal, Morris vehemently denied the charges. In spite of the controversies, however, he has managed to maintain a national platform as a political commentator and analyst on Fox News.

Morris was a late addition to the *National Review* retinue. One of the magazine's final two-page advertisements for the Alaska cruise noted Morris had just "signed on," and it listed his credentials as "ace political analyst and 'Hillary' expert."

Described by *Time* as possessing "a small frame pumped with manic energy," Morris was absent of traditional outdoor male interests and was a shark out of water in Alaska, but by all accounts he found an eager ear in Palin. Morris had long cultivated the ability of placating those in power, of earning their confidence, and he soon had Palin off in a corner by herself, in an intense tête-à-tête. "He's like a cult leader," says former Republican media consultant Stuart Stevens. "The client has to get in there, drink the Kool-Aid and look him in the eye, get the whole mystical connection going."

Whether Palin knew the details of Morris's tawdry past, or simply recognized him as a conservative talking head from Fox, is uncertain. What is most definite is that they had a very long private conversation during which Morris monopolized the discussion. Two days after Palin was tapped by McCain to be his running mate, the ceaselessly self-aggrandizing Morris declared in *The Washington Post*: "I will always remember taking her aside and telling her that she might one day be tapped to be Vice President, given her record and the shortage of female political talent in the Republican Party. She will make one hell of a candidate, and hats off to McCain for picking her."

On that August afternoon in Juneau, however, Morris's advice to Palin, who identified herself as a "reformer" in her opening remarks to her guests, had been far more cautionary, far more ethereal. "What happens to most people is that they campaign as outsiders," advised Morris, "but when they get into power they turn into insiders. If you want to be successful, you have to stay an outsider." Otherwise, he prophesied, she would lose her "outsider cred."

It was a momentous reception. When the time came for Morris and other guests to leave, Hanson recalled that Palin appeared disheartened to see the *National Review* contingent depart. "She said, 'Hey—does anyone want to stay for dinner? We're going to eat right now.' She also invited everyone to come back the next day. 'If any of you are in the area, all you have to do is knock. Yell upstairs, I'll be right down.'" Hanson got the distinct impression that Palin was lonely in the statehouse, that she was eager for intellectual conversation of a political bent.

Bitney doubted that. "Bored is more like it," he said. "She has a remarkably short attention span." Either way, there would be no more visitors from conservative magazines that summer in Juneau, and the *Noordam* was soon to depart that night for Yakutat Bay, more than a hundred nautical miles northwest, to view the spectacular Hubbard Glacier the following morning. Palin may have felt the pangs of the cruise ship's departure, but in the months ahead, as one of the most competitive presidential elections in American history played itself out before a spellbound international audience, she would reap significant rewards from the seeds she had sown with those cerebral power brokers who had come to visit the Last Frontier in the summer of 2007. While Palin barely mentioned either cruise ship encounter in her memoirs, they would nonetheless play a pivotal role in her political destiny.

In little more than a year, Sarah Palin was going to get called up to the varsity.

B UT HER LONGTIME FRIEND and legislative director, John Bitney, would no longer be on the team. Bitney's long hours on the campaign and working on Palin's legislative agenda in Juneau had provided the final strains to his marriage; he and his wife were headed for a divorce. He informed Palin of his impending breakup, but not that he had begun having an affair with someone working in Alaska government—whose husband, in particular, was a close friend of Todd Palin's—and the word eventually got back to the governor and her husband. They were livid. Bitney had a tense meeting with Sarah Palin in her office. He says she was emotional—hurt, disappointed, and very upset—and Bitney knew he was not long for his position as Palin's legislative director. Bitney says that he understood Palin's response—to a point. He acknowledges that he should have been more forthcoming with her, particularly given the tangled web of relationships between all the various parties. On top of that, the Palins were uncompromising about that sort of thing. Everything to them was black and white. They demanded almost a cultlike loyalty.

Bitney had spoken openly with Palin's chief of staff Mike Tibbles, whom Bitney himself had recommended for the position, about securing a job outside of the governor's office where he would have no direct contact with Palin. Tibbles, according to Bitney, seemed to understand the situation, and was sensitive to Bitney's need for employment. Bitney had given up his lobbying work to serve on Palin's campaign and to work in her administration. He knew that the Palins could be cruel—he had seen them cut people off at the knees over the years—but he never thought it would happen to him. They went too far back. He had been her lead strategist on her run for governor. He had been totally loyal. And he had been a key player in her legislative triumphs during Palin's first six months in office. "Whatever you did," Palin had said publicly to Bitney at a May 17, 2007, press conference marking the end of the legislative session, "you did it right." Members of her staff broke into applause in recognition of his effort. There was a celebratory photo of them taken with Bitney at the podium and a smiling Palin at his side. It was another moment of triumph together for the two former bandmates from Wasilla Junior High.

Little more than a month later, however, with the legislative challenges behind them and the long days of an Alaska summer ahead, Bitney had hopes of landing a position with the Department of Transportation. Nothing had been confirmed, but according to Bitney, Tibbles indicated to him that "we'll figure something out," and it put Bitney at ease.

That "ease" was not to last long. During the first week in July—the Fourth of July holiday fell on a Wednesday that year—Bitney decided to spend a few days later in the week fishing on the Kenai River, a popular salmon stream south of Anchorage. One night after fishing, his state issued BlackBerry went out of service. "I thought it was a temporary outage," he says, "and I didn't think much of it." Nonetheless, Bitney thought it might be a good idea to drive back to Juneau to confirm his future with Tibbles. On his way out of town that Sunday, July 8, he stopped off at his Anchorage office before commencing his 850-mile, two day drive back to the capital. But when he tried to enter the state government offices at the Atwood Building in downtown Anchorage, his key card didn't work. With the BlackBerry and now his key, Bitney was growing concerned that something was up.

His first day of driving took him to the small truck stop of Tok, three hundred miles up the Glenn Highway. He spent the night at Young's Motel, next to Fast Eddie's restaurant. The following morning, he checked his e-mail, only to find that communications sent to his state of Alaska address had bounced. He placed a call to his loyal deputy, Christopher Clark, who, in turn, transferred the call to Tibbles. Over the past six months they had earned the nickname "Tibbles and Bits" in Juneau. If you wanted something done in Palin's administration, you went to them. But Tibbles, according to Bitney, was short and to the point with him on the phone. "We cut you off on Friday," he said. There would be no transfer. Nothing. Bitney had been fired three days earlier. No one had bothered to tell him. Bitney felt like he was "in the land of suck, at that point." He went to a nearby gas station. For a few quiet moments he stood watching cars, RVs, and big rigs race by him on the Glenn Highway. He never heard from Sarah Palin again.

Word spread quickly through the small circles of Juneau about Bitney's firing. It was a shock to many involved in Alaska government, and the first big crack in Palin's governorship. The Associated Press reported that "a spokeswoman for the governor says Bitney and Palin mutually agreed he would leave his post for personal reasons." The Alaska Public Radio Network reported Bitney's departure as "amicable." Bitney, who was a valued commodity in Juneau, accepted his fate. Within twenty-four hours he had been offered a job by Alaska House Speaker John Harris, a Republican, as his chief of staff. Once Todd Palin heard about the Harris offer he was not pleased; according to Harris, the "Shadow Governor" called him trying to dissuade him from hiring Bitney.

Harris didn't budge. A year later, Todd Palin would claim to *The New York Times* that he "did not recall" speaking to Harris about Bitney, while the governor's spokesperson Sharon Leighow would tell *The Wall Street Journal* that Bitney had been "dismissed because of his poor job performance." Bitney could only shake his head about how it all came down. "They're bizarre people," he said, "emotionally immature."

B ACK IN COLORADO, BLOGGER ADAM Brickley had no knowledge of the behind-the-scenes drama taking place in Alaska during the summer of 2007, or any idea of the cruise ships carrying conservative pundits to the Alaska Governor's Mansion. But he celebrated when Fred Barnes devoted his entire column in *The Weekly Standard* to Palin and made mention of her "body count" in respect to political foes. Brickley responded with an interesting observation. "Yes, the analogy is a little morbid, but the point is a good one," he declared. "Standing in Sarah Palin's way is political suicide, and you'll have to forgive me for wishing that fate on the 2008 Democratic ticket."

Then the Alaska news channel KTUU-Channel 2 also picked up the story in August 2007, producing a full-length feature on Brickley's blog and Palin's possible vice presidential candidacy—more than a year before she was to be tapped by John McCain. Palin's spokesperson Sharon Leighow responded to the blog by declaring: "Governor Palin is certainly flattered by all this speculation that's out there, but she has no plans to run for another office. She loves being governor of Alaska. And her plate is full with initiatives to move the state forward."

Brickley then took another tack in his postings; he began defending Palin against her critics, even those in Alaska. As national interest in Palin began to mount, Brickley sent out a warning to her critics: "Taking shots at Sarah Palin is somewhat akin to playing Russian Roulette. Remember what happened to the *Voice of the Times* and the State Ag Board? Please don't make fools of yourselves, you may regret it." He also went after Sheila Toomey, the popular "Alaska Ear" political gossip columnist at the *Daily News* who reported on the Palin-for-national-office hype in August:

> Palintology . . . That's the name of a Web site devoted to Sarah-love. Or, as the site defines the word: "the science dealing with Alaska's first female governor." It's a repository for

those ain't-she-the-gorgeous-Republican hope stories making the media rounds lately.

It's produced by Alaska Multimedia Productions, an
Anchorage-based Web production company. Wonder who's
paying them to do it. This is in addition to the site mentioned
a couple weeks ago that's pushing Sarah for vice president.
Vice president? Not hardly.

But Ear is prepared to predict the spin works well enough
that she gets tapped to make a speech at the 2008 national
convention. Then we'll see if she has legs.

OK, that didn't come out right. You know what Ear means.

Brickley's response was to assert that Toomey "wrote an article which essentially asserted that [Alaska Media Productions] was being paid by someone to run her Palin fan site." Toomey had made no such "assertion"; she
merely had asked the question. But his combative response began to be echoed
throughout the Palin sycophantic blogosphere—which only continued to expand in the months ahead.

The push for Palin in August of 2007 had gained considerable traction by
autumn and was clearly being watched by Palin and her cohort in Alaska. An
October 15 *Newsweek* cover package "Women & Power," with media maven
Arianna Huffington, Atlanta mayor Shirley Franklin, and media chef Rachael
Ray on the cover, included a feature story on the emerging role of women in
politics ("Now This Is Woman's Work") that focused on Palin and then Arizona governor Janet Napolitano, a Democrat. It was big ink for Palin—
Brickley was ecstatic—and painted Palin and Napolitano as possessing "a
pragmatic, postpartisan approach to solving problems, a style that works
especially well with the large numbers of independent voters in their respective states." The article, by Karen Breslau, which also described Palin as "a
former beauty-pageant winner, avid hunter, snowmobiler and mother of four,"
praised Palin's ability to work with "lawmakers on the other side of the
aisle."

Obviously, the producers of the *Charlie Rose* television show picked up the
copy of *Newsweek,* because only a few days after the issue hit the stands, Palin
and Napolitano—both in New York to participate in *Newsweek*'s annual
women's event—appeared on the popular PBS interview program for a twenty-
minute segment with Rose. This was to be a momentous media moment for

Palin, one that launched her career nationally, both at the time and later, as it was a YouTube video of this interview that was to be viewed repeatedly by McCain campaign advisers during the long, dysfunctional process of selecting Palin a year later. The interview provides an unfettered look into Palin's raw capabilities several months before the anointment. She cannot really hold a conversation about anything—save a few sound bites about resource development in Alaska—and in comparison to Napolitano comes across as a vacuous lightweight.

Rose begins by mispronouncing Palin's last name—he pronounces it with a soft "a," like a "pal"—while Napolitano hijacks the interview for the first four minutes. Palin had a difficult time even entering into the discussion—until Rose directed a question to her about education (Napolitano had just said that "education is the twenty-first century for the United States. . . . We're not getting the next generation adequately prepared for the world economy"). In answer to Rose's question, "Do you see education the same way . . . ?" Palin, in something of a precursor to the word salads that would later be widely parodied, broke into what was clearly a rote response about energy independence, which had become her mantra—and which she clearly was hoping would thrust her into national prominence:

PALIN: Well, absolutely, it is. For the state of Alaska, though, our biggest issues are energy issues, so that we can pay for a world-class education system up there. Our energy issues surround the fact that Alaska is very, very wealthy in reserves, oil and gas reserves, but we are not given the ability right now, or I guess the permission, by some, to go ahead and develop those resources and flow that oil and gas into the rest of the United States of America to help secure our United States so that we can quit being so reliant on foreign sources of energy, but a clean safe domestic supply of energy being produced in Alaska. Again we are very rich in the reserves, we just need that ability to tap them and flow into hungry markets our oil and our gas, so development of our resources . . .

The awkward and convoluted sentence structure is all there, the vague assertion that unnamed enemies are out to get Alaska (by *some*), the utter inability to get specific. Rose pressed her for clarification: "Are you speaking of conservationists or Washington or who that you think is providing the principal impediment?"

Palin can't really answer. "Those who want to make the decisions for Alaska," she stumbles, "yet, usually from the East Coast, yeah, maybe not trusting that Alaska can—"

Rose cuts her off again. "But is it the Congress, primarily responsible?" She can't give an answer. Within a matter of a few minutes, Palin is clearly in well over her head. "In some respects," she responds, and then her answer shifts toward blaming Big Oil, "but also some of the larger oil companies who hold the leases and have the right to develop our resources, who may look at Alaska's resources as being in competition with their foreign sources of energy that they are developing; so once Alaska is allowed to very responsibly and safely develop our resources we'll lower costs of energy across the United States and that would allow Arizona to fund an even greater education system and we'd be able to secure the United States with a clean domestic supply of energy." She never mentions Alaska's education system.

Rose presses her again. He is trying to get through the sound bites, through the memorized phrasing, through the wild swings in her response. "Why can't you convince environmentalists of that?" he asks.

Then Palin flat-out lies. It's not the environmentalists. They "are right on board with us with our proposal to build a natural gas pipeline through Alaska and then flow that energy into the rest of the United States," she contends. Then who are these unnamed "some" not "giving Alaska the permission"? She obviously has no clue of the converging economic and political processes that determine how energy gets developed. She doesn't mention AGIA by name, doesn't mention her energy tax legislation ACES. "Environmentalists have great concerns about some other development proposals like in ANWR [the Arctic National Wildlife Refuge] and offshore drilling and we are working on that," she claims. "We're working with them. But we have to prove our way, if you will in Alaska, we have to prove that we can do this cleanly, that we can do this safely and that's what I think my administration is standing for, doing it right."

Palin has the look and the tone down, but the substance is barely at the level of a high school civics class.

Later on, Rose brings up the Bridge to Nowhere. Palin takes credit for its demise. "We stopped that because we'll make real sensible decisions using other people's money, you know federal government's money. It is money that is based on the highway transportation formula so it is Alaska's money at this

point, but we'll make some wise decisions on how to build up our infrastructure." She makes no mention of her earlier support for the project.

Palin then tries to establish some foreign policy credentials.

> **PALIN:** National security issues, I think, uh, you know. Candidates are
> gonna be asked, are you doing, even as a candidate, and are your inten-
> tions to do all that you can to help secure these United States and I think
> every elected official needs to ask themselves that. And I say that Charlie,
> even personally, my one and only son, my eighteen-year-old, he just signed
> up for the United States Army, he is at boot camp right now, and I'm
> thinking, you know, this kid is doing all that he can within his power
> with to help secure and defend the United States. Every elected official
> had better be asking themselves, are you doing as much also, are you do-
> ing all that you can, certainly on the presidential election, in that scene,
> that's what's going to be asked of candidates and I think he or she who
> ends up on top of that issue will get those independent votes.

She can't mention a specific foreign policy issue. She brings it back to the
personal, mentioning her son's enlistment in the Army. She can't construct a
single thought on the subject beyond that which is vague and convoluted. And
the speech patterns that would come to be in place—the singsong phrasing, the
racing through passages, the jumping from issue to issue—were all manifest as
well. Given her response, Rose pressed her on who she is supporting for president. Palin is undecided. She doesn't have a horse in the race. She doesn't let on
if she's going Republican or Democrat. The vagueness at this point in the race
is startling:

> **PALIN:** I'm undecided because I haven't heard a lot—a lot of, uh—of
> discussion to the degree that I want to hear about doing all that we can
> to secure these United States, and not just militarily, but again with our
> energy issues, are we too beholden to unstable regimes right now, are we
> at their beck and call, those who would potentially cut off a supply of
> energy to the United States.

Rose asks her somberly, "Do you know what the Bush administration energy policy is?" Palin clearly does not. She turns the question into a joke.

"Well," she says, flashing her smile, "we hear about it through the media, yes . . ." and then she goes silent. Napolitano rescues her with a joke—"You're presuming there is one"—then takes control of the discussion again.

Then comes what certainly will be a surprise for anyone who would later watch Palin's vicious assault on Obama's health care reform package. Napolitano brings up the issue of health care. Rose swings the discussion of the issue back to Palin.

PALIN: Huge, huge, huge, sometimes it's such a huge issue we don't even broach the subject in an interview like this, Charlie, because it is so needed, reform, availability of health care for all.

ROSE: . . . Everybody that I have seen or interviewed who is a candidate is saying that it is desperately in need of attention.

PALIN: Well it is, you know what we are doing up there in Alaska. I don't want to reinvent any kind of wheelbarrow. There have been so many very wise think tanks and task force and user groups and stakeholders coming together for years trying to solve this issue. What we have done in Alaska is to, I guess, create another task force but one to inventory what the good ideas are from across the nation and plug in those the successes, because again no one single governor has a silver bullet and is going cure the ills caused by an inadequate health care system . . .

Palin is stumbling badly in this response, in over her head, and cannot say anything of substance so that she tosses the ball off to Napolitano, "I'm sure you, too, Janet, in your state, it is high, high on your agenda . . ."

There was also a clip of Palin videotaped in Rose's Green Room, not available to his viewers, in which Palin was asked who her favorite authors were. "I love C. S. Lewis—very, very deep," she says mentioning the famed novelist, without noting why, and then shifts to the writings of Dr. George Sheehan, a columnist for *Runner's World*. "Very inspiring and very motivating," she says. "He was an athlete and I think so much of what you learn in athletics about competition and healthy living that he was really able to encapsulate, has stayed with me all these years." Palin, who was to quote everyone from Plato and Aristotle to Lou Holtz in *Going Rogue,* made only the slightest mention of Lewis in her memoir and no mention of Sheehan. She clearly had a difficult time keeping her influences straight.

In the aftermath of the *Newsweek* article and Charlie Rose appearance, Palin was now regularly brought up as a potential Republican candidate for vice president. She took every opportunity to appear on a national platform while Brickley trumpeted every appearance, every reference, and aggressively challenged anything negative about her in the media. Palin's was the first active cybercampaign for the vice presidency.

In December it was announced by the Associated Press that Palin would be posing for *Vogue*, the high-end women's fashion magazine, and that the photo shoot would be taking place at her home in Wasilla.

By then Palin was being dubbed "The Hottest Governor in the Coldest State," and was clearly trading on her looks. "In a state where residents are not shy about voicing their political opinions," AP reporter Steve Quinn declared, "Internet blogs also don't ignore this aspect of the current occupant of the governor's office. One proclaims Alaska and Palin 'Coldest State, Hottest Governor.'" Quinn asserted that Palin was "well suited for the magazine, attractive as she is accomplished. The forty-three-year-old Palin's high cheekbones could rival any runway model's; she's well-dressed, and often wears her brown hair with gold highlights fashionably swept up."

Palin defended her decision to pose for the magazine. "Can you imagine if our administration would choose to shun any kind of national limelight and let them capitalize on some of the negative with the corruption trials?" Palin said. She equated the shoot to "changing Alaska's image." In yet another article about the *Vogue* shoot, she echoed her civic responsibilities. "We've got to make sure the rest of the United States doesn't believe the only thing going on in Alaska is FBI probes and corruption trials."

Palin's shoot appeared in the February issue of *Vogue* with Kate Bosworth on the cover (a faux cover with Palin's face interchanged with another model went viral on the Internet). This time, Palin's pairing was with Kathleen Sebelius, then the Democratic governor of Kansas (and later to become secretary of health and human services in the Obama administration). "At first they had me in a bunch of furs," she told the *Anchorage Daily News*. "Yeah, I have furs on my wall, but I don't wear furs. I had to show them my bunny boots and my North Face clothing."

The accompanying article, written by *Vogue* contributing editor Rebecca Johnson, opened with references to her "naturally good looks (one blogger called her Tina Fey's sexier sister)" and then cut to Palin's inability to take a photo without smiling. "As mayor [of Wasilla]," Johnson noted, "she was seen as a golden girl of the Republican Party, a hard-working, pro-business politician whose friendly demeanor (that Palin smile!) made her palatable to the typical pickup-driving Alaskan man." She also made note of a reference in the Washington, D.C.–based blog *Wonkette,* in which Palin was referred to as "the hottest governor in all fifty states and my total girl crush." At the end of the article there was what was becoming the de rigueur reference to Palin as "a national star" and "maybe even a vice-presidential candidate." Johnson didn't seem to take such talk seriously—a vice presidential nomination, Johnson argued, seemed unlikely—and with only 670,000 residents, "Alaska delivers fewer voters than a medium-size American city."

In spite of Johnson's caution, Brickley was ecstatic. The *Vogue* "issue will be hitting stores just as the presidential primaries draw to a close and VP speculation begins in earnest," he asserted. "Sarah Palin will suddenly be staring thousands of American women in the face and forcing them to consider the fact that Hillary Clinton may not be the best woman running for national office when November rolls around."

None other than Rush Limbaugh soon picked up the beat. Early in 2008, a woman named Julie from Alaska called in to his show.

CALLER: I was calling today because I heard on our statewide news that one of the running mates for McCain being considered would be our governor from the great state of Alaska.

LIMBAUGH: Talked about this I think yesterday or the day before.

CALLER: Yeah. I think that it would create quite the paradox for your Drive-By Media. Our governor, Sarah Palin, is intellectual, she is—

LIMBAUGH: (interrupting) How do you pronounce her last name?

CALLER: Pay-lin.

LIMBAUGH: Sarah Pay-lin. Okay.

CALLER: Yep. She's been heralded throughout the state as being personable, likable, intelligent, strong, and conservative. And she crosses over from conservative to liberalism not in thought, but because she stands by what she believes in. And, surprisingly enough, she has been at the fore-front of ethics reform in our great state . . .

LIMBAUGH: Yeah, plus she's a housewife, before that, she's a babe. I saw a picture.

CALLER: [laughing]

LIMBAUGH: Well, it's undeniable.

CALLER: Well, it is undeniable, and that's why the paradox is there for me. I think that because she's intelligent, number one, conservative maybe number one also, but she is photogenic, she is likable, she is en-gaging. When you meet her, she is interested in you, she speaks well.

LIMBAUGH: By the way, wait a second. I'm not diminishing any of those things by pointing out that she's a babe.

CALLER: Oh, no, no, no.

LIMBAUGH: The babe is the icing on the cake aspect, something the Democrats can't claim on their side.

CALLER: Exactly, especially when the highest Democrat that you can speak of is Mrs. Bill Clinton.

LIMBAUGH: You said it, not I. I just advanced the theory.

CALLER: Well, I can tell you that Governor Palin doesn't have to lift her chin up to twelve o'clock to get a good photo of her.

LIMBAUGH: I just love you. I love you, Julie. I love listening to women talk about other women like this.

Brickley, apparently, had no problem with the manner in which Limbaugh discussed Palin. "I would be remiss if I did not thank Rush Limbaugh for all of the help he has given to our movement in the last few days," Brickley gushed on his blog a few days later. "Mega dittos, El Rushbo!"

THEN ON MARCH 5, 2008, CAME AN announcement from Palin that seemed to arrive completely out of the blue. While leaving her office to attend a reception at the Baranof Hotel, Palin casually mentioned to a trio of reporters that she was expecting her fifth child, which was due sometime in May. No one in Juneau—not a single member of her staff, not even her closest confidants—was aware that Palin was pregnant, much less seven months along. As Wesley Loy of the *Anchorage Daily News* put it, Governor Palin "shocked and awed just about everybody around the Capitol" with her announcement. Loy interviewed State Senator Lyda Green, once Palin's mentor but by then her adversary, who observed that Palin was "very well disguised." When she herself was five months pregnant, noted Green, also the mother of five, "there was absolutely no question that I was with child." One lawmaker who had worked closely with Palin that legislative session was equally taken aback: "Really? No!"

In both her memoir and later, in 2009, at a speech she delivered in Evansville, Indiana, Palin says she discovered that she was pregnant while traveling alone, on a trip to New Orleans, after picking up a pregnancy test kit at a local Walgreen's. She indicates that while she was pleased by the news, she was also worried about the political implications of her pregnancy. She was worried what people would think and what they would say. She suggests that, "for a fleeting moment," she considered terminating her pregnancy. She was out of town. No one would ever have to know."

Palin didn't call her husband to tell him of the results. She says she wanted to tell him in person, when he returned from a stint on the North Slope. They kept the news to themselves. She says she didn't share it with anyone but Todd Palin, not even her children. Indeed, Palin has also acknowledged that she waited about three months until she went to visit her family physician, Cathy Baldwin-Johnson. It was following this first meeting, she declared, that she realized her child might have Down syndrome. She also discovered that it would be a boy. A short time later, Baldwin-Johnson confirmed the speculation about Down syndrome. Palin acknowledges that she was devastated by the revelation and that she again considered terminating her pregnancy.

Back at the Baranof Hotel, in the aftermath of Palin's announcement, the word spread quickly through the capital. Palin made sure not to allow the spin of the news to derail her governorship. She knew that some of the old-school politicians might make political hay out of her having to take time off to give birth and tend to her young child. She cut them off at the pass. "To any critics who say a woman can't think and work and carry a baby at the same time," Palin told the *ADN*'s Loy. "I'd just like to escort that Neanderthal back to the cave."

The news came as a complete shock to Palin's Trooper detail, Gary Wheeler, who had just accompanied Palin to Washington, D.C., for a National Governor's Conference. Not only had Wheeler failed to notice that Palin was pregnant—Wheeler remembers she had changed into jeans upon her arrival in Washington, with no apparent revelation of pregnancy—but, according to Wheeler, Palin had never informed the Troopers of her situation in case of an emergency.

Three days later, the *Anchorage Daily News* melded the rumble surrounding Palin's pregnancy with the ever-growing clamor about Palin's vice presidential aspirations. "Gov. Sarah Palin will be the first to admit that it might be a stretch for a hockey mom from Alaska to be considered for the No. two spot on Sen. John McCain's presidential ticket," wrote *ADN* reporter Erica Bolstad in a lengthy front-page story. "But there's an undeniable national buzz surrounding the first-term governor, seen by many Republicans both within Alaska and outside the state as a fresh, new face to represent the party's future."

Just as she had wanted to stop any spin discounting her role as governor, Palin was also quick to make sure that she would continue to be considered for the vice presidential nomination. "I'm very confident that a pregnant woman should not and doesn't have to be prohibited from doing anything, including running for vice president," Palin said. "Or working in the home or out of the home. The world is our oyster also, whether carrying a baby or not."

A MONTH LATER, PALIN WAS SCHEDULED to make a speech at an RGA energy conference in Dallas. She was slightly less than eight months pregnant at the time. Shortly before her trip to Texas—which involved a stopover in Seattle—her Trooper security detail, Wheeler, says that Palin made a last-minute announcement that she wouldn't be needing a trooper to accompany her on her trip, and that her husband, Todd, would be traveling with her instead. An e-mail written by Palin, obtained through a Freedom of Information Act request, confirms Wheeler's recollection. At 9:26 on the morning of April 14, 2008, the day before her flight, Palin sent the following e-mail to her administrative assistant, Janice Mason:

J- instead of rga paying for staff, and/or rga (or state) paying
for Security on this Texas trip, pls let them know First Spouse
is available to travel instead - they can pay for Todd. Pls chk
on flt availability for him (on my flts). Thanks

Twenty minutes later, Mason wrote Palin back that the RGA was working
on Todd's flight and that "they will pay for him to accompany you."

That first night in Texas, according to information she gave at a news conference following her return, Palin claimed that she called her physician in the
middle of the night from her hotel room to discuss what Palin referred to as
"amniotic fluid leaking." Nonetheless, Palin stayed in Dallas and delivered her
speech later that day. Immediately afterward, Todd sent a message to the Palins'
closest aides—Bailey, Perry, and Frye—noting simply: "Her speech kicked ass . . ."
There was no mention of her medical situation. Rather than getting checked
at a nearby hospital in Dallas before her departure (Baylor Medical Center
was less than ten minutes away), Palin and her husband got on their return
flight home to Anchorage via Seattle. They did not tell flight attendants of
Palin's medical situation. On returning to Anchorage late in the evening of
April 17, Palin claims to have gone directly to the Mat-Su Regional Medical
Center, located just off the Parks Highway, roughly seven miles outside of
Wasilla. "Landed in Anchorage at about 10:30," she said. "Got out to the valley at 11:30 and she [Baldwin-Johnson] met us at the hospital, checked me out
and said, 'Um, yea you, look, you may have it tonight or in the morning.'" It
was reported that Palin gave birth to a baby boy, Trig, the following day, April
18, at 6:30 A.M.

The State of Alaska immediately issued a formal press release:

> Governor Sarah Palin and her husband Todd welcomed the
> arrival of their fifth child this morning. The Palins were thank-
> ful that the Governor's labor began yesterday while she was in
> Texas at the Governor's Energy Conference where she gave
> the keynote luncheon address, but let up enough for her to
> travel on Alaska Airlines back to Alaska in time to deliver her
> second son.
>
> Trig Paxson Van Palin was born at 6:30 A.M. and weighs
> six pounds, two ounces. The Governor and Trig are both do-
> ing well and resting comfortably.

Palin's spokesperson, Sharon Leighow, also issued a statement noting that "the governor's labor began while she was in Texas."

Almost immediately, there were rumors in Alaska and on the blogosphere that the baby was not Palin's and that it was actually that of her seventeen-year-old daughter, Bristol, who was living with Palin's sister Heather in Anchorage; there was also criticism of Palin that she risked her—and her child's—health by taking the long flight back to Alaska. Contrary to her later claims that the criticism came only following her being named John McCain's running mate, in fact, the critics began airing their concerns instantaneously.

However, Palin's family physician, Baldwin-Johnson—who is by all accounts a well-respected member of the medical community in Alaska and who, in 2002, had been named Family Physician of the Year by the American Academy of Family Physicians—later issued a letter in which she said that Palin had "one pre-term delivery at 35 weeks gestation in 2008." The letter further indicated that Palin had "no health risk factor other than her age" and that "she followed the normal and recommended schedule for prenatal care, including follow-up perinatology evaluations to ensure there were no congenital heart disease or other condition of the baby that would preclude delivery at her home community hospital. This child, Trig, was born at 35 weeks in good health. He was able to go home at two days of age with his mother."

Three days after Trig's birth, she and her husband held a news conference in Anchorage, with Trig joining them. The audiotape of the event provides a fascinating glimpse into the Palins' mind-set at the time of Trig's birth and their chafing at criticism of their decision to fly back to Alaska.

REPORTER: You said you felt some signs of labor, what were those signs?

PALIN: Well, not contractions so much because I had Braxton Hicks contractions for months as every pregnant woman does, and nothing real painful but just knowing that, um, it was feeling like, I may not, um, be able to be pregnant a whole another four or five weeks knowing that it would be not a bother to call our doctor and let her know. And, um, she's delivered how many babies over the years did she say?

TODD: Lots . . .

PALIN: A lot. It's been a couple of decades of her delivering babies. We knew to call her and just get her advice and, um, from there we again decided to skip the energy conference reception and come on home and get checked out.

REPORTER: So did your water break?

PALIN: Well, if you must know more of those type of details, but, um . . .

REPORTER: Well, your dad said that and I saw him say it so that's why I asked.

PALIN: Well, that was again if, if I must get personal, technical about this at the same time, um, it was one, it was a sign that I knew, um, could lead to, uh, labor being, uh, kind of kicked in there was any kind of, um, amniotic leaking, amniotic fluid leaking, so when, when that happened we decided OK, let's call her [Baldwin-Johnson].[‡]

TODD: There's a lot of new doctors out there on the streets in the last couple of days.

The *Anchorage Daily News* story the following day, by Kyle Hopkins, reported that Palin had *not* asked her physician "for a medical OK to fly." That said, Baldwin-Johnson was quoted as assessing: "I don't think it was unreasonable for her to continue to travel back."

Palin herself discounted the risk.

PALIN: Everybody's going to tell us what we could have, should have done and even though these folks—especially the critics—they're not doctors. They didn't know the situation. They don't know the situation. They, they certainly don't know our doctor and the consultations that

---

[‡] Palin's account of the birth of Trig appears in *Going Rogue*, pages 193 to 196. There is no mention of "leaking" amniotic fluid anywhere in her memoir.

we've had with her. So we did nothing to put our child nor anyone else in danger, uh, going through this five times I know what labor is and, uh, I am not a glutton for pain and punishment. I would have never, um, wanted to travel if I had been fully engaged in labor.

But Hopkins contacted an obstetrician in California, Dr. Laurie Gregg, active in the American College of Obstetricians and Gynecologists, who said that "when a pregnant woman's water breaks, she should go right to the hospital because of the risk of infection. That's true even if the amniotic fluid simply leaks out." As for the distinction that Palin was trying to make, Gregg was not buying into it. "To us, leaking and broken, we are talking the same thing," Gregg asserted. "We are talking doctor-speak."

The Palins were clearly irritated by the direction of the questioning. An aide to the Palins decided it was time to wrap things up. One final question was allowed.

REPORTER: Was it important to you to have the baby in Alaska?

PALIN: It was very important that we have . . . it was more important that, that Trig arrive safely and healthy and, um, and that is exactly what happened. The extra blessing was that Trig was able to be born into this great state, you know, kind of like, I feel like this extended Alaskan family, that he was here, for that.

TODD: Can't have a fish-picker from Texas.

Immediately following Trig's birth, Palin sent out an e-mail to family and friends—using what has been described as "the voice of God"—to inform them about the challenges of Down syndrome. "Many people will express sympathy, but you don't want or need that, because Trig will be a joy," she wrote. "You will have to trust me on this." She signed the letter, not with her name, but as "Trig's Creator, Your Heavenly Father."

Meanwhile, the announcement of the arrival of a fifth child in the Palin household did little to stem the tide of Palin's vice presidential aspirations. On May 8, 2008, Palin's special assistant, Ivy Frye, sent out an e-mail to Palin's inner circle, noting that The Congressional Quarterly had launched a game called "VP Madness" to select running mates for both John McCain and Barack Obama. Palin had made it into round two on the GOP side of the competition, trouncing Texas governor Rick Perry, 59–40. The results, Frye noted, had been featured in the *Anchorage Daily News*. Palin and her closest aides were keeping their eyes on the prize. Child or no child, she still had her sights set on the varsity.

PART II

AMERICA

The election of a President is a cause
of agitation, but not of ruin.
—**Alexis de Tocqueville**, *Democracy in America: Volume II*

CHAPTER 3

Hail Mary

D URING THE SAME TIME in the summer of 2007 that Sarah Palin was hosting the pundits from *The Weekly Standard* and *National Review* at the Governor's Mansion in Juneau, far away, in the gritty campaign offices of Crystal City, Virginia, John McCain's once highly touted presidential campaign was in severe crisis. His so-called Straight Talk Express had blown its engine and had come to a grinding, nearly catastrophic halt. After months of vicious, often destructive, infighting, and what *The New York Times* dubbed "zigzagging lines of command," several of his most trusted and loyal political advisers were cast off into the political ash heap and prompted to sever ties with the campaign. It was a cataclysm that would have profound consequences in the tumultuous months ahead, and perhaps, most important, foreshadowed several critical decisions that were to be made about the nature and direction of the campaign as it sputtered into the primaries and, eventually, the general election a year later.

In January 2007, according to several sources from inside the campaign, three key McCain operatives requested a meeting with the candidate. The trio included his campaign manager, Terry Nelson, who served as national political director of George Bush's 2004 reelection effort; speech writer Mark Salter, McCain's close friend, longtime chief of staff, and co-author of McCain's five books, including the bestselling *Worth the Fighting For* and *Faith of My Fathers*; and chief strategist, John Weaver, a Republican political operative and also a close friend of McCain's who had first hatched the idea of a McCain presidency a decade earlier. Their mission was to confront McCain and beseech him to demote Rick Davis, a controversial Washington, D.C., lobbyist and former political operative in the Reagan White House, who had been serving as "chief executive" of the McCain campaign. Many cynically viewed his ascent in the McCain hierarchy as the result of an opportunistic cultivation of Cindy McCain, the candidate's wealthy wife, who, in an interview with Katie Couric, once referred to Davis as "our closest friend." The use of the plural possessive was not lost on other staffers. Many viewed Cindy McCain as brittle and distant, but it was her family's money and social status in Arizona that had jumpstarted John McCain's political career a quarter-century earlier, and when it came to pillow politics, she still had significant influence on her husband.

The trio of Nelson, Salter, and Weaver viewed Davis as inexperienced and ineffective, particularly Weaver, who saw Davis as a political parvenu who had bungled McCain's fundraising efforts during the early months of the campaign. Perhaps even more significantly, they felt that his lobbyist ties could present a big public relations problem to McCain in the long run, that they were, at best, a liability, and at worst, a potential torpedo heading straight for the campaign in the weeks and months ahead. Davis, a University of Alabama dropout who, like McCain, had been raised in a Navy family, was a founding principal in the lobbying firm Davis Manafort. In the early years of the decade, according to *The New York Times,* Davis and his associates were paid nearly $2 million by the troubled Federal Home Loan Mortgage Corporation and the Federal National Mortgage Association (known commonly as Freddie Mac and Fannie Mae) for "consulting services," largely because of his rela-

tionship with McCain. In 2006, Davis had also set up a meeting between Mc-
Cain and shady Russian aluminum magnate Oleg Deripaska at an international
economic conference in Switzerland. Deripaska's suspected links to organized
crime figures in Russia were so alarming that the U.S. government revoked his
visa that same year. According to *The Washington Post,* Deripaska later thanked
Davis and his firm for arranging the meeting with McCain "so spectacularly"
and "in such an intimate setting."

The disgruntled McCain triumvirate wanted Nelson placed in charge
of the campaign's operations and a clear hierarchy of leadership established. And
they wanted Davis out of his leadership role. Their pleas created an administrative headache for McCain, who, in spite of his reputation as a war hero
and take-charge kind of guy, was an abysmal organizational leader who seemed
to prefer chaos over an orderly structure of decision making. He denied the
request, and according to *The Washington Post* admonished them to "work it
out," creating, in essence, a four-headed Hydra, battling it out with one another and creating a tension-filled office atmosphere, once again with no clear
line of authority. McCain campaigns were typically dysfunctional, but this
one had gotten seriously out of hand. During the ensuing six long months,
animosities between Davis and the others stewed and eventually boiled over
for a second time. The gap between fundraising projections and what in actu-
ality had been contributed to the campaign was startling. A $45-million pro-
jected war chest going into the third quarter of 2007 was, at best, $2 million,
and expenses were mounting. In spite of his reputation as a fiscal watchdog in
the Senate, the McCain family finances were unwieldy, and the candidate had
developed a preference for being flown around the country by private charter
jets, costing the campaign upward of a quarter-million dollars a month.

Conversely, McCain thoroughly detested fundraising. Many in the campaign viewed him as too proud to stick out a hand. In his early congressional
races and subsequent runs for the U.S. Senate, McCain had relied on his wealthy
wife's moneyed connections in Arizona to support his candidacy. He had, for
the most part, been above the dirty work of raising money. His inclination to
challenge his own party's leadership throughout his Senate career also affected
his fundraising abilities on the national level. His most recent stand on immigration reform, in which he supported a path to citizenship for the approximately 12 million to 20 million illegal immigrants in the United States,
essentially stopped the flow of contributions from the party base. Rock-solid
Republicans—the kind that gave regularly to the party and bundled money on
behalf of candidates—viewed McCain with a jaundiced eye. Coupled with
Davis's inability to raise money himself ("incapacity was more like it," said

one disgruntled staffer), donations to the campaign had come to a near stand-still.

By July, with the campaign nearly broke and apparently little method to the organizational madness, McCain had decided that it was time for a change. McCain had a well-known temper, and he was severely incensed. There were angry phone calls and shouting matches, leading both Nelson and Weaver to tender their resignations on July 10. At least a half-dozen additional staffers resigned in the days ahead.

Nelson, at thirty-eight, the youngest of the trio, had never bonded with McCain, had never established an easy comfort zone with the candidate or his wife, and, by most accounts, was the primary focus of McCain's dissatisfaction. While some have asserted that Nelson was forced out, he claims that he resigned on his own accord. Either way, he was gone.

The ever loyal Weaver, who had originally recruited Nelson to the campaign, left with him. Disgusted by the dysfunctional dynamics of the past several months, and sensing no relief in the immediate future, Weaver also submitted his resignation. It was to be a portentous moment in the political life of John McCain. "Today, John Weaver and Terry Nelson offered their resignations from my presidential campaign, which I accepted with regret and deep gratitude for their dedication, hard work and friendship," McCain declared in a less than transparent statement to the press. "John Weaver has been my friend and trusted counselor for many years and to whom I am greatly indebted."

Tall and angular, with a poetic conception of Republican politics that stretches back to Lincoln, Weaver was raised in the small, working-class community of Kermit, in the desolate reaches of West Texas, just across the border from New Mexico and far from the power hubs of Dallas and Austin. His parents were conservative Democrats and he broke into statewide politics at the age of twenty working for then-Democratic congressman (and soon to be senator) Phil Gramm. It was Weaver who had first envisioned a McCain presidency a decade ago in a Birmingham, Alabama, bar, where he sketched out his political dreams for McCain on a cocktail napkin. Many in the McCain circle thought his idea was "crazy," as he recalls, but he was able to convince the senator's staff and, eventually, the candidate himself, of the plausibility of his vision. It was Weaver who served as chief strategist and political coordinator of McCain's insurgent run against George W. Bush in the 2000 Republican primary; and it was Weaver who fashioned the idea of the Straight Talk Express, the campaign bus on which McCain and his political entourage traveled

with members of the media, who in turn enjoyed nearly full access to the candidate along the long road to New Hampshire.

Perhaps most significant, it was Weaver who most fully grasped the power and uniqueness of McCain's narrative and how it could be translated into a national political commodity. In the ensuing decade, he became McCain's closest strategist and a powerful political soul mate. They both shared a dark sense of humor and a skeptical, if not cynical, perspective of the American political process. Along with Salter, he saw McCain as a war hero and maverick, willing to cross party lines, a moderate on social issues, a fiscal hawk in respect to the federal budget and government spending. McCain's biography—his *story*—underscored a profound commitment to national security and, most important, an open and transparent candidate, comfortable and engaging with the national media. That was the McCain brand as fashioned by Weaver. It had produced overwhelming success in New Hampshire in 2000, where the underdog McCain shocked Bush, the establishment candidate, with a decisive nineteen-point victory. The Straight Talk Express was on a roll.

Then came South Carolina. Weaver and the rest of the team were outraged by the sleazy campaign tactics that Bush unleashed on McCain, including push-poll telephone calls suggesting that McCain had fathered a child with a black prostitute. If McCain would never forget the tactics (his, and his wife's, relationships with Bush were forever strained), Weaver would never forgive them. Shortly thereafter, Weaver bolted briefly from the Republican Party, worked for a handful of congressional Democrats, and, according to rumors, tried to get McCain to consider doing the same. A few years later, Weaver, then forty-four, was diagnosed with leukemia, and went through a tough, nearly fatal three-year battle with the disease. By 2006, he had survived two debilitating rounds of chemotherapy (giving him another bond with McCain as a cancer survivor), but he was through the worst and ready to accompany McCain on another run for the presidency.

In the 2008 primary, McCain would no longer be an underdog (at least not at the outset), but Weaver envisioned another ride on the Straight Talk Express, starting in 2007, this time leading all the way to the White House. He was convinced that McCain could at once shed the Republican shackles of the Bush era and capture the middle ground of the American electorate—"common sense conservatism" was the new mantra—only this time Weaver would not be there at the end. Weaver himself suspected that Davis had undermined him through back-channel gossip and leaks to Cindy McCain. (She and Weaver had allegedly engaged in an intense telephone argument shortly before the apocalypse.)

Whatever the source of the discontent, Weaver's departure was painful and acrimonious. He delivered a terse resignation statement and a week later told *New York* magazine that the problems surrounding McCain's campaign were "nobody's fault but mine." The problem with the campaign, Weaver would later assert, was that "we believed our own bullshit." The "bullshit" was the amount of money that Davis said he could raise. He had come nowhere close.

Several other lower level staffers loyal to either Nelson or Weaver (or both) also stepped down, including Reed Galen, McCain's deputy campaign manager, and Rob Jesmer, the campaign's political director. There were rumors that speechwriter Salter was also going to leave the campaign, but McCain managed to convince him to stay on, albeit in an unpaid position as a special adviser. Several political prognosticators announced the McCain campaign dead in the water. "Stick a Fork in It," read one characteristic headline. "The Straight Talk Express Breaks Down," chimed another. McCain's good pal, Senator Lindsey Graham, was equally emphatic. "The guy's dead, nails in his coffin," he intoned. "Fifth in a four-person race." But McCain refused to cave in. In the ensuing leadership vacuum, the seventy-one-year-old candidate, who has always seemed to be invigorated by crisis, himself played a larger role at the helm.

Weaver was forced to watch the proceedings from afar. While he maintained friendships with several of the remaining staff (and even helped secure the critical endorsement for McCain of Governor Charlie Crist in Florida), from the distance of an outsider, he was impressed with the way that McCain grabbed hold of his flailing campaign. "It was mostly through John's sheer willpower that he pulled it back together," Weaver observed. "That and the fact that [Rudy] Giuliani floundered and [Mitt] Romney wasn't able to pick up any steam. They left John with an opening and, to his credit, he made the most of it." A young campaign staffer, Steve Schmidt, a veteran of Bush's 2004 reelection campaign whom Weaver had brought into the fold, had come up with the idea that the new narrative of the McCain campaign was that of a "comeback"—once again putting the candidate in the more comfortable role of underdog. It was the perfect outside position for McCain. He had found a new groove and was bonding with the disciplined and focused Schmidt.

A T THAT POINT IN THE RACE, just about anyone with any political seasoning was betting on Hillary Clinton to run away with the Democratic Party nomination. The oddsmakers in Las Vegas had Clinton at nearly even money, with the upstart junior senator from Illinois, Barack Obama, as a

seven-to-two long shot. Clinton was, at one point, 33 percentage points ahead of Obama and former North Carolina senator John Edwards in the national polls, a seemingly insurmountable lead.

With the Straight Talk Express back on track, it looked like it would be a McCain-Clinton final in the fall. That's where the smart money was anyway, and the McCain camp liked the matchup. They knew that while Clinton had a large and fervent support base, she also had very high negatives and carried not only her own baggage, but also the considerable freight of her husband, Bill Clinton, the forty-first president of the United States. It didn't take a wide stretch of the imagination in the latter part of 2007 or early 2008 to envision a scenario in which McCain would claim victory in November. While it may not have been inevitable, it certainly was plausible.

The McCain camp wrapped up the Republican nomination with relative ease, although there were a few surprises along the way. Giuliani's campaign imploded early—betting on the ridiculous notion that he could jump-start his campaign in Florida after terrible showings in Iowa and New Hampshire. Romney, stiff and a bit too tailored, never gained traction in the GOP heartland. Mike Huckabee, the congenial evangelical minister and former governor of Arkansas, surprised everyone by winning seven states and, in the end, was the last primary opponent left standing. Finally, on March 4, with the odds in Texas stacked up against him, Huckabee announced that he was giving up his campaign and throwing his support to McCain. With the Democrats still in hot battle, McCain now had plenty of time to regroup his forces, conserve his resources, vet and select his running mate, and refocus his attention on key battleground states. It appeared to give the GOP operatives a tactical advantage in the upcoming general election.

I N THE MONTHS AFTER THE DEPARTURE OF NELSON AND WEAVER, Davis did his best to steer the ship back toward land, but by most accounts the vacuum of leadership was filled by McCain himself and by the savvy and confident Schmidt. While a physically commanding figure, with a shaved head and bulky six-foot frame, Schmidt was not prone to tantrums as were many of the other top McCain staffers, and he exerted a calming influence on an organization that had been stretched to the hilt with dissension and petty animosities. He demanded discipline and loyalty throughout the ranks, not by barking out orders, but by modeling the behavior. Many view him as a protégé of Bush henchman, Karl Rove, though that is both a decidedly unfair and misleading analogy; Schmidt is an ideological moderate who believes in the big-tent paradigm for the Republican Party. In 2006, he fashioned an improbable reelection bid by California governor Arnold Schwarzenegger (whose approval rating had crashed to the low 30s) by steering the Governator's campaign back to the middle of the road. Schmidt had directed Schwarzenegger to lose his gas-guzzling Hummer and to quit acting like a bully in his battles with legislators. Schwarzenegger won his reelection by a seventeen-point landslide.

A former high school tight end from northern New Jersey and a political science major at the University of Delaware (he didn't graduate), Schmidt got along well enough with Davis, and also with Salter, and by late spring of 2008 he had established himself as leader of the McCain pack, if not in title, then by proxy. Although never as close to the McCains as Davis, he had earned the candidate's respect simply by steadying the ship and by shifting the arc of McCain's narrative to that of a comeback, which played perfectly into McCain's self-perception as a dark horse. While Rove had nicknamed Schmidt "The Bullet," McCain gave him the moniker "Sergeant," because of his no-nonsense leadership abilities and take-charge persona. But Schmidt's real strong suit was keeping everyone on message. He allowed no deviance from the narrative.

In the final weeks of June, however, less than a year after his campaign's first implosion, it must have seemed like déjà vu for McCain, as several key staffers—and key Republican operatives outside the campaign, including several governors—solicited him, yet again, to remove Davis from his leadership position. As The New York Times reported, McCain's "campaign is once again a swirl of competing spheres of influence, clusters of friends, consultants and media advisers who represent a matrix of clashing ambitions and festering feuds." There were rumors that Davis was trying to decentralize the national operation by having the campaign run by the organization's eleven regional managers. The proposal had sent many GOP advisers, both inside and outside the campaign, apoplectic.

McCain saw the writing on the wall. A shake-up had proved effective a year ago, so why not another one? On July 2—nearly a year to the day since Weaver-Nelson left—Schmidt was placed in command of day-to-day operations in Arlington, while Davis had been demoted once more, by assignment, if not by title (he kept the moniker of "campaign manager"), in the McCain operation. According to several sources, Davis's role was sharply scaled back to fundraising, assisting with preparations for the upcoming GOP convention, and overseeing the always tricky vice presidential selection process. Davis was none too happy about his second demotion in little more than two years, but he respected Schmidt's leadership abilities and was loyal to the McCains, so he accepted the decision. If nothing else, his new assignment allowed him to focus on specific tasks critical to the campaign.

In February, Davis had accompanied McCain to the winter meeting of the National Governors Association at the JW Marriott Hotel in Washington, where, according to the campaign legend, the soon-to-be Republican nominee first met Alaska governor Sarah Palin. Palin's official state of Alaska calendar for Saturday, February 23, 2008, indicates that she attended a morning coffee sponsored by McCain and both a reception and dinner later that evening featuring McCain, held exclusively for twenty-two Republican governors and their spouses, at the plush Crystal Room of the Willard InterContinental Hotel, located only a few blocks from the White House. During the reception, McCain, his wife Cindy, Davis, and both Sarah and Todd Palin enjoyed a friendly conversation about their respective families and energy policies, which by various accounts lasted no more than fifteen to twenty minutes (McCain would later claim he "came away extraordinarily impressed"). Davis established further contact with Palin—who, ironically, had yet to endorse McCain—and secured a way to keep in touch with her in Alaska. Their communications became more and more frequent as momentum built toward the Republican convention, slated for the first week of September, in St. Paul.

What is often lost in this storied retelling of this propitious first meeting between McCain and Palin are the various contexts in which it took place. Only two days earlier, McCain had been hit with a bombshell from *The New York Times,* charging him with carrying on an inappropriate relationship with Washington lobbyist Vicki Iseman. The article implied that the relationship had been "romantic." The evidence for such an affair was thin and the timing highly inflammatory. (The *Times*'s ombudsman, Clark Hoyt, later criticized the story. He called the implication of a romantic relationship "the scarlet elephant in the room" and that if the newspaper were going to make such an assertion, it owed "more proof than the *Times* was able to provide.") Ironically, the slim sourcing and the unfounded implications of an affair backfired on the *Times* and turned McCain, at least momentarily, into a victim. Perhaps even more importantly, it upped his street cred with the conservative right, who viewed the *Times* as the enemy.*

---

* Iseman initially sued the *Times* for $27 million in damages, charging defamation and damage to her career, and declaring that any claims of "inappropriate contact

In the immediate days after the *Times* story and the impending fallout, McCain was understandably furious. But he also saw the opportunity to turn the story to his advantage. When he addressed his audience that evening at the Willard, he received an enthusiastic standing ovation from a group of Republican elected officials wanting to express its empathy to what was perceived to be yet another unfounded assault on a conservative elected official by the Gray Lady. McCain returned the favor by playing to his crowd. He delivered a strong states' rights address to the assembled governors, repeating over and over his mantra, "Governments matter," and declaring, "I'm a federalist. Only the things that the states can't do should the federal government do. I want to work with you so we can keep more of the money in your state, and that means further tax cuts if necessary." McCain, never a favorite among the Republican mainstream, especially its governors, had won over his crowd.

Most important, those gathered at the GOP governors dinner knew that someone in the ballroom that night could very well be picked as McCain's running mate. It gave the dinner an added jolt of adrenaline. An Associated Press account of the evening duly focused on the positive response to McCain's speech, but it concluded with an interesting caveat: "The audience included a few governors whose names have been floated as possible vice-presidential running mates for McCain, including Charlie Crist of Florida, Mark Sanford of South Carolina, Sarah Palin of Alaska, Jon Huntsman, Jr., of Utah, Haley Barbour of Mississippi and Tim Pawlenty of Minnesota." Although Palin's spokesperson Meg Stapleton would later publicly chastise Palin biographer and *People* magazine editor Lorenzo Benet for his assertion that Palin "learned she was on the short list as a running mate" during her meeting with McCain and Davis in February, Palin clearly knew that she was in the hunt at that time. Moreover, one of the front-runners for the VP slot, Tim Pawlenty, had hurt his chances at the conference by pushing a bipartisan proposal to curb greenhouse emissions, much to the annoyance of coal and oil producing states, like Alaska.

---

with the senator, romantic or otherwise," are false. The lawsuit asserted that other media outlets were investigating McCain's ties with Iseman and that the *Times* was so concerned about being scooped that it printed a story "to pack the maximum sensational impact with the minimum factual support." The lawsuit contended Iseman suffered an "avalanche of scorn, derision, and ridicule" that damaged her health. In 2009, Iseman and the *Times* settled the suit without payment. The *Times* did not retract the article.

The proposal was buried in committee, leading conservative columnist Robert Novak to pen a critical column about Pawlenty entitled "How Not to Run for Vice President." It did little to help the Minnesota governor's standing in the vice presidential sweepstakes. Meanwhile, Palin had come away from the conference making a favorable impression on McCain and clawing her way up in the pack, especially with Davis. The long, cumbersome process of selecting a running mate was clearly underway.

A T A BIG WASHINGTON, D.C., FUNDRAISER IN October of the previous year, Davis had first approached prominent Beltway attorney Arthur "A.B." Culvahouse, then fifty-nine, about getting involved in the "legal policy side" of the campaign and helping to raise money for McCain. Culvahouse demurred. He was a big-time GOP contributor and, in fact, was a co-host of the event. He had given $3,000 to George W. Bush's election efforts over the years and would eventually contribute $7,300 to McCain's. In remarks that he was later to give to the Republican National Lawyers Association, Culvahouse said that he agreed to "help" with the vice presidential vetting process if and when McCain claimed the nomination. He noted that he "didn't hear anything for months" until someone asked McCain at a press conference in Miami who would be handling the vice presidential vetting, to which the candidate answered "A. B. Culvahouse." The Associated Press had picked up on McCain's response, which is how Culvahouse learned he had the job.

Culvahouse is an insider's insider in Washington. He is about as Republican elite as one can get. His style and his demeanor scream out conservative establishment. A Tennessee native, Culvahouse received his law degree from New York University in June 1973, and immediately, at the age of twenty-four, was named chief legislative assistant and counsel to Tennessee senator Howard Baker, Jr., who was then serving as ranking minority member of the Senate committee investigating the Watergate scandal. For Culvahouse, it was a choice position at a choice time and secured his entrée into the Republican establishment. Afterward, he joined a top Beltway law firm, O'Melveny & Myers LLP, later becoming a partner and, eventually, chair of the company. He served as White House counsel to President Reagan, who awarded Culvahouse the Presidential Citizens Medal. During the presidency of George H. W. Bush, he served on the Federal Advisory Committee on Nuclear Failsafe and Risk Reduction, and under Bush II he served on the President's Foreign Intelligence Advisory Board.

Most significant, however, Culvahouse's experience with vice presidential vetting dated back to 1976, when he had handled the vetting paperwork for Baker, widely expected to be Gerald Ford's running mate (he was passed over at the last minute for Bob Dole). Culvahouse knew the ropes of vetting. While he had backed Bush over McCain in the 2000 GOP primary battle, he was firmly in McCain's camp this time around. He told Davis that if McCain won the nomination, he'd "help" with the vetting process.

"The Republicans do it differently than Democrats," Culvahouse explained at a meeting of the Republican National Lawyers Association in April of 2009, at which he addressed the selection of Palin as McCain's running mate. "We always have. There are no rules. The Democrats usually pick a committee that goes around and says, 'Who ought to be on the list?' Republicans always have the largest role—my role, the vetter's role—is to vet. And we are given a list." In the end, Culvahouse explained, he accepted McCain's offer to head up the vetting process on a trio of conditions:

> [McCain was to be] the decider. [Second], there was no one between him and me, there was no committee of folks who are going to say, "This person's on the list and this person's off the list," because if he was the decider, I needed to know that these were his people that we were vetting, and that third, and very importantly, because there were at least two occasions, one in our party and one in the other party, where someone had been selected to be the vice presidential nominee, who had not gone through the formal vetting process, he could not pick anyone that I hadn't vetted. He agreed to that.

McCain and Davis originally came up with a list of roughly two dozen potential running mates (one adviser put the number at precisely twenty-six). None was told that they were on the list. Sources in the McCain camp contend that there were at least five women on the list, including Palin; Meg Whitman, the former chief executive of eBay, (later to run unsuccessfully for governor of California); Secretary of State Condoleezza Rice; Carly Fiorina, the former chief executive of Hewlett-Packard, who was to run unsuccessfully for the U.S. Senate from California; and McCain's Senate colleague, Kay Bailey Hutchison of Texas. Culvahouse says that a coterie of more than two dozen attorneys in his office worked on the process of producing forty- to fifty-page dossiers on each potential nominee, drawn largely from the Internet and public documents, including news reports, speeches, financial and tax return disclosures, court cases, investigations, ethics charges, marriage and divorce records. Those dossiers were then reviewed by McCain, Davis, Schmidt, Salter, and, finally, Charlie Black, a Republican operative and über-lobbyist (he once sponsored the "coronation" of Unification Church leader Sun Myung Moon in the U.S. Senate Dirksen Building) then serving as a senior adviser to McCain.

Once the number was winnowed down to a handful, each potential running mate was then to be asked a series of seventy-four questions in writing. Culvahouse elaborated: "Very specific questions. There was no debate about what the meaning of 'is' is. I've drafted that question. It was 'Have you ever been unfaithful?' 'Has anyone ever asserted you've been unfaithful?' 'Is there anyone who could truthfully assert that you have been unfaithful?' Then you define unfaithful."

On Memorial Day weekend, McCain hosted a three-day gathering of hiking, fishing, barbecuing, and simple relaxing at his secluded retreat, outside of Sedona, for nearly two dozen guests that included Louisiana governor Bobby Jindal, Florida governor Charlie Crist, his former opponent Mitt Romney, Kansas senator Sam Brownback, and his two sidekicks from the Senate, Lindsey Graham of South Carolina, and Joe Lieberman of Connecticut (who many suspected was McCain's choice). Whitman was also invited to the event, leading to public speculation that she might also be in consideration for "number two." Tim Pawlenty, still widely considered the front-runner for the job, was noticeably not on the list (though he and his wife, Mary, had attended a similar McCain Klatch earlier that year). Mike Huckabee had also been invited, but declined the invitation. The press was not allowed.

With major national media speculating that the get-together was something of an audition for the second spot on the ticket, McCain intentionally played down its significance. "It's just having a group of friends for Memorial Day weekend to visit us and enjoy one of the most beautiful places in America," McCain declared. "It's no more and it's no less. I want to assure you." McCain clearly enjoyed his seclusion in northern Arizona. In March, he had told reporters that nothing made him happier than barbecuing at the retreat. "I have so much nervous energy," he enthused, "it keeps me moving." Lindsey Graham helped keep the reporting of the three-day gathering light by noting that McCain "barbecued ribs all night."

Lost in the flurry of speculation surrounding the Memorial Day affair was some Internet scuttlebutt that Culvahouse had been spotted, not in Arizona (he had not been invited to the event), but far away in Juneau, which fueled rumors on the Internet (and on the ground in Alaska) that Palin was on McCain's short list. (Several McCain advisers denied that Culvahouse had been in Juneau for the purpose of vetting Palin.)

The jockeying for number two was shifting into high gear for the summer. Palin's name was beginning to pop up everywhere on the Internet and, more significantly, in the mainstream press. Bizarrely, in her memoir, *Going Rogue*, Palin said that reporters had merely "dropped off-camera hints to that effect," when, in fact, she had been interviewed several times very much *on camera* about her VP possibilities. As early as February, CNN's Joe Johns had noted in an interview with Palin "that people do mention your name as a possible vice presidential running mate." He asked her directly what she thought of the possibility. "I do think there needs to be a *governor* on the ticket," she responded. "At some point in my life, I would like to have an opportunity, if it's handed to me, to serve on a national level"—though she added the caveat, "but I don't think it's going to happen this go-around." In late June, she was described as being on the "short list" in an appearance on the Fox Business Channel, during which time she promoted drilling in the Arctic National Wildlife Refuge (ANWR).

Quietly, albeit steadily, there was a ramping up of her candidacy by the Republican right. That same weekend, in an interview with Larry Kudlow of CNBC, in which she dissed McCain's position against drilling for oil in ANWR ("he's wrong on that issue"), Palin was asked by Kudlow directly if she would accept McCain's invitation to join him on the GOP ticket.

PALIN: Well I'd like the opportunity to get to change his mind about ANWR, I'll tell you that. But Larry, I'm gonna give you the same answer that any other potential VP gives you and that is you know, I really enjoy my job here in Alaska as governor. I believe that there's a lot that Alaska could be and should be doing to contribute to the rest of the U.S. And I think I can do that in my job here in Alaska. And I know that, again, the other potential VPs are saying the same thing that they like where they are today. So I also have to say though that it's really probably out of the realm of possibility to be tapped for that position, so I don't even have to worry about it.

KUDLOW: Well okay. You've got a lot of work to do drilling up there to help the rest of America. But let me ask one final question. In your judgment, is it time for the Republican Party to put a woman on the ticket?

PALIN: Oh, we're overdue for that. Absolutely. I would love to see that happen.

By that point in the game, Palin was the only GOP woman seriously under consideration. Palin's star was rising, at least in the right-wing hemisphere, so much so that her number one promoter, Adam Brickley at the "Draft Sarah Palin for Vice President" blog spot, was nearly giddy: "Maybe it's just me, but watching all of the media attention Gov. Palin is suddenly getting, it's starting to look like there might be something going on behind the scenes."

According to McCain campaign advisers, Davis had leaked Palin's name to select news makers, floating the Palin balloon as a test. On June 29, Palin's biggest mainstream media promoter and former lunch mate, Bill Kristol, in what was clearly a planned promo for Palin, made this fascinating segue from Hillary Clinton to Palin in an exchange on *Fox News Sunday* with host Chris Wallace and contributor Juan Williams:

WALLACE: Bill, how important are the Clintons? And will Bill Clinton stop sulking in his tent like Achilles and behave?

KRISTOL: Psychoanalyzing Bill Clinton is a tough task. I think Hillary Clinton was gracious. She's put behind the horrible sexism and misogyny that Democratic primary voters demonstrated, which I'm appalled by, personally. Never would have happened in the Republican Party, you know.

Republicans are much more open to strong women. And that's why McCain's going to put Sarah Palin, the governor of Alaska, on the ticket as vice president.

WALLACE: Is that your prediction?

KRISTOL: I'm moving from [Bobby] Jindal to Palin. She's fantastic. You know, she was the point guard on the Alaska state championship high school basketball team in 1982. She could take Obama one-on-one on the court. It would be fantastic.

Anyway, I do think—I actually think Sarah Palin would be a great vice presidential pick, and it would be interesting to actually have a woman on the Republican ticket after Hillary Clinton has come so close and failed on the Democratic side.

WILLIAMS: Well, how about Colin Powell on the McCain ticket? Don't you think that would be a winner?

KRISTOL: No, no, no.

WILLIAMS: No?

KRISTOL: That's, again, misogynist thinking, you know?

WILLIAMS: Misogynist thinking?

KRISTOL: You have to go for the gold here with Sarah Palin. She's great. She's a reform governor.

WILLIAMS: Mother of five, I believe.

KRISTOL: Mother of five. Ethics, incredible record of cleaning up—she took on her own corrupt Republican Party in the state, cut spending.

WALLACE: Of course, they'd have a problem on ANWR, since she's for drilling in ANWR and he's against it.

KRISTOL: And she could persuade McCain to take the last step to the sensible position on energy and gas, which is to be for drilling . . .

WALLACE: Can we please get off Sarah Palin?

KRISTOL: . . . for drilling in ANWR.

Note the certainty with which Kristol made his prediction. There's no qualification: McCain is *"going to put Sarah Palin . . . on the ticket."* He's stating it as a matter of fact. As an informal foreign policy adviser to McCain (and a close friend of McCain's neocon foreign policy coordinator, Randy Scheunemann), Kristol clearly had the inside scoop on the vice presidential sweepstakes still primarily in the hands of Davis. Note also his emphatic rejection of Colin Powell. The Republicans' right-wing base was forcing McCain to move to the right in the general election. To even suggest Powell was, in Kristol's words, "misogynist"—read *centrist*. The neocons were forcing McCain to take a decidedly starboard tack.

B EHIND THE SCENES IN THE EVANGELICAL NETHERWORLD, the campaign pushing for Palin was heating up anew. A month later, on Sunday, July 31, 2008, Palin would once more be on Kudlow's show. And while the vice presidential possibility was again a topic, there was now a second line of questioning. After more than a year and a half of her administration's badgering Walt Monegan over her ex-brother-in-law Mike Wooten, Palin decided that now was the time to go after Monegan and get rid of him once and for all. Monegan's attorney, Jeffrey Feldman, says he has no idea to this day why Palin chose that moment to get rid of her popular commissioner of public safety. Monegan speculated that it may have been the fact that he sent Palin an e-mail indicating that a legislator had reported Palin driving with her infant, Trig, without an approved car seat. Palin had fired back an e-mail to Monegan from her private Yahoo account: "I've never driven Trig anywhere without a new, approved car seat. I want to know who said otherwise—pls provide me that info now." Palin could never let even the smallest matter slide.

Whatever her reasoning, it was while she was right in the middle of the vetting process for the vice presidency of the United States—while she was being viewed under one of the biggest microscopes imaginable—that she created a crisis that brought both heat and intense scrutiny on her administration. "She is simply self-destructive," says conservative Alaskan journalist Paul Jenkins. "That is her pattern." His view was echoed by others in the Last Frontier. "I really don't think she can help herself," said a political ally who distanced herself from Palin last year when she resigned from office. "There's something in her psychological makeup that doesn't allow her to let things run smoothly. It's not that she thrives on crisis and conflict—though she does do that, too, to an extent—but this goes deeper than that. Her personality is unstable and she needs the world around her to be unstable. And I don't think she can control it. I don't. It's who she is."

Kudlow could not avoid the issue in his interview:

KUDLOW: Governor Palin, people want to know why you did fire your police commissioner or Public Safety Commissioner Monegan. Is it because he stopped you from getting rid of your brother-in-law or what? People want to know if this is an ethical lapse on your part.

PALIN: I'm glad that you're asking because I never tried to fire a former brother-in-law who's been divorced from my sister for quite some time. No, it was the commissioner, that we were seeking more results, more action to fill vacant trooper positions to deal with bootlegging and alcohol abuse problems in our rural villages especially. Just needed some new direction, a lot of new energy in that position. That is why the replacement took place there of the commissioner of public safety. It had nothing to do with an estranged former brother-in-law, a divorce that had happened some years ago.

It was clearly a distortion of grand proportions—the governor and her family had been obsessed with Wooten and would continue to be long after the election (legal matters between Wooten and her sister Molly were still pending as she spoke)—but that would be the line that Palin would continue to push about Troopergate in the weeks and months to come. She also tried to diminish the scope of the opposition by describing her detractors as "a couple of lawmakers who are pretty angry with me"—again a blatant act of duplicity in that it was a unanimous bipartisan vote of Alaska's Legislative Council (ten Republicans and four Democrats) that had voted in favor of the Troopergate investigation. "A couple of lawmakers who weren't happy with that decision certainly are looking at me as kind of a target right now and wanting to probe and find out why I did replace this cabinet member," Palin added. "And it's cool. I want them to ask me the questions. I don't have anything to hide and didn't do anything wrong there."

Then Kudlow's line of questioning switched back to the potential VP nomination. Contrary to the myth that the Palin selection came completely out of the blue, Kudlow noted that "on the world's largest pay-to-play prediction market, a betting parlor called Intrade, you are in third place with a 20 percent support probability behind former Governor Romney and present governor of Minnesota, Pawlenty."

PALIN: As for that VP talk all the time, I'll tell ya, I still can't answer that question until somebody answers for me, *what is it exactly that the VP does every day?* I'm used to being very productive and working real hard and in administration. We want to make sure that that VP slot would be a fruitful type of position, especially for Alaskans and for the things that we're trying to accomplish up here for the rest of the U.S. *before I can even start addressing that question.*

"*What is it exactly that the VP does every day?*" Palin asked this with less than a month to go before the GOP convention—after she had been quietly promoting herself behind the scenes for more than a year during regular contact with Davis. With all the expressed doubts about the vice president's duties, about whether she was even interested in the job, much less a pending legislative investigation on the immediate horizon, the fates, nonetheless, continued to play in her favor.

Who knows if any of her suitors in the McCain camp even saw the Kudlow interview? They had much bigger fish to fry that weekend. Barack Obama's celebrated trip to Europe that July—during which time he drew a crowd of more than 200,000 to a speech in Berlin—had seriously affected the McCain campaign. They were galled by the arrogance of Obama appearing presidential on foreign soil and by the gobs of fawning media attention he received, not only at home, but from the international media as well.

At some point in July, in an attempt to steal some of Obama's thunder, a "very senior McCain aide" leaked a story to Robert Novak that the announcement of McCain's running mate was imminent. CNN's Dana Bash and Gloria Borger also reported a similar story. It was widely speculated at that point that the pick would be Bobby Jindal, the thirty-seven-year-old governor of Louisiana, viewed by many as the GOP's answer to Obama. But in an interview on Fox News, Novak confessed that the story may have been "a dodge," as he called it, a false story planted by the McCain campaign to bring some of the focus back to the GOP candidate. If so, Novak contended, it's "pretty reprehensible." Another McCain operative called it a "head fake." Novak was none too happy about being played. Meanwhile, Jindal took himself out of the running, saying "we've got a lot more work to do right here in Louisiana."

More than anything else, the Jindal incident underscored the McCain campaign's obsession with Obama and their growing resentment that he was the darling of the media and seemingly given a free pass by the national press. In 2000, McCain himself had been the media's darling (he had dubbed the press that traveled with him "my base") and he stewed over what he saw as fawning coverage of his opponent. That McCain simply did not like Obama—at a visceral level, he did not respect him—also fueled his growing bitterness. In his second year in the Senate, Obama had pulled what McCain viewed as a double cross over lobbying reform legislation. It resulted in a scathing letter back to Obama (reportedly written by Salter and signed by McCain) that declared:

> I would like to apologize to you for assuming that your private assurances to me regarding your desire to cooperate in our efforts to negotiate bipartisan lobbying reform legislation were sincere. When you approached me and insisted that despite your leadership's preference to use the issue to gain a political advantage in the 2006 elections, you were personally committed to achieving a result that would reflect credit on the entire Senate and offer the country a better example of political leadership, I concluded your professed concern for the institution and the public interest was genuine and admirable. . . . I hold no hard feelings over your earlier disingenuousness.

That there was no love lost between the two candidates helped to shape the mood and dynamics of the campaign through the hot months of summer. Rather than focus on McCain's strengths, the campaign was more concerned about stopping what they perceived to be the Obama juggernaut. The McCain campaign was back-pedaling on its heels, recklessly straying from the narrative first crafted by Weaver and Salter. As one McCain aide told Robert Draper in a fascinating account of the McCain inner circle for *The New York Times Magazine*, "For better or worse, our campaign has been fought from *tactic to tactic*." It was a trenchant concession. There was no longer an overarching strategy to the GOP campaign that was both shaped and defined by the McCain narrative. Instead, the McCain campaign was always responding to

Obama, never taking the lead, fighting skirmish to skirmish. This was never more manifest then it was with the so-called celebrity ad, which came out in late July and in which Obama was compared to Paris Hilton and Britney Spears. That the ad seemed to have a momentary impact—it brought down Obama's lead in the polls—may have fostered the idea that McCain could somehow beat Obama in a battle of the trenches. But it proved no way to win a war.

John Weaver, who in spite of leaving the campaign a year earlier had kept in close contact with some of its operatives, told *The Atlantic* that he viewed the celebrity ad as "childish" and that it "reduces McCain on the stage." Even McCain's media strategist, Mike Hudome, felt that the ad was off point and sacrificed "the real McCain maverick message." But only a Weaver or someone with his deep vision of McCain and the bigger picture of national politics and American history could fully understand that such short-term benefits came with a significant long-term price tag attached: namely, that such ephemeral reactionary responses diminished the McCain brand. "The ad was a ridiculous waste of money and a waste of time," Weaver declared in an interview after the election, "both of which were precious resources the McCain campaign couldn't squander." He continued:

> This was a big election, and we knew that—we'd known that
> it's going to be a big election for years. Like 1900 was a big
> election. Nineteen thirty-two was a big election, 1960 was a
> big election. Sometimes there were just big moments in history.
> This was one of them. It was going to be a transformational
> election. This was a big-time election—for us to trivialize
> that—what we ended up doing was trivializing John McCain,
> who had been a big person—a major player on the world stage
> since the day he was shot down over Hanoi. And I just thought
> that at the time it wasn't big-time politics. It was small ball.
> And it hurt McCain.

Obama, whose political instincts seemed to be particularly attuned to the dynamics of the campaign, responded to the McCain ad in much the same way as Weaver. "You know, I don't pay attention to John McCain's ads, although I do notice he doesn't seem to have anything to say very positive about himself," Obama observed with the subtlest strains of sarcasm. "He seems to only be talking about me. You need to ask John McCain what he's for and not just what he's against."

The scuffle over the celebrity ad may have seemed insignificant at the time, but it provided considerable insight into the McCain campaign as it entered into the final stages of selecting his running mate. McCain was not only rudderless without his strategist, Weaver, but he was also without a mainsail, too. He had grown more and more irritated with the many shackles that had been placed on him during the campaign, most notably Schmidt's insistence to keep him away from the press. Eight years earlier, McCain had set sail on a pirate ship with a black patch over one eye. In the summer of 2008, his handlers had placed him aboard a cruise liner, clean and homogenized, with his whites on and with far too many rules. The spontaneous and fun John McCain had receded; the frustrated, bitter, even angry John McCain had emerged. He was not a particularly happy candidate as the summer of 2008 stretched into the dog days of August.

It was about to get worse. To those close to him—and to some even outside his inner circle—McCain had made no secret of the fact that he wanted Joe Lieberman as his running mate. He saw it as a maverick's pick—an "Independent Democrat" who had run on the Democratic Party ticket as the vice presidential nominee only two national elections ago. Lieberman could help carry Florida and perhaps some of the Northeast and Midwest as well; and he could make it harder on Obama in several swing states. A McCain-Lieberman ticket would contest Obama in the bipartisan middle, right where McCain liked to position himself. He could force Obama to the left side of the highway. Perhaps he let too many people in on his preference. Lindsey Graham, who was a strong supporter of Lieberman, let the word out to enough of the party faithful that a backlash developed. "Lindsey pushed it too hard," said one McCain adviser. "It backfired outside the campaign, and it also backfired inside. He was just too much over the top."

Schmidt and Davis were well aware of McCain's preference for Lieberman (and both were supportive of that direction), but they also could see the writing on the wall. Bill McInturff, McCain's seasoned pollster, had done informal polling of GOP delegates and concluded that anywhere from 15 percent to a full third of the Republican convention might walk out in the event of a pro-choice nominee. A walkout had happened before to the Democrats in 1948—when the Strom Thurmond delegates had bolted (Harry Truman still won the nomination and the national election)—but McCain aides were terrified by the prospect of such a virulent, public display of disunity at the convention, particularly after what they expected to be a unified coronation of Obama in Denver, the Clinton wild card notwithstanding. "The possibility of a mass walkout scared the hell out of them," said one GOP strategist. "They were literally afraid of destroying the party."

There was one last-ditch effort to save the Lieberman candidacy. McCain was seventy years old when he contemplated a second run for the presidency, and according to Weaver and other senior advisers, McCain came very close to announcing a single-term pledge when he announced his candidacy for president in April of 2007. He even hinted at it obliquely during the New Hampshire primary at a town hall meeting, at which he declared, "If I said I was running for eight years, I'm not sure that would be a vote-getter." Yet, eight months later, in Las Cruces, New Mexico, when rumors of such a pledge once again rose to the surface, McCain adamantly denied it. "No," he said testily. "I'm not considering it." But behind the scenes the idea of a single-term pledge was resurrected again in respect to the Lieberman vice presidency. "We knew that we were going to have a tough time getting Lieberman by the conservative base, and we felt that such a pledge would help to prevent a total walkout by the base at the convention," said one of McCain's senior advisers. They began to float the idea with several key Republican delegates.

Lieberman—who earlier in the year said that he would never join McCain on the Republican ticket—accepted the deal. Culvahouse began an extensive vetting process and Lieberman's staff began compiling the paperwork. But opposition to Lieberman, even with the concession of a one-term pledge, continued to solidify. In an open letter to McCain dated August 20 (and that was subsequently posted on scores of evangelical Web sites), conservative Republican icon Richard A. Viguerie wrote:

> Your indication that you're willing to put a person who has a clear, unequivocal pro-abortion record within a heartbeat of the presidency is alarming.
>
> Senator McCain, you are exceedingly proud of being a political maverick—you wear it as a badge of honor. Well, poke the base of the Republican Party—the conservatives—in the eye one more time by choosing a pro-abortion vice presidential candidate, and conservatives will show you that two can play the maverick game.

The opposition to Lieberman—and any other pro-choice candidate—intensified in the days leading up to the convention. Another figure in the GOP's evangelical movement, James Dobson, the founder of both the Family Research Council and Focus on the Family who in 2004 had tried to block the appointment of then Republican Arlen Specter as chair of the Senate Judiciary Committee because of his pro-choice views, had publicly stated as early as February that he would not be voting for McCain as "a matter of conscience." He had backed Huckabee in the primary, and when McCain prevailed, he withheld his endorsement out of fear that McCain might pick a "pro-abortion" candidate. In the days leading up to the convention, he also was threatening to support a walkout if the GOP nominated anyone but a pro-life candidate.

Very gingerly, trying not to upset the nominee, Davis and Schmidt convinced McCain to put Lieberman on the shelf. The pro-choice ex-Pennsylvania governor Tom Ridge and New York City mayor Michael Bloomberg were placed there as well. Davis had floated Ridge as McCain's pick in mid-August, probably as a decoy, but there had been too much kickback from the pro-life contingent about him, too. With Jindal out of contention, that left only three viable possibilities: Romney, Pawlenty, and Palin.

Romney brought a considerable amount of traditional GOP pedigree to the table. In recent months he had worked enthusiastically for McCain and had helped to heal lingering wounds from the primary. He was an ex-governor. He would be strong along the northern rim—Michigan, Ohio, Pennsylvania—and even in his home state of Massachusetts. He also brought to the ticket considerable expertise in economics and a strong business background—a growing concern as the American economy continued to deteriorate—and, with those business credentials, he filled the single biggest hole in McCain's résumé. But they weren't exactly a good fit. The scruffy McCain contrasted decidedly with the well-groomed Romney. Perhaps most significant, particularly to Schmidt, Romney's wealth would have further underscored McCain's. "I think between them they owned something like fifteen homes," exaggerated one senior adviser. "The Democrats would have focused on that the rest of the campaign."

Pawlenty came off as more hardscrabble than Romney, down to earth. He didn't have to think about how many homes he owned. The forty-seven-year-old Pawlenty was the real deal, the son of a truck driver and a native son of St. Paul. His mother died from cancer when he was a teenager, and he worked his way through college and law school. He was of the same generation as Obama, and if not as flashy, he was a solid family guy with rock-solid conservative credentials who had won reelection in a toughly fought campaign as a fiscal and social conservative in a blue state. McCain and Pawlenty genuinely liked each other. They first met in the mid-1980s when Pawlenty, then in his twenties, had served as McCain's driver during a campaign swing through Minnesota on behalf of Republican congressional candidates. They had kept in touch ever since, to the point where Pawlenty actually accompanied McCain on the campaign trail through Iowa and New Hampshire Pawlenty had served as national co-chair of McCain's presidential exploratory committee, which, in turn, led to Pawlenty becoming co-chairman of McCain's presidential campaign. There would be no walkout with Pawlenty—he was pro-life—and he would receive a hometown hero's welcome at the convention. He, too, would be solid in the Northern states, and his youthful vigor and environmental sensitivities might help McCain pick up several swing states in the West—New Mexico and Colorado among them—all critical to a GOP victory in November.

Perhaps Pawlenty's most important credential was his innovative approach in Minnesota to expanding the party—reaching out to what he called "Sam's Club Republicans"—social conservatives of modest means (including women, moderate Democrats, African Americans, and Latinos) who didn't necessarily jibe with the GOP's traditional appeal to wealthy white voters. This view of the party created space between Pawlenty and the Bush administration, allowing him to appeal to the base and, at the same time, reach out to moderates and independents. Pawlenty brought turf and credibility, youth and new ideas to the table. He would make a safe and solid bet.

Most significantly, in light of what happened, Pawlenty had been through a thorough vetting process by Culvahouse. According to sources close to Pawlenty, he had been contacted by Rick Davis in early July about serving as McCain's running mate. He indicated that he'd be honored to be considered. Shortly thereafter, he received a letter from Culvahouse's law firm opening the process, and then received an extensive questionnaire and a request for an array documents—tax returns, real estate and invest records. According to Pawlenty's memoir, *Courage to Stand*, he and his wife stayed up late at night for weeks responding to the requests. They joked that "no way was Mitt Romney doing this by himself." By early August, Pawlenty had scheduled a face-to-face meeting with Culvahouse and an associate, in which he was grilled by the "button-downed" Culvahouse for several hours. Then there were follow-up questions and requests for more paper work. The entire process lasted nearly two months. Pawlenty had been through the mill—but he was not to be chosen.

Davis, in particular, was leaning the other way. He was convinced of Palin's political bona fides, he had bought into the Palin myth and spin, and he was certain she was a game changer. "[Palin] is a maverick," Davis would later assert at a post-election conference at Harvard's Institute of Politics. "There were few people walking around, saying 'Pawlenty is a maverick,' but she was one." He then ran through the Palin litany. "She fought corruption. She fought her own party. When you look at her narrative history—dial yourself back to pre–August 29—and you examine Palin's record, you see a lot of John McCain in her." Davis had drunk the Kool-Aid. That there was a major scandal unfolding in Alaska, that her popularity was in descent, that there were enemies of Palin in Alaska across the political spectrum apparently did not register with Davis. He ramped up his support. As an initial first step, he had McCain call Palin at the Alaska State Fair on Sunday, August 24. It was a brief call, five minutes or so—Palin had a hard time hearing McCain over the noise of the fair—and they agreed to talk again.

That same day, at what has become something of a fabled meeting in Phoenix, the McCain brain trust met at the Ritz-Carlton to discuss the vice presidential selection, without McCain present. On hand, according to a variety of sources, were Schmidt, Davis, Black, pollster McInturff, along with advisers Fred Davis and Greg Strimple.

McCain had been playing catch-up ever since Obama had secured the nomination. In July he was down anywhere from eight to a dozen percentage points, depending on the poll, but by late August, he had narrowed the gap. The claim that the McCain campaign was in desperate straits at the time they picked Palin is not necessarily an accurate one. By late August, pollster McInturff would later assert at Harvard, "we had nearly tied the ballot," and there had been a major shift in McCain's favor on voter perception of his ability to "bring change to Washington." At that point, McInturff asserted, there was no longer a need to wage the campaign on Obama's turf. There were signs of light at the end of the tunnel, so much so that McInturff believed that McCain "might be able to cobble a way to win." The message needed to be "change"—which is the term that was polled by McInturff and his staff—and somehow, that was transitioned into the term "maverick," which became the McCain mantra the rest of the campaign.

Unfortunately, there were significant problems with the "maverick" description. Not only did it fail to accurately reflect McInturff's carefully worded polling, but it had little real traction with the electorate. Joel Benenson, the Obama campaign's polling guru, asserted at the same post-election symposium at Harvard that his numbers directly contradicted the claims of Davis and the McCain camp. "When they started using the word *maverick*, we said, 'Do they know something we don't know?' We actually probed it in a couple of focus groups, and then we tested it as a quality in a poll: 'Who is a political maverick?' Actually, 19 percent said it applied to Obama and 17 percent to McCain—very low numbers for either of them—so it was a term we never really worried about." According to Benenson, "voters had no real attachment to the word." But the McCain camp locked in on it.

McInturff then took the floor at the meeting in Phoenix. He had worked for McCain since 1991, was an absolute McCain loyalist, and a seasoned campaign numbers cruncher. McInturff had started early with the McCain II campaign, left when the money ran out in September of 2007, and then returned again in April when contributions began to flow (leading one blogger on the *Wall Street Journal* Web site to dub him a "money-hungry mercenary"). He substantiated his analysis with polling numbers that picking a pro-choice candidate presented the possibility of significant turmoil at the convention. It was the final nail in the Lieberman coffin. Then he presented his polling on "change." Even though the numbers were not all that bleak, McInturff, a fan of baseball's perennial losers the Chicago Cubs who had a reputation for seeing the glass as half-empty ("Mr. Gloom" one GOP operative dubbed him), saw McCain's challenges as contradictory and substantial. Schmidt concurred. He argued that McCain's vice presidential selection needed to: (1) help him distance himself from the Bush administration; (2) energize the Republican base; (3) cut into Obama's decisive edge with women; and (4) reclaim his mantle as a "reformer." As Schmidt would later frame it, "We had to get McCain's reform mojo back."

Neither Romney nor Pawlenty, it was argued, could help in all four of those arenas. It was perceived that the young and "attractive" governor of Alaska could. Some of the McCain Boys Club—there were no women in the McCain inner sanctum—still resisted the Palin choice. Davis had convinced Schmidt, and by the end of the meeting, the other advisers were leaning toward Palin, albeit some more reluctantly than others.

The group then brought in McCain to present their findings. McCain took it all in without much response. He was playing his cards close to his vest. No one knew where he was with the decision (they weren't even sure about Lieberman, or even Ridge, at that point), but McCain seemed to have accepted the fact that he had to go in a different direction. This could not have pleased McCain—being held hostage by the evangelical base of the party—but he was also a practical man on matters of electoral politics, and at this point in the game, he was all in. His focus shifted reluctantly from Lieberman and Ridge to Palin and Pawlenty, both of whom passed the pro-life threshold.

That evening, Davis and Schmidt met with McCain privately at his hotel room in Phoenix. It was there that they urged him to seriously consider Palin. Davis made several assurances. He had been in contact with Palin regularly since early August. She was ready. She presented his only possible path to victory.

Schmidt was still concerned, however, about the vetting of Palin. He had insisted that as many as fifty lawyers be brought in to do in a matter of days what five had done over ten weeks with Lieberman and Pawlenty. And he had gotten down to a "level of granularity" demanding to know the budgetary implications of such a process. Palin had still only been cursorily vetted. Culvahouse's team had assembled a forty-page or so dossier on her, but nothing else. Palin had not yet gone through the more intensive questionnaire process, as originally required by Culvahouse of any vice presidential nominee, and had not yet had a face-to-face vetting. According to a senior adviser, Davis contacted Culvahouse that weekend to see if he could still fully vet Palin at this late date in the game, as demanded by Schmidt. It would be a scramble—and compressed—but Culvahouse assured Davis that he could.

Davis took the lead in easing McCain toward his decision. Schmidt supported him. McCain agreed. They set up a highly secret meeting between McCain and Palin, scheduled for Thursday morning at McCain's retreat, a two-hour drive north of Phoenix. If things went well, McCain would offer Palin the second slot on the ticket; if not, it would go to Pawlenty, who, of course, had already been through a vigorous vetting process conducted by Culvahouse.

O N WEDNESDAY, AUGUST 27, Sarah Palin delivered a keynote speech at the Alaska AFL-CIO convention at the Captain Cook Hotel in downtown Anchorage. More importantly, she also signed the Alaska Gasline Inducement Act (AGIA), legislation at the convention, with union leaders and a trio of Democratic legislators proudly supporting the new law as well. There was considerable tension in the room because of Troopergate, though Palin nonetheless called it "one of the most historic and exciting events to happen since statehood." It was typical Palin hyperbole, but she had much bigger fish to fry that day. She skipped out of the luncheon early, and, along with her aide, Kris Perry, was driven in the family's black Jetta by her husband, Todd, to Signature Flight Support's Executive Terminal, at the southern edge of Ted Stevens International Airport, where a Learjet 35C, with a pair of turbofan engines, was waiting to take Palin and Perry to Arizona. The top secret arrangements had been executed perfectly by McCain's twenty-eight-year-old advance man, Davis White, who joined Palin and Perry on the flight, first to

Seattle, where they refueled, and then on to Flagstaff, less than thirty miles north of the McCains' retreat. Once aboard, White handed Palin a thick packet of materials to study along the way: McCain's speeches, position papers, and campaign schedules.

The contingent from Alaska was greeted at Flagstaff's Pulliam Airport by yet another McCain operative, trusted deputy campaign manager Christian Ferry, who drove them in a white Chevrolet Suburban to the upscale home of Robert Delgado, southwest of Flagstaff, where Schmidt and Salter would be waiting for them. Delgado, the president and CEO of the lucrative statewide beer distributorship founded in the 1940s by Cindy McCain's father, James W. Hensley, has been a close associate of the McCains' for decades. It was Delgado who assumed responsibility for setting up the McCains' initial 1986 investment with Charles Keating, chairman of the failed Lincoln Savings and Loan—an investment that ensnared the then first-term senator in a scandal during the late 1980s and early 1990s. He called it "ludicrous" to think that McCain had initiated the investment. "Business just isn't his thing," he told the *Arizona Republic* at the time.

There was a long night ahead for everyone in the high Arizona desert. From the time Palin arrived at Delgado's at roughly 10 P.M., the McCain team had less than twelve hours to complete the final vetting process in advance of the senator's decision the following morning. The stakes were high. The McCain team was getting ready to push all their chips into the pot. There was no room for error.

Schmidt says that he and Salter had a "very specific assignment" at Delgado's. They were tasked with making a decision "about whether the governor of Alaska should proceed forward" to "a meeting the next day with Senator McCain." Part of their job was to explain to Palin how the campaign functioned and what would be expected of her "if this project goes forward."

Palin would later write that her first impression of Schmidt was that he was "business-to-the-bone." She also called him "imposing and gruff-voiced." So from the beginning there was a conflict in styles, and perhaps, more importantly, a conflict in disciplines. Serious and formal are closer to the mark in describing Schmidt, along with careful and precise. Details matter. So, too, do loyalty and integrity. For someone who has difficulty with the truth—who dances with deceit—Schmidt is not a good matchup.

Schmidt says that he went into a fairly detailed account with Palin of the terrain ahead. He told her that should she be chosen she would "be one of the most famous and scrutinized people on the planet." He asked her, "Have you considered the implications for yourself and your family? And is there anything that we need to know? Because if we need to know, we're going to find out anyway." While acknowledging her oath and obligations to the state of Alaska, he said she also needed to assure the campaign that she could fulfill those duties without returning to Alaska for the next two months. Schmidt said she brought up one request—her son's deployment ceremony on September 11, at which she was scheduled to speak—to which Schmidt immediately acceded. He had close family serve in Iraq and he was sensitive to the issue. He also thought the return to Alaska for a short sojourn could benefit the campaign. Other than that single concession, however, he stressed to Palin that her energies needed to be 100 percent dedicated to the campaign.

Then Schmidt clarified the unique organizational structure of the McCain campaign. He explained that all of the top campaign staff had been volunteers, that theirs was a slim-and-trim operation, and that they were being outspent by upward of $250 million, saying:

> John wants this to be a small, tight-knit team. If you think of it as a partnership, which is how John refers to it with himself as a senior partner, you will get the last chair at the partner table. You may have one or two people with you from Alaska, but you're going to have to take a great leap of faith with the people that have been around John and put your fate into their hands.

This was a particularly important concept to the McCain team. Schmidt wanted to make sure that Palin understood it fully. Schmidt talked about studying, about the need to be prepared, and warned Palin about exhaustion and the need to sleep when the opportunities presented themselves. It would be an incredibly "demanding nonstop process," Schmidt intoned; did she understand that? Palin assured him that she did.

The ever loyal Salter then took over the questioning. The Internet research on Palin had turned up several possible instances where Palin and McCain had substantial differences on policies. The two senior advisers made it clear that while the campaign "will never ask you to change your position on any issue or to say something that you do not believe in," they needed to know if there were issues on which Palin's position was "not compatible with Senator McCain's," how would she react to them? Once again they needed assurances that Palin understood that "if you were to be vice president, that you would be advocating for the policies and positions of the administration, even if you yourself disagreed with them."

What seemed to be the obvious red herring was the abortion issue. Palin believed in "no exceptions"—including in cases of rape and incest—while McCain did. But Palin assured both Schmidt and Salter that she could live with McCain's position.

Then the subject shifted to the science of evolution. There were reports on the Internet that Palin had supported the teaching of creationism in public schools. During the 2006 gubernatorial campaign in Alaska, Palin said she endorsed teaching both evolution and creationism in the classroom. "You know, don't be afraid of information," she declared at the time (apparently indifferent to recent judicial rulings). "Healthy debate is so important, and it's so valuable in our schools. I am a proponent of teaching both." Salter pressed her on the issue.

From this point on, renditions of what happened at Delgado's house vary significantly. While the various parties do agree that Palin was asked about her views on creationism, the accounts of her response differ by as much as 180 degrees. According to Schmidt:

> She said that she believed in science, that her dad was a science teacher, that she believed in evolution. She was direct and specific in asserting her belief in evolution. She did offer that she believed that the hand of God was present in all things in the creation, which is, you know, roughly what John McCain has also said, and that was that.

In *The Battle for America 2008*, by Dan Balz and Haynes Johnson, and for which Salter was clearly a source, the encounter is reported this way:

> Salter asked [Palin] about her statements in support of creationism. Did she disbelieve the theory of evolution? "No," she told them. "My father is a science teacher."

That particular rendition clearly assuaged any fears that Schmidt and Salter might have had on the issue.

But Palin's version of this incident in *Going Rogue* is entirely antithetical to the accounts of McCain's senior advisers. Her rendition of what happened is worth examining in some detail because of the serious and substantive differences between these contrasting accounts. She notes that Schmidt and Salter had a conversation about "theories of origins." She contends that Schmidt knew her position in advance of the discussion; he says that he did not. The position she alleges to have presented that night was that she believed "in the evidence for microevolution—that geologic and species change occurs incrementally over time." But she says that she categorically rejected the grander notion of Darwinian evolution, the "theory that human beings—thinking, loving beings—originated from fish that sprouted legs and crawled out of the sea. Or that human beings began as single-celled organisms that developed into monkeys who eventually swung down from the trees."

Palin agrees that there was a mention that evening of her father being a science teacher, but she says that Schmidt brought it up, rather than her. She acknowledges that she believed in "the C-word: creationism," and that no one—not even her father—had convinced her to change her mind. She said that the very idea of evolution "flew in the face of the evidence I saw all around." Palin contends that she fully explained her creationist beliefs to Salter and Schmidt and that she wasn't going to allow the campaign to alter her views or "put words in my mouth" for political considerations, though she says that she agreed to "go with them reasonably to a nuanced position, based on facts."

Had Palin answered the question as she claims she did in *Going Rogue*, "the project," as Schmidt called the final vetting process, would have ended there. She would not have been selected as McCain's running mate. Palin, knowing that if she were fully forthcoming on the issue it might cost her the spot on the national ticket, either lied to Schmidt and Salter to get through the final hoop of her vetting process, or she lied in her memoir about what she had said so as to not offend her evangelical base. Either way, these wildly contrasting accounts of this discussion provide multiple levels of insight into the tumultuous relationship between Palin and the McCain staff that was to develop in the days and weeks ahead.

The chasm between these two accounts is astonishing; but perhaps an even more significant divergence of events is Palin's contention in *Going Rogue* that she was grilled by Schmidt during that first encounter about the war in Iraq, including distinctions between the Sunni and the Shia. Palin claims she told Schmidt and Salter that "she knew the history of the conflict to the extent that most Americans did." Those in the McCain campaign, however, say she was not asked such questions at Delgado's—that there was a basic assumption by McCain's senior advisers that any governor of one of the fifty states would have a baseline knowledge of foreign affairs—and they would let others in the campaign assess her specific level of expertise in that arena later on. "I did not have any questions," Schmidt says, "any interrogatories, any prep for her on any national security issues until the day after she was announced."

Had those national security issues been broached in the discussion at Delgado's, it's very possible, if not likely, that "the project" involving Palin would have been terminated before daybreak.

T HROUGHOUT THE EVENING, Palin also engaged in a series of telephone conversations with Culvahouse—"it was less than two hours, total" recalled one adviser—during which time the ramped-up vetting process continued and Culvahouse queried her on a series of issues. According to Culvahouse's account, he asked Palin a trio of "lead-in questions" to break the ice:

> I want to hear why do you want to be vice president? Secondly, are you prepared to use nuclear weapons in the defense of the American Homeland? Third, Osama Bin Laden is identified in the Fatah. The CIA is ready to take the shot, but if they take the shot, there'll be multiple civilian casualties. Do you take the shot?

"She knocked those three questions out of the park," Culvahouse asserted, without explaining how or why he would be in a position to make such an unmitigated assessment of a metaphorical home run based on those questions. Had he asked McCain or his senior advisers for the "correct" answers? (Did Palin actually know what the Fatah was? Was she asked?) But being a legal pillar of the Republican establishment does not always bestow upon one a healthy skepticism or uncertainty of perception. Culvahouse was *certain* of his findings. "She has lots of presence. She filled up a room," he concluded. "We came away impressed."[†]

_____

[†] In a forty-minute presentation to the Republican National Lawyers Association on April 17, 2009, Culvahouse used language that may have suggested to some that his vetting of Palin had been done in person. *"She has lots of presence,"* he declared. "She *filled up a room.* Me and two of my most cynical partners interviewed her and we *came away* impressed." (Emphasis added.) He also stated that

Afterward, Culvahouse, ran down his findings by telephone to Rick Davis. A couple of relatively minor items had come up—a DUI arrest for Todd Palin when he was in his early twenties; a misdemeanor citation to Sarah for commercial fishing without proper licensing—and then a bigger bombshell: the Palins' seventeen-year-old unmarried daughter, Bristol, who had been living with Sarah's sister Heather for most of the year in Anchorage, was four months pregnant. The father-to-be was identified as eighteen-year-old Levi Johnston, a former hockey teammate of Track Palin's, whose Facebook posting certified his Mat-Su bona fides: "I'm a fuckin' redneck who likes to snowboard and ride dirt bikes. But I live to play hockey. I like to go camping and hang out with the boys, do some fishing, shoot some shit and just fuckin' chillin' I guess . . . Ya fuck with me I'll kick ass."

It was troubling news, and posed yet another potential distraction for the campaign, but the advisers assembled concurred that it should not be a disqualifying factor in McCain's decision. (Several commentators wondered if Palin had disclosed this information to her vetters; she clearly did, at the eleventh hour, though not in her written documents; many members of the McCain staff still did not know about it by the time Palin was announced as the VP selection the following day.)

While Palin was engaged with Culvahouse, Schmidt and Salter talked over the decision. Schmidt remained solid. He had heard nothing but positive things about Palin coming out of Alaska, nothing too in-depth, admittedly, and in spite of McInturff's recent quasi-optimistic numbers crunch, he was still convinced that McCain needed a major game changer to win. Salter was less certain; he had expressed some concerns about Palin to others. He was still leaning toward Pawlenty; he thought the governor from Minnesota provided a better fit with the McCain narrative.

Which meant that, theoretically at least, back in Minnesota, Pawlenty was still in the hunt. If something came up with Palin, if McCain had any concerns, he was to be the GOP vice presidential nominee. Pawlenty, who had been in

---

Palin "told me when she sent [the questionnaire] in that there was one issue she wanted to talk about when *we met* for the interviews." Senior McCain advisers contend there was no in-person interview conducted by Culvahouse of Palin *prior* to her being named McCain's running mate. Palin's account of the vetting process in *Going Rogue* mentions no in-person interview with Culvahouse. Culvahouse did not respond to two formal e-mail requests for clarification.

close contact with the McCain vetting team the past several weeks, had been asked to clear his calendar. Indeed, there was some confusion as to whether he had actually been offered the number two slot. Some members of the Pawlenty inner circle thought he *had* been offered it. At least one midlevel McCain operative thought the offer had been made to Pawlenty as well. There was some chaos and confusion amid the behind-the-scenes drama involving Palin.

The vetting team worked through the night. Only one person had been contacted in Alaska—Palin's personal attorney, Thomas Van Flein, who obviously had a bias in favor of his client and who had yet to review all the legal documents and evidence that would eventually be produced in Troopergate; he gave Palin a clean slate and assuaged Culvahouse's legal concerns related to the dismissal of Monegan. Moreover, no one in the Alaska congressional contingent in Washington had been contacted, most notably Alaska's junior U.S. senator and McCain's colleague, Lisa Murkowski (Frank Murkowski's daughter), who in her own right was a rising star in the Senate. Nor had there been a call placed to Lyda Green, Palin's onetime political ally and the matriarch of the Alaska Republican Party. *No one* got a call in Alaska with the exception of Van Flein—a fact that astonishes Republican Party elders in Alaska to this day.

The following morning, Thursday—on the same day that Barack Obama was scheduled to give his rousing convention speech before eighty-four thousand supporters at Mile High Stadium—Palin was shuttled secretly to the McCain retreat, which many journalists have identified as being located *in* Sedona, but which is actually situated closer to the small community of Page Springs. It has none of the New Age ambience that has come to define modern-day Sedona. The fifteen-acre McCain spread—replete with rustic cabin, picnic area, and a hawk's nest—is a long way from urban Phoenix, but it is no more remote than many homesteads in the Matanuska Valley and, in spite of the distance between Alaska and Arizona, Palin must have felt in her element when she arrived. It was while Palin and the McCain advisers were en route to the retreat that McCain spoke with Culvahouse about the vetting process. According to Culvahouse, he told McCain "she wouldn't [be] ready on January 20—I don't think many people would. Maybe only a Dick Cheney, who'd been in the White House and a secretary of defense, would. But she had a lot of capacity."

McCain asked for Culvahouse's "bottom line."

"High risk," Culvahouse responded. "High reward."

"You shouldn't have told me that," McCain responded, according to Culvahouse. "I've always been a risk taker."

The entourage—once again driven by Ferry, who had covered the windows of the Suburban with "Baby on Board" sun shields to protect detection by the media—pulled into the McCain retreat just before 7 A.M. McCain greeted Palin, offered her coffee, and took her for a short walk down to a favorite spot of his on Oak Creek. They talked for roughly an hour. What was said between the two of them remains uncertain, though in Palin's account they shared an irritation "with time wasted on games within the political world" and their common "independence" from "the political establishment." Afterward, according to his advisers, McCain took a brief walk with Cindy, confided his feelings to her, and then met again with Schmidt and Salter for a final tête-à-tête. Schmidt pressed the case for Palin; Salter one last time for Pawlenty. Palin won out. McCain then made his way up to the deck where Palin was waiting with Kris Perry. He took her aside and offered her the second spot on the GOP ticket—after spending less than ninety minutes total with her, and after a focused vetting process that had lasted little more than twenty-four hours. Davis and Schmidt had led him to the trough—but it was McCain who drank the water. In the end—all parties agree on this—it was McCain's decision and his alone, one of the biggest he had made in his life. McCain was playing craps again. He still liked being a shooter, shaking the dice and sending them tumbling across the table.

Much has been made of McCain's record as a prisoner of war, and of his five and a half years as a captive of the North Vietnamese. One can only imagine how those impossible years shaped his distaste for the pettiness and pretense that often dominates American presidential campaigns. But there is another side of McCain's military record that is obfuscated by his years in captivity. The fact is that McCain's record in the Navy was uneven and troubling. He had graduated 894th in a class of 899 at the Naval Academy, where he constantly bristled at authority. He had been involved in at least four aviation accidents during his career before being shot down over North Vietnam, including a near-crash over Spain in which he himself, in his memoir *Faith of My Fathers*, admitted he was "daredevil clowning" and "flying too low." Many quietly suspected that if he hadn't been the son and grandson of respected four-star admirals he would have been drummed out of the Navy long before his fateful flight over Hanoi in 1967. That many mishaps "are unusual," Michael L. Barr, a former Air Force pilot with 137 combat missions in Vietnam, told the *Los Angeles Times*. "After the third accident, you would say: Is there a trend here in terms of his flying skills and his judgment?" Now, at the age of seventy-two, after beating cancer and clawing his way back to the top spot on the Republican ticket, he was still spontaneous and fearless to the point of being impulsive, and in some people's minds, reckless.

As a hot summer sun rose high in the Arizona sky, John McCain was being a daredevil once again, this time on a national stage. Pictures were taken, congratulations offered all around. McCain bid his new running mate adieu and said that he would see her the following day in Dayton, Ohio, where the announcement would be made and Palin would be presented to the world.

The McCain camp would vigorously contend, both during and after the campaign, that Palin had been thoroughly vetted, that there had been no shortcuts in the process. That was their public stand. "We put a process in place which was a typical McCain process, very low-key," said Davis, who was theoretically in charge of that very process, at a post-election symposium at Harvard. "We had a lot of advice from a lot of people. . . . We started with a very large screen of people, twenty or more, and narrowed it down through the process on an irregular basis of meetings and discussions."

"I do this very simple checklist on the vetting question," McInturff asserted at the same Harvard symposium. "I say, 'What came out about Sarah Palin that the campaign did not know in advance?' And the answer is, 'Nothing.' So was the vetting process successful? Yes . . . So there is one standard—did anything come out about Sarah Palin that this campaign did not know about prior to her being picked? And the answer is no. She was very honest. She disclosed information. They asked the right questions."

"Governor Palin told us everything," Culvahouse would say. "Everything, except the pregnancy of her daughter was in response to the written questionnaire, and she told me when she sent it in that there was one issue she wanted to talk about with me when we met for the interviews. So we knew everything going in."

There were many both inside and outside the McCain campaign who would disagree.

At one point in the next week or so, the questioning about Palin's vetting got so intense that the usually unflappable Schmidt finally had to issue an unprecedented press release that stated the campaign would take no more questions about the vetting. He came out swinging:

> Gov. Sarah Palin is an exceptional governor with a record of
> accomplishment that exceeds, by far, the governing accomplish-
> ments of Sen. Obama. Her selection came after a six-month

long rigorous vetting process where her extraordinary credentials and exceptionalism became clear. This vetting controversy is a faux media scandal designed to destroy the first
female Republican nominee for vice president of the United
States who has never been a part of the old boys' network
that has come to dominate the news establishment in this
country. Sen. McCain picked his governing partner after a
long and thorough search. Gov. Palin looks forward to addressing the nation and laying out the fundamental choice
this election represents for the American people.

The McCain campaign will have no further comment
about our long and thorough process. This nonsense is over.

But McCain's longtime adviser John Weaver knew better. So did others
still remaining on the campaign. Long and thorough it was not. Under the direction of Rick Davis, the McCain camp had had more than six months to
make the decision, to go over the possibilities, to make sure that each candidate had been vetted thoroughly and properly. Instead, Culvahouse had been
given less than a day to complete the final vetting of Palin—well into the middle of the night before McCain was to make his decision—and he and his colleagues were never given the opportunity of a face-to-face interview. Schmidt
and Salter only had a few hours with her. McCain had never discussed her
with any of his Alaska colleagues in Congress, in part because he had always
despised the likes of Ted Stevens and Don Young and Frank Murkowski due to
their pork-scheming, special-earmark approach to politics, and he had yet to
establish a rapport with Murkowski's daughter Lisa, who had replaced her
father in the Senate.

Weaver says that he heard about the Palin selection early on the morning
of Friday, August 29, only a few hours before it was made public. He had encountered rumors that she would be the choice earlier that summer, but had
not taken them seriously because it was so "far-fetched," to the point of being
"absurd." Weaver said he was immediately "heartsick" about the selection
and left messages with campaign staffers urging them to reconsider. But by
then it was too late. "She was almost a disqualifying choice," Weaver contends. "She was so unprepared as a candidate, and more importantly, as someone who could govern—and that is not the John McCain I know. She was not
prepared to be president, she was not prepared to be vice president, and she

wasn't prepared to be a national candidate. And I don't care what kind of vetting one goes through, you know that automatically."

As for the vetting process itself, Weaver says, "I'm sure the person who did the vetting is very proud about the job they did. And that's fine. But it was not done in a traditional way. Other Republican governors weren't asked about their interactions with her. Some of them had been longtime supporters of John, and I think would have given him a fairly honest assessment—private but honest. And some of them knew. They had interacted with Palin at governors conferences. The same for Republican leaders in Alaska; they weren't asked. In a trial, you never ask a question if you don't know the answer to it. And I think in the case of the Palin selection, the same thing applied. We selected somebody without knowing anything other than the pure, basic information."

It was later revealed by journalists John Heilemann and Mark Halperin in *Game Change* that the attorney who had conducted the paper vetting of Palin was Theodore S. ("Ted") Frank, a former counsel in Culvahouse's law firm who was also a well-known conservative legal activist for tort reform and a fellow at the conservative American Enterprise Institute. Frank, an alumnus of the University of Chicago Law School, had also worked on the vetting of Lieberman. According to Heilemann and Halperin, the document produced by Frank (in "less than 40 hours") highlighted Palin's vulnerabilities and noted that "Democrats upset at McCain's anti-Obama 'celebrity' advertisements will mock Palin as an inexperienced beauty queen whose main national exposure was a photo-spread in *Vogue* in February 2008. Even in campaigning for governor, she made a number of gaffes, and the *Anchorage Daily News* expressed concern that she often seemed 'unprepared or over her head' in a campaign run by a friend." Heilemann and Halperin also reported that Frank's document came with an unheeded disclaimer: "Given the haste in which it was prepared, the vetters might have missed something."

Another Republican strategist was even harsher in his critique. "[McCain] knows, in his gut, that he put somebody unqualified on the ballot," Matthew Dowd would later assert at a Time Warner summit panel. "He knows that in his gut, and when this race is over that is something he will have to live with. . . . He put somebody unqualified on that ballot and he put the country at risk; he knows that."

Across the great divide in the Obama campaign, those in the know quickly assessed what had happened. The two camps watched each other closely and they picked up stories about each other from reporters and other media sources. "The pick increasingly seemed not just political," Obama's campaign manager David Plouffe would write in his book *The Audacity to Win*, "but the result of a haphazard, irresponsible process, if you could even call it a process." *New York* magazine echoed Plouffe's remarks by calling the vetting "hasty, half-assed, haphazard."

Meanwhile, back in Denver, Tim Pawlenty was left hanging. He had been told to clear his calendar that Thursday and to cancel all his scheduled interviews as one of the Republican commentators at the Democratic convention, where he had defended McCain both on television and radio against the steady barrage of Democratic attacks. He was always the good soldier. Some members of the press wondered openly if Pawlenty had gotten "the big call." In fact, several Republicans felt that Pawlenty had been used as a decoy, that the McCain camp left him out to dry. He went through the entire day wondering what was happening, waiting for flight instructions that never came. In his heart, he said afterward, he knew the call wasn't going to come, but it wasn't until the next morning that he was finally learned that he had been passed over for Palin—by watching a scroll on Fox News.

While the McCain team was making final arrangements to bring Palin and her entourage to Ohio and then St. Paul for the convention, Barack Obama was putting the final touches to the speech that he was about to deliver that night in Denver. One of the most telling, stinging lines in his high-reaching oratory would be: "If John McCain wants to have a debate about who has the temperament—*and judgment*—to serve as the next commander in chief, that's a debate I'm ready to have." The challenge drew a huge and uproarious response from the eighty-thousand-plus Democratic Party faithful assembled in Denver. Obama had thrown down the gauntlet. Little did he know how prescient those comments would be in regards to the process that resulted in Sarah Palin's selection as his opponent's running mate.

When he finally heard about McCain's choice the following morning, Obama was nonplussed. He would later tell *Newsweek*'s Richard Wolffe, "It was basically a sort of Hail Mary pass. They were just flailing. It was sort of like, you've got to do *something*." To his campaign manager, Plouffe, Obama was even more emphatic. "I just don't know how this ends up working in the long run for McCain," he declared. "You can't just wing something like this—it's too important."

Those inside the Obama camp said the candidate was calm and collected, although many of his second-level advisers were more than a bit ruffled. Obama assured his closest operatives that Palin would never get up to speed as a national candidate. Obama's chief political strategist, David Axelrod, viewed things similarly. "It's like throwing a baby in the ocean," he observed, "and asking it to swim." It had taken Obama months to get his chops down and no matter how talented Palin was, Obama was convinced she would never catch up. It was one reason he had picked Delaware senator Joseph Biden as his running mate. He had been a national candidate and knew the turf. Obama was convinced the Palin selection was an act of desperation. In the aftermath of her selection, one of his friends had e-mailed Obama a picture of him delivering the speech in Denver, with the caption: "Everyone Chill the Fuck Out. I Got This."

Tactic to tactic. That's what the Palin selection reflected in the McCain campaign, from the candidate on down. Obama had gotten into their heads. They were clearly intimidated by the Obama factor and it forced them off their game. The McCain advisers—and, as a result, McCain himself—misread the playing field. "It wasn't time for a Hail Mary play," said Weaver, who still views himself as a McCain loyalist. "To contend otherwise is intellectually dishonest. There were many other options at that point in the campaign. To this day I don't understand it."

In the war room of the Obama campaign, Plouffe liked what he saw. "My guess is that the more we learn about Palin and the lack of process behind the pick," he declared at the time, "the bloom will come quickly off the rose. No one wins the presidency with stunts. And that's what this smells like—a reckless stunt."

John McCain and his new co-pilot were about to crash it again.

CHAPTER 4

Uncivil Discourse

The Palin candidacy is a symptom and expression of a new vulgarization in American politics.
—**Peggy Noonan, former speechwriter for Ronald Reagan,**
The Wall Street Journal

*Her speech might have ginned up their base,
but apparently it had sent ours into orbit.*
—**David Plouffe, campaign manager, Obama-Biden,**
The Audacity to Win

What I am seeing reminds me too much of another destructive period in American history. Sen. McCain and Gov. Palin are sowing the seeds of hatred and division, and there is no need for this hostility in our political discourse.
—**John Lewis, United States Congress, 5th District, Georgia**

BARACK OBAMA'S CAMPAIGN STAFF WAS hoping to get a much deserved rest following their candidate's momentous speech at the closing night of the Democratic National Convention in Denver. While some Democratic television analysts had been critical of the convention's early going ("If this party has a message, it's done a hell of a job hiding it tonight, I promise you that," James Carville assessed dismissively on CNN), the week had gone relatively smoothly and had built to a rousing crescendo Thursday night before 84,000 rabid admirers at Invesco Field.

A record national television audience of more than 40 million viewers, plus an international audience estimated at more than 100 million, had tuned in for the speech. Not only had Obama made history as the first ever African American nominee of a major political party, he appeared to be riding an even bigger historical crest of global proportions. His triumphant oratory in Denver—"Now is not the time for small plans"—articulated both a promise and a challenge for the American people. At that moment, with all the attendant drama and emotion surrounding the event, Obama's election may have appeared inevitable, if not destined. It was not. As any hardened campaign hack will tell you, it's a long way between the dog days of August and the first Tuesday in November.

On the Friday morning after Obama's historic speech, Democratic operatives had been tracking plane routes across the country in an attempt to figure out who the Republican vice presidential nominee would be. Someone in the Obama campaign identified the plane out of Anchorage on its way to Middleton, Ohio, carrying Palin's family. Several bloggers had figured out the same scenario. David Plouffe, Obama's campaign manager, was called early Friday morning. He, in turn, woke up Jim Messina, the campaign's aggressive national chief of staff, who was in charge of coordinating the oppositional research on the GOP vice presidential selection, with the news about Palin. Messina, who had been up late celebrating Obama's triumphant oration, told Plouffe to "stop screwing" with him. He thought it was a joke. Plouffe assured him it wasn't "a fire drill." Messina pulled himself out of bed and got to it.

While it's true that Palin had not been in the first or second tier of candidates that the Obama team had been assessing—"Who's Sarah Palin?" was Joe Biden's widely reported response—it's a myth that they had no political dossier on her and that they had been caught completely off guard. Ironically, they had far more relevant information on Palin than the McCain team. Anita Dunn, then serving as a senior adviser to the Obama campaign and in charge of communications and research, had worked for Tony Knowles in his 2006 campaign against Palin; so, too, had Steve Murphy, who was working on Obama's communications team; Murphy's business partner, Mark Putnam, was raised in Alaska and was also working on Mark Begich's 2008 senatorial run. Obama's senior adviser, Pete Rouse, was a political operative in Juneau. They had ample political resources on the ground in Alaska.

The Knowles camp had assembled an extensive opposition file on Palin for the Alaska gubernatorial election; this was made readily available to the Obama campaign. It contained hundreds of files, including interview transcripts, questionnaires, newspaper accounts, polls, letters, press releases, articles, photographs, e-mails, and audio clips dating back to Palin's tenure on the Wasilla City Council. Moreover, available online by the *Anchorage Daily News* were several documents critical to the ongoing Troopergate investigation, including transcripts of the interviews with Palin during their ongoing investigation of Mike Wooten.* It all presented a troubling portrait of Palin—of both her limitations and her dysfunctional tendencies—so that there was little surprise to the Democrats when they began to manifest themselves on the campaign trail.

In fact, the Obama campaign had significantly more firsthand experience with Palin than the McCain inner circle. Several had already been through an entire campaign against her. Dunn had quickly assessed that Palin was not ready for prime time but also acknowledged her skills as a campaigner. Murphy had been impressed with her charismatic manner and was nervous that her presence might redefine the political dynamic in the remaining weeks of the campaign. He reportedly had an intense e-mail exchange with David Axelrod over the implications of the Palin candidacy. Axelrod felt that she was not ready for the national stage. End of discussion. Knowles himself, widely respected in national Democratic Party circles, declared unabashedly, "I fear for my country if the McCain-Palin ticket prevails."

Improbably, Palin had told Schmidt and other McCain advisers that she expected several key Democrats in Alaska to champion her candidacy. She had worked closely with them during her tenure as governor, she asserted, and she could count on their endorsement. It was all part of the package she was selling the McCain team, part of the Palin myth that existed in her own mind. One of the legislators who she was certain would advance her cause was Beth Kerttula, the extremely bright and well-liked Democratic leader in the Alaska House of Representatives. Palin assured McCain's advisers that Kerttula would laud Palin's ability to cross party lines and work both sides of the aisle. Schmidt wanted to claim the middle against Obama immediately and to tout Palin's bipartisan administrative experience. Palin had convinced him and other McCain advisers that the Dems in Alaska would line up to back her.

To the contrary, Kerttula was "startled" to receive a call from the McCain

---

* Anita Dunn is no relation to the author; a copy of the Knowles files was made available to the author after the election. Senior McCain advisers acknowledged that they had not seen many of the documents available online about Palin at the time of her vetting.

campaign shortly after the Palin announcement asking her to hold a national press conference on behalf of Palin. Kerttula refused. A lifelong progressive Democrat who had studied at Stanford University in the 1970s, Kerttula "kind of liked" Palin on a personal level ("she's charismatic, she connects with people"), but she was firmly in the Obama camp and had growing concerns about Palin's behavior in the aftermath of the Troopergate revelations. She initially had reservations about going public with her opposition to Palin—not only was Palin a woman and a fellow Alaskan, but Kerttula correctly assessed that she would have to work with her down the road—but a few days later she was convinced that she needed to take a stand. One close friend kept telling her that she had a larger responsibility to act: "It's the country," he said. "It's the *country*!" Kerttula realized that she needed to say something on the record as an act of conscience. "I've worked real well with the governor, but she's not ready for this step," Kerttula finally told the *Juneau Empire*. "She's not ready to be a heartbeat away from the presidency." It was a crushing blow to Palin. More significantly, it would not be the last time that McCain advisers noticed a substantive discrepancy between Palin's perceptions of reality and the truth.

AFTER HER MOMENTOUS MEETING WITH John McCain at his family ranch outside Sedona, Palin and her aide Kris Perry flew first to Texas, then to Cincinnati. It had been a carefully orchestrated journey so as not to alert the Obama campaign—or the press—about McCain's decision. Schmidt sat next to Palin on the plane. Everyone was tired—the final, haphazard selection and vetting process had taken its toll on everyone—and Schmidt, who originally wanted to discuss policy matters with Palin, decided it was best to let her rest and prepare herself for the grueling day ahead when she would be unveiled before the nation in Dayton. Schmidt was a master organizer—he liked leaving little to chance—and the last-minute and frenzied nature of the selection process headed up by Rick Davis had left him a little edgy and uncertain. He still felt comfortable, even excited, about the selection of Palin. He rightly suspected that the Palin announcement would steal the narrative from Obama's coronation in Denver and that it would rev up the GOP base in Ohio, a key battleground for the Republicans; if they didn't win in the Buckeye State, there were few electoral scenarios that would lead them to the White House. The choice of Dayton was both symbolic and strategic.

After landing in Cincinnati, the McCain entourage drove to Middletown, where they were booked into a hotel under assumed names. Schmidt's trusted friend and White House colleague, Nicolle Wallace (the former George W. Bush director of communications and a former political analyst for CBS), and Matthew Scully (the well-known Bush speechwriter who was author of the provocative nonfiction book, *Dominion,* a polemic against abuse of animals) had been selected by Schmidt to meet Palin in Middletown, where they were to prepare her for her debut the following day in Dayton, another thirty miles or so north into the heart of the state. They were expecting the largest crowd of the campaign. Everyone was determined to keep the choice secret until the following day for maximum impact. There was excitement permeating the GOP campaign that Palin represented the game changer that McCain needed to get back into the race. The secretive movement of Palin from location to location had all the trappings of a spy movie. The planning went off perfectly.

Wallace and Scully had no idea who they were meeting in Middletown. None. When Schmidt led them to Palin's hotel suite—telling them very formally that they were the seventh and eighth people to know of the decision—both were surprised at who was behind the door. Scully, who had been hired by Mark Salter in March to serve on the campaign's speechwriting team, had originally anticipated a male nominee and had composed his first draft for the introductory speech in a masculine voice. Given the intense secrecy surrounding the selection, Scully rightly guessed that it would be neither Romney nor Pawlenty. He had heard about the interest in Lieberman, but also wondered if it might be Colin Powell. He sensed that McCain was going out of the box with his choice. When he realized who the selection was (he recognized Palin), he was delighted by the decision and thrilled that McCain had selected a woman as his running mate.

Scully presented an interesting match for Palin. At first glance, there was a seeming irony that someone who had written a bestseller on animal rights was matched with the gun-toting, moose-hunting Palin. But Scully was also a Christian—the title for *Dominion* comes from the celebrated passage in Genesis, "let them have dominion over the fishes"—a spiritual and sincere man, not prone to flights of fancy, grounded and comfortable in his own beliefs. Moreover, he actually respected those who shot their own game, as opposed to those who unthinkingly ate meat resulting from the moral atrocities of the slaughterhouse. Nor was he a stranger to the rough-and-tumble of vice presidential politics. He had previously served as Dan Quayle's speechwriter. He could also throw elbows. In the aftermath of his tenure in the Bush White House, Scully had made a splash with his hard-hitting critique in *The Atlantic* of Bush's top speechwriter, Michael Gerson (who, ironically, was on the initial cruise ship to visit Palin in Juneau). It was a small world—at least the sphere of top Republican thinkers and writers. Just about everyone in the game knew everyone else.

There was, however, one odd, presaging moment leading up to the unveiling of Palin in Dayton, the first of many to come for Steve Schmidt and the top echelon of the McCain campaign. In an interview with Sean Hannity following her selection, Palin was asked about her "family's reaction" to the nomination, about whether there was "time to huddle and have a hockey team meeting?" Palin's response was immediate and full of manufactured enthusiasm. "It was a time of asking the girls to vote on it, anyway," Palin asserted. "And they voted unanimously, yes. Didn't bother asking my son because, you know, he's going to be off doing his thing anyway, so he wouldn't be so impacted by, at least, the campaign period here. So asked the girls what they thought and they're like, absolutely. Let's do this, Mom." It was a pat Palin response, full of the giddy family-bonding shtick that she liked to dole out. Only it didn't happen that way.

When the Palin family entourage landed in Ohio, Palin took Schmidt aside and asked him to tell her daughters the news about her selection. She hadn't told them yet. Neither had their father. The girls had been informed that they were flying to Ohio under the false premise of attending an event in honor of their parents' silver wedding anniversary. Schmidt felt it an odd request, but as he was doing his best to accommodate Palin and put her at ease, he accepted the task. Bristol, as Schmidt knew, was pregnant. There would now be an intense international magnifying glass placed over her and her sisters. Schmidt walked into the family's hotel suite and gathered everyone together. He tried to be as direct and upbeat as possible. He said that he had some "exciting news" for them. "Senator McCain has asked your mother to join him in the campaign as the Republican candidate for vice president of the United States," he began. He said that it was going to be the experience of a lifetime, that it would be a fun adventure, and that there would be a "team of people" to take care of them and their family's needs. It was intended as a pep talk. Schmidt looked around the room. It was an uncomfortable moment for him. His audience was virtually nonreactive. There was no overt excitement, no joy. Just a strained silence. So much for the hockey team huddle and unanimous vote. It never happened. It was another Palin myth concocted out of her imagination as a means of making her look like a good mother to the American people. Schmidt, on the other hand, just wanted to get out of the suite as fast as he could.

I N ADDITION TO BEING THE Palins' twenty-fifth wedding anniversary, August 29 was also John McCain's seventy-second birthday. The crowd in Dayton sang him an uproarious version of "Happy Birthday"—twice—then a third time. He thanked the crowd and then played to their provincialism ("Dayton has contributed much to the prosperity and progress of America," he chortled) before building up to a semi-rousing introduction of his running mate.

To watch the video of the moment is almost painful—McCain struggling through the speech, reading his notes on the podium, halting, grinning his staged grin, struggling to get through it all. "She's got the grit, integrity, and good sense and fierce devotion to the common good that is exactly what we need in Washington today," McCain halfheartedly enthused. "I am very pleased and very privileged to introduce to you the next vice president of the United States . . ."—he actually had to read her name and her title—"Governor Sarah Palin of the great state of Alaska." It still didn't flow from his lips. He had yet to commit it to memory.

The song "Take Me Out," from the football film *Rudy,* blared over the loudspeakers as Palin and her entourage emerged from the bowels of the Nutter Center, located on the campus of Wright State University. It was a perfect choice of music—passionate and uplifting, from a film about an overwhelming underdog and overachiever. The McCain advance team choreographed it flawlessly, a far cry from the gaudy disaster of McCain's speech two months earlier in New Orleans (before a sickly lime green backdrop) when Obama had secured the nomination. Palin waved and flashed her beauty pageant smile. This was her moment of introduction to the nation, to the world. She and Todd and four of her children—Piper, Willow, and Bristol carrying Trig (Levi Johnston had yet to be brought into the picture; Track was in the Army)—made their way across the stage toward McCain, his wife, Cindy, and their twenty-three-year-old daughter, Meghan, all to thunderous applause and a sea of waving American flags.

Dressed in a conservative dark suit, her hair swept into her traditional "updo," an American flag pin on her lapel, and donning her trademark designer glasses, Palin exuded confidence galore, a commanding presence, and a seeming ease that immediately—*instantaneously*—trumped McCain's performance at the podium. She introduced her family, with by far the biggest cheer coming when she named her son, Track, and noted that he was about to be dispatched to Iraq. The crowd went wild, breaking into a chant of "U.S.A.! U.S.A.! U.S.A.!" From that point on, Palin had stolen the mantle from McCain; he was now a sideshow playing second fiddle to her main event. However much of a false projection it was, Palin's glow would burn bright for the next week, if not longer, and the campaign's "mojo," as Schmidt had described it, quickly shifted toward her. McCain simply could not hold a candle to Palin in terms of charisma or personality. It wasn't even close. He knew it. So did she.

Sarah Palin was a political phenomenon the likes of which had never been seen before on the national stage of American politics. Mojo was only the half of it.

But if her glow was bright, the duplicity and distortions transcended the wattage. "I never really set out to be involved in public affairs, much less to run for this office," she declared, trying to keep her drive and ambition in the closet. That this was her *seventh* political campaign for public office since 1992— and that she had actually been *appointed* to yet another state office—was never mentioned. Indeed, Palin had held elected office for most of her adult life; it had provided her with most of her income for the better part of two decades. She was a career politician in the most literal sense of the term—but from the very get-go, she was being portrayed by the McCain operatives as something different, something *oppositional,* to the very thing that she was.

"My mom and dad both worked at the local elementary school and my husband and I, we both grew up working with our hands," she declared. True enough for Todd, but hardly true of her upbringing. Palin's own résumé, with the exception of her fishing business with Todd, showed that hardly to be the case.

Palin trumpeted her tax-cutting ways on the Wasilla City Council and then as mayor, and skipped over all the disfunctions of her tenure. She waxed poetic about her statewide positions in office, referring back to the "good ol' boys network" to which she loved to place herself in opposition. She claimed to be "embarking on a $40 billion natural gas pipeline to help lead America to energy independence," when, in fact, the embarkation was still a long way off, if it would ever happen at all. (It still hasn't.) Palin claimed to have "championed reform to end the abuses of earmark spending by Congress. In fact, I told Congress, thanks but no thanks on that Bridge to Nowhere"—both blatant distortions that would be challenged so often in the weeks ahead that she would no longer be allowed to utter them.

Between the duplicity and the hyperbole, Palin's speech in Dayton provided important clues as to what the McCain camp *thought* they were getting in their choice of the Alaska governor. By playing up her working-class pedigree (which in itself was a distortion), the Republicans thought they were getting someone who could reach out to Reagan Democrats, to moderates and independents, to Sam's Club Republicans. But the biggest catch they thought they were getting with Palin was made clear with an interesting, if often overlooked, passage in Palin's opening speech:

> I think, as well, today of two other women who came before me in national elections. I can't begin this great effort without honoring the achievement of Geraldine Ferraro in 1984 and, of course, Senator Hillary Clinton, who showed such determination and grace in her presidential campaign. It was rightly noted in Denver this week that Hillary left 18 million cracks in the highest, hardest glass ceiling in America. But it turns out the women of America aren't finished yet. And we can shatter that glass ceiling once and for all.

It made for an awkward, uncomfortable moment in Dayton. The mention of Ferraro and Clinton actually elicited a scattering of boos and catcalls from the audience. The applause was forced, at best. The McCain campaign thought they were reaching out to a large population of disenchanted Hillary voters who remained outraged that Clinton had been bypassed by Obama for the second spot on the ticket in Denver. That contingent was much smaller than the McCain team assessed (they had bought into a schism that was much more media hype than fact). More importantly—and this shows how out of touch they were with Democratic Party women—if they thought that Hillary supporters would move toward an anti-abortion, evangelical Christian whose views on evolution were uncertain and equivocal, they were sadly mistaken. That was the political calculus revealed by Palin's speech. It was a horrible misreckoning. McCain's team had no idea what they were getting with Palin. They were finding their way in the dark. "They obviously didn't have a clue," said McCain's old political strategist, John Weaver. "You could read right through the cracks from the very beginning."

If the McCain operatives hadn't gotten what they anticipated out of Palin's selection in respect to women and moderates, however, they made up for much of it in respect to revving up those in the Republican base who had been forced to sleepwalk through the Republican primary and McCain's nomination. They had never liked him and were still not thrilled by his candidacy. (The conservative firecracker Ann Coulter had declared that she would actually "campaign for Hillary" rather than McCain.) But in Palin they had found one of their own—at least on the surface—someone who provided them their raw red meat on which to feed. Suddenly the battle for the presidency shifted once again. It was no longer about leadership and reestablishing America's position in the world. The country would once again be polarized by culture wars—battles over abortion and gay rights, the dividing line between church and state, the Second Amendment and God. It was precisely the campaign that McCain was committed to avoiding. It was Karl Rove and Bush II all over again.

A LMOST AS SOON AS PALIN WAS INTRODUCED in Dayton, the McCain team put her back in the box and kept the ribbon tied. Through all her aspirations of securing the number two spot on the ticket—and she knew she was under consideration for the better part of a year, if not more—she had done absolutely nothing to keep herself abreast of national issues, had not studied McCain's positions, and, in fact, had more closely followed Obama's candidacy than the campaigns of any of the Republicans in the field. (She was fascinated by, if not obsessed with, Obama.) Palin understood the celebrity factor of modern-day American politics—the smile, the hairdo, and the wave—but she was about as far from being a policy wonk as anyone could imagine. When CNN anchor Campbell Brown later complained about the McCain campaign's "sexist treatment" of Palin and publicly called upon senior advisers "to stop treating Sarah Palin like she is a delicate flower who will wilt at any moment," McCain's senior advisers could only roll their eyes. The McCain operatives were absolutely shocked not only by her lack of knowledge, but more importantly, by her "absence of curiosity," as her Republican adversary in Alaska, Andrew Halcro, dubbed it.

The person most astonished by it all was Schmidt. In the aftermath of the Dayton speech, he finally found some time alone with her, to assess her understanding of both domestic and foreign policy issues. It was unnerving. But there was no time to look back. The stories coming out of the McCain campaign about the limits of Palin's knowledge in both national and international affairs have now become legion. The first that would leak out was that she didn't know what countries formed NAFTA, the North American Free Trade Agreement (Canada, the United States, and Mexico). It was said that she didn't know that Africa was a continent and that South Africa was an independent country. She was astonishingly uncertain about municipal, state, and federal distinctions—this after being a mayor and governor. She didn't know what "the Fed" was. One senior adviser said the she couldn't locate Afghanistan on a map. The same adviser said that she didn't know the difference between England and Great Britain. She had no idea why North and South Korea were separate countries. There have been counterdenials by Palin and her allies to many of these allegations, of course; however, in not a single one of her interviews that were to follow did she ever express more than the most superficial of understandings of either domestic or foreign policy issues. "I mean, the proof is in the pudding," said one adviser. "She was clueless." According to John Heilemann and Mark Halperin's *Game Change,* Palin reportedly said, "I wish that I paid more attention to this stuff."

Meanwhile, the national and international media were in a frenzy trying to gather information on Palin. There was instantaneous blowback on her claims that she opposed the Bridge to Nowhere. It was the first of many Palin assertions that would be met with a counterattack; that she was "for it before she was against it" would become a contrasting meme during the campaign, yet another way of calling Palin a liar. With the exception of Fox News, where Palin's candidacy was hyped for most of the summer, the mainstream media was decidedly behind the curve in gathering information on her career. It created a huge vacuum. The Internet went absolutely mad. The more Palin ducked the media, the more everyone figured she had something to hide. And Sarah Palin was good at hiding things. What the McCain advisers quickly discovered—and what was at the root of the discontent between them and the Palin team for the rest of the campaign—was that Palin's rendition of events didn't always coincide with the record. The Bridge to Nowhere was the first example of many more deceptions to come; no matter how much she tried to shade the truth, Palin had been for it before she was against it.

The biggest Palin scandal to hit the Internet in the days following her nomination had nothing to do with politics, but the seemingly improbable matter of whether she was actually Trig's birth mother. In fact, the rumors had developed in Alaska long before her nomination. There were allegations that she had covered up a pregnancy for her daughter, Bristol; or that the baby was someone else's that she clandestinely adopted; or that the scenario she had rendered for the birth (both at the time and, later, in *Going Rogue*) was a complete (and highly dubious) fabrication. At the root of the controversy—and which Palin and her supporters refused to acknowledge—was that Palin's reputation for deceit and duplicity fueled the inferno of doubt.

Whichever scenario might have taken place—and the fact is, *all three of them are troubling*—they raised significant questions about her judgment and capacity to serve as vice president of the United States. There were those in Alaska who felt certain that Trig was her child; there were also many who did not. The issue, for the most part, transcended ideological divisions. It divided households. In fact, there was no conclusive proof either way. The pushback from the McCain campaign on the matter was ferocious. But the biggest lie—and the one that continued to fan the flames of those who followed the matter closely—was that Palin claimed she would make her medical records public. Palin could have (and still could) put the matter to rest. The refusal to release her medical records (or Trig's birth certificate) only contributed to the controversy. Accusations about her medical history escalated. Allegations—none of them based on any medical records—were raised on the Internet that she had a sexually transmitted disease she was trying to hide (genital herpes) and that she was suffering from a bipolar disorder. In an extensive article about all of the major candidates' health, Dr. Lawrence Altman of *The New York Times* reported that "Maria Comella, a spokeswoman for Ms. Palin, said the governor declined to be interviewed or provide any health records."

A few days later in a televised interview, NBC's Brian Williams asked Palin, "Did I hear you just agree to release your medical records?" Palin's response was delivered in her trademark, nondeclarative sentence fragments:

> The medical records. So be it. If that will allow some curiosity seekers, perhaps, to have one more thing that they can either check the box off that they can find something to criticize, perhaps, or find something to rest them assured over. Fine. I'm healthy, I'm happy, had five kids. That is going to be in the medical records. Never been seriously ill or hurt. You will see that in the medical records if they're released.

If they're released. In fact, Palin actually never released them. Ever. That she did is a lie. What was issued, only a day before the election, was a two-page written statement from her doctor—Dr. Cathy Baldwin-Johnson of Providence Health and Services—that recalled Palin's general medical history since 1991 and asserted that Palin "is in excellent health" and has "no known health problems that would interfere with her ability to carry out the duties and obligations of Vice President of the United States." She also indicated that Palin had "one pre-term delivery at 35 weeks gestation in 2008." There were no "rec-ords" accompanying the statement. Nor was there a birth certificate. By the time the letter was released—only a few days before the election—even some high-ranking operatives inside the McCain campaign were quietly wondering if Trig was, indeed, her child.

T HE ONSLAUGHT AGAINST PALIN continued. The firestorm that engulfed the blogosphere eventually spread into the mainstream press. Ironically—given the brutal treatment of both Schmidt and Nicolle Wallace in Palin's memoirs—the two McCain senior advisers were Palin's two staunchest de-fenders in the early days of the campaign. While Republican strategist Alex Castellanos once dubbed Schmidt "the perfect killing machine" in respect to his messaging, Schmidt also has a profoundly human side, particularly when it comes to family life. A father with two young children (whom he missed des-perately during the campaign), close to his parents and a gay sister whose rights he has advocated for, Schmidt has the innate ability to connect with people separately from politics or ideology. He was profoundly disturbed by the at-tacks on Palin at the outset. When questioned about Bristol's pregnancy, he declared philosophically, "Life happens in families. If people try to politicize this, the American people will be appalled." He considered questions about Palin's leadership capabilities to be "sexist" and declared that he couldn't "imagine the question being asked of a man." As the attacks ramped up against Palin, he characterized the mainstream media as being "on a mission to destroy her" and reaching "a level of viciousness and scurrilousness" unprecedented in American political history. He said that the campaign felt "under siege."

Nicolle Wallace also went after the mainstream media in defense of Palin. In an interview on MSNBC's *Morning Joe* in which she appeared with re-porter Jay Carney, who had just written a cover profile of Palin for *Time* magazine, Carney pressed Wallace about Palin not being made available for questions from the press.

CARNEY: We don't know yet, and we won't know until you guys allow her to take questions, you know, can she answer tough questions about domestic policy, foreign policy . . . [interrupted]

WALLACE: Wait, wait. Questions from who? From *you*? Who cares?

CARNEY: I think the American people care . . . [interrupted]

WALLACE: I think the American people want to see her, but who cares if she can talk to *Time* magazine?

Wallace's performance was less than convincing and more than a bit disingenuous. It reflected a tactic that Palin's handlers would push throughout the campaign—that she was being victimized by the mainstream media and that her message didn't need (and would not succumb) to their various filters. As it turned out, it was a brilliant strategy, if only temporarily. They wanted the second unveiling of Palin at the Republican National Convention to take place on their terms, under carefully controlled circumstances, with a precisely scripted rollout in a hermetically sealed environment. They wanted nothing left to chance.

P ALIN HAD BEEN PLACED IN NEAR VIRTUAL SECLUSION in the Minneapolis Hilton leading up to what would certainly be the biggest night of her career, her acceptance speech at the Republican convention, being held at the Xcel Energy Center in St. Paul. Amid the unprecedented firestorm surrounding Palin's selection, McCain's advisers knew that her performance in St. Paul—this time before a national television audience close in size to the one that had watched Obama's speech—could prove decisive in November.

Matthew Scully understood the importance of the Palin speech and put his heart into its initial drafting. In many respects, he rightly reckoned, it would prove to be more significant than McCain's. Part of Scully's appeal to the GOP operatives was that unlike his former colleague Michael Gerson, who favored overtly biblical language in his oratorical compositions for George W. Bush, Scully was able to find a more secular tone, one that satisfied the evangelical base but that didn't turn off moderate or undecided voters. His draft for the convention also had to be redirected for a female voice, and he worked Palin's biography into the draft. He paid no attention to the various news stories that were emerging about her; he didn't want to be influenced by them. He felt that the speech would have transcendent historical significance.

As Scully watched Palin read through the initial drafts of his speech, he was profoundly impressed by her. She had been coached intensively by Priscilla Shanks, a veteran New York stage, television, and film actress who had been brought in to work on Palin's enunciation and to round off some of her more irregular pronunciation habits and shrilly exclamations. Scully was struck by Palin's focus and the progress she was making. Her editorial suggestions, he thought, were spot-on.

This would be the night that forever sealed the nation's impression of Sarah Palin. For all the drama and erratic behavior to come, the Sarah Palin frozen in the memory of the collective body politic was the one who delivered the caustic speech in St. Paul that went after Obama. People who wonder why Palin would emerge so immediately divisive, such a focal point for controversy and liberal wrath, need only to return to her convention speech for the answer. How much of the rewrite was Scully's, and how much was completed by the rest of the McCain inner circle and Palin herself is uncertain, but the final version that she delivered was rich in hyperbole and dripping with sarcasm. While some lines in the speech, Scully acknowledged, were clearly drafted "at Senator Obama's expense," there was nothing in the speech that he "considered unfair." Sometimes in politics you have to pick a few fights, he felt, and engage the opposition. If people thought she should present herself as mild or defensive, Scully thought, they had another thing coming. "She went out there and she tagged him," Scully said, "and that's what you're supposed to do."

Palin was introduced the night of the convention by Rudy Giuliani, who only a year earlier had been leading the GOP polls for the presidency. With his September 11 credentials as mayor of New York and tough-guy persona, Giuliani was selected to introduce Palin not only as a means to shore up her foreign policy credentials but also as a way of melding her Last Frontier charms with Big Apple grit. On paper, such a pairing may have made political sense, but in its execution, at least, the introduction was severely flawed—and permanently problematic in terms of Palin's national reception. It hardened liberal America against her instantaneously.

In introducing Palin, a sneering, albeit stumbling, Giuliani issued a vicious personal attack on Obama. Dressed in a dark blue suit and a red-and-blue striped tie, Giuliani seemed improbably cast, an American hero to some, but by the late summer of 2008, after a disastrous presidential campaign of his own, he looked ever more the villain than the hero. Even in the hearts of the GOP faithful, there were those who detested Giuliani for his various personal indiscretions (three marriages, a public affair with his communications director) and his pro-choice, pro–domestic partnership, and pro–gun control views. For a moment, Giuliani finally found his stride. "In choosing Sarah Palin as his running mate, John McCain has chosen for the future," Giuliani intoned.

"The other guy looked back. John looked forward." His timing was off again, but it didn't matter. His next few lines sealed the deal:

> Governor Palin represents a new generation. She's already one of the most successful governors in America and the most popular. . . . And she's already had *more executive experience* than the *entire* Democratic ticket combined.

The crowd roared. That was going to be the Republican mantra: that Obama and Biden both lacked executive experience. They were *legislators,* not rulers; they were about *process,* not decision making. "She's been a *mayor,*" Giuliani emphasized again, his smile almost turning into a giddy smirk. "I love *that.*" His face broke into a big grin. "She's got an 80 percent approval rating," Giuliani asserted, almost incredulously, then added a self-referential remark. "You never get that in New York City. Wow!"

Then it got even more confusing and quite nearly bizarre. Suddenly Giuliani became a radical feminist. Once again, referring to some of the resulting buzz from the Palin selection, Giuliani grew adamant. "One final point," the thrice-married mayor declared with furious indignation. "How—how dare they question whether Sarah Palin has enough time to spend with her children and be vice president. How dare they do *that.* When do they ever ask a man that question? *When?*" The question rang hollow. The GOP was never at the forefront of feminist issues and it came off as calculating, if not disingenuous, for Giuliani to be bringing it up now, a final bone to Hillary and the disgruntled Democratic women they were hoping to harness by selecting Palin. "And now the job is up to us," Giuliani concluded. "Let's get John McCain and Sarah Palin elected, and let's shake up Washington and move this country forward." Hardly a rousing call to arms—and an odd, ultimately ineffective framing of Palin's entrée to the national political stage.

Palin entered the arena to a thunderous standing ovation. She—and her family—had been hammered by the media in the six days leading up to the convention, and the crowd welcomed her as an underdog with enthusiastic cheers that lasted for more than three minutes. The empathy was real, and the welcoming acclamation was electric. If Palin had any doubts about how she would be received by the delegates, those concerns were quickly and overwhelmingly dismissed.

Palin started right in on "the experts," "the pollsters," "the pundits," the

"Washington elite." She was in her fighting mode from the beginning—possessed by that odd, trademark scowl with her jaw out, her bottom lip up, fists clenched, her eyes seeming ever so slightly crossed, looking as though she was itching for a brawl. Sarah Palin against the world. She began by puffing up the credentials of her running mate and immediately personalized the connection. Palin made everything personal. She described McCain as "a man who wore the uniform of this country for twenty-two years" and then praised him for refusing "to break faith with those troops in Iraq who have now brought victory within sight." Palin was hitting her marks perfectly. She was on her game, and then almost immediately turned the focus back on herself. "And as the *mother* of one of those troops," she offered with a conviction that turned nearly into a snarl, "that is *exactly* the kind of man I want as commander in chief." The crowd cheered. That the segue to her children came from a woman who continually demanded that the media "leave my kids alone" was riddled with an irony that she would never confront. She brought them into the mix whenever she could, not just with notes of introduction, but as political stage props for her own peculiar brand of populism. Unlike Biden or McCain, who also had sons serving in the military, Palin would employ her son, Track, as a verbal rampart throughout the campaign.

She then introduced the rest of the family—which in the week leading up to her speech had been the fodder for constant attack and exposure—and in response to the specific charges swirling on the Internet that she had once had an affair with one of her husband's business associates, she beamed up at her husband seated in the mezzanine. "He's still my guy."

Then Palin moved in another direction that would be unique to her political formulation. "Long ago, a young farmer and haberdasher from Missouri followed an unlikely path to the vice presidency," she declared, in what was an obvious reference to Harry Truman. She then quoted right-wing writer Westbrook Pegler's famous line about Truman—"We grow good people in our small towns, with honesty, sincerity, and dignity"—though she did not quote Pegler by name. Pegler—an avowed enemy of the New Deal and an anti-Semite who would later sympathize with the John Birch Society—had also once expressed the hope, in respect to Senator Bobby Kennedy, that "some white patriot of the Southern tier will spatter his spoonful of brains in public premises before the snow flies." He also, more to the point, would say of Truman that he "is thin-lipped, a hater" and declared during the civil rights movement that "clearly the bounden duty of all intelligent Americans [is] to proclaim and practice bigotry." This is the moment when Palin began carving up the country, dicing it up into red and blue America, us against them, placating the Great Cultural Divide.

> I know just the kind of people that writer had in mind when he praised Harry Truman. I grew up with those people. They are the ones who do some of the hardest work in America . . . who grow our food, run our factories, and fight our wars. They love their country, in good times and bad, and they're always proud of America.

With her homage to Pegler, Sarah Palin—"just your average hockey mom"—claimed her stake in American political discourse and established her brand. From that point on—and that is the moment of its inception—Palin would become the most polarizing and divisive figure in contemporary American history. With the remainder of the speech she sealed the deal. She was a throwback to Norman Rockwell's America—only in a fitted black skirt and pumps, and a $2,500 shantung silk jacket designed by Valentino Garavani and purchased at Saks Fifth Avenue.

After noting that she had "signed up for the PTA," there was an awkward moment of silence—she started giggling with a girlish smile, and looking out at signs in the audience. The crowd, at least in front of her, started chanting, "Hockey moms! Hockey moms!" There was more silence, a nervous expression washing over Palin's face. She quickly regained her composure. "I love those hockey moms," she exuded. "You know, they say the difference between a hockey mom and a pitbull? . . . Lipstick." The crowd went wild at Palin's joke. It was another branding moment.

It would later be claimed that Palin had ad-libbed the joke, when, in fact, it was a line she had used frequently before, including in an op-ed she wrote for the *Anchorage Daily News* as early as December of 2004. It would also be claimed that the teleprompter had gone out on her at that moment, that it was working "sporadically." Perhaps so. But in the television footage of her speech, you can actually read her next line in the teleprompter. It was there, waiting for her delivery. If it went out at all, it was back in operation almost instantaneously, and was certainly in service when the hockey-mom-and-pitbull line was delivered.

Technology aside, Palin had clearly bonded with her audience. She had the crowd in her palm, her confidence once again in ascension. She became combative again—this time with a command force—as the subject of her speech swung back to Obama. Palin was sharpening her dagger. She touted her experience as "a small-town mayor"—the jaw and bottom lip extending outward again—and then she moved into the portion of her speech that would come to define her. "I guess a small-town mayor," she snarled with derision, "is sort of like a 'community organizer'—except that you have actual responsibilities." The crowd went wild as a protester was pulled from the arena. Palin was delivering the raw venison that the base had been craving for so long.

She continued on with the small-town theme and the digs at Obama.

> I might add that in small towns, we don't quite know what to make of a candidate who lavishes praise on working people when they are listening, and then talks about how bitterly they cling to their religion and guns when those people aren't listening. [Cheers] We tend to prefer candidates who don't talk about us one way in Scranton and another way in San Francisco.

Palin was working the crowd, pulling everyone in from the edges. Whatever nervousness she may have had at the beginning was long gone, her confidence soaring. She was heading toward the basket for a breakaway layup. "Well, I'm not a member of the *permanent political establishment*," she declared with dripping sarcasm. "And I've learned quickly, these past few days, that if you're not a member in good standing of the Washington elite, then some in the media consider a candidate unqualified for that reason alone." She was greeted by a chorus of empathetic boos that extended into waves. She let it play out like a pro. Many in the audience broke into a chant of "Shame on you!" directed at the media pit and at the networks, and in particular, at PBS commentator Gwen Ifill (one of the few African Americans in the sea of white faces at the Xcel Center). Palin watched over the moment of choreographed mayhem in delighted approval.

And then she delivered what was to be her biggest hit of the night—the sound bite that would be played over and over in the days ahead—and, in retrospect, perhaps the high point of her candidacy. It wasn't aimed at Obama or even the Democrats; it had nothing to do with policy or governance. It was directed at the "media elite," or the "lamestream media," as she would come to call it in the days and months ahead. "Here's a little news flash for all those reporters and commentators," she said with an evil grin forming on her face, her telltale finger pointing with obvious delight. "I'm not going to Washington to seek their *good opinion*; I'm going to Washington *to serve the people of this country.*"

The crowd rose to its feet. She was their new darling.

Palin wound down by trumping her own experience again—taking on the "good ol' boys" and "the lobbyists" and "the Big Oil companies"—and pledged to govern with "a servant's heart." She talked about "ethics reform" and "earmark spending by Congress." She went back to her canned remark about saying "thanks, but no thanks" to the Bridge to Nowhere—a line that was met with a forced and hollow applause; it had already been debunked repeatedly in the previous week and would soon be excised from her repertoire. She made it seem as though construction on the Alaska gas pipeline had already begun, which it hadn't—and suddenly, Palin was slipping once again down the slippery slope of deceit. "Americans need to produce more of our own oil and gas," she roared to chants of "Drill! Baby! Drill!," describing herself as a "gal who knows the North Slope of Alaska."

Then she pulled out the dagger one more time and went after Obama. The crowd didn't want a policy wonk, they wanted an assassin. "I've noticed a pattern with our opponent," she said, twisting the knife a little deeper. "Maybe you have, too . . ."

> We've all heard his dramatic speeches before devoted followers. And there is much to like and admire about our opponent. But listening to him speak, it's easy to forget that this is a man who has authored two memoirs but not a single major law or even a reform—not even in the state senate.
>
> This is a man who can give an entire speech about the wars America is fighting, and never use the word "victory" except when he's talking about his own campaign.

Palin was back with the rare, red sirloin. "Al Qaeda terrorists still plot to inflict catastrophic harm on America," she said with mock disgust worthy of a B movie actress, "and he's worried that someone *won't read them their rights.*" Palin's moment of oracular grandeur was coming to a close. She blew McCain's Hanoi cell mate Tom Moe a kiss—another signature gesture that she would return to time and time again as conservative America's darling—and then took one final shot at Obama before claiming the stage with her family. "For a season, a gifted speaker can inspire with his words," she concluded. "For a lifetime, John McCain has inspired with his deeds."

Sarah Palin had passed her biggest test with flying colors and had exceeded the campaign's greatest expectations. Those who had seen her struggle through her early practice sessions with her speech coach were astonished by the flawless, seasoned delivery. But she had also shown all her cards. She held nothing back. With Sarah Palin, what the American public saw at the Xcel Center was what they were going to get for the rest of the campaign.

The speech would permanently fix Palin in the American psyche and frame her ideologically. She was the promoter of small-town America. White America. Religious America. She had not mentioned racial divisions once in her speech, made no reference to those in the inner cities, to urban America, but the subtext was clear. She established herself in opposition to Washington, to the media elite. She was an outsider—and proud of it. Indeed that was her calling card. And most important—and perhaps this is what angered those on the other side of the political divide most—she was the "anti-Obama" and she had not been afraid to assault his integrity and to belittle his accomplishments. As John Heilemann of *New York* magazine declared, Palin "was unafraid to wield the stiletto" and "seemed to delight in plunging it into Barack Obama's kidneys."

Palin herself would assess the moment differently. "By God's grace," she wrote in *Going Rogue*, "I was having a ball." So, too, was the opposition. More than $10 million in contributions were pledged to the Obama campaign in the next twenty-four hours. She would become the Democrats' best weapon. "Her speech might have ginned up their base," said David Plouffe, "but apparently it had sent ours into orbit." By the end of the month, Plouffe estimated, Palin would add $20 million to $25 million to Obama's campaign coffers.

The McCain hierarchy celebrated Palin's triumphant speech in the bar of the Minneapolis Hilton. The unassuming and modest Scully received an ovation when he entered. McCain was ecstatic. Wallace claimed that she had cried throughout the speech; she had been moved by the dramatic arc of the evening and by Palin's fortitude in the face of a full-on media assault. Schmidt, in particular, was thrilled by Palin's performance. She had proved herself and then some. "Game on." He smiled. "Game on." When the Palins finally arrived, they were surrounded by a mob scene. They hung out for fifteen or twenty minutes and then retreated to their suite. Schmidt turned philosophical. He was riding on Palin's wave and was intuitively assessing its force. "Arguably at this stage?" he declared. "She's a bigger celebrity than Obama."

By the time the curtain came down on the Republicans in St. Paul, television, magazine, newspaper, and radio reporters had descended on Alaska in droves—in Anchorage and Wasilla, and down in Juneau, too—initiating their first looks at Palin's checkered career in Wasilla and in her year and a half as governor of Alaska. Most had never been to Alaska and had no idea of either the geographical or political terrain. The media descent was like a cloud of locusts swarming across the Arctic, uncertain of their ultimate destination.

For the first several days—and indeed for much of the campaign—the real story was being told by a hardy and ragtag band of bloggers in Alaska who knew Palin only too well, some back to her days on the Wasilla City Council. Most of them had been blogging well before the Palin nomination and had developed a critical narrative of her governorship, particularly in recent months as it related to Troopergate. As Eric Boehlert noted in *Bloggers on the Bus,* his delightful chronicle of the progressive blogosphere (or "netroots nation," as it became known), independent voices from the Internet "influenced and altered the road to the White House" in ways never before imaginable. Moreover, the intrepid band of bloggers from Alaska did the public vetting of Sarah Palin that the mainstream media failed to do. They were ahead of the curve every step of the way.

Two of the Alaska bloggers—Jeanne Devon (AKMuckraker) of *The Mudflats,* and Shannyn Moore of *Just a Girl from Homer*—were soon to receive national platforms, having been invited to blog from Alaska for *The Huffington Post. The Mudflats* would later receive a Blogger's Choice Award for Best Political Blog of 2008 and was to maintain the largest readership of any independent blog site in the state. Moore would receive a Wings of Justice Award as well as a Steve Gilliard Award from Netroots Nation; she also emerged as a regular on-air contributor on MSNBC's *Countdown with Keith Olbermann.* Palin would dub the Alaska bloggers "fringe" and "partisan," but in fact they reported from across the political spectrum. In addition to *The Mudflats* and *Just a Girl from Homer,* some of the more popular Alaskan blogs filing daily reports on Palin-related issues included Dennis Zaki's *The Alaska Report,* Phil Munger's *Progressive Alaska,* Jesse Griffin's *The Immoral Minority,* Andrew Halcro's *AndrewHalcro.com,* Linda Kellen Biegel's *Celtic Diva's Blue Oasis,* Writing Raven's *Alaska Real* (which provided a much needed voice from Native Alaska), along with a pair of conservative voices, Sherry Whitstine's *Syrin from Wasilla* and Paul Jenkins's *Anchorage Daily Planet*. All were rich, charming, frequently brilliant—and loaded with on-the-ground information and insights about Palin and Alaska politics that could not be garnered anywhere else.

Andrée McLeod, the Anchorage-based good-government activist who had filed a Freedom of Information Request for nearly twenty thousand pages of Palin's e-mails in April and who had filed the first Ethics Act complaint against her, also became an important figure in the early days of the campaign as she provided access to her e-mails to Karl Vick of *The Washington Post*. McLeod developed a "comfortable, easygoing" relationship with Vick, whose stories benefited significantly not only from McLeod's prior research but also from her extensive knowledge of Alaska's complicated political landscape. Before the campaign was over, McLeod worked with dozens of reporters from throughout the United States, Canada, and Great Britain.

The morgues of the major dailies in the Last Frontier—the *Anchorage Daily News*, the *Juneau Empire*, the *Fairbanks Daily News-Miner*, and the *Mat-Su Valley Frontiersman*—along with their Web site archives, also provided a wealth of information on Palin. Another key source of coverage was the nonpartisan *Alaska Budget Report*, where its founders, Gregg and Judy Erickson, and editor Rebecca Braun provided in-depth and nuanced analysis of Palin's tenure as a governor and mayor. National wire reporters who had worked in Alaska for years—particularly Yereth Rosen of Reuters—filed important stories about Palin that the mainstream press wouldn't latch on to for weeks.

But perhaps the biggest blow to the Palin narrative in the early days of the campaign came from neither a blogger nor a journalist, but from a longtime local activist in Wasilla, Anne Kilkenny, who simply decided to write a letter to a handful of friends. Kilkenny, who lived little more than a mile as the crow flies from Palin—and less than a ten-minute drive around Lake Lucille—was in "a bit of shock" when she first learned of Palin's selection. Like many Alaskans, she thought it had been "a joke." She knew Palin had charisma and a certain sort of crafted charm, and she had seen how it had worked in Wasilla. Kilkenny was "more than a little disgusted" by it. A self-described "hippie-era Berkeley grad" whom Palin would belittle in *Going Rogue* as "the town crank," Kilkenny felt like she knew Palin "for who she really was," not how she had been reconstructed as governor and as the vice presidential nominee. Kilkenny had been intimately involved in Wasilla politics—she came from a long line of civil engineers—and she had worked to revise Wasilla's municipal zoning code. As such, Kilkenny had kept an extensive file on Palin. It was right at her fingertips. Moreover, she had heard stories about the Palins and Heaths in the

Mat-Su, not all of them pretty, and she felt like Sarah Palin had run something close to a reign of terror in her small community for the better part of a decade. She knew she needed to step up.

Never one to hold her counsel, Kilkenny felt as though she had something important to say to her close friends who didn't know Palin and her history in Wasilla. After watching early Palin coverage dominate network television, where Palin's entrée was being greeted with the favorable spin of her being a "hockey mom" and "maverick" and someone who had taken on the "good ol' boys network," Kilkenny went to her keyboard and began typing out an e-mail intended for a handful of her friends. She felt compelled to tell a different story about Palin than that being constructed by the national media—yet another counternarrative, one that was decidedly at odds with the one being fed to the mainstream press by the McCain camp. Kilkenny is a spiritual woman and she wanted to make sure she wrote the letter "with a clean heart." She took her time composing the first draft, which she sent out to a handful of friends. In it, she described Palin as "like the most popular girl in middle school" and said that Palin and Hillary Clinton had only two things in common: "their gender and their good looks." Kilkenny echoed something that one hears often in Alaska. "Even men who think she is a poor choice and won't vote for her," Kilkenny observed, "can't quit smiling when talking about her because she is a 'babe.'" But she also gave Palin her due: "She is energetic and hardworking," Kilkenny asserted. "She's smart."

Perhaps most significant, Kilkenny documented some important details about Palin's tenure as mayor of Wasilla.

> Sarah campaigned in Wasilla as a "fiscal conservative." During her 6 years as Mayor, she increased general government expenditures by over 33%. During those same 6 years the amount of taxes collected by the City increased by 38%. This was during a period of low inflation (1996–2002). She reduced progressive property taxes and increased a regressive sales tax which taxed even food. The tax cuts that she promoted benefited large corporate property owners way more than they benefited residents.

In addition to chronicling her political record, Kilkenny also included some stinging personal observations about Palin, observations that more than two years later still hold their mark. "She has bitten the hand of every person who extended theirs to her in help," she wrote. "Fear of retribution has kept all these people from saying anything publicly about her." She steered clear of some of the more personal allegations that were heading Palin's way, but challenged the myth that Palin had environmental credentials. Palin, she wrote, "turned Wasilla into a wasteland of big box stores and disconnected parking lots."

The e-mail went viral. Within the week, Kilkenny had personally received nearly 9,600 e-mail responses. Her letter had been posted on thousands of Web sites and e-lists. It became such a phenomenon that it was quoted widely by the mainstream press and Kilkenny appeared on a host of television shows and news programs. The media were clamoring at her door.

After a little more than a week, she took her time to respond to some of the comments, offer up a few corrections, and issue a second missive. The letter (which was to have a life of its own throughout the campaign and which received a Special Award from the Alaska Press Club) prevented Palin from fully deceiving the mainstream media about her early political career.

IN SPITE OF THE RUMBLINGS FROM ALASKA, The McCain campaign was riding high after the GOP convention. Sarah Palin had not only hit a home run with her speech, she had driven it out of the park. It was a grand slam and more. The worn-out baseball clichés and metaphors didn't quite capture the full impact of her performance. All the questions about her personal life had been troubling and a major distraction in St. Paul—her daughter's pregnancy; the disputed parentage of Trig; and the persistent rumors of an affair with a former business associate of Todd's—but for all the cyberspace energy given to Palin's personal life, there was a surging and meaningful pushback from the conservative base. They were contributing money to the Republican National Committee by the basketful and volunteering in droves. Palin had fired them up in a way they had not been since Reagan's candidacy for a second term in 1984. Palin had proven to be the political game changer that McCain's top brass had been looking for, the boost they had needed to capture the narrative away from Obama. Coming out of the box in St. Paul they were ahead in the polls 48–45. It was a stunning reversal.

On September 10, the McCain team and Palin gathered at the Ritz-Carlton in Pentagon City, Virginia, not far from McCain headquarters, for the flight back to Alaska and a three-day stay there, during which time she would conduct the first of her three interviews with the network TV anchors—leading off with Charlie Gibson of ABC. The return to southwest Alaska also allowed Palin the opportunity to spend some time with friends and family and, most important, to see her nineteen-year-old son, Track, deploy to Iraq. Schmidt finally had the opportunity to settle in with Palin, to test her "bandwith," as he described it, as well as her baseline of political knowledge, both domestic and foreign, and her grasp of American and world history. He had made certain assumptions about a seated governor and a two-term mayor that, he would soon discover, proved to be decidedly unwarranted.

Schmidt was one of the most trusted taskmasters in the Republican Party. His credentials were impeccable. During the 2004 Bush-Cheney campaign he had been in charge of "rapid response" directly under Karl Rove. He later served as Dick Cheney's communications director and was tasked with seeing the Supreme Court confirmations of Justices John Roberts and Samuel Alito through the Senate. During all of the turbulence in the last two years of the McCain campaign, he had been the glue that held it together—mostly as a volunteer. Of all the operatives and advisers in the Republican Party, he was the one, said one of his colleagues, "who you want in your bunker." He had a military air about him. In Sarah Palin, however, Steve Schmidt's talents as a tough and effective political strategist were about to be tested, in ways that he never—and could never—have imagined.

Schmidt slowly began appraising Palin's knowledge of foreign affairs. She repeated several times that Saddam Hussein was behind the September 11 attacks. Particularly troubling to Schmidt was the fact that she could not name the enemy that her son would be fighting in Iraq. Schmidt gave her a copy of Lawrence Wright's Pulitzer Prize–winning exposé, *The Looming Tower: Al-Qaeda and the Road to 9/11*—though no one ever saw her reading from it; she preferred *People* magazine and *Runner's World*. (Palin would later complain that "the Middle East was Schmidt's preferred issue" as opposed to "the tanking economy.") When it came time to assess her level of knowledge, Schmidt was brutally direct. Privately, he told aides assigned to prepping her on foreign affairs that their work was cut out for them, that she didn't know anything.

Part of the spin coming from the McCain advisers in the aftermath of the campaign was that Palin passed her major first test in her interview with ABC's Gibson, not with flying colors, perhaps, but with no major gaffes. That wasn't quite the case. For the first time, a national audience could see that she had trouble constructing sentences and that there were huge gaps in her knowledge base. There were those trademark Palin non sequiturs—those series of rattled-off catchphrases that don't link and don't make sense when put to paper. She got caught with what probably was a bit of "gotcha" journalism—when she was asked about the Bush Doctrine—but instead of being honest, what made it a "gotcha" moment was how she handled it. "In what respect, *Charlie*?" she responded testily, almost defiantly. She shuffled in her chair, her anger bristling right at the surface.

Palin's lack of depth on foreign affairs also became nakedly manifest. In explaining U.S. foreign policy toward Russia, she launched in several directions, before declaring: "That manifestation that we saw with that invasion of Georgia shows us some steps backwards that Russia has recently taken away from the race toward a more democratic nation with democratic ideals."

Then, as though she were lecturing a four-year-old, she went into a sing-song response about the geographic significance of U.S.-Russian relations:

PALIN: That's why we have to keep an eye on Russia. And, Charlie, you're in *Alaska*. We have that very narrow maritime border between the United States, and the forty-ninth state, Alaska, and Russia. They are our next-door neighbors. We need to have a good relationship with them. They're very, very important to us and they are our next-door neighbor.

GIBSON: What insight into Russian actions particularly in the last couple weeks does the proximity of the state give you?

PALIN: They're our next-door neighbors. And you can actually see Russia from land here in Alaska.

Gibson cornered Palin on her Bridge to Nowhere claims. Once again she turned combative and defiant. And she simply refused to tell the truth. "You supported the bridge before you opposed it," Gibson declared. "You were wearing a T-shirt in the 2006 campaign [the B-roll illustrated Palin with the infamous "Nowhere Alaska 99901" T-shirt in Ketchikan], showed your support for the bridge."

Palin went into defense mode with an answer that revealed her capacity for deceit. "I was wearing a T-shirt with the zip code of the community that was asking for that bridge," she declared. "Not all the people in that community even were asking for a $400 million or $300 million bridge." Gibson did not yield to her lie. He pointed out that Palin had changed her position only after the bridge had become "a national embarrassment to the state of Alaska." He gave her the opportunity "to revise and extend" her remarks.

PALIN: It has always been an embarrassment that abuse of the ear form— earmark process has been accepted in Congress. And that's what John McCain has fought. And that's what I joined him in fighting. It's been an embarrassment, not just Alaska's projects. But McCain gives example after example after example. I mean, every state has their embarrassment. And, as I've said over and over, if Alaska wants that bridge, 300 million, 400 million dollars, over to that island with an airport, we'll find a way to build it ourselves. The rest of the country doesn't have to build that for us.

GIBSON: But you were for it before you were against it. You were solidly for it for quite some period of time . . .

PALIN: I was . . .

GIBSON: . . . until Congress pulled the plug.

PALIN: I was for infrastructure being built in the state. And it's not inappropriate for a mayor or for a governor to request and to work with their Congress and their congressmen, their congresswomen, to plug into the federal budget along with every other state a share of the federal budget for infrastructure.

Her appearance with Gibson was a far cry from her command performance at the Republican convention. It registered the first significant chink in Palin's armor during the campaign.

Meanwhile, the American economy was in free fall. On September 7, Fannie

Mae and Freddie Mac were seized by the federal government. On September 15, Lehman Brothers collapsed. Only days later, AIG announced that it was on the verge of bankruptcy. The dominoes were falling one by one. "If we don't act boldly, Mr. President," declared Treasury Secretary Henry Paulson and Fed chairman Ben Bernanke in a joint statement, "we could be in a depression greater than the Great Depression."

McCain then made one of the great blunders in recent American political history. In the middle of the crisis, he declared in Jacksonville, Florida, that "the fundamentals of the economy are strong." Obama could only snicker. "No fucking discipline," he remarked to one of his advisers. The Democrats pounced on the statement. The economy was now the biggest issue in the campaign. All of McCain's foreign policy expertise became secondary.

It's become a mantra of McCain-Palin operatives—indeed of the candidates themselves—that the financial collapse of mid-September essentially doomed the Republican ticket. "It's an intellectually dishonest position," says McCain operative John Weaver. "I reject that notion categorically." McCain's Keystone Kops response to the collapsing economy turned the tide—and he had no one riding shotgun to assist.

I N WHAT WOULD COME TO HAVE LASTING implications far beyond the 2008 presidential campaign—Tina Fey's mimicry of this event on *Saturday Night Live* would become a cultural icon—Palin was slated to undergo her second round of anchor interviews, this time with Katie Couric of *CBS Nightly News*. By all accounts, including Palin's own, the Couric interviews were a disaster. Almost overnight, whatever propellant Palin had brought to the McCain ticket had become an unequivocal anchor. Sarah Palin was sinking—and she was sinking fast. She had become a national laughingstock—a joke, a punch line, an object of seemingly endless ridicule—and she would not make it back to the surface for the duration of the campaign. The numbers suddenly turned strongly against her. "We were beginning to see in our research not merely a cooling off in terms of people's views of Palin," David Plouffe observed, "but downright concern about her qualification."

Long afterward, long after snippets of the interviews were played millions and millions of times on news feeds and Internet Web sites, Palin would blame others for her manifest failures during the *Nightly News* interviews. She came up with several spins—most of them directed at Couric and McCain media strategist Nicolle Wallace—and a series of fabricated scenarios about the interviews that bear no resemblance to the truth. She would bitterly refer to Couric "as the lowest rated news anchor in network television" with "a partisan agenda" who hammered Palin with "repetitive, biased questions." In fact, Palin's startling series of faux pas throughout the Couric interviews were all of her own making.

It was a long-established strategy to have Palin participate in prime-time interviews with all three of the major network anchors in the hope that they would establish her as a national heavyweight with vice presidential gravitas. By placing her in the same television frame with the anchors, McCain's strategists were also hoping to erase the novelty of her nomination, to shove her through that first hoop of popular acceptance beyond which she so desperately needed to pass.

Schmidt had called in his trusted aide Wallace to help Palin navigate the interviews. He thought they would be a good match. Wallace had earned her conservative stripes serving as communications director in the Bush White House. And while she was a decade younger than Palin, she also had major media cred through her stint as a national political analyst with CBS. Like Palin, she was tough, could play hardball with the guys, and she was loyal—to Bush and McCain and also to Schmidt. As it turned out, she proved to be a severe threat to Palin. What Schmidt could not have known is that Palin usually surrounds herself with sycophants and is profoundly threatened by women who are smarter than her and who can in any way contest her authority or celebrity. Wallace, just by her presence and her résumé, brought out the worst in Palin. "She hated me from the beginning," Wallace said bluntly afterward. It was a match made in hell.

Palin would go so far in *Going Rogue* to contend that the Couric interviews were an inside job orchestrated by Wallace as a favor to a friend.

> Nicolle went on to explain that Katie really needed a career boost.
>
> "She just has such low self-esteem," Nicolle said. She added that Katie was going through a tough time. "She just feels she can't trust anybody."

It is a contention that is prima facie absurd. Why would Wallace have tried in any way to sabotage a candidate for whom she was dedicating her life? Palin never provides an answer. "The whole notion there was a conversation where I tried to cajole her into a conversation with Katie is fiction," Wallace would assert. "I am not someone who throws around the word 'self-esteem.' It is a fictional description. Katie Couric was selected because we did evening anchors. I did not advocate an interview for anyone I am friends with."[†]

In her widely celebrated appearance on *The Oprah Winfrey Show*, Palin would further contend that her encounter with Couric "was supposed to be kind of lighthearted, fun working mom speaking with working mom and the challenges that we have with teenage daughters." It was another bold-faced lie. Sarah Palin was seeking the second-highest position in the land. Couric— whose extensive celebrity and résumé also posed a threat to Palin—was her second scheduled interview with the anchors. The first major segment of the interview was scheduled in front of the United Nations on a day that Palin was in New York City trying to beef up her foreign policy credentials with photo-op meetings with the likes of Henry Kissinger and President Hamid Karzai of Afghanistan. How and why Palin could contend the interview was supposed to be anything otherwise, said one McCain adviser, "is nothing less than ludicrous."

Wallace also issued a formal disclaimer. "We set up this interview on the day of the U.N. General Assembly with a walk-and-talk in front of the U.N.," Wallace asserted. "It was never made as two working gals. It's either rationalization or justification or fiction. That was supposed to be to highlight her foreign policy savvy. . . . The picture is in front of the U.N. to highlight her expertise and readiness to be Vice President—it wasn't about 'two working gals.'"

According to McCain advisers, the deep background to this story had nothing to do with Katie Couric or Nicolle Wallace and everything to do with Sarah Palin—her ego and eccentricities, her self-absorption and inability to see the bigger picture. She could never see beyond herself.

By the time of the Couric interviews—they were conducted during the week of September 21—Steve Schmidt had developed strong concerns about Palin. He saw her upside—an "innate ability" to connect with the base, as he would put it, that gave the GOP a significant post-convention surge—but he had also grown both wary and weary of her intellectual shortcomings and also of her capacity to lie and to deceive. He felt that she had made it through the Gibson interview relatively unscathed—"not an A," certainly, but no "significant damage" either—and he wanted her to engage in significant preparation in advance of her encounter with Couric.

Palin refused. She had already flung herself into combat mode with McCain

---

[†] Wallace issued a statement to *The Rachel Maddow Show* following the publication of *Going Rogue*.

"headquarters," as she dubbed it. She was focused on other matters. According to Schmidt, Palin "refused to prep for the Couric interview. She did not prepare for it." She had become obsessed with a series of fourteen questions presented by her hometown paper, the *Mat-Su Valley Frontiersman,* with a circulation of little more than six thousand. She willfully refused to focus on the interview and, instead, excoriated her staff for their handling of the newspaper's questions, to which she responded in great detail. (The following day, banner headlines in the paper triumphed "*Frontiersman* Exclusive: Palin Responds to Questions.")

Palin would also contend that CBS had edited the interviews in such a way as to make her look foolish and to distort her responses. "When I saw the final cut," Palin asserted, "it was clear that CBS sought out the bad moments, and systematically sliced out material that would accurately convey my message." If true, it wouldn't be the first time that a deft touch of an editor's hand had significantly altered an interview. But the fact of the matter is, the four most devastating moments in the Couric interviews—her inability to identify a single Supreme Court decision with which she disagreed; her failure to name a newspaper or magazine that she read; her sarcastic response of "I'll try to find you some and I'll bring 'em to ya," to Couric asking her for an example of McCain pushing for economic regulation in the Senate; and, perhaps most important, her bizarre series of non sequiturs in response to a question about the economy—are all clearly unedited, single-take responses. Palin looked alternately confused, angry, and disoriented throughout the interviews—the proverbial deer in the headlights—and many of the questions over which she tripped were softballs that any high school senior should have been able to answer. There wasn't a "gotcha" moment in the bunch.

What is fascinating about re-viewing the entirety of the Couric interviews is how direct and straightforward Couric remains throughout—at some points you feel her even trying to be helpful to Palin—and how uninformed, even childish, Palin appears in almost every question. At one point Palin breaks into a preadolescent response to a query about McCain's credibility on the economy—never one to be tripped over by facts, she defiantly declares, "I'm not looking at poll numbers." It is an embarrassment from beginning to end.

IN THE AFTERMATH OF THE INTERVIEWS AND THE CAMPAIGN, it has long been forgotten what Couric opened the series with: a question posed to Palin about McCain campaign manager Rick Davis's lobbying ties to Freddie

Mac and Fannie Mae. On Tuesday, September 23, *The New York Times* ran a front-page story detailing $15,000-per-month payments to Davis's lobbying firm, Davis Manafort, in which he remained "an equity holder." Couric opened up her questioning with a direct reference to the scandal.

> PALIN: My understanding is that Rick Davis recused himself from the dealings of the firm. I don't know how long ago, a year or two ago that he's not benefiting from that. And you know, I was—I would hope that's not the case.

> COURIC: But he still has a stake in the company, so isn't that a conflict of interest?

> PALIN: Again, my understanding is that he recused himself from the dealings with Freddie and Fannie, any lobbying efforts on his part there. And I would hope that's the case because, as John McCain has been saying, and as I've been on a much more local level been also rallying against is the undue influence of lobbyists in public policy decisions being made.

That much of McCain's campaign staff was composed of lobbyists—from Davis and Charlie Black on down—was a contradiction that Palin refused to address.

After that, Palin could never find solid footing with Couric. She refused to answer questions directly. She was evasive, combative, even hostile. She continued to look down, as if hoping to pull some answer from the ground. The most widely replayed—and satirized—answer by Palin was her response to a question posed by Couric on the $700 billion stimulus package then before Congress. The way Couric framed it should have been a perfect pitch for Palin's supposed populist sensibilities. Instead she butchered it. Palin's comments on the bailout are remarkable to read in their entirety. There's not a single jump cut in the response, and the transcript below is verbatim:

> PALIN: That's why I say I, like every American I'm speaking with, we're ill about this position that we have been put in where it is the taxpayers looking to bail out. But ultimately, what the bailout does *is* help those

who are concerned about the health-care reform that is needed to help shore up our economy, helping the . . . uh, oh, it's got to be all about job creation, too, shoring up our economy and putting it back on the right track. So health care reform and reducing taxes and reining in spending has got to accompany tax reductions and tax relief for Americans. And trade, we've got to see trade as opportunity, not as a competitive, um, scary thing. But one in five jobs being created in the trade sector today, we've got to look at that as more opportunity. All those things under the umbrella of job creation. This bailout is a part of that.

In Tina Fey's brilliant parody of Palin's ramblings on *Saturday Night Live*—she did not change a single word—one nevertheless loses the frantic, if not deranged, quality of Palin's response. In a blistering condemnation of Mc-Cain's vice presidential selection, conservative *Newsweek* columnist Fareed Zakaria described Palin's answer as "a vapid emptying out of every catch-phrase about economics that came into her head." CNN political analyst Jack Cafferty was even more direct. "If John McCain wins, this woman will be one seventy-two-year-old's heartbeat away from being president of the United States," Cafferty angrily declared, "and if that doesn't scare the hell out of you, it should." He characterized the CBS interview as "one of the most pathetic tapes I have ever seen from someone aspiring to one of the highest offices in this country." When Wolf Blitzer tried to temper Cafferty's candor by noting "she's cramming a lot of information—," Cafferty shot back: "There's no excuse for this. She's supposed to know a little bit of this. Don't make excuses for her; that's pathetic."

"It was not her best answer," Blitzer responded almost sheepishly. "I agree with you on that."

In fact, Palin's very next exchange was equally incongruous:

COURIC: If this doesn't pass, do you think there's a risk of another Great Depression?

PALIN: Unfortunately, that is the road that America may find itself on. Not necessarily this, as it's been proposed, has to pass or we're going to find ourselves in another Great Depression. But, there has got to be action—bipartisan effort—Congress not pointing fingers at one another but finding the solution to this, taking action, and being serious about the reforms on Wall Street that are needed.

The switch to foreign policy the following day did little to change either the tenor or content of Palin's performance. By then, Fey's other parody of Palin—"I can see Russia from my house"—had reached iconic status. That Palin had not said those words made no difference; her inference during the Gibson interview had stuck. Couric began a line of questioning that gave Palin the opportunity to make up for the gaffe with Gibson. Instead, she only dug herself a deeper hole.

COURIC: You've cited Alaska's proximity to Russia as part of your foreign policy experience. What did you mean by that?

PALIN: That Alaska has a very narrow maritime border between a foreign country, Russia, and, on our other side, the land boundary that we have with Canada. It's funny that a comment like that was kinda made to . . . I don't know, you know . . . reporters.

COURIC: Mocked?

PALIN: Yeah, mocked, I guess that's the word, yeah.

COURIC: Well, explain to me why that enhances your foreign policy credentials.

PALIN: Well, it certainly does, because our, our next-door neighbors are foreign countries, there in the state that I am the executive of. And there . . .

COURIC: Have you ever been involved in any negotiations, for example, with the Russians?

PALIN: We have trade missions back and forth, we do. It's very important when you consider even national security issues with Russia. As [Vladimir] Putin rears his head and comes into the airspace of the United

States of America, where do they go? It's Alaska. It's just right over the border. It is from Alaska that we send those out to make sure that an eye is being kept on this very powerful nation, Russia, because they are right there, they are right next to our state.

Those were hardly hardball questions. In fact they were more like Sunday afternoon lobs that would have been knocked out of the park by any seasoned politician. Certainly she had plenty of time to think about the Gibson gaffe and should have been ready with her response. Instead, Palin had the gall to contend that it was Couric who was unprepared for the interview. She claimed that there was "much Katie appeared not to know, or care to know about." Yet, as the sequence on Russia and Palin's foreign policy credentials clearly illustrate, Couric had gone out of her way to help a stumbling Palin find a word she couldn't retrieve and gave her every opportunity to present her foreign policy bona fides. Self-examination is not Palin's strong suit. Palin would continue to contend, in her memoirs and elsewhere, that one could indeed see Russia from Alaskan soil, though what foreign policy experience Palin had garnered from the proximity continued to go unarticulated in her interviews— and in her memoirs.

While Palin admitted that her performance in the Couric interviews "had let the team down," she never acknowledged that she had failed to prepare for them. She also included what she clearly thought was a damning cameo coming at the conclusion of one of the interview sessions: "As I walked away," Palin observed, "I glanced back and saw Nicolle and Katie share a friendly hug. Then they posed for pictures." Sarah Palin had been the victim of a *conspiracy*.

T HE RESPONSE TO THE COURIC interviews turned toxic. The concerns that had been aired about Palin's inexperience and capacities became magnified beyond belief. Palin and her supporters have long contended that the attacks on her were entirely "partisan" in nature, but, in fact, the biggest swing against her during the campaign came from Republicans. In what was perhaps the most devastating attack on Palin in the immediate aftermath of the Couric debacle, conservative *Washington Post* columnist Kathleen Parker— who would win the 2010 Pulitzer Prize for Commentary—wrote a scathing, if not downright shocking, screed entitled "The Palin Problem," in which she called for Palin to step down from the Republican ticket. It was a radical, nearly unimaginable proposal that reportedly generated more than eleven thousand responses to the *Post*.

Parker had been an early supporter of Palin's. She had charged Palin's feminist critics with supporting "only a certain kind of woman." Some of the "passionately feminist critics of Palin who attacked her personally" deserved some of the backlash they received, Parker argued, "but circumstances have changed since Palin was introduced as just a hockey mom with lipstick—what a difference a financial crisis makes—and a more complicated picture has emerged." Parker granted Palin her positives—an exciting narrative, "common sense," and "executive experience." Palin "didn't make a mess cracking the glass ceiling," Parker exuded. "She simply glided through it." But in the middle of a growing economic crisis, she argued that Palin's intellectual shortcomings could no longer be overlooked, and they had become plainly manifest during the Couric interviews, from which Parker quoted in her column:

> Palin filibusters. She repeats words, filling space with deadwood. Cut the verbiage, and there's not much content there. . . .
> If BS were currency, Palin could bail out Wall Street herself.

Parker concluded that there was only one option: for Palin to resign. She was dead serious. "McCain can't repudiate his choice of running mate," Parker observed strategically. "He not only risks the wrath of the GOP's unforgiving base, but he invites others to second-guess his executive decision-making ability." Only Palin, Parker argued, "can save McCain, her party and the country she loves. She can bow out for personal reasons, perhaps because she wants to spend more time with her newborn. No one would criticize a mother who puts her family first."

Parker then switched audiences and directed her final line exclusively at Palin: "Do it for your country."

The flood of conservative attacks against Palin continued. Just how many of them came from inside knowledge of the campaign or were simply the product of careful observation remains uncertain. But as the once promising days of September turned into the stretch run of October, they continued to escalate. Conservative *New York Times* columnist and senior editor at *The Weekly Standard,* David Brooks, who had earlier raised minimalist concerns about Palin substituting "a moral philosophy for a political philosophy," called Palin "a fatal cancer to the Republican Party." Christopher Buckley, son of William Buckley, said that "the thought of Sarah Palin as president gives me acid reflux," and he further contended that his late father "would have been appalled" by her candidacy. In an interview with *The New York Times,* former George W. Bush speechwriter David Frum, a frequent conservative voice on weekly television talk shows, said "I think [Palin] has pretty thoroughly—and probably irretrievably—proven that she is not up to the job of being president of the United States."

It was almost as if the conservatives were piling up on her. *Wall Street Journal* columnist and former Reagan speechwriter Peggy Noonan, an early critic of Palin's, amped up her attack a notch. "In the end," Noonan asserted, "the Palin candidacy is a symptom and expression of a new vulgarization in American politics. It's no good, not for conservatism and not for the country. And yes, it is a mark against John McCain, against his judgment and idealism."

Behind the scenes, those in the inner sanctums of the Bush White House— where McCain was always a dreaded figure anyway—were also dismissive of Palin. According to Heilemann and Halperin, none other than Vice President Dick Cheney had said that McCain made "a reckless choice" in selecting Palin. George W. Bush speechwriter, Matt Latimer, contended that President Bush himself had first thought that McCain had picked Pawlenty, and then when he realized it was Palin, whom he had met only briefly on a fueling stop in Anchorage, reportedly joked, "What is she, the governor of Guam?"

P ALIN REMAINED OBSESSED WITH HER reviews and bad press. In spite of admonitions to the contrary, she read everything that she could track down on either of her two BlackBerrys, and her husband, Todd, monitored everything about her on the Internet. Her emotions were riding on a roller coaster.

Schmidt, meanwhile, was concerned about getting Palin through her upcoming debate with Joe Biden. If Palin could pull off another performance like she had at the convention—if she could somehow capture the narrative and lure Biden into making some dreadful mistake—perhaps she could provide another game-change moment to the campaign. On the other hand, if Palin self-immolated as she did with Couric, the campaign would be buried by the debris. Game over.

Palin had gone into a deep funk in the aftermath of the Couric interviews and there was little sign that she was capable of pulling herself out. She had scorched her relationship with Nicolle Wallace—the two women reportedly had an over-the-phone shouting match prior to Palin's final tête-à-tête with Couric—and so Schmidt, for the debate preparation, was forced to assemble a new starting lineup, one that included, rather curiously, Wallace's husband, Mark, an attorney who had served in a variety of capacities in the Bush White House.

By then, Palin, as was often the case with any social configuration she encountered, had been a polarizing figure inside the McCain camp. Palin often split her world in two, partly because she can only see the world in black and white, and partly because she views people as either for her or against her. The McCain campaign had broken into competing factions. Those who had bonded with Palin included Randy Scheunemann, Steve Biegun, and Jason Recher. Those who were somehow cast in opposition to Palin included Schmidt, the Wallaces (who refused to bow to her various neuroses), and, to a lesser degree, the rest of the McCain team loyal to Schmidt.

The debate with Biden was scheduled for Thursday, October 2, at Washington University in St. Louis. Palin and her support team had gone to the upscale Philadelphia Westin Hotel to prepare her for the debate.

Back in Crystal City, Virginia, Schmidt was in dire search of an explanation for Palin's erratic and divisive behavior. He could not reach out to those who knew her well in Alaska for counsel (he couldn't risk word getting out about his concerns), so he was left to his own devices and his own perceptions of what psychic forces were at play in Palin's head. The persistent lying—or saying things "that were not accurate," as he would later phrase it—coupled with her periods of near catatonia had stretched his capacity for understanding. Some in the inner circle suspected that Palin was understandably suffering from acute child separation or, perhaps, postpartum depression. Others were certain she had suffered from nervous exhaustion from the pressure of the campaign and the devastating public humiliation of the Couric interviews. But there were others who simply suspected that she was "bat shit crazy," as one of her former staffers in Alaska called it, living in a fantasy world of her own.[‡]

The news Schmidt received out of Philadelphia was not promising. On Saturday, September 27, Mark Wallace had called headquarters to inform the triumvirate of Schmidt, Davis, and Salter that the scene at the Westin was an

---

[‡] Palin's mental state during the period is covered in *Game Change*, pages 396–400.

unqualified disaster. The prep was going nowhere. Palin was not eating, not drinking, not sleeping. The latest installment of the Couric interviews had destroyed the final thread of Palin's confidence. She had lost several pounds on her 5'4" frame in the recent weeks—perhaps as many as ten—and she was consuming, at most, a half-can of her beloved Diet Dr. Pepper daily.

Schmidt had hoped to call in Karen Hughes, his media-savvy friend from the George W. Bush White House who had been one of Bush's most trusted advisers, to perform the role of Joe Biden in the debate prep. She was a tough conservative woman—pro-life and openly patriotic—and he thought she might be someone Palin could look up to and who could help the faltering candidate focus. But once Schmidt caught wind of the scene in Philly, he knew that he could no longer bring in Hughes due to her close association with the Bush White House. Schmidt assessed that once Hughes fully grasped the gravity of the situation—and Palin's state of mind—she would have felt obligated to inform the president of the impending catastrophe. It put Schmidt in a sticky bind: he couldn't chance putting either Hughes or Bush in the untenable position of knowing what was really going on inside the McCain campaign. It was just this side of madness.

Schmidt and Davis took a train from Washington to Philadelphia. The situation was even worse than Schmidt imagined. The hotel room was dark and stuffy, and reeked of greasy junk food. The half-dozen or so staffers there, as well as Joe Lieberman, who had agreed to help with foreign policy issues, looked morose. Schmidt noticed Atkins energy bars strewn about the room and he was concerned that Palin was on some strange diet that accentuated her mental distress.

Schmidt cleared out the room and quickly assessed his candidate. She looked drawn and pale. She was still downward-looking, depressed, almost emaciated. Schmidt confronted Palin—gently but firmly—about her appearance and about her losing weight. He told her that she needed to sleep eight hours a day so that she got the proper rest that any national candidate needed. Moreover, she needed to get off the diet immediately, get off the Atkins bars, so that she was taking in enough nutrition for her brain to function properly. He talked about bringing in a nutritionist.

There were some matters, however, that Schmidt could not soft-pedal. He told her that the reason she had failed so miserably with the Couric interviews was because she had been woefully unprepared. That was not going to happen again. She was going to have to buck up and get her act together. He did not mince words. He said that even Ronald Reagan had made mistakes during interviews. She could turn everything around with a solid performance against Biden.

That weekend, Schmidt and company had been forced to sketch out the situation for McCain. It had been a delicate process with minimal details, but McCain got a sense of what was happening. He, of course, had survived five and half brutal years in Vietnam and was nearly through his second national campaign, so he was uniquely sensitive to the debilitating psychic pressures weighing down on Palin. In fact, Palin's situation brought out the best in McCain. He immediately suggested that they pack up camp and relocate to his high-desert getaway outside Sedona. Cindy could look out for Palin and she could bring in her family. The open air would do her good. She could run. She could breathe.

Schmidt informed Palin of the change in game plan. Palin took it all in and nodded in agreement. She had little fight left in her.

In *Going Rogue,* Palin's account of the scene in Philadelphia is strikingly antiseptic. The troubling ramifications of Palin's mood swings do not figure anywhere in her narrative. She blames the problems on Wallace's temper and attempts to force Palin to say things she didn't believe. It was the staffers who needed a new diet and fresh air, most of all Schmidt, whom she mocked for his beefy build and for smoking cigarettes. She attributed the idea of moving the debate prep out of Philadelphia to Cindy McCain, though she did not explain why or how that had happened. Indeed there's no explanation for moving the debate prep across country save for the stuffiness of the hotel room at the Westin.

"Fiction," Schmidt would say later of Palin's account. "Total fiction."

MARK MCKINNON, THE QUIRKY TEXAS DEMOCRAT–turned–Bush media strategist who had left John McCain's campaign in May when Obama secured the Democratic nomination (he had pledged to do so the year before), had a hard-earned reputation as both a calming influence on political candidates and as a message maven. McCain had dubbed him "almost a genius." Although it was largely unpublicized at the time, he had been brought to St. Paul a month earlier as a favor to help prepare Cindy McCain for her convention speech. In their moment of near desperation, the McCain team thought he might be a good match for Palin and was brought in to serve, in Todd Purdum's words, as her "horse whisperer" in the Arizona desert.

A great deal of lore has been generated about McKinnon's role in prepping Palin for the debate, when, in fact, his time in Arizona was limited to little more than three hours and he is reported to have responded "Oh . . . my . . . God," following his initial encounter with her. He later gave a more detailed rendition of his first impression. "She knew she was in trouble," he observed in an account he wrote for the *Daily Beast*. "She knew she wasn't prepared. And she knew it would be difficult, maybe impossible to be ready. And the brief session I witnessed, verified as much, and I was convinced the debate would be a disaster."

Palin's recovery in Arizona was much more gradual, much more drawn out, than she or the pundits would later claim, but McKinnon also saw that Palin had found some of her old fight at the McCain compound, some of the tenacity that had driven her to the national stage, and according to his depiction, Palin made it clear that she "was not, under any circumstances, going to let John McCain down."

People forget that Palin's initial foray on the campaign trail was really her first time out on her own. Her erratic collegiate career was marked by frequent retreats to Wasilla, and when she finally landed long enough to graduate from the University of Idaho, she had been close to friends and family there as well. Forget about never having a passport until only the year before, Palin never felt comfortable in Juneau—for that matter, even in Anchorage—and returned to Wasilla whenever she could. On her official junkets to the Lower 48, Palin mostly hunkered down in her hotel rooms or hung by the pool with her aide and friend Kris Perry. She showed little interest in the world outside of her hotels, conference sites or scheduled tours. Gary Wheeler, Palin's director of security who had been born and raised in Alaska, traveled with Palin on several out-of-state trips, including those to Washington, D.C., Southern California, and even to Deadwood, South Dakota, for a meeting of the Western Governors Association in June 2007, and said of Palin, "The only thing she wanted to do was shop. She wanted us to take her to the mall." Wheeler noted that while she liked to get up and take a jog—usually by herself—she rarely engaged locals in discussions about their communities. "She was pleasant and polite, but not really talkative," he said. "She wasn't especially interested in exploring local history sites or museums or even local politics. She often seemed more interested in her two BlackBerrys when talking to other people, to the point of being rude at times." Some conversations with Palin, he said, "were a bit like to talking to a wall."

Troopers didn't necessarily like drawing the Palin detail. If they talked too much or tried to engage her, she would often report them to her superiors. "Working with the governor was a bit like being a cat on a hot stove," says Wheeler, a well-liked twenty-six-year veteran of the Troopers who worked under several administrations, both Republicans and Democrats. "You never knew when you were going to get burned." According to Wheeler, she once complained that a detail assigned to her chatted too much in the car. "She really wasn't interested in other people," Wheeler says. As for personally exploring communities to which she traveled, "never, not once," he recalled. "She seemed completely uninterested." Palin had never really walked the streets of urban America on her own—anywhere—and had never driven across the continent in search of her country. In addition to the horrible onslaught against her and her family on the campaign—and one can probably never fully imagine how horrifying that crush was—it is possible that she was experiencing a very real culture shock on her first real and extended journey Outside as a fully mature adult.

The decision to move the debate prep proved to be a wise one. Those who believed that Palin suffered something of a breakdown in the aftermath of the Couric interviews saw her slowly come back to life. She was surrounded by family and was able to go off on jogs along dirt roads through the high desert. She seemed revived.

It was while in Arizona that Palin bonded significantly with Randy Scheunemann, yet another controversial lobbyist attached to the McCain campaign (his firm, Orion Strategies, had represented the governments of Macedonia, Georgia, and Taiwan since 2003), who had been paid more than $56,000 in the second quarter of 2008 serving as McCain's top foreign policy officer. Scheunemann, who often mixed foreign policy advocacy with generating personal income, served as founder of the Committee for the Liberation of Iraq and had played a significant role in advocating for the U.S. invasion of that nation since the 1990s. More significantly, he had lobbied McCain's office on behalf of Georgia as recently as the fall of 2007 and reportedly introduced the senator to the foreign ministers of Albania, Croatia, and Macedonia as they tried to win admission to NATO. He and his pal, Bill Kristol, both served on the neoconservative Project for a New American Century.

According to New York Times reporters Elisabeth Bumiller and Larry Rohter, many members of the GOP's "realist" or "pragmatic" foreign policy wing of the party—one that included Colin Powell, Brent Scowcroft, George Shultz, James Baker, and even Henry Kissinger—had privately expressed concerns about the neocon Scheunemann's role in the campaign. As Palin prepped in the debate, she likely knew none of those details about Scheunemann and none of the controversies. The bulky and bearded Scheunemann was comically playing Joe Biden in the practice debates, and he provided a friendly, supportive face amid the varied antagonisms of the campaign. "They hit it off famously," said one McCain adviser. Scheunemann, rather than McKinnon, proved to be Palin's true horse whisperer.

Following her practice sessions in the afternoon, Palin would break out on a jog with the Secret Service following close behind. On one of her runs, she took a header and severely scraped the palm of her right hand while breaking her fall. In both an interview with *Runner's World* and also in *Going Rogue,* Palin concocted a story that the fall was top secret. She claimed that she made the Secret Service agents "swear to secrecy" about her accident and added that she had "great respect" for them keeping silent about it months later. That was another of Palin's oddly fabricated scenarios: there were AFP/Getty photos of her bandaged hand sent out over the wires the following day with the caption describing her injury "as a result of falling while jogging." Wolf Blitzer even mentioned it on CNN. A secret it was not.

O NE SMALL VERBAL TIC THAT Palin couldn't seem to shed in the high desert was her constant reference to her vice presidential opponent as "O'Biden." In all of the practice debates, she kept tripping over it. Finally it was suggested that she simply call Biden "Joe." It worked.

In the lead-up to the debate, there was a newfound confidence in Palin by the McCain team that she could probably hold her own. She had done well in the practice rounds, at one point earning an ovation for her work. She had clearly climbed back from the abyss. Those who thought that Biden was going to dice up Palin in the debate were in for a surprise. Biden himself was prone to verbal gaffes and long-windedness. There were concerns that he would appear condescending against Palin or overly confident. He had his own challenges during his prep for the debate (in which Jennifer Granholm, the then-governor of Michigan, had stood in for Palin) trying to establish the proper tone. It was also his debate to lose. He was an odds-on favorite. Nobody gave Palin a shot.

Right before the debate, staged at Washington University's athletic complex, Palin and her senior staff joined together in a side room before Palin was to take the stage. Palin's always present companion, Kris Perry from Alaska, walked into the room and declared in a roaring voice: "Be still in the presence of the Lord!" Palin bowed her head (later she would complain that she had no one to pray with at that moment) but the force and over-the-top nature of Perry's order was unsettling to some of the McCain staff present, who hurried out of the room.

The vice presidential debate—watched by an estimated 70 million viewers—turned out to be more of a sparring match than a bare-knuckled brawl. While Palin held her own, she did manage to unleash some of what Maureen Dowd of *The New York Times* called her "homespun haikus" on Biden. When asked about the use of nuclear weapons, Palin responded: "Nuclear weaponry, of course, would be the be all, end all of just too many people in too many parts of our planet, so those dangerous regimes, again, cannot be allowed to acquire nuclear weapons, period." ("Mostly the end-all," as Dowd wryly observed.) And then she committed what Dowd dubbed a "dizzying verbal loop-de-loop" in an answer to a question about energy issues and climate change:

> We have got to encourage other nations also to come along with us with the impacts of climate change, what we can do about that.
>
> As governor, I was the first governor to form a climate change sub-cabinet to start dealing with the impacts.

She winked her way through other challenging questions—literally—and at one point stated in response to a follow-up query about McCain's position on health care reform, "I may not answer the questions that either the moderator or you want to hear, but I'm going to talk straight to the American people and let them know my track record, also." It was a canned line and she went on to deliver another self-promoting haiku.

While most commentators had scored the contest for Biden—his emotional reference to his daughter's and first wife's deaths in a car crash provided the one truly memorable moment—the GOP was also claiming victory. For Palin it had been a personal triumph—she had just held her own against a thirty-eight-year veteran of the U.S. Senate and one of Washington's most celebrated "good ol' boys." She was nearly giddy with excitement. Palin was through her last formal test of the campaign. She put the Gibson and Couric disasters behind her, and set herself on a new course. No more studying, no more index cards. She told Bill Kristol that she found the debate "liberating." She was now free of Schmidt and all the other senior advisers at McCain headquarters. Sarah Palin was unshackled.

Palin celebrated the aftermath of the debate by popping a bottle of champagne with campaign aides in a suite at the Four Seasons Hotel overlooking the Mississippi River. It was there that she reportedly first brought up the idea of attacking Obama's controversial former preacher, Jeremiah Wright. Mc-Cain had expressly forbidden bringing up Wright because he didn't want to be accused of playing the race card. It was a sensitive issue for McCain and he remained adamant in his position. Palin persisted. It was all about winning the election, she asserted eagerly, let's take it to them. According to Scott Conroy and Shushannah Walshe, Palin also blurted out: "I just don't want to go back to Alaska."

The following morning, an article appeared in *The New York Times* that carefully chronicled the slim relationship between Barack Obama and William C. "Bill" Ayers, a former member of the Weather Underground and presently distinguished professor of education at the University of Illinois, Chicago. The *Times* reported that their paths had "crossed sporadically" in recent years and noted that Obama had described Ayers as "somebody who engaged in detestable acts 40 years ago, when I was 8." The right-wing blogosphere had been on fire with reports about the Obama and Ayers friendship, attempting to portray Obama as a secret radical hell-bent on destroying the country and Western world. Television ads had been prepared by fringe Republican organizations hyping the connection. Palin wanted to play up the relationship on the campaign trail. Although it was originally claimed otherwise, e-mails between Palin and staff confirm that she was granted permission to do so as long as her comments stuck to a script based on the *Times* story. "The gloves are off," she declared, "and the heels are on."

At her ensuing campaign stop in Englewood, Colorado, before a group of private donors, Palin went on the attack. "Our opponent . . . is someone who sees America, it seems, as being so imperfect, imperfect enough, that he's pal-lin' around with terrorists who would target their own country," she declared. "This is not a man who sees America as you see America and as I see America."

The tenor of the national debate had shifted significantly toward the angry. It didn't take a weatherman to know which way the wind was blowing. Doug-lass K. Daniel, an editor of the Associated Press's Washington Bureau, wrote a scathing indictment of Palin's new attack entitled "Palin's Words Carry Racist Tinge." Palin, Daniel asserted, was trying to fire up "a faltering campaign"—and charged that she had crossed the line with "a racially tinged subtext." Palin's inflammatory rhetoric, Daniel declared, avoids "repulsing voters with overt racism. But is there another subtext for creating the false image of a black presidential nominee 'palling around' with terrorists while assuring a predominantly white audience that he doesn't see their America?" Daniel did not hold back. "Whether intended or not by the McCain campaign," he concluded, "portraying Obama as 'not like us' is another potential appeal to racism."

Palin was tapping into a largely unarticulated and visceral opposition that had developed nationally—mostly in white enclaves—against the idea of an Obama presidency. How much of it was fueled by racism was uncertain, but Palin's code words most certainly tossed fuel on the sizzling inferno. She had become the embodiment of the anti-Obama sentiment sweeping across parts of the country.

Georgia congressman John Lewis—a seminal figure in the civil rights movement and a longtime congressional colleague of McCain's—was outraged by the emerging currents of the campaign. Only a few months earlier, McCain had identified Lewis as one of the "three wisest men" he would consult during a time of crisis. He had also singled out Lewis in his book *Why Courage Matters* (written with Salter). "John Lewis was one of the bravest of those who stayed true to the faith," McCain had written. "They couldn't scare the courage out of him."

Lewis had no delusions about the increasingly hostile rhetoric being leveled at Obama. "What I am seeing reminds me too much of another destructive period in American history," Lewis declared in a statement he released in *Politico*'s Arena forum. "Sen. McCain and Gov. Palin are sowing the seeds of hatred and division, and there is no need for this hostility in our political discourse."

Lewis drew similarities to George Wallace, the segregationist governor of Alabama during the height of racial unrest in the South. "George Wallace never threw a bomb," Lewis asserted. "He never fired a gun, but he created the climate and the conditions that encouraged vicious attacks against innocent Americans who were simply trying to exercise their constitutional rights. Because of this atmosphere of hate, four little girls were killed on a Sunday morning when a church was bombed in Birmingham, Alabama." Lewis's charges were clear and unequivocal. They were more than a pushback; they were a challenge. He accused the Republican candidates for the highest offices in the land of "playing with fire," a fire he declared that "will consume us all."

McCain responded with indignation. He described Lewis's remarks "as a brazen and baseless attack on my character and the character of the thousands of hardworking Americans who come to our events to cheer for the kind of reform that will put America on the right track." He called upon Obama "to immediately and personally repudiate these outrageous and divisive comments." What was fascinating about McCain's response is that he made no defense of Palin.

Bill Burton, Barack Obama's national press secretary during the presidential campaign, was selected to issue a response. "Senator Obama does not believe that John McCain or his policy criticism is in any way comparable to George Wallace or his segregationist policies," he said. "But John Lewis was right to condemn some of the hateful rhetoric that John McCain himself personally rebuked just last night, as well as the baseless and profoundly irresponsible charges from his own running mate that the Democratic nominee for President of the United States 'pals around with terrorists.'" The message from Obama and the Democrats to McCain was clear and direct: Sarah Palin was out of control.

CHAPTER 5

Rogue

At some point, the McCain campaign will realize that their veep candidate is a couple of sandwiches short of a picnic.
—Andrew Sullivan, *The Atlantic*

And now that the debate is over, and also—you know, yes, I kind of feel like, all right. The wings are flying here. Let's soar, let's get out there and speak to voters and let them know what their choices are. And I'm excited about this opportunity in this last month.
—Sarah Palin, in an interview with
Carl Cameron of Fox News

I don't believe she's ready to be president of the United States, which is the job of the vice president. And so that raised some question in my mind as to the judgment that Senator McCain made.
—Colin Powell, former chairman Joint Chiefs of Staff, on CNN

ON SUNDAY, OCTOBER 5, WITH LESS THAN A month to go until Election Day, readers of *The New York Times* were greeted with an opinion piece by Bill Kristol entitled "The Wright Stuff." Kristol—who had come north to meet Palin little more than a year earlier and had fawned over Palin that summer as his "heartthrob"—had conducted a lengthy telephone interview with her that may have seemed relatively innocuous to the general readership, but to those inside the McCain campaign, it was nothing less than an outrage.

Forget about upsetting Schmidt and the Wallaces—Palin had betrayed her running mate, John McCain, at his very core. For all her posturing about "respecting" and "honoring" McCain, in her interview with Kristol she was insubordinate and shamelessly disloyal to the man who had selected her. There is no other way to put it. Country first? Hardly. It was always—and only—about Sarah Palin.

In his column, Kristol acknowledged having met Palin in Alaska the previous summer. This had been the first time, he asserted, that he had spoken to her since. He described her as "confident and upbeat"—she indicated that she wanted to challenge Biden to another debate (Kristol absurdly volunteered to moderate it). He rolled out some hockey mom bathos and then, finally, cut to the chase. Palin, he revealed, had "made clear—without being willing to flat out say so—that she regretted allowing herself to be overly handled and constrained after the Republican convention." She was attacking her own campaign and her own senior strategists, but her political apostasy did not stop there. Her remarks would soon border on mutiny.

Kristol noted that Palin had gone after Bill Ayers that weekend in Colorado and that she was eager "for the McCain-Palin campaign to be more aggressive in helping the American people understand 'who the real Barack Obama is.'" Kristol, who would last only a year as a *Times* columnist before he was dumped unceremoniously in January of 2009 (Scott Horton of the *Daily Beast* reported that it was because of "sloppiness and uneven quality"), then brought up the issue of Jeremiah Wright, Obama's longtime pastor of Trinity United Church of Christ in Chicago.

Palin most assuredly knew McCain's position on Wright. He had made it abundantly clear throughout the campaign. His senior advisers had also made it clear. In an interview with Sean Hannity earlier in the year, McCain commented on Obama's relationship with the controversial pastor. "Obviously, those words and those statements are statements that none of us would associate ourselves with," McCain said very somberly and deliberately. "And I don't believe that Senator Obama would support any of those. . . . I do know Senator Obama. He does not share those views." McCain himself had been the victim of racially charged accusations by the George W. Bush campaign during the 2000 campaign in South Carolina. He did not want his campaign to be associated with anything that smacked of racism. There had been no changing his mind. Palin, however, in addressing the issue with Kristol, didn't hesitate to undermine McCain's authority, openly and brazenly:

To tell you the truth, Bill, I don't know why that association isn't discussed more, because those were appalling things that that pastor had said about our great country, and to have sat in the pews for 20 years and listened to that—with, I don't know, a sense of condoning it, I guess, because he didn't get up and leave—to me, that does say something about character. But, you know, I guess that would be a John McCain call on whether he wants to bring that up.

Palin was brashly confronting the top of the ticket and airing the campaign's laundry in the national press. She was asked if she had any advice for McCain. Once again, she didn't hesitate providing a response: "Take off the gloves."

McCain's senior advisers were livid by Palin's open taunting of the campaign hierarchy. McCain could not have been happy either. He may have lacked discipline, but he was loyal to his core values and to his senior staff. Palin had clearly gone off the reservation. In *Going Rogue,* Palin is utterly absent of remorse about her behavior. She admits that she was told "not to discuss Obama's pastor of twenty years, Jeremiah 'God Damn America' Wright." And then she betrayed McCain again. She said that she will "forever question the campaign" for imposing a sanction on such discussions, without acknowledging that the directive came straight from McCain himself.

I T WAS ONLY TO GET WORSE. On the same day as the Biden debate, the McCain staff had made the decision to abandon Michigan as part of its national electoral vote strategy. It had been a tough determination wrought with some internal strife. Michigan had been a blue-state target for McCain, a so-called pickup in the parlance of national party strategists. The McCain advisers thought they might be able to make a move on Obama there. Obama did not resonate particularly well with working-class voters and he had withdrawn from Michigan's problematic Democratic primary, giving Clinton an easy victory. But in the days after the country's financial collapse and McCain's haphazard response (along with Palin's devastating performance in the Couric interviews), the poll numbers in Michigan had shifted dramatically in Obama's favor. In one poll, a virtual dead heat had shifted to a ten-point Obama edge. On September 25, the highly regarded polling firm Selzer & Company reported Obama's lead at 51–38. By the end of the month (when the decision was finalized), the *Detroit Free Press* poll had Obama with a sixteen-point lead (precisely the margin by which Obama-Biden eventually won). The Wolverine State had moved out of reach.

Given the GOP's limited resources and an Electoral College strategy that was absolutely dependent on Ohio, Wisconsin, Pennsylvania, and Florida, it was incumbent upon the McCain campaign to focus its energies and resources on must-win states. They could no longer work the fringe. Palin was apparently oblivious to such a strategy. Her mantra of "every vote matters," which she repeated time and time again in respect to the Michigan pullout, indicated that she had little grasp of basic presidential campaign strategy. Once again, it was only about her.

In an interview with Carl Cameron of Fox News, conducted with the St. Louis Gateway Arch framed directly behind her, Palin publicly challenged the McCain campaign's decision to pull resources out of Michigan. "Do we haveta?" she said to Cameron, returning to her emphasized Wasilla drawl. "Do we haveta call it there?"

> Todd and I would be happy to get to Michigan and walk through those plants of the car manufacturers. We'd be so happy to get to speak with the people there in Michigan, who are hurtin' because the economy is hurtin'. Whatever we can do and whatever Todd and I can do in realizing what their challenges in that state are, as we can relate to them and connect with them and promise them that we won't let 'em down in the administration. I want to get back to Michigan and I want to try.

This was the moment that McCain advisers would identify later as Palin "going rogue." She was openly challenging campaign strategy in front of the national media. In a post-election interview she gave to Oprah Winfrey at the time of her book release, Palin would assert that she was caught off guard by the Cameron question, and that she hadn't known about the Michigan decision in advance of the interview.

WINFREY: Didn't several times they say to you when actually you mentioned, when you were talking about pulling out of Michigan and you said I wished we'd stayed in Michigan. Weren't you told then, Sarah just stay on script?

PALIN: Right, *told afterwards* and that, that was always puzzling to me because if I were to respond to a reporter's questions very candidly, honestly, for instance, they say, "what do you think about the campaign pulling out of Michigan" and I think, "darn I wish we weren't. Every vote matters, I can't wait to get back to Michigan" and then told afterwards that, "oh, you screwed up. You went rogue on us Sarah, you're not supposed to be." And my reminder to the campaign was, *I didn't know we pulled out of Michigan.* My entire VP team, we didn't know that we had pulled out. I'm sorry, I apologize, but speaking candidly to a reporter.

In *Going Rogue* itself, Palin gives pretty much the same explanation. She says that no one had told her about the Michigan strategy and that she had been "caught a bit off guard." She says that she "answered truthfully" when claiming to have first learned about the decision from a newspaper story.

Palin's rendition of events in respect to the Michigan decision reveals a fascinating glimpse into her psyche. Palin is the victim. She is caught "off guard." Her reference to having "answered truthfully" is an indication in and of itself that perhaps she is being less than candid. In fact, when Cameron brought up the Michigan decision to Palin, she had prefaced her remarks with: "Well, that's *not a surprise* because the polls are showing we're not doing as well there, evidently, as we would like to. But, I read that this morning also. *I fired a quick e-mail and said, oh, come on.*"

Palin clearly had known about the Michigan decision *before* her interview with Cameron and had been in contact with McCain senior advisers before it as well. (Palin never mentioned that portion of the Cameron interview in *Going Rogue* or with Winfrey.) The e-mail trail tells the story. "If there's any time, Todd and I would love a quick return to Michigan—we'd tour the plants, etc.," Palin wrote. "If it does McC any good. I know you have a plan, but I hate to see us leave Michigan. We'll do whatever we had to do there to give it a 2nd effort."

The response from the McCain command post was direct: "Michigan is out of reach unless something drastic happens. We must win [Ohio] and hopefully [Pennsylvania]." Palin replied that she "got it." Obviously she hadn't—though she would go to great lengths to lie about it in the months ahead.

But that wasn't the end of it. Immediately after the Cameron interview, Palin knew that she had gone too far. "Oops," she wrote in the cutesy way of hers when she was trying to avoid disapprobation. "I mentioned something about [Michigan] to Carl Cameron and it's now recorded that I'd love to give Michigan something of the ol' college try."

Palin couldn't let Michigan go. Some have speculated that she was thinking about 2012 already, that it had nothing to do with the election at hand. Republicans in Michigan were also upset about the decision (while Obama's senior advisers were ecstatic). She more than likely had encouragement from her own staff and regional GOP officials to reverse course. But McCain headquarters remained adamant. In what was a persistent pattern of Palin's after the Biden debate, she would not take no for an answer. She would ask the same thing several times of different staff, hoping to find someone who would momentarily let their guard down and cave to her willpower. "It's a cheap 4hr drive from [Wisconsin]," she e-mailed again. "I will pay for the gas." She continued to badger headquarters, much to the growing perturbation of Schmidt. When the reasoning was explained to her yet again and she was told to cease and desist, she replied with what had become her campaign meme: "I know what I know what I know."

Palin had become addicted to the emotional high of the rope lines where her adoring fans had come to greet her. She had felt the love in Michigan on two separate swings through the state and was ready for the encore adrenaline rush. She reportedly concocted a plan of commandeering the campaign bus at night and having either Jay Leno or David Letterman report on her clandestine sojourn as she crossed the state line. The idea was comical—and showed the power of Palin's capacity for self-promotion—but it exacerbated tensions between the Palin bus and McCain headquarters in Virginia. According to Conroy and Walshe, "Rick Davis was so concerned about the possibility that the governor would ignore orders and travel to Michigan on her own that he attempted to order Secret Service agents to prevent it."*

B ACK IN ALASKA, PALIN'S STAR WAS FALLING back toward earth. Her approval ratings had tumbled precipitously, as she embarrassed many Alaskans with her erratic performance on the campaign trail. For some, it was her hubris and arrogance in the face of her disastrous performances with Gibson

---

* Scott Conroy and Shushannah Walshe, *Sarah from Alaska: The Sudden Rise and Brutal Education of a New Conservative Superstar* (New York: Public Affairs, 2009), pp. 151–53.

and Couric. For others, it was her bitter attacks on Obama. She was coming across as a right-wing hack in a state that much preferred substance over ideology.

On the streets of Anchorage, there was another political battle being waged, far from the national spotlight. McCain headquarters sent in a full-force ensemble of attorneys and political operatives to Alaska—dubbed the "Truth Squad"—who essentially conducted the vetting of Palin that hadn't been undertaken prior to her nomination. Led by New York lawyer Ed O'Callaghan and former Palin administration spokesperson Meghan Stapleton (working in conjunction with Palin's attorney Thomas Van Flein), the Truth Squad held a series of press conferences throughout the early days of the campaign castigating the Troopergate investigation. To many in southwest Alaska, the Truth Squad had the feel of an occupying military force.

All told there were eventually more than fifty honorary members named to the Truth Squad, most of them women who held public office or who served as party operatives in swing states critical to a GOP victory. The Squad—broken into "state" and "national" membership—included congresswomen Michele Bachmann of Minnesota, Shelley Moore Capito of West Virginia, and Virginia Foxx of North Carolina. The national squad also included Palin's political crony from Wasilla, Kristan Cole. But the public face of the Truth Squad was assumed by O'Callaghan and Stapleton.

O'Callaghan and Stapleton made for an interesting pair. O'Callaghan, an alumnus of Georgetown University and the New York University School of Law, spent nearly a decade as an assistant United States attorney for the Southern District of New York. The last three years of his government service were spent as co-chief of the Terrorism and National Security Unit. He was tough and reeked of the East Coast—an outsider where outsiders are always suspect. He openly acknowledged that he was advising Palin's private attorney Van Flein and there were many who suspected that he was advising Attorney General Talis Colberg behind the scenes as well. Stapleton, on the other hand, was something of a beloved figure in southwest Alaska. A native of Auburn, New York, where her father is a prominent attorney, Stapleton also completed her undergraduate degree at Georgetown, during which time she served as a speechwriter for the Republican National Committee. She then earned a master's in broadcast journalism at Syracuse before following her dreams west to serve as an on-air television reporter in Anchorage. Stapleton had ingratiated herself to her new Alaskan audience with a series of heartfelt personality profiles and had once been knocked over by a reindeer while she was wearing a Santa suit, all on camera. But there was another side to her persona that Alaskans had not seen. In an interview with the *Alaska Journal of Commerce* she once said that the word that described her best was "tenacious," and close associates said that she privately entertained political ambitions of her own. Now, on a daily basis in Anchorage, O'Callaghan and Stapleton were playing bad cops to each other. They now dubbed her Meg "Staplegun" or "Stapletongue" or simply "Meg the Mouth."

"The Truth Squad Days were dark," says *The Mudflats'* Jeanne Devon. "It was personal. Alaskans are so protective of our state. We're almost like an island nation and the feeling of McCain 'outsiders' arriving in the night and literally taking over the Department of Law was very disconcerting." Devon likened the arrival of the squad to that of "an invasion from a foreign power—a bloodless coup." What was particularly troubling to many Alaskans, Devon added, was seeing the once popular journalist Stapleton "standing shoulder to shoulder with Ed O'Callaghan and publicly eviscerating Walt Monegan, Hollis French, Les Gara, Kim Elton, and other respected public servants. It felt like a betrayal. It was like watching family members getting flogged on TV. It was painful." Devon's pal Shannyn Moore likened the Truth Squad members to "national political assassins" invading Alaska. "The McCain-Palin ticket," she wryly observed, "has become a poster child for partisan politics on steroids."

During what would become a notorious moment in Alaska street theater, several television crews captured an intense and impromptu confrontation on the streets of Anchorage between Stapleton and Democratic legislator Les Gara on West 4th Avenue, just outside the Alaska legislative offices. With cameras circling around them, Gara asked Stapleton if she was going to apologize to Walt Monegan for the attacks made by her and O'Callaghan during the campaign. After several minutes of back-and-forth bantering, during which it became clear that Stapleton would refuse to issue any such apologies, Gara cut to the chase. "You don't have to apologize to people," he noted. "You get to insult them. You don't have to apologize to them—"

Stapleton interrupted Gara. "It is unfortunate," she asserted, "that some are perceiving it as anything but laying out the facts . . ."

Gara was not biting into her spin. "I think you should probably take a look at the videos," he asserted. "I think you should take a look at the three times a week press conferences. I think you should take a look at the pictures you put on TV. . . . The little fake thing you did to try to tell people in the Lower 48 that Republican prosecutor Steve Branchflower was somehow a Democrat."

Stapleton then put on a feigned look of being aghast at Gara's accusations. There were more interruptions. "You know why they hired Steve Branchflower,"

Gara responded, amazingly able to keep his cool. "Because Branchflower had issued the only public report which was critical of Walt Monegan. So they hired him knowing that they had a guy who couldn't be accused of being biased by anybody *other than you*, actually."

The video of the Gara-Stapleton exchange symbolized to Alaskans across the political spectrum the dark side of Palin's national candidacy. The Truth Squad had left a sour taste in the mouth in the Last Frontier. Gara, for his part, would charge the Truth Squad with "witness tampering" in the Troopergate investigation. "Until McCain campaign staffers flew to Alaska to stop this investigation," Gara said, "the governor and her staff agreed to comply with what we all know is a bipartisan investigation. After August 29, the campaign started working to block this investigation, and witnesses began joining that effort by ignoring their subpoenas and risking jail time. Something obviously changed the minds of these witnesses."

The event that had precipitated the Gara-Stapleton tête-à-tête was the formal release of the Legislative Council's investigative findings on Palin—known popularly as the Branchflower Report. The Truth Squad was trying to spin the report as partisan and undertaken by a Democratic Party conspiracy to smear Palin. It was anything but. By a *bipartisan* and *unanimous* 12–0 vote—eight *Republicans* and four Democrats—the Alaska Legislative Council agreed to make the report public. There were four different findings included in the report, but the first was the one that hit home: Branchflower found "that Governor Sarah Palin *abused her power* by violating Alaska Statute 39.52.110(a) of the Alaska Executive Branch Ethics Act." (Emphasis added.)

It was a clear and unambiguous violation of the Ethics Act. Branchflower found that Palin had abused her power in her concerted efforts, along with her husband and staff, to have Walt Monegan fire Palin's former brother-in-law, Alaska State Trooper Mike Wooten. The report further found that in respect to her husband, Todd Palin, that "[Governor] Palin knowingly permitted a situation to continue where impermissible pressure was placed on several subordinates in order to advance a personal agenda." Branchflower exonerated Palin for the actual firing of Monegan, which he viewed as "a proper and lawful exercise of her constitutional and statutory authority to hire and fire executive branch department heads." He further found that Wooten's workers' compensation case had been handled properly by the privately owned contracted agency engaged to do so. But he also sent a stinging rebuke to the attorney general's office for failing to comply with Branchflower's requests for e-mails related to the case.

Palin's response to the findings was nothing less than bizarre. Outside a convenience store in Altoona, Pennsylvania, she claimed that Branchflower had completely exonerated her. "There was no abuse of authority at all in trying to get Officer Wooten fired," she told a gaggle of news media standing outside an idling McCain campaign bus. "Thankfully the truth was revealed there in that report that showed there was no unlawful or unethical activity on my part." When pressed by NBC's Matthew Berger with a direct question about abusing her power, Palin responded, "No, and if you read the report you'll see that there was nothing unlawful or unethical about replacing a cabinet member. You gotta read the report, sir."

The following day, Palin conducted a telephonic press conference—moderated by Stapleton no less—with a trio of Alaska news outlets, the *Anchorage Daily News* and two television stations, KTVA-Channel 11 and KTUU-Channel 2, both in Anchorage. In what was a shameful bit of homegirl posturing, Palin tried to butter up the Alaska reporters, declaring at the outset, "Even hearing your names makes me feel like I'm right there with you at home." She said that "I'm very very pleased to be cleared of any legal wrongdoing, any hint of any kind of unethical activity there. Very pleased to be cleared of any of that." Lisa Demer of the *ADN* pressed Palin by noting that the first finding of the Branchflower Report asserted "that you abused your power by violating state law" and asked Palin directly if she felt like she did "anything wrong at all in this Troopergate case?" Palin broke into more of her classic double-speak constructions.

> Not at all and I'll tell you, it, I think that you're always going to ruffle feathers as you do what you believe is in the best interest of the people whom you are serving. In this case I knew that I had to have the right people in the right position at the right time in this cabinet to best serve Alaskans, and Walt Monegan was not the right person at the right time to meet the goals that we had set out in our administration. So no, not having done anything wrong, and again very much appreciating being cleared of any legal wrongdoing or unethical activity at all.

Whatever hometown advantage Palin might have expected from the Alaska media was not forthcoming. People in Alaska across the political spectrum had been appalled by the behavior of the Truth Squad and were fully aware that Palin had been found guilty of "abuse of power" by Branchflower. The *Anchorage Daily News* came down hard on her. In a blistering editorial entitled "Palin Vindicated? Governor Offered Orwellian Spin," the paper declared that Palin's reaction was "an embarrassment to Alaskans and the nation." It characterized Palin's response as "the kind of political 'big lie' that George Orwell warned against. War is peace. Black is white. Up is down." Palin was either "astoundingly ignorant" or a liar. "You asked us to hold you accountable, Gov. Palin," the editorial concluded. "Did you mean it?"

Ironically, the *Daily News* suggested that Palin's duplicitous response may have been concocted by "McCain campaign spinmeisters." It had not. In fact, the campaign had crafted a carefully textured response to the findings that acknowledged the abuse of power charges while focusing on the exoneration regarding Monegan's firing. Palin once again refused to adhere to the script. Palin's palpably deceitful response to the Branchflower Report proved to be yet another headache for Schmidt and his colleagues. It gave the story two more days of play—and more negative spin—than it otherwise might have had in the rapidly transitioning 24/7 news cycle. Even worse, the story provided concrete evidence of Palin's persistent challenges with the truth. She was being dubbed Orwellian even in her hometown newspaper. Much to Schmidt's chagrin, the cement of that particular narrative was starting to settle.

By mid-October, Palin and her coterie were engaged in an ongoing rebellion with McCain campaign headquarters—and the McCain hierarchy was in no mood to coddle them any longer. There was relentless pushback both ways. Palin was full of herself, albeit on edge, feeling that the election was now about her, about her political future and, perhaps, 2012. The conflict between the two camps threatened to explode into open warfare at any moment.

Precisely a week after his first column publicizing Palin's dissension about the Jeremiah Wright strategy, Kristol was at it again, with a singularly off-the-wall commentary containing the opening salvo, "It's time for John McCain to fire his campaign." Kristol was clearly privy to some inside information from McCain staffers. That a major Republican figure should be writing such a column in *The New York Times* during the final weeks of a national campaign was nothing less than extraordinary. "The McCain campaign, once merely problematic, is now close to being out-and-out dysfunctional," Kristol proffered. "Its combination of strategic incoherence and operational incompetence has become toxic." Kristol's solution? McCain and Palin should run as "cheerful, open and accessible" candidates. "The two of them are attractive and competent politicians," Kristol concluded. "They're happy warriors and good campaigners. Set them free."

Kristol appeared to be doing someone's bidding inside the campaign—it was a direct volley at Schmidt—and given Kristol's own formal role in the McCain campaign (as a foreign-policy adviser), he was seriously crossing the line in respect to both conflict of interest and loyalty. Schmidt was furious. There had been other leaks coming out of the campaign slamming Mark and Nicolle Wallace, one in particular about Nicolle Wallace by Fred Barnes at Fox News that Schmidt forced to be retracted the following day. It was absolute chaos. Schmidt and Rick Davis later ordered a system-wide e-mail check to see who in the campaign had leaked material to Kristol. It was Palin's horse whisperer Scheunemann. One exchange came after CNN's Dana Bash had quoted a "McCain adviser" as having said of Palin:

> She is a diva. She takes no advice from anyone. She does not
> have any relationships of trust with any of us, her family or
> anyone else. Also, she is playing for her own future and sees
> herself as the next leader of the party. Remember: Divas trust
> only unto themselves, as they see themselves as the beginning
> and end of all wisdom.

Scheunemann believed the leaks had come from Mark Wallace. He openly revealed his speculations to Kristol in a revelatory e-mail exchange:

FROM: Randy Scheunemann
TO: William Kristol
SUBJECT: Re: who is this?
He [Mark Wallace] is beyond pretentious—and knows something about divas, being married to one Mw is arrogant, incompetent, annoying

FROM: William Kristol
TO: Randy Scheunemann
right—very weird quote: "Divas trust only unto themselves, as they see themselves as the beginning and end of all wisdom." kind of

pseudo-literary . . . doesn't sound like Schmidt or Salter—is Mark W a little pretentious in this way

FROM: Randy Scheunemann
TO: William Kristol
My very educated guess is mark wallace defnding his wife. Knows [CNN's John King] well, gives her deniability, spent several weeks through debate with her, not there now. Real piece of shit.

As it turned out, Scheunemann was completely off base in his accusations. The leak had been made, according to senior advisers, by McCain's national finance co-chair (and a close personal friend of McCain's), Wayne Berman. Another controversial über-lobbyist in the McCain inner circle, Berman had made headlines earlier in the campaign when it was revealed that he had lobbied on behalf of oil companies involved in a sex-for-access scandal involving the Department of the Interior. He had also taken a lead role in raising large contributions for the Scooter Libby Legal Defense Fund, while his wife, Lea Berman, served as social secretary to the Bush White House. This was hardly a leak from the Schmidt-Wallace inner sanctum. It was more like an extension of the Bush White House.

Being wrong didn't stop Scheunemann. According to senior advisers and Palin herself, an irate Scheunemann (Palin's latest knight in shining armor) confronted Schmidt about the leaks, blaming the Wallaces. In Palin's telling (which she says came to her directly from Scheunemann), "Randy stormed Schmidt's office" and confronted Schmidt angrily about the alleged leaks. Schmidt called the story "another fabrication—more fiction." One lower level McCain aide said that the "idea that Scheunemann played tough guy with Schmidt is a joke. [Schmidt] would have chewed him up and spit him out."

I F THE CAMPAIGN WAS COMING APART internally, it was also fully dismantling in the hinterlands as well. It was a repeat of every political process in which Palin had found herself involved during the past twenty years: with dissension, division, anger, attacks. Although her supporters would later claim otherwise, Palin fueled talk of her being a diva with her own behavior—not with those outside the campaign but with her allies. She had sent out an e-mail to senior staff demanding to know who the "invited travellers" were going to be so that she could "know my comfort level with an association with politicians whom I've never met before they jump on the bus or plane with the *VP campaign*." (Emphasis added.)

The *"VP campaign."* That Palin clearly saw them as separate entities by this point was clear to all parties involved. As early as September 18 in Cedar Rapids, Iowa, she let slip a reference to a "Palin-McCain administration." She was obsessed with the amounts of money she was raising for the ticket and wondered openly why it wasn't being directly credited to a separate account for the vice presidential campaign. According to *Newsweek*'s Evan Thomas, it had trickled back to McCain headquarters that Todd Palin had called potential big-money GOP donors in Alaska "to hold their powder" until 2012.

On October 15, as the Palin road show landed in New Hampshire—an auspicious state in U.S. presidential politics and particularly significant to John McCain—Palin was informed that she was slated to appear at a trio of Granite State rallies with Senator John Sununu (the son of the former White House chief of staff of the same name and a close colleague of McCain's in the Senate) and congressional candidate Jeb Bradley (a GOP moderate who was vying to reclaim the congressional seat he had lost two years earlier). Palin had apparently conducted an Internet search of Bradley and discovered that he was a pro-choice Republican who also opposed drilling in the Arctic National Wildlife Refuge. Palin was chafed by the news and refused to appear on the same stage as Bradley and wanted nothing to do with either candidate as long as Bradley was present. As a quick fix in Dover, the campaign had both Sununu and Bradley deliver their speeches before Palin's arrival at the local high school gymnasium. While Palin was gracious with the two men and allowed photos backstage, she balked at having them on the campaign bus with her, although she was to appear with them at the next stop at Weirs Beach in Laconia, overlooking picturesque Lake Winnipesaukee.

Enter Steve Duprey. He was a unique figure in the McCain campaign, a native of New Hampshire and a Republican leader there who had bonded closely with McCain two years earlier as McCain began his second quest for the White House. He often drove McCain through the back roads of New Hampshire in his own Chevy Suburban. Duprey was a real-world guy with an irreverent sense of humor. He loved to joke around with reporters and could ease tension-filled situations along the campaign trail. He described himself as the campaign's "chief morale officer" and said that "if you can't laugh once in a while life's really not worth living." As a seasoned veteran of New England politics and a successful businessman in his own right, Duprey, however, was far more than a court jester and also served as both a sounding board for Mc-Cain and as a gauge for how the campaign was playing in the streets. The bond between the two was so great that McCain's brass invited him to join the Straight Talk Express for the duration of the campaign.

Duprey, who served as a volunteer, had been called back to New Hampshire to make sure that things went well on the Palin junket. There had been growing problems with the Palin entourage, particularly with her advance man Jason Recher. McCain headquarters wanted smooth sailing through New Hampshire while McCain readied himself for his final—and absolutely critical—debate with Obama. They sensed that a shift might be taking place in their favor and there could be no more gaffes from the vice presidential side of the campaign.

When Duprey heard about Palin's position toward Sununu and Bradley he was "extremely aggravated." (Other GOP operatives were "outraged" and "incensed.") Duprey was of the mind that campaigns weren't supposed to "go cowboy" in midstream and that if "command central" had approved a plan, as it had for New Hampshire, it was to be followed explicitly. It was Duprey's distinct understanding that Sununu and Bradley were to appear on stage with Palin at the various rallies and ride with her on the bus for some "quality time with the VP nominee." Recher was trying to place Sununu and Bradley in a separate van. He claimed that he had received permission to do so from Mc-Cain campaign aide Carla Eudy. Duprey wasn't buying it. He called Eudy. She was livid. She ordered Palin on stage with the two candidates and told Recher they were to ride with Palin on the bus.

Palin's body language in Laconia told the tale. She stood awkwardly distant from Sununu and Bradley on the stage and refused to acknowledge their presence in her remarks—though she did manage another classic Palin gaffe by referring to the state as part of "the great Northwest."

It was a glorious time of year in New Hampshire—the colors along the rolling hillsides had turned gold, orange, and crimson in the autumn sun—as the Palin entourage swung south again toward Salem. Palin finally granted the two candidates a brief moment with her on the bus. "She wasn't rude but she really wasn't engaged," said one McCain staffer. "She excused herself quickly and said that she needed to get back to her e-mails." At the final stop in Salem, Palin once again refused to mention either candidate in her stump speech, even though both had praised her lavishly in their introductory remarks. The GOP operatives who had traveled through the state that day with Palin were livid. It was another tarnished moment on the Palin Express.

In the Obama camp, Democratic strategists were wondering why Palin was campaigning in New Hampshire in the first place. Obama's campaign manager, David Plouffe, openly questioned the strategy, saying that he didn't think that Palin was "the best messenger" for the McCain campaign in the Granite State. "It's puzzling that she'd go to New Hampshire," Plouffe noted, adding that internal Democratic Party polling indicated the voters who viewed Palin unfavorably had soared to a high of 56 percent, while those who viewed her favorably had bottomed out at 36 percent. Some speculated that they were trying to hide her there so that there was no way for her to steal the spotlight from McCain in the news cycle on the night of the campaign's final debate. Perhaps Palin agreed with them—at the very last moment, Palin tried to cancel the campaign stop in Dover.

P ALIN HAD NO INTENTION OF GOING GENTLY into that good night on her two-day sojourn through New England. She was about to engage in yet another battle with McCain's campaign management. Earlier in the week, *Salon.com* had published an investigative report by Max Blumenthal and David Neiwert that chronicled both Sarah's and Todd Palin's ties to the Alaskan Independence Party (AIP) and that included explosive and extremist remarks from a pair of active AIP members who had long-term associations with the Palins. While Palin was campaigning in New Hampshire, CNN followed up on the AIP story with a special segment entitled "The Palins and the Fringe"—which led to her heated e-mail encounter with Schmidt demanding that he respond to the charges.

Schmidt was then focused on what he felt could be the campaign's stealth weapon—the so-called Joe the Plumber imbroglio that had ensnarled Obama on the streets of Holland, Ohio—which they planned to unveil that very night in the final debate of the campaign at Hofstra University in New York. Palin seemed to be absolutely clueless about the potential impact—and urgency—of the climactic debate with Obama.

In *Going Rogue*, Palin would claim that her troubles with the McCain campaign resided with a handful of people centered around Schmidt, certainly, and which also included Nicolle and Mark Wallace. That Palin was intimidated and unnerved by Schmidt grew more and more obvious throughout the campaign and afterward. But he and the Wallaces were hardly the only source of Palin's difficulties.

The day after the debacle in New Hampshire, Palin was at it again in Maine, as McCain operatives were trying to put a series of events together involving moderate Republican senator Olympia Snowe, with whom Palin also expressed political differences. Through her advance man Jason Recher, Palin demanded that changes be made in several events involving appearances with Snowe. A detailed e-mail chain never before made public reveals the dept and breadth of the discontent with both Palin and Recher.

Randy Bumps, Northeast regional political director of the National Republican Committee, sent out the initial red alert just after midnight:

FROM: Randy Bumps
SENT: Thu Oct 16 00:25:36 2008
SUBJECT: Maine Program

It is imperative that we discuss the changes that have been made in tomorrow's Maine program in the last couple of hours.

Specifically, someone from Gov. Palin's trip office or Advance needs to contact John Richter, Sen. Snowe's Chief of Staff, immediately to discuss the changes.

Please advise whether Jason, Ed or someone else will be making the call.

Thanks,

Randy

One of the recipients of the e-mail, Jim "Mad Dog" Barnett, director of the campaign's New England operation, responded to Bumps with a quick query early that morning: "What has been changed?"

Bumps explained that Snowe's introduction "has been split." He indicated that this was "objectionable to Snowe. . . ."

Barnett, a young and widely respected Republican operative out of Vermont, expressed his frustration with the Palin operation:

Barnett, a 32-year-old, widely respected Republican activist out of Vermont, had served as the state director for McCain's critical win in the New Hampshire primary. He knew his way around New England, was well versed in the nuances of local political culture, and was disturbed by the way in which those unfamiliar with the state's political terrain were upending, at the spur of the moment, a well thought out on-the-ground strategy. Barnett was candid about his annoyance with the Palin operation:

> I don't understand why the program is changing hours before every event? We work on it all week making all kinds of political and advance calculations, then without exception over the past two days, it changes at the last minute. I think the time to chime in on the program has passed and these requests are complicating things at a very, very bad time when everyone on the ground has responsibilities to tend to. I would urge these conversations take place earlier or not at all.

Bumps responded directly, but this time included Davis White, director of advance, in the e-mail chain. White forwarded it to director of scheduling, Amber Johnson, and senior advisor Carla Eudy. The problem was once again working its way up McCain's chain of command. "We seem to have talked the Snowe people off the ledge," Bumps wrote, "but it is embarrassing. Think we're all set on this one. On to the fact that we have 2 honor guards now. . . ."

Barnett, who had captained his high school football team and was viewed as a tough political operative, had had his fill of the Palin entourage. He responded with a detailed missive that ran down all of the problems that he and his associates were having with the Palin advance team. It provides an extraordinary window into the day-to-day machinations and frustrations wrought by Palin and her courtiers.

> Fellas—
> Ok, there were many issues that arose yesterday and continue into today with this Palin trip. Sorry in advance for the lengthy recitation, but there were quite a few problems.
>
> 1. We worked for many days on the programs taking into consideration all the political implications and working with advance to get everything flowing smoothly. Then, at literally the last minute, for 3 of the 4 events, someone with some apparent authority calls our advance on the ground and fucks everything up. This has so far resulted in pissing

off two United States Senators and the creation of a total cluster which has reflected very poorly on the campaign.

2. Last night in Salem, I arranged . . . to have Gov. Cellucci (a great surrogate for us here) greet Gov. Palin upon here exiting the bus. I get Gov. Cellucci to the drop point and the US [Secret Service] starts giving me a hard time because they were told no greeters and that he would have to get permission from the advance guys to allow this. Mind you, I'm wearing my hard pin and reminding him I have full access and escort privileges. He continued to say no until advance would permit it. Even then, Advance felt compelled to double check with the bus and interrogate us about Gov. Cellucci's plans after greeting her. At which point an remarkably restrained, but clearly perplexed Cellucci responded he planned to watch the speech like everyone else. Finally, after achieving 3 layers of permission on top of my personal escort, I was permitted to allow Gov. Cellucci to shake her hand. Thoroughly embarrassing to the campaign. Both Advance and USSS should be reminded that hard pins have full access including escort access (at least that's how it was explained to me). Or take away the hard pins from RCMs so we know that we have to ask the advance guys for permission for such things.

3. The mag situation [a reference to Magnetometers, metal detectors used for security purposes]. With 45 min. left last night I had a line of people stretching over a quarter mile. We told them we expected at least 5K right from the start. The final USSS certified tally was 6500. But 2/3rds of the people were flooded in at the last minute with no magging whatsoever. This meant advance had to rush to build a second barricade to accommodate unmagged people even though the inside barricade was not full, and the bleachers in the cut shot were half empty. The USSS could not handle anywhere near the 5K we told everyone to prepare for,

much less the extra turnout. I recognize this is probably all the USSS, but we ought to push them for more mags.

4. In Dover, we had at one point 1K people in the overflow area and by the time the bus arrived probably 600 or more after some people left. We urged that Gov. Palin speak to the overflow crowd. I got a lot of resistance to this initially, with no one willing to commit to this obvious and simple arrangement, until someone saw the crowd with their own eyes. Even then, the bus drove right by them and parked 50 yds away in sight, she went inside and made her remarks, conducted a couple press interviews and finally, an hour and a half later, emerged and made 2 min of remarks to the remnants of the crowd, many of who were now into their 5th hour of waiting to see her. If we could have gotten a firm decision early, we could have told the crowd of 1K to stick around and they'd hear from her shortly. No such luck and a lot of people left pissed off, and the press reports on the crowd size were significantly diminished . . .

5. We were also asked to recruit a large number of vols for each event, as many as 80 in Salem. We did. But then only 40 volunteer credentials were made available, so half the volunteers were given a hard time trying to get around and staff was having to contend with that, and it obviously caused a fair amount of distress for the vols.

6. We were supposed to have the flexibility to have Shonda Schilling ride the bus. Her & Curt's schedule were in flux so it was going to be an on the fly thing, but Carla signed off on that with Ashley.

Shonda Schilling is the wife of New England baseball hero Curt Schilling, one of the pitching stars of the 2004 and 2007 Boston Red Sox World Series Champions and a budding Republican Party activist. Shonda Schilling herself is a celebrated melanoma survivor, the founder of the Shade Foundation of America and a national advocate for the prevention of skin cancer. Barnett was aghast that Palin's advance team had "vetoed" Shonda Shilling's ride on the vice-presidential bus from Laconia to Salem, where Shilling was scheduled to introduce Palin at Salem High School. Eudy had placed Shilling's name on the bus manifest, but when Recher denied her access, Shilling was left to her own devices for transportation to Salem.

That was not the last of it. At an unscheduled event in Concord, Barnett wrote, "we were to prepare a normal size crowd for Palin to stop in to see after visiting the shoe store. We were explicitly [told] not to advertise her plans to be there and that there should not be a bunch of people." With only a half-hour notice, according to Barnett, Palin's advance team changed the directive and demanded they get 30 to 40 people there or that Palin "wasn't stopping." Barnett noted that "we got it done," but the way that Palin's advance team treated people in the process "was not pleasant."

Barnett then summed up his dissatisfaction with the Palin contingent:

> In any case, there seems to be a new way of doing business that significantly limits our authority on the ground and resulted in several very bad calls. I don't know if this new way is deliberate and necessary, or someone just throwing their weight around. The events generally went fine and to the outside observer it was alright (except for the extraordinary waits for the mags and the resulting sparseness in some of the shots). But internally, it was not pretty. In the nearly 2 years I've been doing this, I've never had issues with Advance. Without exception they have been professional and appropriately deferential, as have we to them I think. I know times have changed and the production is bigger and not everyone knows each other anymore, but these new guys must be told that they can't just come into town and run roughshod over Political and leave a mess in their wake that we are left to contend with.
>
> I'm very sympathetic that we have lots of new people and an operation that bears no resemblance to the primary, and we all need to try and navigate it with sensitivity. But there are some basic things that need to be conveyed universally so that we all understand the rules of the road. I really do not want to go into the events next week and find that nothing has

changed, or just tell me nothing will change and we will adjust our expectations accordingly, but from what I witnessed I
think that will create more problems than it will solve.

Barnett's dispatch provides a remarkable, unfiltered glimpse into how the
sausage was being made on the Palin bus. It also presented clear and detailed
evidence to the McCain senior advisers that Recher was enabling Palin in respect to her "rogue" behavior on the campaign trail. Eudy, who was overseeing
the day-to-day operations of the Palin entourage in the waning days of the
campaign, was livid. She forwarded the e-mail chain up the ladder, this time
including Nicolle Wallace, who had originally brought Recher on board.

Eudy stated that she needed to discuss the matter directly with Wallace. She
indicated that Recher's behavior had not been an "isolated" incident, and that
every regional campaign manager had issued similar complaints. She expressed
her gratitude that Steve Duprey had been there to clean up Recher's mess from
the day before. While she acknowledged that Recher was not the sole source of
the problem—"some of this," she noted, "starts with her" (meaning Palin)—
Eudy insisted that the manner in which Recher dealt with people on the campaign trail had to change. She was firm. She wasn't impressed by the fact that
Recher had worked at the White House or for George W. Bush or anywhere
else. She said that volunteers were refusing to work on the campaign because
of "the way they are treated by Recher." He needed to know that this was a
John McCain operation—one that was "respectful and nice to other people"—
and that it was a political necessity for the campaign to hold onto its supporters and gain new ones. Eudy had been pushed to the brink. She asked Wallace
for guidance in handling Recher before "I totally take his head off."

Wallace then sent the e-mail chain straight to the top of the McCain hierarchy. Ironically, given how Palin has demonized Wallace since the election,
Wallace came immediately to Recher's defense and saved him from being fired.

FROM: Nicolle Wallace
SENT: Thursday, October 16, 2008 11:50 AM
TO: Carla Eudy
SUBJECT: Re: Maine Program
If you fire recher, the palin thing explodes and steve and rick are well
aware of the consequences. I have no advice about palin. I can serve as a
character witness for recher's professionalism, humor, kindness and re-

sponsiveness to the person he works for, in this case, a very, very challenging person. He is the glue. He handles the palin family in a way that
no one will ever fully understand. My advice is to cheer him on and
mentor and support him as only you, carla, can do.

Eudy's response was simple and straight to the point. "I have no desire to
fire Recher," she responded. "I have a desire for him to treat other people as he
treats you and Schmidt."

Wallace then acknowledged that she understood the frustration and agreed
to "deliver the message" to Recher. "Do you want to send me some additional
specific complaints and examples of unacceptable behavior," she queried, so
that "I can have a talk with him and tell him he is making himself, and me,
look unprofessional?"[†]

There was no reining in Palin's entourage. The same thing happened again
in North Carolina, where she refused to let Republican U.S. senator Richard
Burr on the campaign bus. She was also refusing to do any more talk radio
interviews in her car because she found it "too distracting." A member of the
Palin teamed reluctantly informed headquarters of her latest fit. On October
26, after a long day of stumping in North Carolina, Palin issued an edict to
her traveling staff. "We were informed today that she no longer wishes to do
TV or print interviews post-rally. She's drained," he wrote. "I don't know
what else to tell you."

By this time in the campaign, Schmidt & Co. could only apply Band-Aids
to what was an untenable situation. Nevertheless, the string of episodes, occurring with only three weeks until Election Day, illustrates the challenges the
McCain brass had in keeping Palin in check. Most significant, it fueled concerns in the highest echelons of the McCain camp that Palin was not fit to
serve as vice president. It presented them with a compelling moral dilemma—
wanting to win the election for John McCain while knowing that the number
two slot on the ticket simply should not be just a heartbeat away from the
presidency. They began discussing the possibility that should McCain pull out

---

[†] In an interview with *The Atlantic*'s Marc Ambinder in November 2009, Recher
described the chronology depicted in the e-mail exchange as false. "Maybe the
McCain aides would have been better served trying to get McCain's positive message out," he declared, "and less time clustering away e-mails like squirrels before
winter."

yet another magical come-from-behind victory, they would have to limit Palin's role in the administration severely.

F OR ALL OF PALIN'S BRAVADO and newfound independence, the world around her was unraveling, and unraveling fast. Her candidacy had been a disaster from the get-go. The controversies and perpetual screwups had piled up beyond anyone's imagination. Her private Yahoo e-mail account had been hacked by a twenty-year-old University of Tennessee student whose father served in the Tennessee legislature (largely because she had failed to make sure that access to her account was properly secured). Then there was the controversy over her clothing and makeup expenditures. Various reports indicated that the McCain campaign had spent more than a quarter-million dollars on Palin's and her family's wardrobe and various makeovers.

But perhaps the biggest blow to the McCain-Palin ticket came, once again, not from the Democrats but from the most distinguished Republican voice since Ronald Reagan: General Colin Powell. Powell's bona fides were unmatched—former secretary of state, national security adviser, and chairman of the Joint Chiefs of Staff during Desert Storm—and he had been a "beloved friend" of McCain's for the better part of a quarter-century. They were born within a year of each other and they were both decorated heroes during the Vietnam War. They were of the same generation and of the same mind-set. In recent years, Powell had joined McCain in his criticism of American torture of prisoners. But Powell's sterling reputation had been sullied by his role in generating international support for the invasion of Iraq based upon fabricated reports of weapons of mass destruction. He described his role as a "blot" on his record and he had grown more disgusted by George W. Bush's foreign policy during his second term. He had been careful, even cautious, in weighing in on the 2008 presidential election and had told close friends that he would likely stay neutral. As recently as September he had said publicly that he hadn't "decided who I'm going to vote for yet." But the right-wing shift of the GOP ticket and the ugly tone of the campaign trail had concerned him. On October 16, in Greensboro, North Carolina, Palin took once again to the theme of small-town America that she had unleashed at the GOP convention seven weeks earlier. "We believe that the best of America is in these small towns that we get to visit," Palin intoned, "and in these wonderful little pockets of what I call the real America, being here with all of you hardworking very patriotic, very, pro-America areas of this great nation."

Powell—born in Harlem and raised in the South Bronx—had heard and seen enough. In a televised interview three days later with Tom Brokaw on NBC's *Meet the Press*, Powell decided to take a stand. Many considered it the final turning point in the campaign, the final blow to John McCain's candidacy. Powell had been impressed with Obama, he said, called him a "transformational figure," and he also expressed concerns about McCain's erratic performance on the economy. But then he addressed what was clearly the deciding factor in his decision: Sarah Palin. While he described her as a "distinguished woman," he was clearly not impressed by either her experience or her performance in the campaign. "Now that we have had a chance to watch her for some seven weeks," Powell observed. "I don't believe she's ready to be president of the United States, which is the job of the vice president. And so that raised some question in my mind as to the judgment that Senator McCain made."

It was a devastating assessment. Powell lavished more praise on Obama (he noted that he was possessed by "a steadiness, an intellectual curiosity, a depth of knowledge" that he found impressive), but then criticized what he observed as "the approach of the Republican Party and Mr. McCain [that] has become narrower and narrower." He praised Obama for providing "us a more inclusive, broader reach into the needs and aspirations of our people." And he contrasted those directly with Palin's view: "Obama's thinking that all villages have values, all towns have values, *not just small towns have values.*" It was another broadside against Palin and what she represented.

The response from the conservative attack dogs was predictably vicious and racist. "Secretary Powell says his endorsement is not about race," Rush Limbaugh declared. "Okay, fine. I am now researching his past endorsements to see if I can find all the inexperienced, very liberal, white candidates he has endorsed. I'll let you know what I come up with." Glenn Beck made it sound like an echo chamber. "Kind of leads you to believe it might be about something *other* than qualifications, doesn't it?" he declared. "Where would I get the impression that *race* just might have something to do with it?" Powell didn't flinch or take the bait. Even after the campaign he would hold his position. "Governor Palin, to some extent, pushed the party more to the right, and I think she had something of a polarizing effect when she talked about how small-town values are good," he declared. "Well, most of us don't live in small towns. And I was raised in the South Bronx, and there's nothing wrong with my value system from the South Bronx."

Sarah Palin made not a single mention of the Powell endorsement of Obama in *Going Rogue*. Not a word.

O N SATURDAY, NOVEMBER 1, WITH THE election now only four days
away, Palin was the all-too-willing victim of what would become an infamous prank by the Montreal disc jockeys known as Les Justiciers Masqués
(The Masked Avengers), Sébastien Trudel and Marc-Antoine Audette, the latter of whom portrayed himself as French president Nicolas Sarkozy in a pro-
tracted telephone conversation with Palin. The call took place while Palin was
traveling on her campaign bus from a rally in New Port Richey, Florida, where
Palin had drawn a crowd of 5,500, to Polk City, in the heart of the Florida
panhandle. She had a full staff on board, along with Florida's Republican governor, Charlie Crist, who had joined Palin on the initial leg of the tour but had
not spoken at the rally.

The prank was to be portrayed as yet another minor stumble by Palin on the
campaign trail—a joke gone bad—and the campaign's initial response tried to
play into the humor. "Governor Palin was mildly amused to learn that she had
joined the ranks of heads of state, including President Sarkozy and other celeb-
rities, in being targeted by these pranksters," Palin campaign spokeswoman
Tracey Schmitt declared in a formal press release. *"C'est la vie."* But of all Palin's troubling incidents throughout the campaign—and they were many and
varied—a close examination of the transcript and the audio recording of the
incident provides an illuminating glimpse into Palin's interpersonal capacities
and social skills.

In *Going Rogue,* Palin thoroughly distorts her role in the prank and her response. She says that she initially thought that some of Sarkozy's comments
were "a little off" and "weird" and that she suspected he was "drunk." This may
be the biggest cover-up in Palin's career. What is "weird" is the way that Palin
responded throughout her conversation, from the beginning until the very end,
lasting *nearly six minutes.* She engaged every remark from the faux Sarkozy
with a fawning—even flirtatious—enthusiasm that bordered on the freakish.

That the call had not been cleared properly with McCain senior advisers
only added to the problematic nature of the conversation. Why she would be
taking a phone call from a head of state—one who had enthusiastically and
publicly embraced Barack Obama during his trip to France earlier in the
summer—without full and formal clearance from senior advisers (or the State
Department, for that matter) says a great deal about her judgment and probity.
Palin contends that "headquarters let the B team know the President of France
would be calling." That, too, was an overt fabrication. The initial query from

the Avengers had been placed to Palin's staff in Alaska and had been routed through one of her foreign affairs advisers, Steve Biegun, who was part of Palin's inner circle and who had not properly informed the McCain command of the impending confab. In fact, the chat had not been identified on the daily staff schedule as a communication from Sarkozy but merely as "a personal call." McCain "headquarters" knew nothing about it. Palin also rationalized taking the call by contending that "she'd received calls from presidents from other countries and our own, and had met elder statesmen and other dignitaries, so it didn't surprise us too much that we'd be speaking with the French leader." Who those presidents were from other countries, Palin didn't say.

There were so many moments in the conversation that should have alerted a candidate for national office. Indeed, Audette went through so much audacious, over-the-top material that he eventually ran out of gag lines; he never imagined that the conversation would go on so long.

When Palin first answered the phone, thinking that Sarkozy was on the line, she uttered a coquettish, elaborated "Huh-lowwwww!" only to be told that Sarkozy was waiting to come on. When the faux Sarkozy did get on, Palin returned to her flirtatious, girlish demeanor, "*Hello*, this is Sarah, *how . . . are . . . you?!*" Then Palin fully immersed herself in the call. As Audette's questions became more cheeky and inappropriate, Palin continued to engage him. Her vocal inflection remained animated throughout. She was clearly awestruck by Sarkozy's international celebrity and status.

PALIN: Oh, so good, it's so good to hear you. Thank you for calling us.

AUDETTE/SARKOZY: Oh, it's a pleasure.

PALIN: Thank you, sir, we have such great respect for you, John McCain and I. We *love you* and thank you for taking a few minutes to talk to *me*.

AUDETTE/SARKOZY: I follow your campaigns closely with my special American adviser Johnny Hallyday, you know?

PALIN: Yes, good.

Yes, good? Johnny Hallyday is the Elvis Presley of France, hardly a political liaison to the United States. Palin was forty-four and had never been to France, even as a tourist. By this point, Audette's accent is so ridiculous that it sounded as though he were in a Hollywood comedy playing a Frenchman. He asked Palin if she were "confident." Palin responded with vigor, "Very confident and we're thankful that polls are showing that the race is tightening and . . ." Then came what should have raised suspicion to anyone. "How do you feel right now, my dear?"

My dear. In *Going Rogue*, Palin said the remark made her suspicious that he might have been drinking before he placed the call. But the audiotape makes clear that she harbored no suspicions, as she earnestly engages the question: "I feel so good. I feel like we're in a marathon and at the very end of the marathon you get your second wind and you plow to the finish." Then came one of Palin's most serious political gaffes. "You know I see you as a president one day, too," Audette says. Palin laughs. She is taking him seriously. "Maybe in eight years," she responds. If anyone ever doubted that Palin had presidential ambitions, it was now on the record. Then the conversation turned downright bizarre. Palin responded at every turn, at some points giggling at Audette's comments.

AUDETTE/SARKOZY: You know, we have a lot in common because personally one of my favorite activities is to hunt, too.

PALIN: Oh, very good. We should go hunting together.

AUDETTE/SARKOZY: Exactly, we could try to go hunting by helicopter like you did. I never did that. [Laughs] Like we say in French, *on pourrait tuer des bébé phoques aussi* [we could kill baby seals also].

PALIN: Well, I think we could have a lot of fun together while we're getting work done. We can kill two birds with one stone that way.

AUDETTE/SARKOZY: I just love killing those animals. Mmm, mmm, take away life, that is so fun. [Palin lets out an odd giggle.] I'd really love to go, so long as we don't bring along Vice President Cheney.

PALIN: [Laughs] No, I'll be a careful shot, yes.

AUDETTE/SARKOZY: Yes, you know we have a lot in common also, because except from my house I can see Belgium. That's kind of less interesting than you.

PALIN: Well, see, we're right next door to different countries that we all need to be working with, yes.

Why Palin would think that the real Nicolas Sarkozy would ever pursue this tack of questioning is baffling. But then Palin revealed her utter battiness when it comes to foreign affairs, and in so doing once again disclosed her capacity for deceit. Palin would mention frequently during the campaign that Canada was a neighbor of Alaska and assert that she was well versed in Canadian politics (she was to do it just a few moments later in the conversation). The following exchange revealed just how poorly versed she was.

AUDETTE/SARKOZY: Some people said in the last days and I thought that was mean that you weren't experienced enough in foreign relations and you know that's completely false. That's the thing that I said to my great friend, the prime minister of Canada, Steph Carse.

PALIN: Well, he's doing fine, too, and yeah, when you come into a position underestimated it gives you an opportunity to prove the pundits and the critics wrong. You work that much harder.

AUDETTE/SARKOZY: I was wondering because you are so next to him, one of my good friends, the prime minister of Quebec, Mr. Richard Z. Sirois, have you met him recently? Did he come to one of your rallies?

PALIN: I haven't seen him at one of the rallies but it's been great working with the Canadian officials. I know as governor we have a great cooperative effort there as we work on all of our resource development projects. You know, I look forward to working with you and getting to meet you personally and your beautiful wife. Oh my goodness, you've added a lot of *energy* to your country [giggling] with that *beautiful* family of yours.

Palin had no idea who was the prime minister of Canada, much less the "prime minister of Quebec." Steph Carse is a famous Canadian country singer; the prime minister of Canada at that time was Stephen Harper. Richard Z. Sirois was a radio colleague of the Avengers. Even though Palin was ostensibly negotiating a major pipeline deal through Canada, she was clueless about the country's leadership. And the only subject that Palin ever introduced in the entire conversation was Sarkozy's wife, Carla Bruni, the former model and songstress. Palin was still starstruck by celebrity.

But if none of that was enough to alert Palin, then surely what followed should have. Audette declares, "You know my wife, Carla, would love to meet you, even though you know she was a bit jealous that I was supposed to speak to you today."

Palin giggles again in response. "Well, give her a big hug for me."

Audette reponds immediately: "You know my wife is a popular singer and a former top model and *she's so hot in bed*. She even wrote a song for you."

Palin still follows merrily along. "Oh my goodness, I didn't know that."

Perhaps Palin thought that's what heads of state talked about. "Yes, in French it's called *de rouge a levre sur un cochon*, or if you prefer in English, Joe the Plumber . . . it's his life, Joe the Plumber."

Palin could not be blamed, of course, for not knowing that Audette had just said "lipstick on a pig" in French. But Palin is still with him, still throwing out catchphrases from her stump speeches in response. "Maybe she understands some of the unfair criticism but I bet you she is such a hard worker, too, and she realizes you just plow through that criticism."

Audette asks, "I just want to be sure. That phenomenon, Joe the Plumber. That's not your husband, right?"

Palin still earnest, still wanting to get out the talking points of the campaign, answers proudly, "That's not my husband, but he's a normal American who just works hard and doesn't want government to take his money."

AUDETTE/SARKOZY: Yes, yes, I understand we have the equivalent of Joe the Plumber in France. It's called Marcel, the guy with bread under his armpit.

PALIN: Right, that's what it's all about, the middle class and government needing to work for them. You're a very good example for us here.

Palin is still responding enthusiastically.

AUDETTE/SARKOZY: Governor Palin, I love the documentary they made on your life. You know *Hustler*'s *Nailin' Paylin*?

PALIN: Ohh, good, thank you, yes.

AUDETTE/SARKOZY: That was really edgy.

PALIN: Well, good.

AUDETTE/SARKOZY: I really loved you and I must say something also, Governor, you've been pranked by the Masked Avengers. We are two comedians from Montreal.

It was only then that Palin finally caught on. She took the bait all the way to the end. She finally announced to the bus what had happened. Governor Crist must have thought that he was in the middle of a bad French soap opera. He jumped off at the next stop.

Palin, always wanting to play the victim, later claimed that an irate Schmidt called the bus, "and the force of his screaming blew back my hair." She alleged that he went into a "rant" about people being stupid and wondering why anyone would think that the president of France would be calling Palin a few days before the election. She placed the blame on Schmidt for setting up the phone call in the first place.

Only Schmidt never made such a call. He denies it. And another McCain campaign aide also says he did not make the call. In fact, yet another telltale e-mail disputes Palin's claims. It was an e-mail that Schmidt sent that made the charge—not a personal phone call to Palin—and he sent it to everyone.

> Who set this up? Are you kidding me? Did it occur to anyone that the french president wouldn't be looking to have a conversation with the vicepresidential candidate 3 days before the election. From this moment forward, no interview occurs without my direct signoff. Nothing. I want to know the exact details of this. I want to know who is responsible.

Once again, Palin's rendition of events was *total fiction*. And the Palin bus was heading straight into *The Twilight Zone*.

Later that evening, John and Cindy McCain would be appearing on *Saturday Night Live* sans Palin, engaging in a little comedy of their own. McCain poked fun at his own diminished campaign war chest (and Obama's recent half-hour infomercial on the three major networks) in a sketch that had Cindy and him appearing on QVC selling off campaign-themed items, with Tina Fey returning to her role as Palin. Fey held nothing back in her portrayal of McCain's running mate. As McCain sold a set of knives for "cutting the pork," Fey-as-Palin went to the side of the stage and whispered to her audience. "Okay, listen up everybody, I am goin' rogue right now so keep your voices down. Available now, we got a buncha' these," she said, holding up a "Palin in 2012" T-shirt. "Just try and wait until after Tuesday to wear 'em okay? Because I'm not goin' anywhere. And I'm certainly not goin' back to Alaska. If I'm not goin' to the White House, I'm either runnin' in four years or I'm gonna be a white Oprah so, you know, I'm good either way." When McCain tried to ask her what she was doing, Fey-as-Palin responded with a dramatic wink, "Oh . . . just talkin' about taxes."

O N ELECTION DAY, PALIN SURROUNDED herself with a huge entourage— one that included dozens of family members and friends from all over the country—at the Arizona Biltmore in Phoenix where John McCain was expected to deliver a concession speech that evening and where his closest advisers had gathered to steel him for what looked like an inevitable defeat—if not a landslide, then one of momentous political proportions. The McCain-Palin ticket had lost significant sections of the country that Republicans had held for the past three decades. Indeed, Obama was on the verge of recording the highest winning percentage by a Democratic presidential candidate—52.9 percent—since Lyndon Johnson's landslide over Barry Goldwater forty-four years earlier.

Contrary to what she has promulgated afterward about believing in victory until the end, Palin had long believed the loss was inevitable—she had clearly set her sights on 2012—and she wanted to use the concluding days of the campaign to secure pole position in the GOP's next presidential cycle. The McCain inner circle was outraged by Palin's behavior and they were doing whatever they could to marginalize her presence at the Biltmore during the denouement of the campaign.

Completely unbeknownst to the McCain inner circle, in the final seventy-two hours leading up to Election Day, Palin had been working with speechwriter Matthew Scully to draft both victory and concession speeches for the concluding night of the campaign. She hadn't cleared the speech with anyone in McCain headquarters—nor had her handlers on the plane—and Scully had initiated the process "just in case" one was needed. The last thing he wanted anyone to be was unprepared. Who could know in advance what the plans would be for Election Night? If the McCain-Palin ticket pulled off an unlikely upset, it was probable that she would be called to the podium. If they lost, it would be someone else's call, but who knew what the mood would be? Scully wanted to make sure that all options were available.

In the ragtag final days of the campaign, communication between McCain headquarters and those in the field was less than optimal. Scully let some people on Palin's plane know of his intentions and he also let some lower level staffers at headquarters know that he would be flying to Phoenix ahead of schedule to work on the speeches.

Steve Schmidt hadn't been brought into the loop. "There was never a formal communication from Palin's plane [about her intentions to deliver a speech]," Schmidt stated unequivocally. "As a result, it was never considered, never even discussed prior to her arrival in Phoenix. No one thought it was appropriate."

No matter who initiated the idea (and everyone acknowledges that Scully's motives were thoroughly professional and appropriate), Palin knew that such an address would give her a final appearance before a national audience—an opportunity to look presidential in a scripted setting, to regain some of the luster of her acceptance speech in Minneapolis that had been lost and soiled over the past two months—and provide her with a claim to the mantle in the Republican Party in the months and years ahead. It would also appear as though McCain was passing her the baton.

Scully had interviewed members of Palin's staff and her friend Kris Perry for anecdotes from the campaign to work into the speech. He drafted the concession speech first—concession speeches, Scully felt, were always more important than victory speeches, and it was also easier to turn a concession speech into a victory speech rather than the other way around—and then he spent about ninety minutes turning that version into a victory address. He and his writing partner, Lindsay Hayes, issued a first draft, to which Palin made several handwritten changes, and they had sent the draft back to Palin for final changes and corrections so that it would be ready for the teleprompter at the Biltmore.

Scully was one of the McCain staffers who got on extremely well with Palin, and he had "enjoyed the process" of working with her on the campaign. He viewed her as a highly capable candidate, pleasant to work with, who had stepped into a really "difficult and tough situation" and performed extraordinarily well. "I think very highly of her," he said after the campaign. "I think the world of her and consider her a friend."

Mark Salter woke from his nap and was busy putting the final touches to McCain's speech. The McCain inner sanctum knew it would take nothing less than a miracle for the speech to turn into a victory oration, but the ever loyal and dutiful Salter, like Scully, crafted both, just in case.

According to Scully, he first ran the idea of a Palin speech past Rick Davis in Phoenix. Davis said, "Yeah, that could work," and then went on to explain that in the case of victory there were plans for a grand fireworks show in the Arizona sky and that perhaps Palin could introduce McCain. Almost immediately afterward, Scully ran into his friend and colleague Salter and brought up the idea of Palin delivering a speech with him. Salter, beaten and trying to catch a few minutes of sleep before putting the finishing touches on his speeches for McCain, acknowledged Scully's remarks but made no commitment either way. Scully was never given any indication by either Davis or Salter, formal or otherwise, of a green light.

For most of the night, the McCain and Palin entourages watched the election returns in separate suites at the Biltmore. The fact that Palin and her advisers had not been invited into McCain's suite earlier—even though they were in the same building—said much about the frosty relationship that had developed in both camps. Meanwhile, Obama was running the table in those swing states that he needed to claim the presidency—North Carolina, Virginia, then Pennsylvania (where Palin had spent a considerable amount of time) went for Obama by double digits, and, finally, the game breaker, Ohio—and the writing was on the wall. There would be no victory speeches for the GOP that night at the Biltmore. John McCain's once dynamic Straight Talk Express had slowly skidded off the tracks. It was all over but the crying—quite literally.

Later, Palin would claim her speeches were crafted to do "two things: reminding Americans of what kind of man John McCain was and what he had promised to do for the country." That was not what the speeches were about. There was little substantive reference to McCain in either. Copies of both speeches, leaked out after the election, clearly show that the main bodies of each speech center almost exclusively on Palin and her family.[‡] A substantial portion of both focused on her husband, Todd:

[‡] Final versions of the speeches were first made public by Scott Conroy and Shushannah Walshe prior to the release of *Sarah from Alaska*.

As for my own family, well, it's been quite a journey these past 69 days. And we are ready to return to a place and a life we love. I told my husband Todd to look at the upside: Now, at least, he can clear his schedule, and get ready for championship title number five in the Iron Dog snow machine race! Along the way in this campaign, it was Todd, as always, who helped with the children, gave me advice, and kept me strong. There are a lot of men in this world could learn a few things from Todd Palin. And I am so lucky that after a couple of decades, five kids, and a presidential campaign, he is still my guy.

Among Todd's many winning qualities are the gift of optimism and thankfulness in all situations. And I suppose I'll be counting on those qualities a little more than usual in the days to come. But far from returning to the great State of Alaska with any sense of sorrow, we will carry with us the best of memories . . . and joyful experiences that do not depend on victory.

The speech was intended as a mechanism of bringing back the "narrative" of the campaign to Palin, of reframing the campaign as *her* campaign, historic because of her presence in it.

I will remember all the young girls who came up to me at our rallies, sometimes taking off from school, just to see only the second woman ever nominated by a major party in a national election. They know that in America there should be no ceilings on achievement, glass or otherwise. And if I could help point the way for these young women, or inspire them to use their own gifts and find their own opportunities, it was a privilege.

While she praised Obama for his "grace and skill," and acknowledged his "beautiful family," it included an awkward reference with a racially strained undertone: "When a black citizen prepares to fill the office of Washington and

Lincoln, that is a shining moment in our history that can be lost on no one." A *black citizen?*

Then came the tell-all conclusion:

> Now it is time for us go our way, neither bitter nor vanquished, but instead confident in the knowledge that there will be another day . . . and we may gather once more . . . and find new strength . . . and *rise to fight again.*

Those were words straight out of the Confederacy—and were to serve as a signal that Palin had no intention of leaving the national stage, that she would be back for another run at the White House, on her terms, without the cumbersome McCain to hold her back.

In fact, Palin tried to deliver the speech by stealth that night in Phoenix. She had to be told several times no, she would not be delivering a speech, that McCain would be flying solo on this last mission of the 2008 campaign. Neither John nor Cindy wanted Palin to speak that evening. They were clear and adamant about that. For the most part, it would have been unprecedented. In recent history, it had happened only twice—Dan Quayle had given a concession speech in 1992, following the defeat of the Bush-Quayle ticket to Clinton-Gore; and John Edwards had delivered a concession speech in 2004. In Quayle's case, however, he was a sitting vice president and in a separate location from Bush—his hometown of Huntington, Indiana. In the case of Edwards, his were introductory remarks, brief and to the point, and he had clearly used the occasion to advance his own candidacy four years hence. The McCain camp wanted none of that.

Ever the opportunist, Palin got dressed in her suite and tried to place her furtive plan in motion. She and Todd made their way to McCain's suite, where the senator was with his pals Lindsey Graham and Joe Lieberman, along with Schmidt, Davis, and Salter—who were now all aware of Palin's plans. Schmidt consulted with McCain and informed him of Palin's intentions. He let McCain know that his advisers did not think it a good idea and McCain concurred. "John McCain made it clear that there would only be one person speaking and that it would be he," Schmidt recalled. Schmidt was tasked with the purpose of telling Palin—in front of McCain—that she would not be delivering her speech. "I understand, Governor, that you have a speech," Schmidt told her in his most serious tone possible. "Only Senator

McCain is going to speak tonight. It's not appropriate for a vice presidential candidate to speak."

Schmidt was gravely concerned about the historic moment immediately facing the country. He and the campaign's senior advisers had held "discreet discussions" in the week leading up to Election Day about the campaign ending on a "high note, a positive note." McCain had been a part of these discussions. The candidate had decided to end his long journey in New Hampshire—for nostalgic reasons much more than strategic purposes—and he had done so in the final days of the campaign, engaging in a series of town hall meetings in the Granite State where he had triumphantly began his run in 2000, before returning to his adopted home state of Arizona for the finale.

Schmidt and his colleagues felt a larger duty at hand than advancing personal agendas. To Schmidt, the moment of concession initiated the process by which "power is transferred peacefully," and that the social and historic forces at work in 2008 demanded that it be done thoughtfully and deliberately. "We were very much focused on our role and our responsibility in the moment where the process that culminates with inauguration on January 20th that—peaceful transition of power gets off to as good and smooth a start as possible," he stated. "We've had uninterrupted peaceful transitions of power in this country going back to 1797, between the Civil War and two world wars, great depressions and everything else, and with the election of the first African American president after a long and tough campaign, we felt that it was very important for the losing candidate, particularly in the context of how the last two presidential election nights have gone—because of the closeness of those elections—that the losing candidate—our candidate—needed to go out and affirm the legitimacy of the election and to affirm the legitimacy of the president elect."

Those who know Schmidt well describe him as a fierce competitor—one junior aide described him as being like a "warrior from another century"—and the thought of being on the losing side of a national election could not have been pleasant for him. "We would have rather been on the other end of the phone call," Schmidt concedes, but he also grasped both the political implications of McCain calling Obama to congratulate him and referring to him as "President-Elect."

It is disturbing to compare Schmidt's concerns that evening to those of Palin as expressed in *Going Rogue*. She said that she worried about family members who had arrived from Washington and Texas and who didn't know where the speech was supposed to be delivered. She complained about the chaos of the campaign, without acknowledging how she had contributed to it.

And she felt that she wanted to recognize those partisans "who had put their lives on hold and had dedicated everything they had, everything, to fight for what's right." She wanted one last chance to fire up the troops, for her friends and family to assume center stage.

Sarah Palin refused to take no for an answer. As the McCain and Palin entourages made their way to the front of the Biltmore, where McCain was to issue his remarks, Palin was still trying to get a final copy of the speech in hand. Her manner was "almost desperate," said one adviser. Schmidt and Salter were astounded by her gall and tenacity. Salter, pulling off his sunglasses and looking directly into Palin's eyes, told her in the clearest manner possible that only McCain would be speaking at the podium. Palin's problematic advance man Recher also tried to assert her case. Just then, the candidate and his wife, Cindy, appeared at the platform. Palin was still trying to take the stage with speech in hand. With a group that included Palin, both McCains, Salter, and Schmidt, Salter asked McCain very directly, "You're speaking alone, right?" McCain affirmed. After trying to push herself onto the stage, Palin finally got the message. It had taken at least four times being told no to convince her that she would not be speaking.

In addition to the historical significance of the event, McCain's senior advisers, particularly Schmidt, did not trust that Palin would stay on script. There was little certainty that she would not try to steal the show. They wanted the focus of the evening to be solely on McCain—a vanquished American hero courageously acknowledging his defeat—not on a political parvenu in constant (and haphazard) search of the political limelight. Perhaps most importantly of all, they were aware of what Palin had become on the campaign trail—a divisive figure in respect to the American body politic—and they did not want her to be featured at a time when the country needed to come together, to claim its indivisible legacy.

Of all the problematic accounts in *Going Rogue*—and there are literally dozens now that have been challenged—Palin's duplicity surrounding the final night in Phoenix is remarkable. She went to great lengths in her memoir to explain why she didn't cry. But Palin wept deeply and openly that night in Phoenix, before a national and international audience, as McCain delivered a generous, if not particularly eloquent, concession to Obama. Her tears were not shed for a higher purpose. If they had been, she would have noted it. Sarah Palin was not crying for John McCain or her country; she was crying for herself.

As McCain wound down to his concluding remarks, there was a troubling moment that went overlooked by the national media. "This campaign was and will remain the great honor of my life," McCain declared. "And my heart is filled with nothing but gratitude for the experience and to the American people for giving me a fair hearing before deciding that Senator Obama and my old friend Senator Joe Biden should have the honor of leading us for the next four years." The largely all-white audience assembled in Phoenix booed and catcalled McCain's conciliatory remarks. The crowd had an edge to it, one that augured the temper and tone of American politics in the weeks and months that were to follow. McCain held up his hands to stifle the anger—"Please, please . . ." he intoned—and then the crowd broke into a raucous chant of "Sar-ah! Sar-ah! Sar-ah!," as Palin's tears suddenly turned into a bright smile. She had gotten her final moment on the national stage and a nod toward the future.

After McCain's speech, the two camps went their separate ways, only to encounter each other awkwardly in the parking lot of the Biltmore, as McCain drove away to his nearby Phoenix home. Palin's entourage remained restless. The stage on which McCain had delivered his speech was still in place and fully lit. Most of the media assembled were still huddling around their equipment. Palin decided that she would assemble her friends and family there for a final group portrait. Some worried that she still might attempt to deliver her speech. It was another moment of chaos on the long strange trip of Sarah Palin's bid for national office, and Palin was once again at the center of it. She was trying to upstage the fallen McCain a final time.

According to reporters Scott Conroy and Shushannah Walshe, Recher tried desperately to stop her, then gave in. Palin had no lingering loyalties to McCain, or to anyone else beyond her immediate sphere. "My loyalty is to my family," she reportedly told Recher. She indicated she had every intention of going on stage and taking the group photograph.

Carla Eudy, who had upbraided Recher only a few weeks earlier, was furious when she heard the news. She reportedly ordered Recher to "get her ass off the stage." Eudy called Schmidt. He ordered his staff to shut down the stage—cutting off the sound feed and turning off the lights. It was an apocalyptic moment. The bright promise of the campaign closed down quickly on Palin and her entourage, leaving only the desert stars of the Arizona night to illuminate the final, awkward act of her failed dream and her uncertain political future.

PART III

ALASKA

---

*Here is an old tradition badly in need of return: You have
to earn your way into politics. You should go have a life,
build a string of accomplishments, then enter public service.
And you need actual talent: You have to be able to bring
people in and along. You can't just bully them, you can't just
assert and taunt, you have to be able to persuade. Americans
don't want, as their representatives, people who seem empty
or crazy. They'll vote no on that.*
—Peggy Noonan, *The Wall Street Journal*

CHAPTER 6

Cold Comfort

Sarah Palin has left us to freeze and starve.
—Nicholas Tucker, "Letter from Emmonak"

She just never made it home. She just never came back.
—Beth Kerttula, Minority Leader,
Alaska House of Representatives

And did they get you to trade . . .
Cold comfort for change?
—Pink Floyd, "Wish You Were Here"

T HE WINTER OF 2009 WAS PARTICULARLY harsh in the Alaska bush. With decimated salmon runs far below average in the previous summer—combined with skyrocketing costs for both gasoline and heating oil—the conditions in Native villages were nothing less than brutal. Piercing hunger and an unrelenting arctic cold defined many Alaska Natives' existence, as thousands in these vulnerable communities scattered across the Last Frontier knew not from where their next meal might be coming nor their next gallon of heating fuel. It was a tenebrous time. In the isolated Native community of Emmonak (or *Imangaq* in the language of Central Yup'ik), located on the vast Yukon-Kuskokwim Delta, which fans out to the Bering Sea in western Alaska, conditions were particularly harsh. In what would eventually become a rallying cry sent out in January of 2009 by Nicholas Tucker, a village elder in Emmonak, the calamitous situation in the Alaska bush first became public to those inside Alaska, and in a brief matter of time, to the Lower 48 and the rest of the world.

Tucker, sixty-three years old, with his wife and extended family living in his home, was suffering. "For the first time," he wrote in a landmark letter dated January 9, 2009, "I am forced to decide between buying heating fuel or groceries. I had been forced to dig into our January income to stay warm during December. Again, for this month, same thing happens. I am taking away my February income this month to survive. Couple of weeks ago, our eight-year old son had to go to bed hungry."

Tucker very carefully and precisely provided the background to the current crisis. He explained "the king salmon fisheries disaster" that had taken place the previous summer when his community was prevented from commercial fishing. There had been no net income from fishing. In fact, they had lost money in the process. Once winter hit, they were already in the hole financially. "Our income from the meager, small-scale commercial harvest," Tucker explained, "is basic to and vital to our seasonal subsistence fishing and hunting, berry picking, plant gathering, motor oil and gas, supplies, equipment, and cash for repairs of our outboard motors and our snowmachines used for winter wood gathering. This income pays for our many household bills."

Only this year, there had been no income. The economic foundation for many of Alaska's subsistence communities had been shattered by forces beyond their control. In his lifetime, Tucker noted, he didn't "recall anything having occurred as cold as it has been and its length that we have to endure." He suspected that he was not alone. Over a shortwave radio, he began documenting the conditions of other members of the community—twenty-five households in all—and, in painful detail, constructed a composite picture in Emmonak of widespread fear and destitution. Using only initials, so as not to embarrass others in his community, Tucker laid out the desolate conditions:

> **A. & L. M.:** Middle aged couple, family of eight. Family is buying heating fuel over food all this winter. They have no choice. Wife has a part time job. Husband's health, including a bad back, is preventing work—had lost his last job due to health.

> **P. J.:** Widower and provider of five children. As of December 31, 2008, his food stamps have been cut off. He debates

between buying heating fuel or food. His kids have to eat. He has to keep his kids warm at night during these very cold winter days. He is having hard time getting heating fuel and is piled up on bills, rent, water/sewer. He is behind in payments.

G. & K. F.: Young couple with family of five. Wife is unable to sleep and stressed out not knowing when they will be able get their next heating fuel. A 100-lb. bottle of propane gas that usually lasts four months is now lasting only two months because they use it to heat water. This costs them $200 every two weeks. They do not have hot water heater. Wife has very little income and uses $375, the one-half of her gross income every two weeks, to get heating fuel. She has no food for her family sometimes, because she has to split the rest of what little is left for water/sewer and electricity. Gasoline for her 4-wheeler is very expensive. Her parents help her with food and firewood. They cannot afford a snowmachine or a boat to get logs. Heating fuel and propane is taking her food money away. Her added worry is that the village native corporation is running out of heating fuel and is being airlifted in. New cost is expected to be near $9 to $11 per gallon or higher.

G. & F. H.: Near middle aged couple, family of six. The husband cried as he was talking to me. He says he is not doing good. He receives a very small unemployment income and is out of fuel a lot. He is able to get his heating fuel five gallons at a time. His family has been out of food for quite some time now. Their one-year-old child is out of milk, can't get it and he has no idea when he will be able to get the next can. He has been borrowing milk from anyone he can. His moose meat supply is running out. He has been out of work since October 2008. There are no jobs available. Because of this very high cost of heating fuel, he is in this situation . . . He is mainly concerned about his one-year-old child, his wife and thinks that his wife may be pregnant. They do have some pilot bread. There are days without food in his house. He is not concerned about himself, but about his wife and children. He calls other family members for a can of milk. Whatever little bit of meat they have left, they are trying to make it last. They have little bit of it at a time and out of that, eat as much they can so that they would not be too hungry during the night. They almost lost their child last year with [a respiratory virus]. She is sickly. Their house is not well insulated. The five gallons of heating fuel they are able get last four days. They use their electric stove for heat. Without any work, it is very hard.

One after another, Tucker laid out the stories. He did so matter-of-factly, without emotion, but occasionally he noted that he "could sense choking over the phone from trying not to cry" or "could tell the wife was crying as she related these to me." The very act of accumulating the stories placed an added burden on Tucker. "Just to think about all this is very hard," he wrote. "It hurts." The stories Tucker gathered foretold a potential genocide in rural Alaska if something wasn't done and soon.

Tucker sent out his letter to a handful of politicians, a food bank, and rural newspapers. Within a matter of days, his plea had gone viral on the Web, as a variety of primarily progressive organizations began a grassroots response to the crisis. Churches and business organizations soon followed. Tucker was interviewed on public radio, and throughout the initial process he carefully stayed away from assigning political blame, and sought only assistance and a solution to the immediate rural crisis. The governor of Alaska, Sarah Palin, was not mentioned in his initial letter. "Help is needed," he concluded simply. "We have work to do."

Support efforts in the private and nonprofit sectors quickly mushroomed. Alaska Newspapers, Inc.—a subsidiary of the Native Alaska Calista Corporation—published Tucker's letter and launched a food drive on behalf of the village. Meanwhile, various spokespeople for the Palin administration promised action—mostly meetings and "fact finding" efforts—but the governor herself offered no response. There were pleas for Palin to deploy emergency fuel and food supplies to Emmonak and other crisis-stricken villages in the bush and that she declare a formal "economic disaster" in the region. She resisted.

It was clear throughout the process that Tara Jollie, the director of the Alaska Division of Community and Regional Affairs and a staunch Palin ally, was well behind the curve in assessing the crisis. She admitted that she had no idea of the extent of the fishing emergency throughout the Yukon and had no knowledge, for instance, that Emmonak's fish-processing plant had shut down as a result of the decimated salmon run the previous summer. "I know the governor's very concerned," Jollie said to the press, but there was still no direct action taken by Palin or her upper-level staff. Jollie told others, privately, that she had been "overwhelmed" by the crisis. One colleague said that she was "in over her head." Another said that she was afraid to do anything counter to Palin's wishes. "She was afraid of encountering Sarah's wrath," said one close associate.

"I wish I could take Governor Palin and walk her around in the houses here," Tucker told the *Anchorage Daily News* earnestly a few weeks later. But while Palin originally promised to visit the bush to get a firsthand assessment of the emergency for herself, she never made the trip to Emmonak. Her lone statement during the early days of the crisis was quintessential Palin. "We want to make sure, of course, that no individual is hungry out there. And that nobody is cold out there," she declared. "And we want to know if the community itself—if anything fell between the cracks, between [the power-cost equalization subsidy program] energy rebate checks that were sent to each individual." It was a classic case of Palin trying to blame the victims for their plight and to advance her own political agenda on the backs of others. She would continue to do so in the weeks and even months ahead.

News agencies from around the world began reporting on Emmonak's plight. One particularly thorough report by Kim Murphy of the *Los Angeles Times* pointed out with no small amount of irony that many Alaska Natives were looking for assistance from Venezuelan president Hugo Chávez, hoping that he would follow through once again on his pledge to deliver free fuel to Native Americans—a promise that could mean one hundred gallons for many families. It was not to happen. While Alaska's U.S. senators, Mark Begich and Lisa Murkowski, set aside partisan differences to secure federal assistance, Palin simply refused to do anything tangible. The crisis was becoming, as one blogger noted, "Sarah Palin's Katrina." The governor was completely out of touch.

S ARAH PALIN'S WELCOME IN ALASKA in the aftermath of the grueling national campaign was hardly a homecoming. As she and her entourage returned to Anchorage from the final denouement in Phoenix, she landed at Ted Stevens International Airport late at night (ironically, the day after Stevens had just been voted out of office). Snow was on the ground and she was hardly dressed for late autumn in the Last Frontier. Something had changed. AKMuckraker (Jeanne Devon) of *The Mudflats* had braved the chill and witnessed Palin coming off the plane, "teetering on the most ridiculous shoes I've ever seen in my life. . . . She knows what it's like when it's 10 degrees in November at the airport, but there she was tromping through the snow cover in five-inch black stiletto heels. She reminded me of a little girl playing dress up." The governor had been caught off guard by video journalist Dennis Zaki of *The Alaska Report* responding to a question about the "hurt feelings" experienced in the Alaska legislature during the campaign. Her face broke from her beauty-pageant smile into a hardened glare.

> Well, I don't know what specifically you're talking about "hurt feelings," then, because that's so subjective. Kinda tough to answer, but, um, as I have for the last couple'a years, worked in a bipartisan manner and in my administration, of course, that being made manifest by appointing Republicans, Democrats, and Independents to help serve the, the people of Alaska. I'm gonna continue to do that; continuing to reach out. Nobody should have hurt feelings. My goodness, this is *politics*. Politics is *rough-and-tumble* and people need to get thick skin. *Just like I've got.*

There was anger in her tone as though she were forcing herself back into combat mode with the media, but she remained unconvincing.

According to a close family friend, Todd Palin expressed concern that she was gaunt and had lost weight and that he was worried about her "fragility." Her son-in-law-not-to-be, Levi Johnston, who would soon add plenty of drama to the daily soap opera that seemed always to surround the Palin family, would write in *Vanity Fair* that she was "pouting" and "stressed" after the campaign and that she frequently expressed the desire to quit her governorship and "take this money" that was being offered her. There was a continual stream of revelations from the McCain camp that made their way to the front pages of newspapers and Web sites. The damage from the campaign was unrelenting. According to Johnston, who was living with the family at the time, Palin was livid about the "backstabbing" by McCain's staff; she maintained, according to Johnston, that the "majority of people were out there voting because of me!"

Palin gave interviews in which she couldn't help but mention the possibility of running for president in 2012. In an interview she gave in her Anchorage office with Greta Van Susteren shortly after her return, Palin signaled that she most certainly had her eye on the presidency.

> Faith is a very big part of my life. And putting my life in my creator's hands—this is what I always do. I'm like, OK, God, if there is an open door for me somewhere, this is what I always pray, I'm like, don't let me miss the open door. Show me where the open door is. Even if it's cracked up a little bit, maybe I'll plow right on through that and maybe prematurely plow through it, but don't let me miss an open door. And if there is an open door in twelve or four years later, and if it is something that is going to be good for my family, for my state, for my nation, an opportunity for me, then I'll plow through that door.

But for every two steps she tried to move forward, to distance herself from the campaign, to reframe the narrative that had solidified around her and her candidacy, she seemed to always be taking three back. On Thanksgiving Eve she gave an absolutely bizarre interview with Anchorage television station KTUU, conducted at Schmidt's Triple D Farm and Hatchery, just down the Parks Highway from Palin's home in Wasilla. She was there in what has become something of a traditional Thanksgiving turkey pardoning. The interview turned macabre when Palin left the pen where the turkey pardoning had taken place and then gave an extended interview while not one—but two—turkeys were slaughtered by a worker at Triple D in a funnel-shaped turkey "killing cone," with a blood-filled trough below it—all of which appeared on camera, while Palin gave her interview within a few steps of the bloody action.

According to the KTUU news team, they checked with Palin about the backdrop before they began filming her, but Palin's staff said they hadn't. Palin's friend and aide Kris Perry stood right by the news team during the shoot. The raw footage reveals that no one made even the slightest suggestion about changing the backdrop—indeed at one point Palin appears to look over at the action and make eye contact with the Triple D employee. The video of the event went viral—more than two million hits on YouTube in a matter of a few days—and the late-night comedians and political commentators were brutal in its wake. On his MSNBC show, Keith Olbermann quoted a conservative friend of his who said of Palin, "Not only is she the dumbest politician I've ever heard, but she doesn't even have a clue that she's the dumbest politician I've ever heard. Wow!" David Letterman featured the event in his Top Ten list of Sarah Palin's excuses for the interview, one of which was: "I can see Russia, but I can't see what's going on five feet behind me."

As usual, Palin and her staff exacerbated the coverage and gave the story legs by blaming the news team for the slaughter being televised. Alaska blogger Linda Kellen Biegel witnessed the interview and asserted on her Celtic Diva's Blue Oasis blog that she believed Palin was clearly aware of what was happening: "Give me a break! There is *no way* she couldn't have known!" Later, in an interview with an Alaska radio station, Scott Jensen, the videographer who filmed the interview, said it was Palin who actually "chose the spot."

The humiliation from the interview further exacerbated Palin's funk and sense of alienation from Alaska, where she appeared on the verge of becoming something of a laughingstock. It seemed that she could only find solace outside the Last Frontier, on the campaign trail. Little more than a week after what became known as "Turkeygate," Palin was off to Georgia where she was scheduled to campaign on behalf of Georgia's Republican U.S. senator Saxby Chambliss on the eve of a special runoff election in early December. Palin spent the day campaigning with Chambliss at four events, in Augusta, Savannah, Gwinnett County, and Atlanta. Chambliss, who won the race decisively by 300,000 votes, was ecstatic about Palin's charismatic performance. "I can't overstate the impact she had down here," Chambliss told Sean Hannity on Fox News. "She truly is a rock star. I mean, she came into town to help us electrify our base, make sure that these folks get fired up and turn out tomorrow, and she did exactly that. We had huge crowds, and they were enthusiastic and very electrified." In many respects, the Chambliss race was a harbinger of events to come for Palin and a resurgent bounce-back by the Republican Party in the aftermath of Obama's victory a month earlier. "When she walks in a room, folks just explode," Chambliss continued. "And they really did pack the house everywhere we went. She's a dynamic lady, a great administrator, and I think she's got a great future in the Republican Party."

But her future in her home state was beginning to look dim. She got caught in a lie about whether she had urged Democratic senator Mark Begich to step down from his seat in the aftermath of the U.S. Justice Department dropping its corruption case against Ted Stevens. She sent out an e-mail confirming her position about Begich to the *Fairbanks Daily News-Miner,* and then later her spokesperson Meg Stapleton did the same to *Politico.* The following day, however, Palin claimed at a news conference that she "didn't call for Begich to step down, either." When pressed by the media on the obvious discrepancy between the two statements, she admonished them for "splitting hairs."

Palin's speech kicking off the 2009 Alaska legislative session was clearly intended for a national audience. She offended legislators on both sides of the aisle, many of whom noted that Palin had failed to make eye contact with any of them during her delivery. Her nominee for attorney general—Wayne Anthony Ross, who had served as Palin's personal attorney—was turned down by the legislature, the first time in Alaska history a governor's nominee to head a state agency had been rejected. Her establishment of a national political action committee, SarahPAC, further confirmed suspicions in the Alaska State House that Palin's attentions were elsewhere.

Alaska House minority leader Beth Kerttula—whom Palin refused to name as a state senator following the departure of Kim Elton to the Obama administration, despite overwhelming support for her nomination—sensed from the moment Palin returned that "her heart wasn't in it anymore." Kerttula said she hoped that Palin could have come back to Alaska and refocus her energies on the Last Frontier. "Would that she could have come home," said Kerttula, whose family's roots stretch back three generations in Alaska. "Would that she could have come back and said, 'Well, that was fun. But here I am, and I'm here and I'm gonna be a good governor and I'm gonna put my head down.' But it didn't work that way: she just never made it home. She never came back."

IN OCTOBER OF 2007, PALIN had named Rhonda McBride, a newscaster at Alaska's KTUU-Channel 2, as her "rural adviser," a subcabinet position in Alaska government. Palin had waited nearly a year to fill the position since her election, a sign to many of her disregard for the position in particular and rural affairs in general. While McBride was widely respected for her coverage of Native issues during her career as a journalist, Palin's decision to name a non-Native to what had traditionally been an Alaska Native position angered many in the rural community. The rural adviser had often provided an institutional link between rural Alaska and the state government bureaucracy. McBride, who is of half-European and half-Japanese ancestry, had spent part of her childhood in Alaska and had returned as a young professional to the isolated Native community of Bethel, some four hundred miles west of Anchorage.

There, she worked closely with the Yup'ik community as news director at the public television and radio station. She developed a firsthand understanding of rural Alaska issues and the hard-earned respect of the community. Hers was a connection of the heart, perhaps, but not of blood. When she was tapped for the rural affairs position, McBride says, she was surprised by the selection, but also excited by it. She viewed the position as a way "to help promote better understanding about the challenges of life in rural Alaska and the exciting possibilities for the future." McBride also viewed Palin as a "fresh voice" in Alaska politics and said she was filled with "hope" about a new political dynamic in the Last Frontier.

McBride recalls going for her interview with Palin and meeting with what Palin called her "inner circle"—Palin's husband, Todd; her close friend, Kris Perry; and her director of commissions, Frank Bailey. McBride says that Palin expressed her hope that McBride's communication skills could help "give voice" to some of the many issues facing rural Alaska. In her press release announcing McBride's appointment, Palin declared, "I am delighted that Rhonda will be working on behalf of the citizens of Alaska. Her experience will provide an important link in areas that are essential to rural Alaska, including economic development, land use, and energy issues."

During her campaign for governor, Palin had issued a pair of press releases establishing her positions on Native issues. She played upon her husband's Yup'ik heritage in appealing to Native voters. "My kids are Alaska Natives," she proclaimed. "And my commitment to rural Alaska is unwavering." She pledged that her administration would find a solution to the "subsistence impasse," and promised to work closely with various Native leaders and organizations. "I personally feel the language, stories, traditions of Alaska Native cultures are a national treasure to be nourished and held close to our hearts," she asserted. "It is our rural lifestyle and diverse cultural heritage that distinguishes Alaska from the rest of the world and makes it our wonderful home."

As with many of Palin's campaign promises, the words rang hollow to many Natives. McBride said she realized almost immediately after her appointment that Palin really had little interest in rural affairs. Palin had developed a rocky relationship with Alaska's Native community during her first ten months as governor. She had allied herself with urban sports fishermen and hunters in the state, in opposition to rural subsistence; she had opposed tribal sovereignty; and she had refused to support language assistance to Native speakers. After a momentary rapprochement with Native leaders at the Alaska Federation of Natives convention in the fall of 2007 when she announced McBride's appointment, Palin's relationship with Alaska Natives was only to get worse.

During McBride's first visit to Juneau following her appointment, Mc-Bride recalls that a Native member of the Alaska Senate, Al Kookesh, a Democrat from Angoon who had served as rural adviser under Tony Knowles, confronted her about assuming the position. He told her in no uncertain terms that the post should be held by an Alaska Native; the job, he said, needed a "Native perspective." Still another Alaska Native, Andy Ebona of the Tlingit tribe in Alaska's southeast, handed her a pamphlet about structural racism. While one response to her appointment was overt and direct, and the other subtle, McBride said both made her sensitive to her position—and to perceptions about her position—in the greater Alaska Native community.

McBride recounts a pattern of neglect and rejection during her tenure as rural adviser under Palin. She says she tried to meet with the governor on numerous occasions over the next several months only to be put off by Palin and her staff or flat-out rejected. McBride says that Palin also refused to meet with several Alaska Native leaders. "It became very clear what her priorities were and what they were not," McBride said. "Alaska Native issues weren't on her radar. I think she thought she would get a pass because of Todd."

One matter that particularly irked McBride was Palin's refusal to visit with Alaska tribal leaders, most notably Dr. Walter Soboleff, the respected Tlingit elder living in Juneau and the pastor emeritus of the Northern Lights Presbyterian Church in the capital city. Soboleff was about to celebrate his one hundredth birthday—still in sound mind and strong spirits—and Mc-Bride made several attempts to secure a meeting for him and his family with Palin in Juneau. Soboleff had specifically wanted to discuss the alcohol crisis in the bush. "Her failure to meet with him really offended me," McBride recalls. "How often do you get the opportunity to have a discussion with a hundred-year-old man? He's so precious and very cogent. I certainly would have thought that she would have met with him, because you know, she purports to have these Christian values and he was a Christian leader. That really disappointed me that it didn't happen." McBride made several attempts to set up a meeting, all to no avail. She was beginning to grasp the dark side of Palin's governorship.

A few months after McBride was named rural adviser, Palin callously appointed a trio of non-Natives to the state's seven-member Board of Game, leaving this important Alaska body absent of any Native representation. The board is responsible for establishing hunting and trapping policies throughout the state, issues that are of vital concern to subsistence Native communities living in the bush. There had always been at least one Native representative on the board since its creation in 1976. Myron Naneng, president of the

Association of Village Council Presidents, saw Palin's appointments as a direct reflection of her "anti-rural and anti-subsistence" sentiments, which if allowed to become policy, he argued, could result in the "total annihilation of our subsistence way of life." The appointments were a calculated move on Palin's part, representative of the simultaneous hubris and disconnect that she had developed during her first year in office, and one intended to impose her conservative, ethnocentric (if not institutionally racist) will on Alaska government in general and on Native Alaska in particular.

Since Palin was a relative recluse in Juneau during the rare periods when she was there, McBride felt the direct wrath resulting from Palin's Board of Game appointments. Kookesh was once again vocally critical of Palin's decision, declaring it "morally wrong" for Palin not to name a Native to the board. Other Native leaders and state legislators also registered their opposition to Palin's decision, including several Republican allies in both houses of the legislature. Palin liked to say her administration was "color-blind" and that she was looking for those with "servant's hearts," an oft-repeated meme. She also asserted that she was not "necessarily going to look for race, or gender" in her appointments— which meant more often than not that people of color, in this instance, Alaska Natives, were excluded from positions of power in Palin's administration. "She was supposed to be a breath of fresh air," Kookesh asserted, "but it is certainly not turning out that way for Native Alaska." Palin's claim of being "color-blind" was code for renouncing affirmative action programs and the corrective measures to institutionalized racism that they represented.

The uproar over the Board of Game appointments grew so great that eventually one of Palin's appointees, Teresa Sager Albaugh, a staunch hunting advocate who had not even applied for the position, withdrew her name from consideration. Palin shortly thereafter named a Native, Craig Fleener, to replace her, which momentarily appeased her Native critics, but did little to heal the deeper schism. "Governor Palin blundered with her recent appointment to the Board of Game," the *Anchorage Daily News* noted in an editorial. "It's hard to imagine how a governor who is so committed to a fair public process could have settled for such a skewed membership on the Board of Game."

Palin continued to oppose Native interests not only in respect to subsistence hunting and fishing, but also in respect to a wide variety of social and cultural issues. McBride did her best to continue her outreach efforts with Native communities, but she felt frustrated by Palin's—and the entire administration's— seeming indifference to Native interests and concerns.

Ironically, the one member of the Palin administration that McBride felt was sensitive to Native issues was Walt Monegan, who, of course, was both part Yup'ik and Tlingit, a shareholder in the Calista Corporation who had been raised in the bush. McBride had been impressed with Monegan's promotion of a "vertical prosecution model," in which a single prosecutor is assigned to a case from the initial filing of a crime to the completion of the prosecution. This method results in continuity and improved prosecution success, particularly in rural areas. A 2005 U.S. Department of Justice survey found that Alaska Native women were two and half times more likely to be sexually assaulted than the Alaska norm (which was also higher than national averages). In the aftermath of that study, McBride had heard a particularly painful story from a teacher who told her that most of the girls in her school had been sexually abused. Monegan's grant proposal specifically included community outreach and a prevention component on the issue of sexual abuse.

By the time McBride looked to support this effort in the summer of 2008, Monegan and the Native sensitivities he brought to the Palin administration were nowhere to be found. His departure and the ensuing Troopergate scandal had a significant impact on McBride, who felt that the Monegan dismissal had been mishandled and shamefully disrespectful of a longtime public servant. When she complained about it to Mike Nizich, Palin's icy chief of staff, he told her simply "that's how things are done." There was no further explanation. Nizich, according to McBride, made it clear he had no intention of addressing the matter again.

Ironically, in July of 2008, in a letter responding to his firing, Monegan had warned about problems in the bush in the coming months ahead. "Given the gathering storm of a questionable fishing season, and the escalating price of fuel in our state, there will be serious stress placed upon communities and residents who will struggle with the coming winter's challenges," Monegan wrote. "Last week I had asked our Troopers and Fire Marshalls to outreach both to these communities, and to your departments in a cooperative effort to mitigate issues that will arise like: theft, domestic violence, substance abuse, suicide, and accidental death that all can come from sinking reserves of fuel, money, and hope. Teamwork will never be so important."

A short time later, when Palin was selected as McCain's running mate, McBride says she was "shocked." In an article she later wrote at the one-year anniversary of Palin's nomination, she compared the announcement of Palin's candidacy to the assassination of President Kennedy in terms of personal impact on Alaskans. She was "startled" and not sure "if Palin was up to the task." Nonetheless, McBride tried to be a team player in the days after Palin's nomination. She had been requested by Meg Stapleton, then a contract employee with the state, to write a letter of support for Palin explaining why her job as governor of Alaska was comparable or even "more demanding" than governing a state with a larger population. The ever-dutiful McBride complied. But as the campaign wore on, she became further disenchanted by the Palin administration's continued disregard for Native issues, particularly as Alaska's truncated autumn promised to turn into a piercing winter. By October, she could no longer balance the constant tension between the demands of her job and her conscience. She decided to step down.

On October 13, 2008—the same day that the Branchflower Report would find Palin guilty of abusing her power in office—McBride announced her resignation. While she was politic and described the Palin administration as "well-intentioned," McBride also declared bluntly that "the Native community deserves more." She acknowledged that she "never felt authentic in my role" and then made suggestions for creating a cabinet-level position for Alaska Native Affairs. She was done with Palin and the dysfunction of her administration.

A s McBride's troubled tenure at Rural Affairs illuminated, the Alaska Native issue presents one of the most complex—and complicated—sets of political, economic, and cultural challenges facing any state in the union. The myriad problems stretch all the way back to the 1740s, when the Russian Empire first claimed the lands then known as *Alyeska* primarily for its lucrative fur trade and also as a geopolitical counter to British and Spanish colonial expansion in the Americas. Although the Russian presence in Alaska never totaled more than seven hundred colonists, they treated Alaska Natives quite nearly as slaves, herding them into camps and attempting to convert them to Russian Orthodoxy. At that time, Alaska's indigenous population totaled approximately 74,000. Their various regionally identified cultures dated back twelve thousand years or more. Anthropologists believe that Alaska was originally populated by the Inuit, later followed by Native peoples commonly referred to in popular culture as "Eskimos," the Inupiat and the Yup'ik. Alaska Natives also include its southeastern communities— Tlingit, Haida, and Tsimshian—along with the Aleut and Athabascans. The geographical span of Alaska reflects a vast and intricate mosaic of Native cultures, traditions, and languages.

While the purchase of Alaska from Russia by the United States in 1867 left the region essentially without effective governance or political oversight for decades, the formal declaration of Alaska as a U.S. territory in 1912 reified what was essentially a structure of neocolonialism in the region. At that time, Alaska's indigenous peoples composed roughly 40 percent of the territory's population of sixty thousand. Statehood brought little change to the colonial dynamic (the Native population had dwindled to roughly 20 percent of the state's population), but the discovery of oil in Prudhoe Bay in 1968 augured the beginning of a new social equation in Alaska's political economy. Three years later, in December of 1971, the U.S. Congress passed the Alaska Native Claims Settlement Act, which transferred ownership of 44 million acres of resource-rich land to a newly established network of Native organizations, including a dozen Alaska Native regional corporations and more than two hundred local village corporations. A thirteenth regional corporation was later created for Alaska Natives who no longer resided in Alaska.

The advances from the Alaska Native Claims Settlement Act were significant; however, the legislation did little to stem the tide of isolation, marginalization, and good-old-fashioned racism that marked urban-rural relations since the first sustained European contact in the eighteenth century. In 2002, the United States Commission on Civil Rights issued a stinging report entitled *Racism's Frontier: The Untold Story of Discrimination and Division in Alaska.* The report outlined what anyone who spent any length of time in Alaska understood simply from direct observation: that in addition to long-standing racial prejudices throughout Alaska, there are also substantial institutionalized racial fissures in respect to educational and employment opportunities, and in the administration of justice.

Palin's inaction amidt the bush crisis in the winter of 2009 further augmented those fissures and outraged Alaskans from across the political spectrum. The community of bloggers that had generated so much information and background on Palin during the national campaign once again lit up the Internet with reports of hunger and destitution throughout the bush.

Contrary to Palin's robotic complaints that the opposition to her handling of the crisis was "partisan," the sense of shock at her seeming inaction was both widespread and deeply felt throughout Alaska. For all the tensions and racial prejudices that define urban-bush relations, there is also a profound sense of common interest and community spirit that trumps partisan politics in the Last Frontier, particularly when someone is in need or vulnerable. Jay Ramras, a conservative Republican legislator and successful restaurateur and hotelier in Fairbanks, organized a massive food-and-supplies drive below the radar of publicity. Ramras was a native of the interior, with a bachelor's degree in history from Syracuse University, and at times like this felt that "partisan politics didn't matter." He viewed the situation as a "humanitarian crisis" and simply wanted to help.

The one missing element in the process was air transport to get the supplies from Fairbanks to the bush. Initially, Ramras tried to make arrangements for the use of Department of Public Safety aircraft. As a successful businessman in Fairbanks, Ramras had long organized volunteer efforts in his community. With little fanfare, he went about securing donated food supplies and cash to support the effort in the bush. Contributions came in from all quarters and from across the political spectrum. The Fairbanks Walmart kicked in $1,000. The rock band Spank the Dog in Juneau—featuring a pair of Palin's discarded allies, John Bitney and Paul Fuhs—raised $4,500 at a benefit concert held at Juneau's Hangar Ballroom.

But Ramras's requests to obtain state assistance for air transportation through the Governor's Office and various State of Alaska departments went unheeded. After failing with Public Safety, he approached the Department of Military and Veterans Affairs for their C-130s (which they used each year to fly in Christmas presents to rural villages) and again was turned away, as he was told that an official "state of emergency" needed to be declared in order to make use of the aircraft. It was a classic Catch-22—the circular pathway of government bureaucracy that Palin allegedly so detested—and Palin was right in the middle of the logjam. Moreover, it was becoming clear to many that Palin's failure to assist in any way reflected her seemingly un-Christian outlook of punishing the villages.

Never one to be afraid of Palin's wrath, Ramras issued a press release condemning her inaction. "We have Alaskans in a rural area in need of our assistance and have been able to amass needed food but have no way to deliver it to communities," Ramras declared. "I am saddened that Governor Palin has created a vacuum of leadership by not making state transportation assets available. Many of the cash donations raised will be needed for transportation instead of being used to purchase necessities for these communities. That is a shame."

As always, Palin took the bait. She could not avoid a street brawl, even when it made her own behavior look worse. Ever since her stint on the national campaign trail, she had become increasingly hypersensitive to any form of criticism back at home. In what was to become a battle of dueling press releases, she fired back at Ramras. "We are working cooperatively with the communities, many legislators, Native corporations, and other entities to address the needs in these areas," Palin declared, albeit disingenuously. "I am disappointed that Representative Ramras failed to express his concerns to my office before issuing a press release with incomplete and misleading information. This is particularly concerning since he knew I would be attending a meeting with his entire caucus that evening."

Ramras fired back a last time. "I am shocked and appalled that Governor Palin would stoop to making derogatory statements about me," Ramras retorted. "My question to her during our caucus last night was 'where is the food?' That the governor would accuse me of politicizing the current economic situation in the Lower Yukon strikes me as fool-hardy and Clinton-esque." This was a particularly nasty slur in what was essentially an intra–Republican Party squabble. Ramras denied playing politics, stating that Palin had simply "been too silent and her administration has taken too long to help in relief efforts. We are already weeks late." Ramras put together legislation authorizing use of state-owned aircraft for "compassionate aid." The exchange underscored Palin's pettiness and how badly her relationship with the Republican caucus in both houses of the legislature was deteriorating. It further isolated her from the legislature as a whole and from the social and political dynamics that shape the Alaska legislative session in Juneau.

O UTSIDERS WHO HAVE NOT EXPERIENCED the Alaska bush in the middle of winter simply have no concept of how cold and how isolated village life can be. When storms blow through for days at a time, a darkness settles in, both literally and figuratively, that defies description. As Willie Hensley, the celebrated Native leader and writer, has noted, the Inupiat have a word— *itraliq*—that means "bitter cold, so cold it hurts."

Without fuel and foodstuffs, and at a time when daylight is a rare and precious commodity, the Arctic nocturne can be both terrifying and deadly. Nearly two months into the crisis—and eight months after she had first been warned of it—Palin finally announced that she would be traveling to the interior villages of Marshall and Russian Mission (more than three hundred miles up the Yukon River from Emmonak) with evangelist Franklin Graham. The son of famed evangelical icon Billy Graham who heads up the international Christian relief group Samaritan's Purse, Graham announced that he and Palin would be delivering forty-four-pound boxes of food to every household in the two villages. As a gesture of relief, it was modest at best; as a solution to the wide scope of the crisis, it was dismissive beyond comprehension. And it was conspicuous in its avoidance of Emmonak.

It was equally clear from the outset that Palin intended to squeeze every bit of national self-promotion she could out of the event. In what was little more than a glorified Palin-and-Graham photo op, Palin advanced her peculiar brand of bootstrap conservatism to a small assemblage of the press. "The solutions to meeting a lot of the challenges in Alaska," Palin declared ungrammatically in a videotaped interview with Kyle Hopkins of the *Anchorage Daily News,* "government's not going to be the solution. It can't be the entire answer that is sought from those who are in need, but it's working with the faith-based community, with other nonprofits, with charitable individuals who know that Alaskans and others . . . we all pull together when others are in need. This is going to illustrate that."

Palin's conservative critic in the Alaska legislature, Jay Ramras, couldn't hold his tongue. "I applaud her for following in the footsteps of what Alaskans and nonprofits and churches have already been doing over the last four to six weeks," he declared acidly. "I think she's setting a great example for the next wave of giving."

If doing little to solve the crisis in the bush, the Samaritan's Purse mission nonetheless provided an astounding example of Palin's innate capacity for deceit. Of all the baffling lies that Palin was to utter throughout her career—of all the exaggerations and deceptions and outright duplicities—this one was probably the grandest of them all. And the mainstream media never called her on it. Not once.

That Graham served as Palin's partner in crime on this "mission" to the bush should have come as little surprise. The heir apparent to his father's evangelical "crusade," if not his stature (one critic called him the "error apparent"), the younger Graham had first arrived in Alaska in 1970 as a high school dropout (from a Christian boarding school on Long Island), where he worked briefly on the North Slope in his self-described "wild" youth, during which time he overtly rejected the Christian teachings of his father. He was fond of beer, fast cars, faster motorcycles, and, reputedly, even faster women. He had scrapes with the law. He was later kicked out of LeTourneau College in Longview, Texas, for keeping a female classmate out past curfew.

Graham fits perfectly into the pattern of religious leadership described by Max Blumenthal in *Republican Gomorrah,* one in which the evangelical calling is the result of a personal trauma or a fall from grace. Graham reportedly "turned his life over to God" on his knees in a Jerusalem hotel at the age of twenty-two. Palin and Graham shared the same dark view of humanity. "Man's heart is the same everywhere," he asserted in a *USA Today* profile. "It's evil. It's wicked. The human soul is a putrid sore of greed, lust, and pride." In *Going Rogue*, Palin would echo Graham's view of the human spirit by declaring that "man is fallen." Her politics, she declared, spring from this dark view of human nature, and in Graham she had found a national minister to match her political ambitions.

Like Palin's, the younger Graham's career has been steeped in controversy. He was criticized on several occasions for trying to convert victims of natural disasters when they were especially vulnerable. Unlike his father, who sought to build spiritual bridges with his evangelical mission, Franklin Graham is an unrepentant Christian zealot, adamant in his belief that the only way to God is through Christianity and belief in Jesus Christ. He had generated no small amount of controversy in the aftermath of 9/11 by calling Islam "a very evil and wicked religion," and he has been a vociferous critic of homosexuality. He also came under intense criticism in 2006 when he countered his mother, Ruth's, stated wishes over her burial site, unleashing an internecine family squabble that *The Washington Post* said grew to "Biblical proportions" when Franklin Graham insisted that his parents be buried at the $25 million Disneyesque Billy Graham Library in Charlotte, North Carolina, replete with a talking cow. ("It's truly tacky," said Ruth Graham's biographer Patricia Cornwell.)

At a private meeting of spiritual leaders in June of 2008, according to Blumenthal, Graham sat next to soon-to-be president Barack Obama and "peppered" him with "pointed questions, demanding to know whether the [then] senator believed that 'Jesus was the way to God or merely a way.'" He also reportedly inquired about the Muslim faith of Obama's father, "suggesting that Obama himself might be a Muslim."

Graham has also come under fire for his excessive annual income of $1.2 million, drawn from both Good Samaritan and the Billy Graham Evangelistic Association (BGEA). The $535,000 he drew annually from Samaritan's Purse was the highest salary of any international relief agency based in the United States, including eight with larger annual budgets. His $699,000 annual draw from BGEA went up even when its revenues had dropped 18 percent. It was only after his exorbitant compensation was made public that Graham decided to scale back on payments to his retirement fund, but his holdings are vast. To this day, he keeps a getaway on picturesque Lake Clark in southwest Alaska (replete with a 1958 cloth-winged Piper Cub airplane for local travel) and an office in Soldotna on the Kenai Peninsula.

Graham, who had spoken the previous two years at Palin's annual prayer breakfast in Alaska, used the trip to the troubled Alaska Native communities to advance his religious views. "Every mission, every trip I take is a ministry mission," he declared. "I'm a preacher of the Gospel of Jesus Christ."

Palin took a different tack. Speaking in her peculiar syntax and sentence structure without subject and predicate, Palin championed "public-private" partnerships. She also acknowledged from the beginning that her mission was to send a "message." Rather than acknowledge the hardships that those in rural Alaska were experiencing, Palin launched into a litany of neocon economic theory laced with Horatio Algeresque mythologies.

> Another purpose of the trip today is not just delivering food for a short-term solution, but to remind those, especially young people, in rural Alaska of the job opportunities that are available, albeit it requires in some cases leaving the village for a short time. Perhaps for seasonal work or with shift work, either on the slope or in mining operations, or in the fishing industry, or state service. We're going to look for those who would perhaps want to become VPSOs [Village Public Safety Officers] or troopers or teachers in their own community, remind people of job opportunities, because it is a cash-based society right now.
>
> We can help with providing food and providing fuel, but in a cash-based society, there needs to be income, also, in the community. There needs to be some economic vitality. The only way that that happens is for people to know that there are job opportunities to get to work, and make sure that that is part of the solution here.

Palin then went after the leadership in the village communities. It was classic Palin behavior; at a time of crisis, she chooses to attack the victims.

> Some of these areas, they may need to see some change in leadership within the community, also. For the leaders whom are looked to for guidance with the young people, that these leaders show them where opportunities are also. . . . And in

some of the communities I would say that perhaps new leadership would help provide solutions.

Palin's attack on rural leadership angered many. In the aftermath, she kept
tripping over her remarks. When pressed for specifics, she refused to provide
any. "I'm not talking about anybody specifically," she ducked. "I'm just talking about young people who are desiring those who will help them see what
the opportunities are in Alaska and not just seek government to provide solely
for all the needs in rural Alaska."

Palin's attack on the village leadership took her to a troubling place. In response to a question posed to her by Annie Feidt of Alaska Public Radio and
videotaped by Kyle Hopkins of the *Anchorage Daily News,* Palin decided to
use her husband, Todd, as "an example." In doing so, she manufactured facts
out of thin air, reconstructed chronologies, and distorted her husband's life
history beyond recognition. This was no accident or slip of the tongue. It was
another strange—even bizarre—instance of Palin saying what was politically
expedient, the facts be damned:

> [Todd] grew up in Dillingham in a fishing village on the west
> Coast of Alaska also. He recognized after high school that he
> perhaps would need to leave that village in order to provide for
> his family, and he capitalized on an opportunity up on the
> North Slope to work with his hands and—and to build things
> and to fix things—those things that he had learned growing up
> in rural Alaska. Todd left the village, uh, has been working up
> on the slope, but for those first years especially, it was such a
> win/win for him, because he would get to come back to the
> village after a one and one, or a two and two week schedule—
> come back to the village and still live the subsistence lifestyle
> that he wants, still enjoy, um, uh—the—the culture out there
> and the subsistence lifestyle—those things that he wanted to
> do, at the same time recognizing the world has changed so
> much, and in a cash-based society, he had to have a job.

This was a purely fabricated biography of her husband. It is difficult to
imagine how the governor thought she would get away with it, given that the

facts were so readily available. But just as she had lied on the campaign trail about her husband's membership in the Alaskan Independence Party, she would lie again about his family history. Todd Palin is, in fact one-eighth Yup'ik, on his mother's side, and he did spend part of his childhood in Dillingham, where his family owns and operates a hardware and building supply store. As many would note, Palin had never identified as Alaska Native, and, in fact, his father, Jim, with whom he resided while in high school, was of European descent and served as general manager of the Copper Valley Electric Association, in Glennallen, more than five hundred air miles northeast of Dillingham. The Palins then moved to the Mat-Su, where Palin's father was named general manager of Matanuska Valley Electric Association; his stepmother, Faye, served as vice president of the Matanuska Telephone Association. Todd Palin had been raised in a comfortable middle-class home (one of his classmates said he was born with "a silver spoon in his mouth"), with two administrative incomes far from the Alaska bush. After high school he did not "leave that village in order to provide for his family"; he went to college in Washington state, where he failed at basketball, dropped out of college, came back to Wasilla, and, according to his Wasilla High classmate, J. C. McCavitt, worked as a laborer for Alagco, a gravel company just outside Wasilla, at which he eventually became a member of the Laborer's Union. He also inherited his family's commercial fishing business in Dillingham, and, finally, took a job on the Slope only when he was in his late twenties, long after he was married to Sarah Heath and had become a father and while his wife was on the Wasilla City Council. Todd Palin has never gone back to the "village," never lived a "subsistence lifestyle." It was all an absolute and chilling lie—one that underscored the fraudulence of not only her administration's Alaska Native policy but of her very integrity as governor. In its boldness and absolute concoction, Palin's lie was astonishing.

S ARAH PALIN NEVER WENT to Emmonak. Not once. Her shunning of the very community that first called attention to the bush crisis reflected not only her inability to confront her critics but also her palpable disregard for engaging the real world outside her narrow, immediate circle. So when she arrived in Marshall with Graham—reportedly with a batch of homemade cookies as a gesture of goodwill to help solve the crisis—Nicholas Tucker was forced to travel up the Yukon Delta.

It was a painful encounter from the get-go. As Tucker first met the Palin entourage, Lieutenant Governor Sean Parnell inexplicably referred to Tucker as a "blogger" in a tone oozing with condescension, while Tucker responded quite curtly: "I am not a blogger." Parnell looked very much like a herring out of water. In video of the event provided by Alaska Newspapers, Inc., one can hear Palin in faux sincerity mode ("Ohhh, so nice to meet you!"), as Tucker approaches the governor.

Of medium height, lean, and graying at the temples, Tucker has a low-key, serious demeanor that connotes dignity and sincerity. Dressed in a faded blue baseball cap and a fur-lined parka, Tucker, in the video, introduces himself to Palin and identifies that he's from Emmonak. It's clear Palin initially has no idea who he is. She reaches out and gives him a hug. He explains to the governor that her mission represents "temporary help but we need sustainable jobs, fisheries." Palin then goes into a lecture mode and her faux policy-wonk-speak—talking about economies needing to be "revitalized"—and Tucker says "that's barely enough. We want to get restored back to who we are. The Native people are very strong people and this is probably the only time that they cried out for help." It was a heartfelt—if not heartbreaking—plea for assistance from a proud Native elder. And right in the middle of it—as Tucker hands Palin a copy of his original letter (and his identity finally sets in on her)—she rudely breaks away from her discussion for a photo op with some women. Then she returns to Tucker, who continues his remarks—and Palin cuts him off and returns to the same lie about her husband "leaving his village."

> Also, Mr Tucker, we'll let people know, young people in these areas also, that it's not just the jobs inside the villages, but good resource development jobs with the mining and with the oil production and fisheries even if they are outside the villages. Like my husband, who grew up in Dillingham, the native village of Dillingham. He's worked on the North Slope these years, so he could come back to the village and participate in the community, then go off to work again, then come back. That's the ideal way to work.

Tucker refuses to accept Palin's patronizing response. "Our culture is too tied into us," he asserts. "It's hard for us to live in Anchorage because of all the discrimination." She interrupts him again. Their energies and focus are so remarkably different—Tucker is steady and patient, Palin flighty and unfocused—that they are clearly talking past each other, as though existing in parallel universes. Palin interrupts him yet again. "See, that's what these resource development jobs allow," she utters, going back to her rote response. "Just like with my husband, he didn't have to leave forever the village, he would be gone, week on, week off . . ." Her attention span is obviously running on overdrive, and she starts scanning the room, planning her escape.

"I don't do politics," Tucker says to her, looking her straight in the eye. "I come from the heart and the sorrow of our people."

S ARAH PALIN HAD ANOTHER CRISIS LOOMING during the winter and spring of 2009, far from the bush and rooted in the more urban confines of Anchorage, though it, too, was born of neglect and arrogance and bad judgment. Andrée McLeod, a "good-government activist" in Alaska and a onetime close political confidante of Palin's, had become outraged by what she viewed as Palin's cavalier approach to governance. Palin, she thought, was as corrupt as all the rest or even worse. Palin, she says, "sailed into the Governor's Office on an anticorruption wave and failed to deliver on it." She considered Palin a fraud and it troubled her deeply. "There finally came a time when I could no longer handle her almost daily public pronouncements of being open, honest, ethical, and transparent," McLeod said, "when her official conduct didn't square with her rhetoric. And since the Alaska media and legislators wouldn't address her abuses of office, I decided to take matters into my own hands." She openly accused Palin of "making a mockery of our system of government."

In March 2008, McLeod, who was a registered Republican and had run for both the school board and state legislature in Anchorage on the GOP ticket, attended the Republican State Convention at the Hotel Captain Cook in downtown Anchorage. There was a showdown brewing at the convention pitting two of Alaska's GOP heavyweights against each other again—Palin and her perpetual GOP nemesis, state party chairman Randy Ruedrich, with whom Palin had waged a battle when they sat together on the Alaska Oil and Gas Conservation Commission (AOGCC) earlier in the decade. There remained bad blood between the two of them. They hadn't spoken since Palin had been elected governor, and Palin's name had been excluded from the state GOP Web site.

Palin took it as a serious affront. She recruited GOP interior regional chair Joe Miller (the same Joe Miller who two years later would run for the U.S. Senate against Lisa Murkowski) to execute a political coup d'état against Ruedrich at the convention. It was no secret—both the Associated Press and the *Anchorage Daily News* picked up on the story in advance of the three-day gathering—and both sides were ready to engage in battle. Ruedrich's term wasn't to be up until 2010, so it would take a two-thirds party vote to suspend party rules and oust him. Palin's GOP rival Jay Ramras was having none of her machinations. "I think it's incredibly divisive, distracting, and demoralizing because it ignores the process of election cycles," Ramras told the Associated Press. "It shows a base level of immaturity; it's not the hallmark of a healthy debate." Miller, then working as an attorney for the Fairbanks North Star Borough, had used his government-issued computer and had also hacked into those computers of three of his associates as part of an Internet campaign against Ruedrich. (He later tried to cover up his efforts and subsequently lied about it to his supervisors.)

At the convention, McLeod observed two members of Palin's staff, director of commissions Frank Bailey and special assistant Ivy Frye, both of whom were part of the governor's inner circle, clearly involved in the effort to overthrow Ruedrich, along with Miller. Palin was there briefly, then left. She watched as they tried to orchestrate the coup over cell phones. It was a futile effort—Palin was the ringleader of yet another gang that couldn't shoot straight—and Ruedrich survived easily, by a vote of 167–133 in his favor. One Democrat who had worked in the administration of Tony Knowles and watched the proceedings from afar was astonished at how little power Palin wielded within her own party. "A seated governor?" she said. "Are you kidding me? She couldn't even execute that?"

McLeod suspected that Palin and members of her administration had used their state-assigned e-mail accounts and phones to conduct partisan political activities directed at Ruedrich—much as Palin had charged Ruedrich six years earlier. She made the first of several Alaska Public Records Act requests at the time—for e-mails and phone records from Bailey and Frye—and in so doing first discovered the inner workings of the Palin regime, including its use of a private e-mail system and personal Yahoo accounts for government business. And she also discovered that Todd Palin had been included in many of the e-mail chains, the first concrete example of his shadow role in the state government.

While McLeod didn't find any e-mails directly linking Palin, Bailey, and Frye to the partisan machinations involving Ruedrich at the convention, she did discover e-mails indicating that Palin and Bailey had sidestepped proper state personnel protocols in the hiring of surveyor Tom Lamal, who once co-hosted a Palin fundraiser at the Pagoda restaurant in North Pole (on Santa Claus Lane, no less), for a state right-of-way agent position in Fairbanks. Palin's acting chief of staff, Mike Nizich, was also included in the e-mail chain.

"Looks like Tom Lamal finally got on in DOT Fairbanks," Bailey wrote. "This was a long battle but [deputy commissioner of administration Kevin Brooks] pushed it through the road blocks to get Tom Lamal hired into a classified [position] in [Fairbanks] with the [Department of Transportation]."

"Great," Nizich wrote back to Bailey. "Long time coming."

These initial findings prompted McLeod to dig deeper—along with another fiscal-conservative watchdog, Zane Henning, of the Last Frontier Foundation—and to seek more Palin administration e-mails. "For her to be portrayed as a role model by the media is an absolute travesty," McLeod declared. "The more people find out about Palin . . . the more they learn that a 'servant's heart' does not beat within her."

On August 6, 2008—three weeks before Palin would be tapped by McCain as his running mate—McLeod filed the first of what would eventually be several Executive Branch Ethics Act complaints against Palin and her administration, arguing that Palin and several of her underlings "had exerted undue influence and misused their official positions" to secure Lamal's hiring by the state. Three months later—on the same date that he would issue his findings exonerating Palin in her Troopergate scandal—Personnel Board investigator Tim Petumenos found that while Palin herself did nothing wrong in the hiring, he did recommend "ethics training" for Bailey because of the "troubling" nature of his e-mails. Although it may have seemed trivial, the recommended ethics training for Bailey had drawn blood. Palin's reputation as a reformer had been tarnished. Soon others, including Henning, were inspired to file other complaints. And McLeod filed a pair of lawsuits against the state, one challenging Palin's use of private e-mail accounts to conduct state business and the other seeking access to the e-mails of Todd Palin when they related to government affairs.

ONCE SARAH PALIN RETURNED TO ALASKA after her campaign for vice president, McLeod began the slow process of filing four more ethics complaints against Palin involving misuse of state resources for partisan political purposes; accepting undisclosed gifts; misuse of her office; and campaigning for the vice presidency while receiving her governor's salary (McLeod argued that Palin should have taken official leave and handed the reins to

Lieutenant Governor Parnell). She also acknowledges working on several others—including those charging Palin with: using her state offices to conduct partisan interviews after the campaign; wearing promotional clothing at an event in which she was serving in her official capacity as governor; collecting a per diem while living in her home in Wasilla; and, most significant, using her position as governor to collect contributions to a legal defense fund.

In the end, perhaps as many as thirty ethics complaints were filed against Palin by a variety of Alaskans (the exact number is uncertain, as some of them remain confidential) and while Palin would refer to them incessantly as "frivolous" (a term the media eventually parroted as well), the fact is that many of them had significant bearing on state government.

Palin would also boast that she had won them all (in a misleading posting on Palin's Facebook page, her attorney Thomas Van Flein would claim a record of 26-0-1, as though he were keeping score in a hockey game), but the fact is that four of the complaints ultimately resulted in negotiated settlements and sanctions. In addition to the very first complaint filed by McLeod—which resulted in Palin's director of boards and commissions, Bailey, being required to take ethics training—Palin also agreed to repay the state for family travel expenses and to pay back income taxes on thousands of dollars in expense money she received while living at her Wasilla home. By the time of Van Flein's Facebook posting, there had already been an initial "probable cause" finding presented by independent counsel for the Alaska Personnel Board Tom Daniel that would require Palin's legal defense fund to return roughly $386,000 in contributions, as it was found that "there is probable cause to believe the trust violates the Ethics Act," although the Personnel Board also concluded that "the evidence supports Governor Palin's contention that any violation of the Ethics Act was not a knowing violation." (In June of 2010, the Personnel Board upheld that finding.) Of course, Van Flein's scorecard also failed to take into account the ruling by Alaska's Legislative Council a year earlier, which found that Palin had "abused her power" in the Troopergate matter by violating the Ethics Act. So when it came to ethics complaints, Palin hardly had a clean record; 26-0-1 it was not.

McLeod has further argued that the entire ethics complaint process has been conducted in a "culture of corruption" stacked against the plaintiff. The three-member Personnel Board that presided over the vast majority of the other Ethics Act complaints was established by the Alaska State Legislature to be bipartisan. The legislation states that "not more than two members of the board may be members of the same political party"—an objective that has been conveniently sidestepped by three successive Republican governors (including Palin) who have made sure that at least one of their appointees is a Republican-turned-"declined to state"; there hasn't been a Democrat serving on the board in years. Moreover, board members all serve at the pleasure of the governor—making sure that the appointees are beholden to the administration in power. (Indeed, the most recent appointment to the board, made by Palin's successor, Sean Parnell, is a member of the Republican National Committee.) As a result, the board is bubbling with biases and hidden agendas. Board hearings have often deteriorated into partisan gamesmanship; in one instance a board member hurled invectives at McLeod: "Just keep *bitching*, Andrée. Just keep *bitching* . . . until you're all through . . . just keep *bitching*." All throughout its findings in Palin's favor, the Personnel Board was never a neutral body.

McLeod refused to back down in the face of attacks levied against her. "Clearly you do not serve the public," she retorted at a board meeting. "You have allowed the Governor's Office to use state resources to malign and vilify. You should all be ashamed of yourselves. . . . What is the cost of corruption? What is the cost of the culture of corruption that you are now complicit in?"

Throughout her final days as governor and in *Going Rogue*, Palin would malign McLeod as the "falafel lady," a racially loaded term of derision aimed at McLeod's ethnic background. McLeod is of Armenian descent by way of Lebanon, but she was raised in New York (her family immigrated to the United States in 1963) and you can still catch the trace of a Long Island accent in her voice. Energetic, spunky, and uniquely tenacious (she makes Palin's infamous barracuda persona look more like that of a goldfish), McLeod first arrived in Sitka in 1978. She began working in Alaska government in 1984, serving in a variety of positions for the departments of Fish and Game, Education, Administration, Health and Social Services, Transportation and Public Facilities, Military and Veterans Affairs, and Labor and Workforce Development. She also worked as an aide for a couple of Alaska legislators and completed a degree in economics at the University of Alaska at Anchorage.

What is widely unknown about McLeod and her relationship with Palin is the close nature of their political alliance, beginning in 2002, in the aftermath of Palin's failed bid for lieutenant governor. Ironically, they worked together during Palin's highly publicized battle with Ruedrich—none of which is included in *Going Rogue*. Palin supported McLeod politically during her runs for the Alaska State House. Prominently displayed on McLeod's campaign brochure was a quote from the former mayor of Wasilla: "Like many of us, Andrée wants good government. She's not afraid to stand up for what's right.

Though she ruffles a feather or two now and then, this intelligent Alaskan is exactly what we need during these times."

During their period of working together, Palin often sent McLeod e-mails full of praise and support. One from 2003 reads as follows:

> That was a great letter to the ed. this week Andrée. I haven't had time to call but wanted to tell you it was, again, insightful & educational & good writing. I'm still disenchanted with the whole issue of RR [Ruedrich] and state politics and am not even very optimistic about the call for an independent investigation. We'll see. I guess I'll believe it when I see it. Hope you're doing well, staying warm & staying on top of all these state issues I'm hearing about on the news! Love, SP

Other Palin e-mails to McLeod refer to her as "intelligent," "bold," "powerful," and "encouraging." In one e-mail Palin wrote: "Ugh! I know you must get so frustrated because you're all about accountability!" Still another declared in classic Palinese: "wow! again! YOU ARE A WRITER . . . I'll bet your son is, too. You will be thanked for summing up for others what many believe: that there's nothing wrong with healthy debate and challenges to the status quo when something is wrong & it can easily be fixed!"

Unless, of course, it was directed at Sarah Palin.

IN THE AFTERMATH OF HIS ENCOUNTER WITH THE PALIN-GRAHAM ENTOURAGE IN MARSHALL, Nicholas Tucker would no longer be diplomatic in his dealing with the Palin administration. He issued a second letter and this time he took off the gloves. If his first epistle was tempered, this one bristled with emotion. "First off," he wrote, "I am outraged." Tucker was incensed that he had to travel to Russian Mission and then Marshall to meet with Palin. "Why did she not come here to Emmonak?" he asked. "It took away the most precious time of my life to have to be absent from my granddaughter's and nephew's first Yup'ik dance in Alakanuk that evening." His journey had been a challenge. Moreover, he was incensed that Palin had used the visit to promote what was a veiled anti-Native political perspective, one that was an attack on their subsistence way of life. He challenged her on the underlying duplicity of her remarks. Where were the ten thousand jobs in Alaska required to eliminate unemployment in the villages? Were the elderly expected to complete the job exodus as well?

Tucker was equally incensed by Palin's comments about changing the leadership in the villages. Tucker took it as a personal affront.

> I was there. About whom and to whom was she referring that top leadership in what village(s) should be changed? This is a blow to all rural villages telling each one of us that our past and current leadership isn't worth being there!
>
> Why and on what basis? This message is dismal, not of hope. How do I take things? Here, I had a person whom I voted for and who turns around and stabs us. I tell you, I want things done for Emmonak. And now, for all rural villages. We deserve better than that respect.

Tucker noted that in his original letter he had simply stated the conditions of those in need. He had not pointed any fingers or engaged in any debates. But, Palin, as was her wont, struck back at anyone who she thought she could bully. "Usually, I refrain from this type of outrage," Tucker wrote, "but I am hurt to the core of my heart and spirit." He saw the Palin-Franklin mission for what it was—"talk and PR are cheap until you have solid accomplishments to back them up."

Tucker sounded a call for Alaska Native unity. He expressed "faith in my fellow rural villages and their leadership" and complimented them for meeting the vast, contemporary challenges that were confronting them in the bush. He threw down the gauntlet. "I think all rural Alaska deserves an apology and never to be treated like this again," he asserted. "I feel insulted myself and on behalf of our rural native villages."

It was a passionate statement coming from deep in the Alaska bush. And while this exchange was lost to most Alaskans, much less to those in the Lower 48, it served as something of a rallying cry for those whose lives had been affected by the crisis.

Later that year, Palin would boast on her state-funded Twitter account: "Good update re Rural Advisor John Moller's recnt Emmonak trip, great news he reports; we'll twitter assuming press won't pick up good news." Then came her report: "50% of residents have subsistence needs met already, others confident they can do the same."

It was another instance of Palin distorting reality. When Kyle Hopkins of the *Anchorage Daily News* asked the governor's spokeswoman, Sharon Leighow, about Palin's assertion, Leighow e-mailed: "The good news—At the Federal Subsistence meeting in Emmonak last week, Nick Tucker reported that 50 percent of the residents have met subsistence needs and other 50 percent are confident they will meet their needs."

Tucker was now livid. "I want them to take it back," Tucker responded to a query from Hopkins. "I've never said that. Ten times over, I've never said that." In an interview with videographer Dennis Zaki of *The Alaska Report,* Tucker was even more adamant.

> When I'm talking with people I'm straightforward. OK, I expect to say my piece, just the way things are, and I want that in return . . . just the way they are. No buttering up, nothing added. Just the truth. *Now, I did not say that. I want a public apology and I want that taken back.* That statement was made by an Alakanuk fisherman at our meeting, and that represented Alakanuk.

Alakanuk is a village located roughly eight nautical miles from Emmonak, on a different arm of the Yukon Delta, with an entirely separate and distinct village leadership. John Moller, who had replaced Rhonda McBride at Rural Affairs, later admitted that he may have been mistaken; according to Tucker, he received an e-mail apology from the rural adviser admitting his error. Tucker accepted Moller's mea culpa and called him "a man of honor." Neither Palin nor her spokesperson Leighow ever issued an apology or a retraction. In the end, such niceties were of little concern to Tucker. His burdens were far more immediate and substantive: "I don't know what we are going to do for this coming winter." The governor of Alaska didn't seem to care.

CHAPTER 7

Unraveling

When the going gets weird, the weird turn pro.
—Hunter S. Thompson, *Kingdom of Fear*

Oh the jealousy, the greed is the unraveling . . .
—Joni Mitchell, "All I Want," *Blue*

Only dead fish go with the flow.
—Sarah Palin, resignation speech

A S THE WONDERS OF ALASKA'S late spring burst into all their glories in early June of 2009, with wildflowers ablaze in the valleys and high meadows and the magnificent king salmon runs beginning in the snowmelt and glacially fed rivers surging throughout the state, Sarah Palin seemed very much like a whirling dervish off-kilter, spinning madly out of control, unable to maintain—or sustain—her political equilibrium. Whatever she said or did, wherever she went, Palin seemed to unleash a wild rage of anger and vitriol that inevitably left a wide swath of destruction in its wake: collateral damage. For Palin it was the typical series of controversies and misunderstandings, lies and half-truths, vengeful charges and bitter recriminations that always follow her and on which she appears to feed and thrive. This time, however, the turmoil seemed to be taking its toll. Anyone paying close attention could see that her governorship was an abject failure—the legislature was literally circling her from all sides—and it was about to collapse from the weight of her apparent psychological turbulence, her inability to focus, and her seemingly reckless personal ambition, which was now national in scope.

Palin was clearly flailing—she had taken to the social network Twitter to vent her frustration with the press and with her critics, posting as many as ten tweets a day, many of them descending into petty bitterness. Palin's tweets provided a fascinating glimpse into her mental life and thought process. On what was a public account paid for by the state of Alaska, Palin recorded observations about her family and concerns about the media. In only her second tweet she contested an Associated Press article about her position on the federal stimulus package and directed followers to a state-run Web site refuting the contentions of the article. She offered medical advice and promoted private business interests. She took on President Obama (whom she referred to only as "Obama," while with other public officials she employed their proper formal title) on a variety of fronts, including foreign policy. On May 7, for instance, she posted:

> Outraged Obama's budget includes major cuts to missile defense programs, when N. Korea refuses to abide by UN

In many respects, Twittter was a perfect medium for her. It was spontaneous and quick and, with a limit of 140 characters per message, freed Palin from the confines of grammar and coherent thought processes. She could wander all over the map however she wanted. And she was in direct contact with her faithful followers without the snarly institution of the media interfering with her and calling lie to her various deceits and fabrications.

WEDNESDAY, JUNE 3, WAS THE type of day that most residents of southwest Alaska choose to stay outside until after darkness descends, to get out of the city and take in the glories of the Last Frontier. The last two summers had been gray and dreary. On that day, it was approaching 70 degrees, the Alaska sky cerulean blue, and the imposing mountain ranges framing Anchorage rose up majestically toward the heavens. For Sarah Palin, however, it was more embattlement, as she woke to find herself in the middle of an imbroglio with former Alaska governor Frank Murkowski, yet another Republican mentor turned enemy, who had written a harsh critique of Palin in the opinion pages of the *Fairbanks Daily News-Miner*:

> As a former governor who negotiated a draft contract with
> North Slope oil and gas producers, it is hard not to compare

where the gas line project is now to where it would have been, had Gov. Sarah Palin's administration simply proceeded to improve the draft contract we negotiated pursuant to the Stranded Gas Development Act. . . . The bottom line is that by the end of the Palin administration, Alaska will have wasted four years in attempting to get a gas line that could be far along by now had the Palin team simply picked up the SGDA contract we handed it.

Palin was getting it from all sides. And she was dishing it, too. She responded with an official press release from the Governor's Office: "I am so very proud of our gas line team which works hard every day to make progress on this vital project for our state, without any need to seek publicity or achieve political advantage. With no need for grandstanding, they have moved this project along with stakeholders and federal regulators, and that is going to pay enormous dividends in the future." Of course, Palin had sought political advantage and had "grandstanded" at every opportunity along the way in respect to oil and energy policies, but it was the only way she could strike back at the likes of Murkowski. The facts spoke for themselves.

Palin had other fish to fry that day. There's an old joke that Anchorage is just thirty minutes from Alaska and, of course, the reverse is true, too, so that residents of Alaska's urban center are only a half-hour away from the splendors of the Last Frontier. The roadways out of town were filled with traffic in both directions that evening, but several Alaskans were opting to remain indoors. Michael Reagan, the late president's adopted son (with actress Jane Wyman), was making the rounds on the lecture circuit and his next stop was Anchorage. While President Reagan's two living biological children—Patti and Ron Jr.—had famously rejected their father's (and mother Nancy's) cold brand of conservatism, Michael had not only embraced it, he was capitalizing on the family name and legend. He was a minor-league right-wing radio host for American Family Radio, had written a book with a ghostwriter, Joe Hyams, entitled *Michael Reagan: On the Outside Looking In,* and had even served as host for *Lingo,* a marginal half-hour game show that was filmed in Canada but syndicated for a year in the United States. He would occasionally claim brief moments of fame for remarks on the air, including his call to kill babies who had been named for the Lebanese militant group Hezbollah and its leader, Hassan Nasrallah:

Naming their children "Hezbollah." You know what I'd get
'em for a first birthday? I'd put a grenade up their butts and
light it. Happy birthday, baby. Bye bye.

In response to a caller who pointed out that children are not responsible
for the names they are given, Reagan repeatedly asserted, "So what's wrong
with killing the *mothers and the babies*?" (Emphasis added.) Such comments
have made Reagan a fringe political player, even in the right-wing underbelly
of the Republican Party, but in Alaska, it put him square in the thick of things.
So there he was in downtown Anchorage on this glorious evening, scheduled
to make an appearance at the Alaska Center for the Performing Arts, a lovely
venue and yet another community perk of the gas and oil money flowing
through Alaska. The title of his talk was "What Would Ronald Reagan Do
Today?" and the person selected to introduce him was—who else?—none
other than Sarah Palin, who was herself trying to claim the Reagan mantle in
the aftermath of her failed vice presidential candidacy and as she assessed
her prospects for the 2012 Republican Party presidential sweepstakes. Right
before the event, Palin sent out a post on Twitter: "On my way to intro Michael
Reagan & hear him speak re: what his wise, innovative father, Pres. Reagan,
would do in these challenging times." At $34.50 a pop, there were no cheap
seats to this affair, and, in spite of Palin serving as a barker on its behalf, the
venue was at best half-filled.

Palin was introduced by her portly and crude court jester, local radio
shock jock Eddie Burke, Anchorage's excuse for Rush Limbaugh, who weirdly
lingered on stage playing with an electronic gadget while Palin began her
speech. A scattering of Palin family members and associates were in the
audience—her brother, Chuck Heath, her husband, Todd (whom she actually
introduced as the "First Dude"), along with Lieutenant Governor Sean Parnell—
as Palin took to the stage, dressed in a contrasting combination of dark suit,
pearls, and red patent-leather wedge sandals that had caused a controversy a
week earlier when she had worn them at a somber Memorial Day weekend
event in Fairbanks (in her ever-increasing slide toward self-reference and narcissism, she even referred to her "Franco Sarto red high heels" in her speech,
predicting that her critics were "going to be loaded for bear and they're going
to start unloading because, because I dared speak up"). She proceeded hap-
hazardly in her remarks, reverting to her tortured phrasing, jumping from serious to cutesy in a single breath. She seemed to speed-read through certain
passages that clearly were not hers, her singsong phraseology rising octaves to

the grating high pitch that her speech teacher had rid her of before her remarks at the Republican convention. The triumph and glories of St. Paul seemed a long way off.

It was another one of Palin's lazy attempts at speechwriting, pulling phrases, jumbling sentences, contorting ideas. Matthew Scully's fine hand was nowhere to be found. But the remarks were certainly calculated. She wondered aloud why "today do we feel we have to pussyfoot around our troublesome foes," without ever saying specifically who those "foes" might be, employing simply the word "terrorists" to identify foes as she tossed verbal chunks of red meat to the crowd. She praised Reagan *fils* for being willing "to screw political correctness," a metaphor that surely was intended to reflect on her own penchant for "going rogue" and to identify him as an important ally.

Dennis Zaki videotaped the speech, and it was later transcribed, nearly in full, for *The Mudflats* by Jeanne Devon (AKMuckraker), designating the "word salad award" for a particularly peculiar Palin construction:

> Today the things that some in Washington would do to take away our freedoms, it's absolutely astounding, and we would do so well to look back on those Reagan years as he championed the cause for freedom and then he lived it out as our president—*cheerfully, persistently, and unapologetically.* Reagan knew that real change and real change requiring shaking things up and maybe takin' off the entrenched interest thwarting the will of the people with their ignoring of our concerns about future peril caused by selfish short-sighted advocacy for growing government and digging more debt, and taking away individual and state's rights and hampering opportunity to responsibly develop our resources, and coddling those who would seek to harm America and her allies.

While the phrasing was uniquely Palin's, the content seemed largely foreign to her, as if she had somehow borrowed piecemeal phrases of cloth and tacked them together in a strangely shaped verbal patchwork quilt. As it turned out, she had indeed borrowed them, from an obscure opinion piece written by Newt Gingrich and Craig Shirley for the *New Hampshire Union Leader* in November of 2005 that was posted on the Internet and in which they declared:

"*Cheerful persistence* rather than easy victories were the keys to Reagan's career." Note the clarity and directness of the Gingrich-Shirley article. And while Palin's garbled oratory lacked none of those qualities, as many as a dozen passages were strikingly similar to those in their article. Palin opened her remarks by noting:

> First, I think what we're going to learn tonight via Michael is that Ronald Reagan's ideas were the "right" ideas and all we have to do is look back at his record, his economic record, and his national security record to know that his ideas were right.

Gingrich and Shirley had asked:

> What should Americans learn from this remarkable man and his remarkable Presidency? . . . The "right" ideas really matter (the left was wrong and Reagan was right about virtually every major public policy issue and the historic record is clear for those willing to look at it).

After her opening remarks, Palin awkwardly, almost dismissively, acknowledged that, "Recently, Newt Gingrich, he had written a good article about Reagan . . ." (Recently? It had been written four years prior to her speech.) Without ever mentioning Shirley, the title of the article, or from whence it came, Palin paraphrased the article at length, without clear acknowledgment, in each instance, mangling it at virtually every turn.

> PALIN: He said, regarding your dad Michael, he said that we need to learn from his example that courage and persistence are keys to historic achievement and with Reagan's example, D.C. politicians calling the shots for our country, they had better rely on the good sense of the American people and bag their alliance on the entrenched bureaucrats and the elite self-proclaimed intellectuals, and the smug lobbyists who dominate Washington, and the liberal media that is imposing its will on Washington, embracing that status quo, that business as usual.

GINGRICH/SHIRLEY: Courage and persistence are the keys to historic achievement. . . . Relying on the good sense of the American people beats relying on the elite intellectuals, entrenched bureaucrats and smug lobbyists who dominate Washington.

From this point on, Palin continued with her speech, presenting her remarks as if they were her own, while seamlessly using almost verbatim words from the Gingrich/Shirley piece, at several points, without ever citing it.

PALIN: We have to remember first that Ronald Reagan never won any arguments in Washington. He won the arguments by resonating with the American people.

GINGRICH/SHIRLEY: Reagan never won an argument in Washington. Reagan won his arguments in the country with the American people.

———

PALIN: So Ronald Reagan spoke to us then with us here in our hearts is where he reached us. . . . He captured our hearts so he could affect positive change by what he did. He focused on our kids, on our children, on their future, on the future of America.

GINGRICH/SHIRLEY: The key to capturing the attention and, yes, the hearts of Americans is to focus on their future and their children's future. Reagan understood this . . .

———

PALIN: Reagan knew that real change—and real change requiring shaking things up and maybe takin' off the entrenched interest thwarting the will of the people . . .

GINGRICH/SHIRLEY: Reaganism is about real change both at home and overseas and that real change requires upsetting the entrenched interests . . .

———

PALIN: He stood strong on his knowing that the framework through which he believed that positive change that framework for our kids, it was freedom.

GINGRICH/SHIRLEY: Successful governance means having a framework through which to lead the American
people. For Reagan, that framework was freedom.

At this point, Palin offered her second (and final) reference to the article
that Gingrich and Shirley wrote. She said: "What Newt had written in this
article, he wrote, remember how refreshing it was with his [Reagan's] outrageous directness that Americans loved, and craved and deserved." Ironically,
that quote *isn't* in the article—and isn't from any other Gingrich article available on the Internet. The closest wording she may have been referring to was
from the Gingrich-Shirley article: "Candidate Ronald Reagan responded to
the failures of the left with enormous clarity and directness."
Palin continued, once again without attribution or reference:

PALIN: Remember this? His vision for the Cold War? We
win, they lose.
GINGRICH/SHIRLEY: On the inevitability of the Soviet
Union, Reagan responded with a then shocking vision for the
Cold War—"we win, they lose."

———

PALIN: And with detente, speaking of detente, he used two
words: "Evil Empire."
GINGRICH/SHIRLEY: Reagan replaced the entire vision of
detente with two vivid words: "Evil Empire."

Like a ravenous vulture, Palin had scavenged all the meat there was in the
750-word Gingrich-Shirley article—the only apparent source for the initial
segment of her speech—and then segued off the beloved Gipper and shifted
back to what had become her favorite subject those days: the embattled Sarah
Palin.
There was an interesting backdrop to the whole Palin-Gingrich affair: earlier in the spring, when Gingrich had been asked directly in an interview with
Christianity Today who he viewed as the "emerging leaders" in the GOP, the
former House Speaker had distinctly refused to name Palin, wondering instead
when pressed: "Is she willing to do the kind of development of national issues
and development of a national profile that would be required? . . . [B]ecoming
a national leader would take a significant amount of work." The pilfering of

his intellectual labors may not have been the "significant amount of work" that Gingrich had in mind. There was also background with Shirley, a respected Reagan biographer and Republican operative, who had been brought into the McCain campaign for a few months in early 2008.

In response to plagiarism charges, that Palin had borrowed from the Gingrich-Shirley article, Palin's attorney, Thomas Van Flein, immediately sent out a letter threatening the *Anchorage Daily News* and other publications that reported the similarities as "actionable." He called the allegations "defamatory." As an attachment to his letter, Van Flein included a transcript of the speech in which the portions that had been taken from the Gingrich-Shirley article are indented, giving the impression that they had somehow been verbally "indented" in Palin's delivery. He also failed to note those passages that came before and after Palin's brief references to Gingrich. Van Flein also did not provide a copy of the Gingrich-Shirley article with his letter in order to compare. Finally, like Palin, Van Flein never once referred to the actual article or mentioned Shirley, in spite of the fact that Shirley was the co-author. It was intellectually misleading and an overt attempt to stifle journalistic criticism of Palin.*

When confronted later with the charges, Gingrich, not wanting to get entangled with Palin, had called the story "silly," but did not call the charges false. Shirley, who had been left out of Palin's attributions entirely, blamed Palin's staff for what he suspected was sloppy and ineffectual support. He told the *Huffington Post*'s Sam Stein that what really bothered him was that Republican politicians "adopted only [the ideas] in rhetoric and not in action." At its worst, it was a conscious act of intellectual theft on Palin's part (doubting that anyone would ever notice to call her on it), while at best it was an act of oratorical recklessness, reflecting Palin's utter lack of respect, or interest, really, in

---

* The author first reported Palin's unattributed use of the Newt Gingrich and Craig Shirley article on June 6, 2009, in *The Huffington Post*. Van Flein's letter was in response to the *Anchorage Daily News* posting the article on its Web site. In his letter, Van Flein asserted that: "It is abundantly clear in context, and even in sub-context, that the overview of President Reagan's legacy was attributed to Newt Gingrich . . . Thus, the commentary, paraphrase and analysis were acknowledged, attributed and sourced at the outset of the commentary—and at the end of the commentary." The original article by Gingrich and Shirley, "Another View: Republicans Need to Relearn Lessons of the Reagan Revolution," appeared in the *New Hampshire Union Leader,* November 1, 2005.

intellectual ideas and real political theory. When it comes to politics, Palin is all id. She is lazy beyond belief and carelessly impulsive. Immediately after Reagan's talk, she tweeted: "Great talk by Michael Reagan tonight. Encouraged by his conservative ideals and commonsense."

A MIDST THE TURMOIL OF THE GINGRICH AFFAIR, Palin and her family were getting ready for an East Coast swing, though the details were not yet fully in place. As with virtually all of Palin's travels, there were last-minute changes at all turns. In an article foreshadowing Palin's sojourn, *Politico* had reported, ironically, that "Sarah Palin takes low-key return to the road." Low-key it would not be.

Palin had carelessly canceled on several commitments since her return to Alaska, most notably the National Republican Congressional Committee and the National Republican Senatorial Committee. In April, the joint chairmen of fundraising for the committees' marquee event held in Washington, D.C., each June, sent out a national press release announcing that Palin would be serving as keynote speaker. A representative for the committees had contacted "representatives" of Palin, presumably at her political action committee, SarahPAC, located in Alexandria, Virginia, and had invited Palin to serve as the event's keynote speaker, a plum assignment. They believed that she had accepted. But Palin claimed that she had not. The governor's ever spinning political spokesperson, Meg Stapleton, put the blame on Palin's staff at SarahPAC, telling the *Anchorage Daily News* that Palin didn't even know about the invitation. "Someone helping me out on the East Coast," Stapleton declared, "in the enthusiasm of Sarah Palin and the enthusiasm of providing some sort of response, confirmed that the governor was coming, and that wasn't appropriate." It was a classic Team Palin response: (a) never accept responsibility; and (b) blame someone else.

Palin's political staff at SarahPAC, with whom she would break her association shortly thereafter, were just as adamant that Palin *did know* and *had confirmed* her appearance. They were outraged by Palin's explanation. The elected officials, however, tried to put a positive spin on the controversy. In a joint press release sent out by the committee chairs, Texas senator John Cornyn called Palin one of the "most popular and recognizable faces" in the GOP and one of its "brightest rising stars." Texas representative Pete Sessions said that Palin had "electrified" audiences during the 2008 campaign and that he expected her to "generate a similar amount of enthusiasm at this spring's dinner." But Palin didn't budge. She let the egg harden on Cornyn's and Sessions's faces. "She was a disaster," one Republican source complained to Fox News, more often than not a bastion of support for Palin. *"We had confirmation."* Sources familiar with the Palin snub fumed about how the governor—and her staff—handled the invitation. Rather than smooth things over with a gracious acceptance, they turned what should have been a win-win situation for the governor into a lose-lose.

The congressional fundraising committees were livid, and in a matter of only a few hours announced that none other than Newt Gingrich had come on board to take Palin's place. There was no small amount of irony in the replacement. GOP spokesman Ken Spain asserted that the GOP had "decided to go in another direction," further declaring in what was an obvious critique directed at Palin, "Speaker Gingrich is a *leader*." The affair led Republican insiders in the Beltway to dub the Palin circle as "the gang who couldn't shoot straight."

Beyond the troubled organizational shortcomings reflected in the scuffle was Palin's explanation that she would have to wait until after Alaska's legislative session to make her decision to attend. It was another lie. She had just confirmed other events during the Alaska legislative session (which was scheduled to end in mid-April), and had even left Alaska for Indiana during some key votes in the final days of the legislative session to give speeches at the Vanderburgh County Right to Life dinner and a breakfast event for S.M.I.L.E., a nonprofit organization that supports families with Down syndrome. She had also confirmed a pair of appearances in New York state during the very same weekend that she was balking at the GOP leadership. So the explanation "that her gubernatorial responsibilities in Alaska prevented her from committing" simply did not ring true to those who were closely following Palin's schedule. "She may go, she may not go," Stapleton casually declared, further irritating those in Washington who plan events like the Senate-House dinner several months in advance.

Moreover, there had been other Palin scheduling mix-ups two years running with the Conservative Political Action Conference, at which the governor was supposed to be the keynote speaker in 2008 and again in 2009, when she pulled out of her commitment with less than two weeks to go, leaving CPAC to replace her with Rush Limbaugh, who went on to generate national headlines with his bombastic attacks on President Obama. In May, Palin had also skipped out at the last moment on the White House Correspondents Dinner in Washington, and a long-standing event in New York City honoring the Alaska fishing industry, sending Todd in her stead. It was a pattern that was becoming all too predictable.

The Palin ensemble was clearly a three-ring circus—though with no apparent ringmaster. Some in Washington dubbed them the Keystone Kops or the Not-Ready-for-Prime-Time Players. Kathleen Parker, a conservative critic of Palin's, opined that Palin clearly "isn't ready. For whatever reason—skittishness, distrust, or, quite possibly executive weakness—Palin has been unable to make the transition from Alaska politics to the Big Game hunt of the national arena." But there may well have been something more at work here than naïveté and inexperience. Palin liked to view herself as a "maverick," and her penchant for not showing up for scheduled appearances and making people guess whether she was coming dated back decades. It was a deep-seated pathology of hers, one of many that she did not seem capable of transcending. "She is a complete and utter diva," said Andrew Halcro. It was another example of her *going rogue,* a euphemism for her duplicity and, perhaps, for her seeming instability.

I N SPITE OF ALL THE SCHEDULING snafus, the governor and her entourage—her husband, Todd; fourteen-year-old daughter, Willow; Palin's sister, Heather Bruce; and the Bruces' fourteen-year-old son, Karcher—finally departed from Anchorage on their way to New York for what would prove to be a momentous journey to the Empire State. The weekend would culminate in a series of charges and countercharges, finger-pointing and denial involving Palin and late-night talk show icon David Letterman, along with a series of lesser imbroglios involving the congressional leadership of the Republican Party and assorted bit players. Palin, always good at assuming center stage, had forced herself there once again, straight into the vortex of the swirling winds. This time, however, it would consume her governorship.

As it turned out, Palin did execute a pair of commitments that weekend, one of which was in upstate New York, in the small Finger Lakes community of Auburn, home of William Seward, the former secretary of state who, under Andrew Johnson, negotiated the purchase of Alaska. Auburn was also, not so coincidentally, the home of Palin's then-political confidante, Meg Stapleton, whose father, prominent Auburn attorney T. David Stapleton, sits on the board of the Seward House Foundation, the nonprofit organization that raises money on behalf of the Seward House and, which, by state law, must steer clear of partisan activities.

A gorgeous spring day, much like that what they left behind in Alaska, greeted the Palin entourage in Auburn. The governor, donning what had become a trademark corsage, rode most of a mile-long parade in a classic 1959 red Cadillac convertible, holding small American and Alaska flags and waving to the crowds. Many cheered her on to seek the presidency, with chants of "Run, Sarah, Run!" rumbling throughout the parade. There were also smatterings of protests, too, including members of the Defenders of Wildlife Action Fund, an organization that had targeted Palin nationally for her support of the aerial hunting of wolves. In respect to the 2008 presidential campaign, it was déjà vu all over again—but it was also, more probably, a portent of things to come.

Auburn Police Department crowd estimates for the event were listed at five thousand to six thousand, though Stapleton would later claim twenty thousand—a nearly four-fold exaggeration. Although the events in Auburn were intended to be nonpartisan, Palin used the occasion as yet another platform to craft a narrative about herself that linked her to national historical figures. "We are blessed that William Seward recognized what Alaska could offer with our strategic location, with our resources that today could help secure the United States and make us less reliant on foreign sources of energy," she said, sounding a frequent political theme of hers. "He took a path that wasn't necessarily real easy, but it was the right path." What she did *not* note in her speech was that Seward, an ardent abolitionist in the years leading up to the Civil War, had been attacked for spending so much of the Federal Reserve on the purchase of Alaska at a time of fiscal constraints in the aftermath of the war. Nor did she mention that Seward had survived a plot to assassinate him, along with Lincoln, by ardent secessionists conspiring with John Wilkes Booth. Those particular details did not properly accompany the Palin-as-national-figure narrative that had become the operating theme of all her public appearances.

During her speech at the Seward House later that evening, which cost $100 per head to attend, Palin ramped up her attack on President Obama, her perennial foil as she set her sights on a run for the White House in 2012. If anyone had any doubts of what she was really doing in New York, this speech should have settled it. "It's clear to many that some of our priorities as a nation are reversed," Palin declared. "Alaskans get tired of hearing that Washington bureaucrats know what's best for us so we push and fight and challenge decisions made inside the Beltway when they are not in the best interests of the country, and we know that decisions that are being made recently are not in the country's best interests." She then made an oratorical beeline directly at what she perceived to be Obama's jugular—his economic stimulus package intended to jump-start the flailing American economy. Palin railed against federal monies with "strings attached," a favorite claim of hers about so-called mandates, saying that they are more "like ropes." "It is not free money," she declared in that peculiar syntax of hers. "It is not free money, and taking it is taking away anything that is free." What she did not say was that she had accepted more than 98 percent of the $1.24 billion federal stimulus package offered Alaska; she had turned down *less than 2 percent of it*—a $28.56 million program directed toward energy efficiency—about which the Alaska legislature was threatening to override her veto just before her departure. Those kinds of details typically escaped Palin in her positioning with "the Feds," as she consistently negotiated a fine line between exaggeration and deception in her proclamations on the stimulus bill.

Palin had a second event to attend the following afternoon, Sunday, where she was to receive an award from the Independent Group Home Living Foundation, a nonprofit organization on Long Island that supports families dealing with disabilities. Hearing that Alaska's first couple was in the vicinity, former New York mayor Rudy Giuliani, whose own presidential aspirations had fizzled in Florida in 2008 but who was contemplating the New York gubernatorial race in 2010, invited the Palins to take in a game at Yankee Stadium between the Yanks and Tampa Bay Rays.

Giuliani, a regular at big-time Yankee games, always liked to flash some celebrity bling in the Bronx. Palin, who came to the game in her trademark designer sunglasses and plenty of bling of her own, was heavily made up for her Big Apple public viewing at the newly christened Yankee Stadium, where she and her family joined Giuliani and his third wife, Judith. But there was a considerable backstory to Palin's appearance in Yankee Stadium that day as well. Records obtained through the state of Alaska later revealed that Giuliani had spent a rather phenomenal $4,250 on the three tickets for the Palins (Sarah, Todd, and Willow attended the game). Moreover, Giuliani was actually courting the state of Alaska at the time for work in the Last Frontier in his capacity with Bracewell & Giuliani's Environmental Strategies Group (ESG), a legal and public relations consortium that assists "clients with a number of high-profile environmental and energy issues," including "climate change" legislation and litigation. Giuliani was to visit Alaska only a few days later, having lunch with Palin's former legislative director John Bitney (then working for Alaska state senator John Harris), who said that Giuliani expressed concern about Palin getting "too far ahead of the issue" and drawing fire from Democrats "just by virtue of who she is."

(Giuliani also told Bitney that he was "amazed" by the buzz that Palin created at the Yankee game, even among Democratic season ticket holders who had box seats near his.) According to the New York *Daily News*, the couples exchanged "laughs, smiles and small talk" (Bitney's conversation with Giuliani confirmed this) until the sixth inning, when the Palins left for their commitment on Long Island, with the Yankees trailing 3–1, long before the seventh-inning stretch that would cause so much commotion in the days ahead.

T HE PALINS MADE IT TO ST. James, about halfway out on Long Island, just in time for the thirtieth Annual Gala of the Independent Group Home Living Foundation, where the governor was to be honored before a sold-out crowd of more than a thousand. The organization's mission is to: "provide programs, services and support for people with developmental disabilities so they can realize their full potential as human beings and contributing members of their community," along with coordinating community activities and developing "progressive legislation" to "protect the right of our constituents and their families to access appropriate care." The founder of the organization, Konrad J. Kuhn, when asked by New York's *Newsday,* acknowledged that he didn't know "what type of advocacy work Palin has done on behalf of developmentally disabled children"; nonetheless Palin's celebrity had clearly drawn a crowd. While rocker Dave Mason, whose 1960s hit (with Traffic) "Feelin' Alright" would become a minor anthem for baby boomers, served as the event's featured performer, several patrons paid $1,000 to attend a special cocktail hour with the Palins, where they took photos with the guests. Palin declared, "Every single person has purpose, no matter what their developmental abilities" "Independence and freedom: they're cherished rights for every citizen regardless of their ability level." As in virtually all Palin speeches, she turned the spotlight back on herself and on her family.

> God has blessed us, and we don't ask why me? why us? . . .
> Without Trig, I don't think we would ever have had our
> hearts, and our minds, our souls, and ourselves opened up to
> the passion that you all have and had for many years for the
> special needs community. Without Trig, I think that that would
> be absent from us.

Ironically, the Palins had traveled to the event *without Trig*—he had been left in the care of Bristol and her parents—and she would claim, without explanation, at the event that "we couldn't bring him on the airplane" because he was "too rowdy," though she had clearly flown with him before. She was, however, joined at the event by Sean Hannity, who would assert that Palin had delivered her acceptance speech "without a teleprompter"—a clear partisan dig at Barack Obama at what was supposed to be a nonpartisan event and one that was also disingenuous, as video of the event shows that Palin had clearly walked to the podium with prepared remarks and was reading from them throughout her seventeen-minute speech. There was no mention of "screwing political correctness" at the event, however, and she expressed hope that addressing the needs of those with special needs could be a "unifying issue" and "nonpartisan cause" in this country—right before Hannity's digs at Obama.

WITH THAT, THE PALIN ENTOURAGE was off to Washington, D.C., where Sarah and Todd Palin's on-again, off-again appearance at the National Republican fundraising gala was becoming something of a slapstick joke. Palin had been told she would be allowed to address the gathering briefly, but behind the scenes, National Republican Congressional Committee chairman Peter Sessions had indicated he didn't want Palin to upstage Newt Gingrich, the fundraising gala's keynote speaker. "A great deal of effort has been put into this fundraising event, and Speaker Gingrich has gone above and beyond the call of duty," asserted gala spokesman Ken Spain to *Politico*. "It is our hope that Governor Palin will attend the dinner and be recognized, but we understand if her busy schedule doesn't permit her to do so." It gave Palin a polite out. According to an unidentified campaign official, the "disinvitation" to Palin was done "out of respect" for Gingrich. "You dance with the one who brung ya."

Since the mainstream American media rarely discuss matters of real political theory—strategy and policy, yes; but overarching theory, no—the issues underlying the Gingrich-Palin tensions went largely overlooked. In fact, they were rooted in the former Speaker's broader theoretical vision for the GOP. His latest book, *Real Change,* was a political manifesto for the big-tent theory of Republican Party politics. "The Republican Party cannot win over time as the permanently angry anti-government party because neither appeals to most voters," Gingrich asserted. Moreover, he argued that Republicans must be "pro–good government" and resist the temptation "to allow their campaigns to be dominated more and more by pandering to small, specific segments of the activist wing of the party." Although he refrained from criticizing Palin openly, Gingrich's GOP mantra was the direct antithesis of Palin's realpolitik.

At the last minute, Palin and Todd decided to show up at the gala, and while Gingrich and Palin were civil, her very presence at the Monday night event, even if only in an introduction, thoroughly upstaged Gingrich's message. "Newt Gingrich was the keynote speaker at Monday night's fundraising dinner for the Senate and House Republican campaign committees," CNN reported, "but it was Sarah Palin who stole the show." The Palins' arrival brought a cheer from the two thousand assembled party faithful, and during a break in the program Palin was swarmed by well-wishers and GOP dignitaries. According to reports, Palin's former running mate, John McCain, tweeted: "Great to see Sarah and Todd at the dinner tonight—nice reunion!"

Later that evening, however, an even greater upstaging would take place when David Lettermen took Palin squarely into his sights. Palin's East Coast sojourn, particularly her weekend foray to Yankee Stadium with the Giulianis, had made headlines in all the New York papers and presented itself as an easy target for Letterman. He opened his show with his standard Top Ten list, this time the "Top Ten Highlights of Sarah Palin's Trip to New York":

10. Visited New York landmarks she normally only sees from Alaska.
 9. Laughed at all the crazy-looking foreigners entering the U.N.
 8. Made moose jerky on *Rachael Ray*.
 7. Keyed Tina Fey's car.
 6. After a wink and a nod, ended up with a kilo of crack.
 5. Made coat out of New York City rat pelts.
 4. Sat in for Kelly Ripa. Regis couldn't tell the difference.
 3. Finally met one of those Jewish people Mel Gibson's always talking about.
 2. Bought makeup from Bloomingdale's to update her slutty flight attendant look.
 1. Especially enjoyed not appearing on *Letterman*.

Nine out of ten could have been offered in good humor, but the "slutty flight attendant" reference had certainly crossed the line and, by overtly sexualizing Palin, Letterman had opened himself up to all sorts of charges. Letterman had been particularly hard on the Republican ticket during the 2008 campaign, bitter about John McCain canceling on his show in late September and then lying about it ("something doesn't smell right," Letterman declared), and there was a certain amount of leftover vitriol fueling his humor toward Palin.

Later, in his opening monologue, Letterman took it a disturbing step further when he declared that "the hardest part of [Palin's] trip was keeping Eliot Spitzer away from her daughter." It was dangerous territory he was heading into, now sexualizing Palin's daughters (his reference was vague as to which one) and using Bristol's out-of-wedlock pregnancy as satirical fodder. And then he went sideways. "One awkward moment for Sarah Palin at the Yankee game," he deadpanned, "during the seventh inning . . . her daughter was knocked up by Alex Rodriguez." It was a typical Letterman joke construction—bringing together two disparate public figures, in this case, the allegedly promiscuous Yankee slugger who had been linked with women from Madonna to former New York madam Kristin Davis; and Palin's eighteen-year-old unmarried daughter, Bristol, whose out-of-wedlock pregnancy had created such a stir during the campaign. Only Bristol hadn't been at the game. Her fourteen-year-old sister, Willow, had. Letterman never said Bristol's name and it left open the possibility that the joke was alluding to the governor's fourteen-year-old daughter.

The Palins were livid—and understandably so. But Palin also saw an opening to trump much of the bad national publicity she had received in recent days and to wage a holy war against the liberal media elite personified by Letterman at her hated broadcast network, CBS. Once again, Palin went to her Facebook page to launch an incendiary attack:

> Concerning Letterman's comments about my young daughter (and I doubt he'd ever dare make such comments about anyone else's daughter): "Laughter incited by sexually-perverted comments made by a 62-year-old male celebrity aimed at a 14-year-old girl is not only disgusting, but it reminds us some Hollywood/NY entertainers have a long way to go in understanding what the rest of America understands—that acceptance of inappropriate sexual comments about an underage girl, who could be anyone's daughter, contributes to the atrociously high rate of sexual exploitation of minors by older men who use and abuse others."

Palin was being persecuted again. (Hers was the only daughter about whom Letterman would ever make such a joke.) And she milked it to the hilt. Todd Palin also issued a statement on Palin's Facebook page, declaring that "any jokes about raping my fourteen-year-old are despicable. Alaskans know it, and I believe the rest of the world knows it, too."

The entire debate was now slipping into Neverland. Todd Palin had turned the joke about Bristol—vulgar and offensive as it was—into a reference to "rape." The following night, Letterman apologized by calling Palin "an absolutely lovely woman" and claiming that they were "just jokes." But Letterman's apology came off as less than sincere. "These are not jokes made about her fourteen-year-old daughter. I would never, never make jokes about raping or having sex with a fourteen-year-old girl," he asserted, then inexcusably went back to the source of the joke, making fun of Bristol. "Maybe these are questionable because the girl who, excuse me, but is knocked up, is eighteen years old."

He issued a direct apology to Palin, but couldn't resist attaching sarcasm to it all. "Governor Palin, if you're watching, I would like you to consider coming to New York City—you and Todd as my guests, or leave Todd at home—I'd love to have you on the show. It'd be exciting," he mocked. He wanted to put it all behind him, but he made light of it along the way. "All right, so there, I hope I've cleared part of this up. Am I guilty of poor taste? Yes. Did I suggest that it was okay for her fourteen-year-old daughter to be having promiscuous sex? No."

The comedian, known for his sarcasm and acerbic wit, simply couldn't find his sincerity button. It was particularly ironic, given the sexual scandal that was heading his own way four months later, but the Palins weren't biting. They fired back again, this time through Meg Stapleton. "The Palins have no intention of providing a ratings boost for David Letterman by appearing on his show," Stapleton posted on Palin's Facebook page. "Plus, it would be wise to keep Willow away from David Letterman." That parting shot was classic Palin-Stapleton overkill. Just when they finally had generated an unusual amount of sympathy for Palin across the political spectrum, they once again found a way to cross the line.

The incident soon became a national cause célèbre. There were threats of boycotts. The ever-harder-to-take-seriously right-wing shock jock John Ziegler went apoplectic and called for Letterman to be fired. His attempt to organize a national protest at the Ed Sullivan Theater, where Letterman's shows are taped, drew a "crowd" of fifteen people. Indeed, there were far more members of the media there than protesters. Whatever moral traction Palin had generated by her initial response was dissipating rapidly. Letterman finally put an end to it. In an unprecedented eight-minute monologue, Letterman issued a second apology. This time, he took the high road. "The joke really, in and of itself, can't be defended," he acknowledged, explaining again that he thought he was referring to the eighteen-year-old Bristol and not fourteen-year-old Willow. "I've never made jokes like this as long as we've been on the air, thirty long years, and you can't really be doing jokes like that. And I understand, of course, why people are upset. I would be upset myself."

It was a fascinating moment in American television history. Letterman assumed full responsibility for the joke.

> I was watching the Jim Lehrer "NewsHour"—this commentator, the columnist Mark Shields, was talking about how I had made this indefensible joke about the fourteen-year-old girl, and I thought, "Oh, boy, now I'm beginning to understand what the problem is here. It's the perception rather than the intent." It doesn't make any difference what my intent was, it's the perception. And, as they say about jokes, if you have to explain the joke, it's not a very good joke. Well, my responsibility—I take full blame for that. I told a bad joke. I told a joke that was beyond flawed, and my intent is completely meaningless compared to the perception. And since it was a joke I told, I feel that I need to do the right thing here and apologize for having told that joke. It's not your fault that it was misunderstood, it's my fault. . . .
>
> So I would like to apologize, especially to the two daughters involved, Bristol and Willow, and also to the governor and her family and everybody else who was outraged by the joke. I'm sorry about it and I'll try to do better in the future. Thank you very much. [Audience applause]

Letterman's full-fledged mea culpa suddenly turned a good deal of the public sympathy back in his direction. For all his biting humor (and ensuing personal turmoil), Letterman remains a beloved figure in American culture, and after nearly three decades of hosting late-night television programming on both NBC and CBS, his audience wasn't about to abandon him over a single faux pas, particularly one involving the polarizing Palin. Indeed, *The Late Show*'s ratings shot up during the Palin skirmish. In a Facebook posting titled "Governor's Reaction Regarding Letterman's Apology," Palin declared:

> Of course it's accepted on behalf of young women, like my daughters, who hope men who "joke" about public displays of sexual exploitation of girls will soon evolve.
>
> Letterman certainly has the right to "joke" about whatever he wants to, and thankfully we have the right to express our reaction. And this is all thanks to our U.S. Military women and men putting their lives on the line for us to secure America's Right to Free Speech—in this case, may that right be used to promote equality and respect.

Palin found it necessary to get in one final dig and some holier-than-thou moralizing. And so the controversy extended through one more news cycle. Many commentators who initially sided with Palin turned back around to condemn her for making bigger political hay out of what had initially been a complaint about exploiting her daughters. Others were appalled by how the Palins had twisted Letterman's joke into something it clearly was not intended to be—a glib rift about the "rape of a fourteen-year-old."

In *Going Rogue*, Palin used the controversy not particularly to go after Letterman, but to take a cheap shot at feminists. She accused them of "staying silent too long" and of being "hypocrites." In fact, the National Organization of Women, on the day immediately following Letterman's first ill-advised apology, issued a formal statement asserting that Letterman and other comedians "in search of a laugh should really know better than to snicker about men having sex with teenage girls (or young women) less than half their age. The sexualization of girls and women in the media is reaching new lows these days—it is exploitative and has a negative effect on how all women and girls are perceived and how they view themselves." NOW then went a step further. The organization also condemned Letterman for joking about "what he called Palin's 'slutty flight attendant look'—yet another example of how the media love to focus on a woman politician's appearance, especially as it relates to her sexual appeal to men. Someone of Letterman's stature . . . should be above wallowing in the juvenile, sexist mud that other comedians and broadcasters seem to prefer." The condemnation was clear and unequivocal—but Palin refused to acknowledge it, either at the time or in her memoirs.

While those defending the Letterman joke were few and far between, there was a backlash against the Palins for taking it a step—or two—too far. In a column posted on the Web site *Open Salon*, J. E. Roberts issued a counter-narrative to the Palin-Letterman controversy in which he noted how Palin finds herself "time and again in these hostile confrontations on the national stage over her family life." The act, he argued, was wearing thin. He pointed out accurately that Palin "repeatedly sought to use her family in order to score political points." Roberts also criticized Palin for "inflating" Letterman's comments and returned to a familiar theme in the litany of criticism directed at the governor. "Sarah Palin is lying, and she is exploiting her own daughter, by way of a fabricated scandal, in order to gain attention for herself," he intoned. "It is a disgrace to the value of family and honest and forthright public service as virtues in our society that she would do this. It is a disgrace to conservatism that she so willingly props herself up by lying about other people."

Back in Alaska, a place where Palin seemed less and less comfortable as spring burst full-bloom into summer, Palin's governorship was spinning rapidly out of control. She had also appeared to many to have gone off the deep end. Almost immediately following the Letterman brouhaha, Palin found herself in another public battle, this time with Alaska blogger Celtic Diva (Linda Kellen Biegel), who had posted an image on her Web site in which the face of shock jock Eddie Burke had been superimposed over her son Trig's in what was clearly a joke aimed at Burke. This one didn't reach a national buzz, but the buzz was thick on the streets of Anchorage and Wasilla and every bit as ferocious as the Letterman affair. Once again Palin's spokesperson Stapleton took it too far:

> Recently we learned of a malicious desecration of a photo of the Governor and baby Trig that has become an iconic representation of a mother's love for a special needs child.
>
> The mere idea of someone doctoring the photo of a special

needs baby is appalling. To learn that two Alaskans did it is absolutely sickening. Linda Kellen Biegel, the official Democrat Party blogger for Alaska, should be ashamed of herself and the Democratic National Committee should be ashamed for promoting this website and encouraging this atrocious behavior.

Then Stapleton took it even further, linking Biegel incredibly with Obama. "It is past time to restore decency in politics and real tolerance for all Americans," she wrote. "The Obama Administration sets the moral compass for its party. We ask that special needs children be loved, respected and accepted and that this type of degeneracy be condemned." Biegel responded that she was simply making fun of Burke. It was a form of political commentary. Nothing more, nothing less. And it had nothing to do with Trig.

Many suspected that this dark conspiracy in which everything was linked to Obama may well have been fueled by Stapleton. Those in south-central Alaska said that Stapleton had been articulating bizarre theories about a conspiracy linked directly to the White House for some time.

In a portrait of Palin in *Time* magazine in July, Stapleton also alleged that attacks on Palin in Alaska were emanating from Obama's inner circle. "The trail is pretty direct and pretty obvious to us," Stapleton declared. According to *Time*:

> Palin and her Alaska circle find evidence for their suspicions about the White House in the person of Pete Rouse, who lived in Juneau for a time before he became chief of staff to a young U.S. Senator named Barack Obama. Rouse, they note, is a friend of former Alaska state senator Kim Elton, who pushed the first ethics investigation of Palin, examining her controversial firing of the state's public-safety commissioner. Both Rouse and Elton have joined the Obama Administration.

What didn't make the printed version of the magazine, but was included in a blog by *Time* correspondent Jay Newton-Small, were two additional comments by Stapleton. "I just hope to God Rahm Emanuel isn't using taxpayer money to come after Alaska," Stapleton declared. She then offered that the reason for this conspiratorial effort was because Palin "represents the biggest threat to Obama. She's the only one who can get the base excited."

Comments like these by Stapleton created a buzz in Alaska that added to a growing suspicion that Palin would not seek reelection the following year.

I N LATE JUNE, THE CONDÉ NAST publication *Vanity Fair* published online a devastating portrait of Palin by national editor Todd Purdum entitled "It Came from Wasilla." The story broke little that was new about the governor for those paying close attention, but it marked the first time since the presidential campaign that much of Palin's history and her sordid behind-the-scenes political machinations had been brought together under a single headline. It was also clear to those that read it that some McCain senior staffers had dished to Purdum about Palin's erratic behavior on the campaign trail, revealing that she was "casual about the truth and totally unfit for the vice-presidency." Perhaps most significantly, the article also asserted that "some top [McCain] aides worried about her mental state." It did not a pretty picture paint.

The story caused yet another round of negative national media attention directed at Palin. Then came Skirmish Two. Not to let Purdum's piece go by without a response, Palin's would-be knight in shining armor, Bill Kristol, once again came to her defense with a blog posting on the *Weekly Standard* Web site. Pigeonholing Purdum as a "lefty journalist" and describing the article as a "hit piece" full of "dubious claims," Kristol asserted that the article was dependent "on self-serving stories provided on background by some of the people who ran the McCain campaign into the ground."

He then challenged Purdum's contention that several of his sources in Alaska had "consulted" the *Diagnostic and Statistical Manual of Mental Disorders* and had come to the conclusion that Palin suffered from a "narcissistic personality disorder."

> Is there any real chance that "several" Alaskans independently told Purdum that they had consulted the *Diagnostic and Statistical Manual of Mental Disorders?* I don't believe it for a moment. I've (for better or worse) moved in pretty well-educated circles in my life, and I've gone decades without "several" people telling me they had consulted the *Diagnostic and Statistical Manual of Mental Disorders.*

That Kristol runs in narrow and elite circles goes without saying. But he apparently had yet to arrive to the New Millennium, at which the *Diagnostic and Statistical Manual of Mental Disorders* is available to anyone with a Web link and in which anyone with an idea can disperse it immediately and widely on the Internet. Nor had Kristol been to Alaska recently, where, in fact, people were widely discussing Palin's mental state that summer at backyard barbecues and on Alaska's varied blog sites. Palin's "narcissistic personality disorder" was the diagnosis du jour.

Perhaps Kristol could be excused for this oversight. But then he suggested that the leaks to Purdum from the McCain campaign had been initiated by senior adviser Steve Schmidt. In particular, there were the charges in Purdum's account about Palin suffering from "postpartum depression" on the campaign trail. "In fact," Kristol wrote, "one aide who raised this possibility in the course of trashing Palin's mental state to others in the McCain-Palin campaign was Steve Schmidt."

The former tight end did not take kindly to Kristol's speculative accusations and Monday-morning quarterbacking. While Schmidt had gotten down and dirty in the trenches during the last decade with the likes of Bush, Cheney, Rove, Schwarzenegger, McCain—and, yes, even Sarah Palin—Kristol had pontificated from the comfort zone of his various ivory towers without having to get his tailored suits dirty. Schmidt was not going to let this one slide.

It was hardly a fair fight. Schmidt came back swinging. "I'm sure John McCain would be president today if only Bill Kristol had been in charge of the campaign," Schmidt deadpanned in an e-mail to Jonathan Martin at *Politico*. "After all, his management of [former vice president] Dan Quayle's public image as his chief of staff is still something that takes your breath away." Asked directly in a telephone interview with Martin if he brought up the prospect of Palin suffering from postpartum depression, Schmidt said: "His allegation that I was defaming Palin by alleging postpartum depression at the campaign headquarters is categorically untrue. In fact, I think it rises to the level of a slander because it's about the worst thing you can say about somebody who does what I do for a living."

Then Kristol's (and Palin's) ally Randy Scheunemann jumped into the fray. "Steve Schmidt has a congenital aversion to the truth," Scheunemann told *Politico*. "On two separate and distinct occasions, he speculated about Governor Palin having postpartum depression, and on the second he threatened that if more negative publicity about the handling of Governor Palin emerged that he would leak his speculation [about postpartum depression] to the press. It was like meeting Tony Soprano."

Schmidt denied it all, then elaborated on the history of Scheunemann being "fired" after being discovered as the leaker of negative information about the campaign to none other than Kristol. It was November 2008 all over again. The old war wounds had reopened. Skirmish Two, covered delightfully by Jonathan Martin, then descended into the mud, where it might have stayed and ended in obscurity.

But then came Skirmish Three. On Wednesday, July 1, CBS News posted on its Web site an article by its own Scott Conroy and special contributor Shushannah Walshe, who were then finishing up their book, *Sarah from Alaska,* in which several highly secret e-mail exchanges between Palin and Schmidt had been posted for the first time. The Kristol-Schmidt exchange had provided the opportunity for Conroy and Walshe to enter the fray with a bomb of their own. Conroy and Walshe's framing of the e-mails made it clear that Palin had lied about her husband's membership in the Alaskan Independence Party and that Schmidt had called her on the lie (see Prologue). The e-mail evidence provided by Conroy and Walshe was excruciatingly revelatory. In what had been a summer of bad news cycles for Palin, this one was particularly damaging.

Palin had a relatively heavy schedule that day out of her Anchorage office. Her official calendar indicates that she met that morning with Senator Mark Begich and others regarding congressional earmarks for Alaska infrastructure, followed up immediately with various members of the attorney general's office, at which she discussed recent Supreme Court decisions affecting Alaska. At noon she was scheduled for a bill signing at Alaska Pacific University. She tweeted about it: "Gorgeous day in ANC for bill signing! Many thanks to APU for use of campus to ceremonially sign HB 172, re: student loans & ASLC." She had time to herself in the mid-afternoon to catch up on her relentless Web surfing, then was scheduled to attend the mayoral inauguration of Dan Sullivan in Anchorage later that afternoon, replete with a barbecue outside the Discovery Theatre at the Alaska Center for the Performing Arts Center. She tweeted about that, too, though there's no official record of her actually being in attendance. There were several adversaries scheduled to be included in the municipal ceremony that day—among them former Anchorage mayors Begich and Tony Knowles—and perhaps Palin simply did not want to confront ghosts from her political past. "Congratulations to Anchorage Mayor Dan Sullivan as he is sworn in today!" Palin tweeted earlier in the morning. "I look forward to working with him."

Those who saw Palin that Wednesday say that she seemed preoccupied and agitated. She had been losing sleep over the constant onslaught; she looked thin and wan. According to an interview given to *The New York Times* by her hairdresser in Wasilla, Palin's hair was thinning and needed "emergency help." In fact, Sarah Palin had had enough.

The latest release of Palin's private e-mails by members of the McCain staff had obviously shaken her. Palin detested Walshe and Conroy and was outraged about their forthcoming book. They had ridden on the vice presidential airplane with her and her kids, and she had never connected with them. Several months earlier, Palin had accused the young journalists of "stalking" her while covering the legislative session in Juneau, and, bizarrely, of "cornering" her daughter Piper when they had accidentally run into her strolling home from Harborview Elementary. The governor had gone so far, according to Walshe and Conroy, as to have her deputy press secretary Sharon Leighow leave them an accusatory phone message. Palin would later claim that Nicolle Wallace had identified Walshe and Conroy as the reporters "who didn't like us very much." The fact that they had obvious access to the deep inner sanctums of the McCain campaign could not have been comforting either. Moreover, the much-detested Schmidt was quoted in the article. None of it sat well with Palin.

With her two closest confidantes out of town (Todd in Dillingham and Stapleton on vacation in New York), Palin was left to her own devices. Her Twitter account went quiet. She had made up her mind to quit as governor.

At some point during the process, Palin claims that she had a phone conversation with her son, Track, then in Iraq, about her decision. "But are you going to let those idiots run you off?" he asked her. "You can't tap out." According to Palin, he told her that she could only leave office if she were going to "move up to something more worthy." Palin convinced him that she was: "I asked if breaking free of the bureaucratic shackles that were now paralyzing our state was 'worthy.'" Apparently his answer was in the affirmative.

Very discreetly, Palin called a series of secret meetings Wednesday evening. According to sources in the Governor's Office, Palin met privately with Lieutenant Governor Sean Parnell, along with his wife, Sandy, in Palin's downtown Anchorage office on the seventeenth floor of the Atwood Building. Palin's frustrations with the "shackles" of serving as governor became clear that evening to the Parnells. She focused on the ethics complaints and reiterated her frustrations in dealing with the media. She also broke the news to her communications director, David Murrow, who later told the *Anchorage Daily News* that he took the announcement like "a punch in the gut." A handful of other top aides and friends were also let in on Palin's secret. They were directed to keep it quiet. Palin would break the news at a press conference Friday morning, at the start of the Independence Day weekend.

The ethics complaints were soon to become Palin's chosen cliché for explaining her stunning decision, but the myriad of forces that led to her resignation were clearly more complex than that. Sarah Palin had painted herself into a very small political corner. Her relationship with the Republican-led Alaska legislature had deteriorated so badly that she was facing veto overrides and a runaway legislative session in 2010. The psychic forces that spurred Palin's ambitions were the same ones that prevented her from repairing individual relationships with legislators. It was not in her skill set to do so. She also detested Juneau—with a vengeance. Moreover, her various national activities—her book project, speaking engagements, and campaigning for other candidates—had become the target of her critics and would certainly lead to even more ethics complaints. She had no other alternative—save to finish out the next year and a half in disgrace and perpetual chaos. She was simply cutting her losses.

On Thursday, Palin had a single ten-minute event scheduled—a meet-and-greet with the Czech Republic ambassador to the U.S., Petr Kolar, scheduled at 11 A.M.—and went back to familiar themes on Twitter. At 1:46 in the afternoon she declared: "Best of luck to Scotty Gomez, AK's greatest hockey player, as he joins up w/ Montreal Canadi[e]ns." Then later she recorded two postings about the so-called Parent Notification Initiative: "I'm ready to be 1st in line to sign petition supporting AK's families." And then at 4:36, Palin's Twitter went dark for the second day in a row and it would stay dark until later the following afternoon. From that point on, she worked furiously on the speech that she was to deliver the next day in Wasilla.

Palin had managed to keep her secret from going viral. No leaks, no surprises. Her office sent out a press release that Palin would be making an "announcement" at her Wasilla home at 11 A.M. Only a handful of local reporters, photographers, and camera operators were able to scramble together to make the scene. State Troopers blocked late-arriving media outside her home. Todd had hustled back from Bristol Bay the previous night to be there, along with various members of Palin's family and her administration. People weren't quite sure what was coming, though many speculated that Palin might be announcing the fact that she wasn't going to be running for reelection. Her nemesis Randy Ruedrich, still head of the Alaska Republican Party, had said earlier that Palin should make up her mind by October so as to allow others to enter the fray if she were going to bow out. What else could it be?

Wearing a bright red coat and dark skirt, Palin seemed anxious as she huddled with Todd and Trig on the sidelines. Shortly after eleven, she broke from the scrum, hustled down to the podium, and, with Lake Lucille providing a background for the few photographers and video cameras assembled, she hurriedly (and quite nearly breathlessly) began her speech. Her introduction strayed from the prepared text, thanking everyone for being there, and she particularly noted that Todd had come in "to stand by my side as always."

The speech was raw Palin—Palin Unplugged—riddled with bizarre sentence construction and nonlinear argumentation, strange punctuation (even in the version released on the state of Alaska Web site), and the complete absence of a narrative arc. It was self-serving and self-congratulatory on the one hand, accusatory and mean-spirited on the other. It positioned Palin as being persecuted—by "political operatives [who] descended on Alaska last August"—and cast Palin as the victim of "the politics of personal destruction" and "wasteful political blood sport." There were no attempts at humor, no laugh lines, no hints of self-deprecation.

Palin went through a long litany of her administration's accomplishments before noting,"And I really wish that you would hear more from the media. More from the media of your state's good progress and how we tackle outside interests, special interests daily we're tackling." Again she whined, in a tone eerily reminiscent of Richard Nixon's famous "You Won't Have Nixon to Kick Around Anymore" speech, delivered in 1962, "You don't hear much about the good stuff in the press anymore, though, do you?"

As Palin moved into her speech, rather than finding her comfort zone, she seemed more agitated, almost to the point of hyperventilating. She took deep breaths between each phrase, large staccatod gulps of air that were magnified by the sound system. She seemed on the verge of breaking down. There was none of the joy that had marked her speeches on the campaign trail, nor even the perverse glee she seemed to take when she was digging the stiletto into Obama. This was not a pleasant journey for Palin. And she was all over the map.

More than halfway into her speech, it was still uncertain why Palin and her entourage had assembled. She had really done nothing except deliver a variety of laundry lists. And there was no hint of where she was going. Finally, more than twelve minutes into her delivery, Palin began a circuitous explanation for her presence, finally stating that "I will not seek reelection as governor." But it did not seem to be her final destination point. She quite nearly skipped over the line.

And then she went into another circuitous bit of argumentation that once again bordered on the bizarre:

> And so as I thought about this announcement, that I wouldn't run for reelection and what that means for Alaska, I thought about, well, how much fun some governors have as lame ducks. They maybe travel around their state, travel to other states, maybe take their overseas international trade missions. So many politicians do that. And then I thought, that's what's wrong. Many just accept that lame duck status and they hit the road, they draw a paycheck, they kind of milk it, and I'm not going to put Alaskans through that.
>
> I promised efficiencies and effectiveness. That's not how I'm wired. I'm not wired to operate under the same old politics as usual. I promised that four years ago and I meant it. That's not what is best for Alaska at this time. I'm determined to take the right path for Alaska, even though it is unconventional and it's not so comfortable. With this announcement that I'm not seeking reelection, I've determined it's best to transfer the authority of governor to Lieutenant Governor Parnell.

Sarah Palin just couldn't bring herself to say that she was resigning, that she was, in fact *quitting*. Neither of the terms can be found in her speech. Rather, this was a "transfer of authority," a "transition" as she would euphemistically characterize it, that would take place at the end of the month in Fairbanks. Her reference to being a "lame duck" was patently absurd. There was still another legislative session to complete in the winter and spring of 2010. What she was really saying was that she was not going to fulfill her oath of office, not going to complete her job or finish her term. She did everything she could to spin the theme of the day away from her quitting. "My choice is to take a stand and [e]ffect change," she declared, "and not just hit our head against the wall and watch valuable state time and money, millions of your dollars, go down the drain in this new political environment."

She equated completing her term with being "apathetic." She proffered that "a problem in our country today is apathy. It would be apathetic to just hunker down and go with the flow. Nah, we're fishermen. We know that only dead fish go with the flow." Her facial expression was riddled with disgust and disdain.

Then she shifted gears one last time.

> Let me go back quickly to a comfortable analogy for me—sports, basketball. And I use it because you are naïve if you don't see a full-court press from the national level picking away right now. A good point guard, here's what she does. She drives through a full court press, protecting the ball, keeping her head up because she needs to keep her eye on the basket. And she knows exactly when to pass the ball so that the team can win. And that is what I'm doing—keeping our eye on the ball that represents sound priorities—you remember they include energy independence and smaller government and national security and freedom! And I know when it's time to pass the ball for victory.

Although the national media had a field day with Palin's metaphorical ramblings, her basketball reference was probably as close as she came to a real explanation for her decision. The correct basketball metaphor for Palin's plight, however, was that she was boxed in—trapped—and she had no alternative but to call a time-out and regroup. She "passed the ball," all right, only Palin took herself out of the game.

She claimed that all five of her children had voted unanimously to support her decision—she did not mention Todd's opinion or refer to him in her prepared remarks. "It was four yeses and one 'hell yeah!' And the 'hell yeah' sealed it," she proclaimed, in a reference to her telephone discussion with Track. She then shot an elbow at bloggers who had forced her children to endure "seeing their baby brother Trig mocked and ridiculed by some pretty mean-spirited adults recently"—a vague reference to the doctored Eddie Burke photograph—but clear enough for those Alaskans paying attention.

Palin concluded with a seemingly endless string of catchphrases and clichés. She mixed sports metaphors a final time and praised herself for having "enough common sense to acknowledge when conditions have drastically changed and are willing to call an audible and pass the ball when it's time so the team can win." It was starting to get painful. Sarah Palin was playing both football and basketball at the same time. She struggled for a final, closing cliché. "Take the words of General MacArthur," she concluded. "'We are not retreating. We are advancing in another direction.'"

Advancing in another direction. That was a perfect way to describe Sarah Palin's entire political career.

PART IV

AMERICA

The blood-dimmed tide is loosed, and everywhere
The ceremony of innocence is drowned;
The best lack all conviction, while the worst
Are full of passionate intensity.
—William Butler Yeats, "The Second Coming"

CHAPTER 8

The Absence of Fact

*The Palins didn't have dinner together and didn't
talk much as a family.*
—Levi Johnston, *Vanity Fair*

With the truth so far off, what good will it do?
—Bob Dylan, "Jokerman," *Infidels*

*John King (CNN):Does the president believe that
Sarah Palin is a liar?*
*Robert Gibbs (White House press secretary): I'll let Webster
define what one calls her. I think in the absence of fact . . .
sometimes what happens is we fill the void with stuff that
quite frankly isn't true.*
—CNN, *State of the Union*

T HE NEWS OF PALIN'S UNEXPECTED ABDICATION crackled like a summer wildfire burning out of control in Denali National Park. There was
instant and spontaneous combustion, and it spread everywhere. Both national
and international media were consumed by Palin's rambling resignation announcement over the Fourth of July weekend and left flailing in their attempts
to deconstruct her mostly incoherent remarks. People throughout Alaska and
the rest of the world were startled and bewildered by it all, though those who
had kept close watch of Palin had noted the signs.

Condemnation of Palin's decision—particularly from Republicans—was
swift. In the *New York Daily News,* anonymous sources from the GOP fired

on her mercilessly: "She proved she couldn't play in the big leagues last fall and now she's proven it again," one of the party's "most prominent kingmak-ers" was quoted as asserting. "If you can't even handle a governorship, there's no way you can handle the White House. She couldn't win—but now she can't even run." Another "top Republican" political operative was quoted as remark-ing: "She has an incredibly thin résumé, a serious lack of *gravitas,* no coherent philosophy and the people around her are amateurs. She's finished." The GOP's controversial chairman Michael Steele said bluntly, "I take 2012 off the table right now." That was pretty much the consensus.

In Alaska, the response was equally harsh, once again from Republican elected officials. The *Anchorage Daily News* reported that state representative John Harris had called Palin's resignation "strange." His colleague Mike Hawker saw little logic in Palin's assertion that she was somehow avoiding a "lame duck" session. "Seated governors just don't resign in the last year of their term no matter how successful or for that matter unsuccessful they've been," Hawker asserted. "Right now there are a lot more questions than answers." U.S. senator Lisa Murkowski, who had her own difficult history with Palin, issued a terse statement: "I am deeply disappointed that the governor has de-cided to abandon the state and her constituents before her term has con-cluded."

Palin's approval rating in Alaska had plunged nearly forty points over the last year. (She herself conceded that they had "plummeted.") Few Alaskans bought into the idea that she was leaving to "help the state progress." In-stead, they saw the resignation as "all about Sarah. It's always about Sarah." Many suspected it was simply a self-serving decision to capitalize on her na-tional fame, to rid herself of the shackles imposed by her governorship, to "cash in."

On the other side of the political aisle, one garnered more of a sense of disgust and good riddance. "It is disturbing that she is leaving her post," said Democratic state representative Beth Kerttula, Palin's onetime-ally-turned-foe. "On the eve of the Fourth of July, in Alaska's fiftieth year of statehood, to have the governor stand down is a terrible statement about commitment to public service and our state." Laurel Carlton, a waitress in Juneau's Baranof Hotel and the very type of Alaskan who had previously given Palin high marks, was even more dismissive. "I think she has a game plan that's not Alaska, and hasn't been for a while," Carlton scoffed to the *Juneau Empire.* "If you're re-ally not going to stay and do your job every day, you should leave anyway, and the sooner the better so somebody can step in and actually do the job." As for

Palin's explanation for her departure, Carlton was even more succinct. "We don't care. We just want her gone."

All across the political spectrum, pundits came not to praise Palin but to bury her. One national GOP figure called her decision "one of the most politically tone deaf moves in years." Beyond the political implications, the incoherent nature of Palin's remarks led several in the media to question her mental state. Dahlia Lithwick from the political Web site *Slate* had the most trenchant response, calling Palin's speech "a lengthy political communication from her that explained nothing, clarified nothing, and expounded upon nothing, save for the fact that she speaks in riddles and koans. Watch it as many times as you like; you still come away feeling you've been treated to a cozy chat with the Mad Hatter."

There was a handful of political analysts who saw beyond the manic behavior and recognized the potential upside to Palin's decision. Larry Persily, Palin's former aide who had challenged her on her opposition to the federal stimulus funds in Alaska, brought it back to a basketball metaphor: "It's like the kid who leaves college early for the NBA draft and says, this is when I am at my height in the market and I'm going for it." This was the explanation that resonated most frequently in Alaska. Palin was going while the getting was good.

Perhaps the most astute political observation, however, came from Bill Kristol, who posted on his *Weekly Standard* Web site:

> It's an enormous gamble—but it could be a shrewd one.
>
> After all, she's freeing herself from the duties of the governorship. Now she can do her book, give speeches, travel the country and the world, campaign for others, meet people, get more educated on the issues—and without being criticized for neglecting her duties in Alaska. I suppose she'll take a hit for leaving the governorship early—but how much of one? . . .
>
> All in all, it's going to be a high-wire act. The odds are against her pulling it off. But I wouldn't bet against it.

This may have been the one time in Kristol's career that he "got it right." What Kristol did not say was that Palin's failed governorship left her with no other options, that she and she alone had created a situation in which she had only one way through the lookingglass—out. Palin had been forced into a political checkmate, and there was little left for her to do save to knock down her king. In respect to realpolitik, however, and given what was to transpire in the months ahead, Kristol's assessment, to give him his due, was both prescient and accurate. There was a gaping hole in the Republican Party in the aftermath of the Bush presidency and the 2008 presidential election: McCain had no juice; Romney and Huckabee no traction; Gingrich and Pawlenty no charisma; Cheney no soul. Palin had every intention of filling the gap. Moreover, Palin's constituency in the Lower 48 was essentially clueless as to what went on in Alaska and had little interest in the political dynamics or the down-and-dirty details of the Last Frontier. She could commit anything short of a capital offense without having to pay political consequences Outside. That isolation provided Sarah Palin with her political parachute.

Kristol's assessment, it should be noted, was utterly devoid of ethical considerations. What did it mean for Palin to abandon her governorship for personal gain after taking an oath of office to the state of Alaska? What did it say about her sense of commitment to Alaska's citizenry that she was abandoning her post? What did it say about her leadership capabilities and capacities? Kristol didn't address those issues. That assessment was left to the thoughtful Alaska Native voice Willie Hensley, who wrote a provocative response to Palin's resignation in *The New York Times* entitled "In Alaska, *Qiviters* Never Win." Hensley began his response by putting Palin's resignation in the context of Alaska Native history. "Ten thousand summers have come and gone here in Alaska," Hensley observed, "and the village people are already preparing for another cold winter . . ." On the other hand, Hensley noted, Palin "has called it quits eighteen months before the end of her four-year term." It was a deft framing. It made Palin's commitment to Alaska and its people seem insignificant, if not inconsequential, in the sweep of Alaska history. Hensley explained that the Inuit have a word— "*qivit,* that you do not want to have applied to you. It means to quit or give up when the going gets rough." In traditional times, Hensley noted, if you give up a leadership position you were jeopardizing your community in the "bitter cold of the Arctic."

After enumerating the many problems facing modern-day Alaska, Hensley gave Palin her due. He acknowledged that she "had the stature within the state, nationally and internationally, to deal with our problems." But Palin did not honor her leadership position or her commitment to her constituents. In so doing, Hensley argued, she became "the first Alaska governor in our state's history to '*qivit*' in the true sense of the word." It was a trenchant critique coming not from Outside, but from a true Alaska voice. Hensley displayed no animus. He wished Palin's successor, Sean Parnell, good luck. "May the great Arctic spirits be with you," he concluded.

T HE ONGOING RESPONSE to Palin's resignation would last weeks, if not months. The following day she was scheduled to appear in the annual Fourth of July parade in Juneau, but she, Todd, Bristol, Willow, Tripp, and Trig, along with her parents, hung close to the sidelines. As was often the case with Palin in the final days of her governorship, her whereabouts were unknown, and there was controversy about whether she was going to participate in the parade. She was spotted briefly by photographers—wearing casual green khaki pedal pushers and a dark T-shirt—and never made formal contact with parade organizers, who were expecting her to ride along the parade route down Main Street in an open convertible, as she had done the previous year. In typical Palin fashion, she left them high and dry. Juneau parade director Jean Sztuk had made up banners in case Palin showed up, but as the last of the parade's clowns and marching bands prepared to depart, Sztuk realized that Palin would be a no-show. "What governor wants to be at the end of the parade?" she asked rhetorically.

For many people—once again across the political spectrum—Palin's explanation for her decision did not add up, particularly in Alaska. The suddenness of her announcement and her jittery behavior at the news conference suggested to some that there was more of a backstory than she let on; perhaps an impending revelation or controversy was the real reason behind the act. While the Palin-Heath clan was in Juneau, rumors around Palin's resignation swirled throughout the more densely populated southwest Alaska. The most persistent of the rumors was that a "federal investigation" focusing on the building of Palin's home on Lake Lucille—along with kickbacks from the construction of the sports complex in Wasilla—were at the root of the resignation. This speculation, which was rampant in the hours following Palin's resignation speech, took on a life of its own. The blogosphere, for the most part, followed by the mainstream press, reported on the rumor. Both *The New York Times* and *The Washington Post* dispatched reporters to cover the story. The energy around the speculation was frenetic. One of the noted Alaskan bloggers who weighed in on the story was Shannyn Moore. A frequent commentator on national television as well, Moore went on MSNBC with David Shuster in the aftermath of Palin's resignation and clearly reported on what she had heard—*rumors* of a federal investigation. Indeed she carefully used the word "rumor" twice. "There is a scandal rumor here that there is a criminal investigation into some activities and that's been rumored for about, I don't know, probably six weeks or two months," Moore told him. Moore presented nothing as fact. She was merely reporting on the buzz in south-central Alaska— and it was extensive.

The Palin fire hose team of Thomas Van Flein and Meg Stapleton went into crisis mode—which once again amounted to throwing gasoline on the flames. Van Flein drafted yet another threatening letter, which was, in turn, sent out by Stapleton to various media outlets. The correspondence posited that "several unscrupulous people have asserted false and defamatory allegations that the 'real' reasons for Governor Palin's resignation stem from an alleged criminal investigation pertaining to the construction of the Wasilla Sports Complex. This canard was first floated by Democrat operatives in September 2008 during the national campaign and followed up by sympathetic Democratic writers."

The letter once again reflected Palin's persecution complex and Stapleton's conspiracy thesis linking attacks on Palin with the White House. In what can only be described as a bizarre legal formulation, Van Flein noted that an article in the "left-wing *Village Voice*" had first advanced the rumors of corruption regarding the building of the sports complex and the Palins' home as far back as October 2008. "This was written," Van Flein contended, "in the style of one pretending to be amazed that so many people in a small town like Wasilla appear to know one another, support one another, and take on big projects together. Apparently that is uncommon in New York." That last cheap shot at the Big Apple was particularly pernicious and disingenuous given that Palin had just returned from small-town New York (where Stapleton was raised) and, perhaps most significant, that New York City had been rebuilding since the September 11 attacks for most of the last decade. No community had paid anywhere near the price in respect to the terrorist attacks on the United States as had New York. It was a typical Palin–Stapleton–Van Flein dig, full of small-minded, petty, backwater venom. Van Flein then provided a detailed account of how the sports complex was built (carefully avoiding any of the many controversies that surrounded it or the debt the city of Wasilla assumed as a result of its construction) and how the Palins built their home. Van Flein declared that "we can categorically state that we are not aware of any 'federal investigation' that has been 'pending' for the last seven years." As always, however, it was never enough to simply state the facts. Team Palin felt compelled to exact a pound of flesh in the process.

To the extent several websites, most notably liberal Alaska blogger Shannyn Moore, are now claiming as "fact" that Governor Palin resigned because she is "under federal investigation" for embezzlement or other criminal wrongdoing, we will be exploring legal options this week to address such defamation. This is to provide notice to Ms. Moore, and those who re-publish the defamation, such as Huffington Post, MSNBC, the *New York Times* and the *Washington Post*, that the Palins will not allow them to propagate defamatory material without answering to this in a court of law. . . . These falsehoods abuse the right to free speech; continuing to publish these falsehoods of criminal activity is reckless, done without any regard for the truth, and is actionable.

Moore had claimed nothing as "fact." It was another Team Palin distortion. As a media strategy, it bordered on the ridiculous. The attack on Moore—viewed as an attack on the First Amendment itself—turned Moore, already a popular figure in Alaska, into another sympathetic target of Palin harassment and revenge. Moore herself called a press conference in Anchorage and issued a statement that received international circulation. It was delightfully Moore-ish, full of pushback and humor. Moore was one of the few national commentators on Palin who could challenge the soon to be ex-governor on her Alaska pedigree. A native Alaskan raised in Homer at the scenic tip of the Kenai Peninsula, she had toiled her way through working-class Alaska in ways that Palin would claim but never actually did. She was also tough as nails and not about to be bullied by Palin. "On the Fourth of July, when Americans everywhere were celebrating our most sacred national holiday with parades and barbeques," Moore declared, "Governor Sarah Palin was busy having me, Shannyn Moore, declared an Enemy of the State." Moore articulated the visceral response that people everywhere were experiencing in the wake of Palin's resignation. And she made it clear she was not intimidated by Palin or her Alaska mafia.

In a rambling quasi-legal letter, the most powerful person in this state accused me of defaming her for pointing out the fact that there have been *rumors—rumors* of corruption—

rumors that have been around for years. When Sarah Palin gave her three-weeks' notice to the people of Alaska, aborting her term as governor, a lot of people wondered why she quit. Mid-level managers turn in their notice, not elected public officials. It didn't make sense. It still doesn't. People have been trying to guess why she really quit, and everyone in Alaska has been playing the guessing game. They're rumors. There are a lot of rumors. And with all the corruption we've had here in Alaska, of course we wonder what's really behind her resignation.

Governors don't just quit. But Governor Palin did.

The governor's massive overreaction—on the Fourth of July no less—should make any reasonable person wonder what's wrong with her. The Lady protests way too much. Eventually, we'll all find out why she really walked off the job.

Moore then went for the jugular. She described Palin as "a coward and a bully." "What kind of politician attacks an ordinary American on the Fourth of July for speaking her mind?" Moore wondered. "What's wrong with her?" Moore was particularly irate about the overt attack on free speech. "The First Amendment was designed to protect people like me from the likes of people like her," Moore asserted. "Our American Revolution got rid of kings. And queens, too. Am I jacked-up? You betcha." She then issued a threat of her own: "Sarah Palin, if you have a problem with me, then sue me. Shannyn Moore will not be muzzled!" It all made for great political theater.

Even more ludicrous was Van Flein's expressed concern in the *Anchorage Daily News* that *The New York Times* and *Washington Post* were "asking questions" about the sports complex. "What I've been informed is that they've been interviewing people in Wasilla about this, and have tried to interview the governor's parents about it," Van Flein declared. In essence, he had threatened the *Times* and the *Post* to stop their investigation in advance of publishing a single word. Palin further accused the two news organizations of "stalking" her parents and other family members. It had become her favorite verb when describing the inquisitive media. As always, she and her family were the victims. As always, they were being persecuted.

But in what could only be described as a rare, if not inexplicable, move that same weekend, the FBI's chief division counsel in Alaska, Eric Gonzalez, issued a statement to Sean Cockerham of the *Anchorage Daily News* that "we are not investigating [Palin]. Normally we don't confirm or deny those kind of allegations out there, but by not doing so it just casts her in a very bad light. There is just no truth to those rumors out there in the blogosphere." Gonzalez gave a similar interview to the *Los Angeles Times*, in which he added that there was "no wiggle room" about any type of FBI investigation. Gonzalez later refused to answer questions or provide an explanation for his announcement. Nor would he provide answers about who had authorized the statement—on a weekend, no less—and why the FBI was concerned about what was appearing about Palin in the "blogosphere" and why it should be a pressing concern of the FBI about whether a sitting governor was being cast in a "very bad light."*

Palin trumpeted the announcement on Twitter, providing a link to the *Los Angeles Times* report: "Trying to keep up w/getting truth to u, like proof there's no 'FBI scandal.'"

In spite of the FBI seemingly coming to her defense, Palin's behavior remained manic in respect to her Twitter account. During the next day she kept up a steady diet of tweets.

> See letter from my attorney on baseless allegations of past 24hrs . . .

> To see full text of the letter from my attorney on baseless allegations of past 24hrs check [Web page listing] . . .

> Critics are spinning, so hang in there as they feed false info on the right decision made as I enter last yr in office to not run again . . .

> so I'll make attempt to keep up w/attaching corrected info. I head 2 West AK villages today, look forward to their busy comm fish activity!

---

* In a phone call interview on February 3, 2010, Special Agent Gonzalez refused to answer any questions regarding the Palin announcement to the press. There has never been any evidence presented substantiating the rumor linking the building of Palin's house to the sports complex in Wasilla.

Attached is my "thank you" sent yesterday to express gratitude, & smack down lies at same time

As has been the case for decades, family is commercial fishing in Bristol Bay—I look forward to joining the work crew for
1 day picking fish

Palin had more in mind than picking fish in Bristol Bay. In spite of protestations that she didn't realize why her resignation was "such a darn big deal,"
Palin clearly recognized that she was a hot national news commodity yet again.
She and her advisers decided to hold a series of glorified photo ops on Bristol
Bay—her "home turf" as she dubbed it—surrounded by family dressed in their
working clothes in the far, isolated reaches of western Alaska. Palin invited
four television news crews—Fox News, ABC, NBC, and CNN—to interview
her on the shores of Kanakanak Beach and aboard the Palins' open aluminum
skiff. (MSNBC's Rachel Maddow dubbed it "The Sarah Palin 'I Quit' Clarification Tour.") The one major broadcasting network, of course, that Palin did *not*
invite was CBS News, an exclusion that she emphasized with glee in her memoirs.
    With Fox News (where Palin was, apparently, auditioning), Palin played to
her audience. "The critics want to put you on a course of personal bankruptcy,
so you can't afford to serve," she said, calling the allegations "bull crap." She
then took a swipe at Obama. "Average, hardworking Americans need to be
able to get out there, unrestrained, and fight for what is right," she declared.
"Fight for energy independence and national security, fight for a smaller government instead of this big government overgrowth that Obama is ushering in."
    With ABC's Kate Snow, she started out friendly—"we're chasin' the tide, it's
ebbin' and flowin', of course"—but then became defensive when asked why she
was resigning. "You mean I didn't do a good job in my twenty-two or twenty-
four minutes of explanation the other day?" She then took a swipe at her constituents. "You know why they're confused," she declared. "I guess they cannot
take something nowadays at face value."
    When asked about running for national office, Palin indicated that she
would not face the same controversies that haunted her in Alaska because: "I
think on a national level, your department of law there in the White House
would look at some of the things that we've been charged with and automatically throw them out." The ABC News Web site pointed out that "there is no
'Department of Law' at the White House."

Palin kept up the jitterbug dance in her explanations. It was the "ethics complaints"—but it wasn't. She kept mentioning the half a million dollars that defending against the ethics complaints was costing her family—she mentioned "personal bankruptcy"—but that wasn't it, either. It was to "progress the state." Her answers at Dillingham were every bit as circuitous and contradictory as her explanation had been at Lake Lucille.

NBC's Andrea Mitchell wasn't buying into Palin's explanation. While the urbane Mitchell seemed particularly out of her element in Dillingham—just as Palin knew she would be—she had lost none of her bite. Mitchell had met Palin at the dinner for Palin and McCain hosted by Fred Malek earlier in the year and she had established a personal, if slim, rapport with the governor. The pre-established familiarity gave her space to push her game.

Mitchell's report from Dillingham began almost freakishly, with Palin running along the beach toward Mitchell, her waders flapping, asking of Mitchell in a patronizing tone, "Are you staying warm?" In her voice-over introduction to the segment, Mitchell said she went to Bristol Bay seeking an "explanation" for Palin's decision to resign. Palin then went through the same scripted answer she had gone through with each of the other camera crews. "I knew that I wasn't going to run for reelection," began her rote response. "I knew that everything changed on August 29th in politics in Alaska. That's the day that I was tapped to run for vice president of the United States. Things changed, and it was quite obvious that nothing would ever be the same for our administration."

Mitchell raised the issue of the legal fees. "Oh, we have a legal bill of about half a million dollars," Palin acknowledged. "But that's—that's not the consideration."

Mitchell didn't take the bait. Palin finally conceded, "That's just one aspect of the insanity of the political game that's being played, you know, that's kind of distracting but that still isn't all of it."

Palin began talking in circles again. "What is all of it is knowing I wasn't going to run for reelection," she began. "So Alaskans, being perfectly honest with them, not wanting to play that political game that most politicians do, and that's kind of pretend like they don't know if they want to run again—well, I knew. I didn't want to run again. So, I'm going to be honest with Alaskans and say one term was enough." Palin still couldn't acknowledge the fact that she had quit midterm. She continued to frame it as not running for reelection. Mitchell refused to issue Palin a pass. She interrupted the governor. "You haven't finished the job, some would say." Palin responded with a flash of anger and frustration. She was on her home court—back in the Wasilla Gym—and she felt no compunction about being polite with Mitchell.

PALIN: You're not *listening* to me as to why I wouldn't be able to finish that final year in office without it costing the state millions of dollars and countless hours of wasted time, wasted—we have true, worthy, public causes.

MITCHELL: Some people have said that you saw the bright lights from the national campaign and came back, and it was very hard to readjust to the nitty-gritty work of being . . .

PALIN: The nitty-gritty, like, you mean the fish slime and the dirt under the fingernails and stuff . . .

MITCHELL: No, Juneau, the state capital. The hard, legislative slog.

PALIN: No. That's not—I am a fighter. I'm—I thrive on challenge.

Palin's voice was cracking as she spoke and she hardly seemed convincing. Mitchell had broken her rhythm and her confidence, even on Palin's home court. Earlier that weekend Mitchell had reported that "people very close to Sarah Palin" were contending that Palin "is out of politics, period. She is fed up with politics. She doesn't like her life. . . . And she really does not want to run for higher office"—a proclamation that was widely quoted in the media, but one that did not jibe with those following the Palin story closely in Alaska.

Mitchell seemed intent on substantiating her earlier report. She asked Palin if she regretted saying yes to John McCain. Palin shot back emphatically, "Not in the least! Absolutely not! It was a great honor to stand by a true American hero." Palin refused to give Mitchell the political obituary for which she was fishing. As she told every other reporter when asked about her intentions for national office, "I don't know what the future holds. I'm not going to shut any door that—who knows what doors open? Can't predict what the next fish run's going to look like down on the Nushagak. So, I certainly can't predict what's going to happen in a couple of years."

To watch all four of Palin's interviews conducted that evening in Bristol Bay—it was bright daylight at 9 P.M.—it was thoroughly clear that Palin remained in deep and dark denial about the implications of her resignation. Indeed, she steadfastly refused to use the term—or any others—that acknowledged her abdication. More importantly, she was emphatic that her decision would have no impact on her future national political aspirations. She kept uttering the phrase, "You know, politically speaking, if I die, I die. So be it," but she also made it clear—several times—that she wasn't going to miss any "open doors." Palin was as slippery as the chum salmon slithering in her family's set-nets. In the words of *Slate*'s Dahlia Lithwick, Palin remained "lost in translation."

T HE FINAL DAYS OF PALIN'S GOVERNORSHIP were marked by more bizarre behavior, bitterness, and recrimination. She kept up with her tweeting, still posting as many as ten a day. She signed bills in isolated communities throughout the state—Kotzebue, McGrath, Unalakleet—leaving some to describe it as Palin's "farewell tour." Her longtime critic, Fairbanks lawmaker Jay Ramras, told the *Anchorage Daily News* that "it's wonderful for her to go pursue adulation in the far corners of Alaska and do precisely what she said she wasn't going to stay in office for—which is to spend state money to go around and be a lame duck." He urged her instead to get to work, "go sit behind a desk and help with the transition of office."

That wasn't how Palin was wired. In mid-July, she shuttled by floatplane to the McNeil River State Game Sanctuary, site of one of the world's largest annual congregations of brown bears gorging themselves on summer chum salmon runs up the McNeil River to McNeil Falls. Demand for viewing the bears at the sanctuary is so great that the state conducts a lottery for entrance. Admission is limited to no more than ten permit holders at any given time and visitors are protected by armed Alaska Department of Fish and Game guides who double as naturalists on the tour. Palin used the waning powers of her governorship to secure permits—not only for herself, but for her parents as well—through her controversial commissioner of fish and game, Denby Lloyd. Afterward, Palin issued a manic series of tweets (what AKMuckraker would dub the "Bear Trilogy," replete with an Afterword) on mama grizzly bears that she couldn't keep within the 140-character limit imposed by Twitter:

> Great day w/bear management wildlife biologists; much to
> see in wild territory incl amazing creatures w/mama bears'
> gutteral raw instinct to

protect & provide for her young; She sees danger? She brazenly rises up on strong hind legs, growls Don't Touch My
Cubs & the species survvives

& mama bear doesn't look 2 anyone else 2 hand her anything; biologists say she works harder than males, is provider/
protector for the future

Yes it was another outstanding day in AK seeing things the
rest of America should see; applicable life lessons we're blessed
to see firsthand

While this particular Twitter posting would serve as fodder for late-night
comedians, it was clear to anyone who read between the lines of these tweets
that Palin was using the "mama grizzly" as a metaphor for her own life, and
perhaps for her own family. The primacy of the matriarch in this Mama Grizzly story was not lost on those speculating about troubles inside the Palin marriage leading up to her final days as governor.

Two days later, Palin sent out another tweet that was to serve not only as a
precursor of things to come, but which also provided a keen insight into the
mental state of Palin as she finished her final frantic run in state politics:

elected is replaceable; Ak WILL progress! + side benefit=
10 dys til less politically correct twitters fly frm my fingertps
outside State site

Sarah Palin was ready to cut loose, but before she was able to shed the bonds
of political correctness, she was to have a final formal hurrah as governor, a
three-day series of farewell picnics in the strategically chosen loci of Anchorage, Wasilla, and Fairbanks—all with pockets of solid Palin support—and far
from the contested terrain of the state capital in Juneau where, by any standard of state protocol, the transition of power should have taken place. It was
a last final snub of the capital.

As for Fairbanks—which Palin referred to so many times as the Golden
Heart City that it had become a cliché—it provided the perfect venue for
Palin's farewell. Little more than two and half years earlier she had broken

traditional protocols by scheduling her swearing-in ceremonies there, and it was home to an amalgam of military bases, mining, and railroad interests.

A crowd of more than five thousand greeted Palin in Fairbanks, along with balmy weather—into the mid-80s—and the Palin faithful gathered en masse for a last word from their departing governor. What they got was fire and brimstone—and for those paying close attention, it was a speech full of the vindictiveness and revenge that would characterize so much of her forthcoming memoir, *Going Rogue.*

Palin made it clear from the onset that although Sean Parnell would be sworn in during the ceremony as the twelfth governor of Alaska, this was not to be his day. It was all Palin's, and as soon as she took to the podium, she made that eminently clear. There were only a couple of references to Parnell in Palin's self-absorbed, nearly twenty-minute speech—and even then she wove the narrative back to herself.

Although not as rambling and circuitous as her initial farewell remarks in Wasilla, the Fairbanks address nonetheless had the bizarre sentence construction, non sequiturs, and singsong elocution that marked all of Palin's self-composed oratory. Nearly all of the images of Palin that day had a singular gesture—her finger was pointing from beginning to end—and her speech began by taking a shot at the Outsiders in attendance, replete with classic Palin sentence structure: "In the wintertime it's the frozen road that is competing with the view of ice-fogged frigid beauty, the cold though, doesn't it split the Cheechakos from the Sourdoughs?" When she said "Cheechakos" she went into the highest range of the Palin screech, emphasizing the derisive term for those who came to Alaska for short-term visits but did not live there. It was a way of bonding with her constituency in the audience, of separating the faithful from those who no longer believed in her.

Palin then conducted what had become a signature segue for her—acknowledging those in the military while mentioning the right to free speech, which she then giddily declared, "I'm going to exercise." She then came out swinging, and with her face and hands in full animation, went directly after the media—again bringing up "the troops" in juxtaposition with the First Amendment. "Democracy depends on you," she asserted forcefully to "some" of the press in attendance, "and that is why, that's why our troops are willing to die for you." Then with voice dripping with disdain and sarcasm, "So, how 'bout in honor of the American soldier, *ya quit makin' things up?*" She didn't stop there. In what was another curious formulation she declared: "And don't underestimate the wisdom of the people, and one other thing for the media, our new governor has a very nice family too, so leave his kids alone." Her anger was palpable.

Her speech then circled back to Palin's favorite subject—herself and her alleged accomplishments—and in the ensuing minutes she uttered the phrase "I promised" (or "we promised") no fewer than ten times, on each occasion assuring her audience, even when the evidence was quite the contrary, that Sarah Palin had kept her word. Along the way she warned Alaskans that they were "going to see anti-hunting, anti–Second Amendment circuses from Hollywood and here's how they do it: they use these delicate, tiny, very talented celebrity starlets, they use Alaska as a fundraising tool for their anti–Second Amendment causes." (It was a biting, ludicrous dig at actress Ashley Judd, who had filmed an advertisement earlier in the year condemning the aerial hunting of wolves in Alaska and who is actually several inches taller than Palin and known for her portrayals of strong women.) Palin concluded the passage with one of her trademark clichés: "We eat, therefore we hunt."

She then stepped once again into Neverland. Palin claimed to have "resisted the stimulus package" and warned Alaskans to be "wary of accepting government largess"—this after she herself had *accepted* 97.2 percent of the federal stimulus package and all that she left on the table was a $28.56 million allocation for energy conservation. She talked the talk of resisting "enslavement to big central government that crushes hope and opportunity," but when it came time to walk the walk, she had only made a symbolic gesture aimed at appeasing her national Republican base. When she asked her audience in Fairbanks if they remembered the old bumper sticker "Alaska, We Don't Give a Darn How They Do It Outside," it was clear to anyone who watched Palin's speech that all she cared about anymore was precisely what was happening Outside. Sarah Palin had abandoned her governorship and she didn't give a darn about Alaska anymore.

F OLLOWING HER FINAL ADIEU in Fairbanks, Sarah Palin all but disappeared. On August 1, she gave a talk to a National Rifle Association gathering, hosted by the Alaska Gun Collectors, in Anchorage, where she reportedly delivered a speech on Second Amendment rights and received an NRA Benefactor Life Membership and a Gold Medal Award of Merit. It was the last time she would be seen publicly in Alaska for more than a month. Her Mad Hatter communications network had gone dark. The frantic, incessant nearly incoherent postings on Twitter came to an abrupt halt. She promised to start up a new Twitter address outside of her government-issued (and paid for) account, but none was posted for several months.

There had been yet another dispute over Palin's withdrawal from a public event—this time a benefit for the Alaska Family Council at an Anchorage megachurch, ChangePoint—where she was to deliver a speech in support of a ballot measure aimed at making it illegal for teens to obtain an abortion without parental notification. Organizers were irate that Palin had left them hanging at short notice. Palin's name had been prominently included on the publicity for the event for weeks. Palin's spokesperson Meg Stapleton, again blaming the other party and invoking the plural pronoun, told the *Anchorage Daily News* that "this is the first we have ever heard of a speech." That was a revelation to Alaska Family Council president Jim Minnery, who said it was news to him when a reporter told him that Stapleton was saying Palin had no knowledge of the speech, which his group had been promoting. He said organizers had been talking to Palin "contacts" for weeks about it. "All we can do is take people at their word that we've worked with in the past," Minnery said. "We've been working for several weeks on the event, promoting it very heavily. It would be a grave disappointment if she doesn't show up but the show will still go on." Palin did not appear.

That there was a political backdrop to the ChangePoint incident went unacknowledged in the mainstream press, but those who followed Palin closely knew exactly what had happened. A posting at Conservatives4Palin indicated that it was a direct payback to Minnery for having "slammed the governor" by opposing Palin on a pair of issues during her governorship. Palin's vengeance apparently knew no bounds.

One of those irate about the ChangePoint incident was Frank Bailey, Palin's once-loyal director of boards and commissions, whom she had tossed under the bus in the final days of her governorship. Indeed, the way in which Palin handled this matter marked a turning point for Bailey in his relationship with the former governor. He could no longer accept the manner in which Palin and Stapleton continued to lie about this matter, leading him to begin work on a critial Palin memoir of his own.

Palin's erratic behavior was once again cause for widespread speculation throughout Alaska. There were continued rumors on Alaska blog sites and in supermarket tabloids that she had suffered a mental breakdown in recent months, that she was anorexic or finally forced to confront a serious psychological disorder. Her hyperventilated breathing during her resignation speech had given cause to all sorts of psychological supposition. There were others who surmised that she had gone through a plastic-surgery operation. And there were those who claimed she had sunk into a serious bout of depression. Each day produced another series of crises and rumors although none were ever substantively confirmed.

Palin's actual whereabouts were unknown to the public. Her father said that he didn't know where she was but he informed the press that she was working on her book. This seemed to be confirmed by sightings of Palin in San Diego, near the home of her ghostwriter Lynn Vincent, where, in fact, she was sitting poolside dictating her memoirs into a recording device and pulling together her journals and scrapbooks. Palin's publishers at Harper-Collins had moved up her publication date to November, hoping to catch the holiday shopping season, but also not wanting her to be out of the public's mind for too long and wanting to avoid the possibility of further leaks and revelations about her political career, particularly those emanating from the McCain campaign.

Palin stayed off Twitter, but she began using Facebook as a means of countering charges not only in the press, but also in the blogosphere. She could still let none of it go. There were stories that she was pursuing a radio career and negotiating a contract. A July 31 posting on Palin's Facebook page was headlined "Barnett Disputes Radio Rumors" and indicated that:

> Radio might be in former Alaska Governor Sarah Palin's plans, but her attorney says a decision hasn't been made. Robert Barnett disputes reports members of Palin's team have been testing the waters to gauge syndicators' interest.
>
> Barnett says, "Many individuals and entities have expressed strong interest in Governor Palin. To date, she has not spoken with any of them, negotiated with any of them or made deals with any of them."

The following day another bomb hit. Alaska blogger Gryphen (Jesse Griffin), at the Web site *Immoral Minority*, had posted a blog entitled "Exclusive! Sarah and Todd Palin are Splitsville!" Citing "one of my best sources," Gryphen listed a plethora of allegations, including that "Sarah is finished with Todd and has decided to end their marriage"; Palin was buying land in Montana; that she had tossed her wedding ring into a nearby lake ("it sleeps with the fishes"); that Todd Palin had pulled a gun on Levi Johnston; and that Palin had been interfering with the prosecution of Johnston's mother.

Like many of those in Alaska positioning themselves in opposition to Palin, Gryphen was a lifelong Alaska resident, born and raised in Anchorage, where he graduated from Dimond High School in the late 1970s, a few years before Palin. During the summer of 2009, he was working as a part-time assistant in an Anchorage kindergarten, while keeping up with his extensive blogging activities. His posting on Palin's marital status went viral.

Inside Alaska, the entire state was abuzz discussing the rumors. At the weekly midsummer Anchorage Market & Festival, with more than three hundred vendors spread across seven acres of pavement, the state of the Palin marriage was part of the collective conversation—even if there was no concrete evidence to back up any of the allegations. Those in Wasilla had been startled by accounts of the Palins' marriage for some time. Most of those rumors could be traced to high school sources—friends of the Palins' children or friends of friends—and Levi Johnston was then in the midst of spilling his guts about the Palin household to *Vanity Fair*. The Sarah Palin described by Johnston in the October 2009 issue—revelations that were made right about the time of the divorce rumors—was a far cry from the image projected by Palin's spin machine. A center of "family values" this was not. Johnston said that "Todd and Sarah pretty much led separate lives." He went on to write:

> After the nomination, Sarah and Todd wouldn't go anywhere together unless the cameras were out. They're good on television, but once the cameras would leave they didn't talk to each other. In all the time Bristol and I were together, I've never seen them sleep in the same bedroom. (I don't know *how* she got pregnant.) Even during the Republican National Convention they slept in different bedrooms at opposite ends of her suite. Todd slept in the living room, on his little black recliner, with the TV going in the background—usually with the news or an Ultimate Fighting Championship match on—wearing clothes he wore that same day.

Johnston depicted Todd as hot-tempered, flying off the handle behind closed doors. "He often got mad that Sarah wasn't looking after the kids," Johnston wrote. Todd was described as a closet drinker, hiding his beer from Sarah in the garage, where he often went to tinker with his snow machines.

Johnston recalled an incident in the summer of 2007—when the family had gone off to Hawaii—during which Sarah had stormed back to Wasilla, leaving the kids and Todd by themselves in the islands.

Johnston's bleak and singular portrayal of Sarah was that of a modern-day couch potato. In the aftermath of the 2008 campaign loss, he alleged, she had returned depressed—"sad," "pouting," and "stressed out." She showed zero interest in the governorship. Johnston says that she read gossip magazines and skipped over the local newspapers that arrived at the Palin home each morning—the *Mat-Su Valley Frontiersman* and the *Anchorage Daily News*. She watched home decorating shows and wedding shows on television in her Walmart pajamas. She constantly sent the kids on errands into the sprawling Wasilla strip mall—for videos, for pizzas, for Crunchwrap Supremes from Taco Bell. "Sarah's got a way of getting her way," Johnston said matter-of-factly. She guilt-tripped her kids constantly, he observed, especially Bristol. According to Johnston, "those two didn't get along much."

For those watching the family through the lens of a television camera, the startling reality TV depiction of their home life may have seemed brutally distorted, if not implausible. But for many of those living in the Mat-Su—including some friends and family members—it was neither. Even those in the region who liked the Palins—and there were plenty of those still around—knew that there were problems in the Palin household. "There was a lot of talk of divorce in that house," Johnston asserted, "and there were times when Todd and Sarah would mention it and sound pretty serious. Sarah would say something, and I don't know how it would make Todd mad, but his anger would elevate so fast. Todd would say, 'All right, do you want a divorce? Is that what you want? Let's do it! Sign the papers!'"[†]

So the scenario presented by Gryphen on his blog may have come off as hyperbolic, even melodramatic, but it did not seem that far from the mark.

[†] In July 2010, during the middle of his on-again-off-again marriage plans with Bristol Palin, Johnston issued a public apology through *People* magazine in which he declared that he had "said things about the Palins that were not completely true." The following month, on the *CBS Early Show*, Johnston rescinded his apology in an interview with correspondent Betty Nguyen, saying that he had done it solely to "make his fiancée happy . . . The only thing I wish I wouldn't have done is put out that apology," he said, "'cause it kind of makes me sound like a liar. And I've never lied about anything."

And the inimitable Palin tag team of Stapleton and Van Flein was about to make sure that it received international attention. Stapleton issued a statement on Palin's Facebook page decrying the blogs.

> Yet again, some so-called journalists have decided to make up a story. There is no truth to the recent "story" (and story is the correct term for this type of fiction) that the Palins are divorcing. The Palins remain married, committed to each other and their family, and have not purchased land in Montana (last week it was reported to be Long Island).
>
> Less than one week ago, Governor Palin asked the media to "quit making things up." We appreciate that the more professional journalists decided to question this story before repeating it.

It was prototypical Stapleton riding in on her high horse and taking swipes wherever she could. While there were those in Alaska (and elsewhere in the country) who marveled at Stapleton's willingness to grant credibility to the blogosphere by responding to the charges, the greater marvel is that Palin allowed her to keep on doing it. Then Van Flein issued a formal legal threat to Gryphen in which he asserted that his story was "categorically false" and composed of "complete fabrications." He presented Gryphen with a series of short-term deadlines to remove the story. It had all of the bravado accompanying a shoot-out at the O.K. Corral:

> Although it is likely you knew your statements were false when you published them, you certainly are on notice as of 1:00 p.m. AST that your alleged facts are false and constitute malice. By 3:00 p.m. today AST please post a retraction with an apology for printing false and defamatory statements. In the event you refuse to do so, please give me the contact information for your attorney. If you do not have an attorney, please let me know if you want to be served with the summons and complaint at the kindergarten where you assist or at your residence.

Once again, Van Flein had managed to turn one of Palin's adversaries into an empathetic figure by threatening to serve papers at the kindergarten at which he worked. Moreover, some of Palin's supporters issued death threats directed at Gryphen and tried to charge him with being a pedophile. "People were really outraged by that," says Gryphen. "Most people at the school had no idea who I was—I kept my politics and my blogs away from my work—so when Van Flein threatened to serve papers at 'a kindergarten' it just confirmed for most people that those who were working for her were mean-spirited. And that her supporters were really weird. By then, people in Anchorage had pretty much grown sick of Palin. They were tired of her act."

Like those before him who had been threatened by Palin and Van Flein, Gryphen refused to be intimidated. He was never served and, oddly, never heard from Van Flein on the matter again. "This dubious legal strategy appeared to do one thing, and one thing only successfully—make Alaska bloggers relevant to the conversation," AKMuckraker noted on her *Mudflats* blog. "If you give someone power, they have it. So, unless Palin's strategy is to shine the national media spotlight on everything the Alaska bloggers have been reporting about her transgressions, and her track record in Alaska, and the big fat mess she's left the state to clean up, it might be a good idea to have Van Flein and crew take out one of those little roll-up rugs, and lie down in the corner with a book for some quiet time." It was splendid advice but went little heeded. Palin enjoyed the national spotlight, no matter how much it revealed about her—or her family.

A UGUST REMAINED UNSEASONABLY WARM in southwest Alaska. A few days in Anchorage the temperature had risen past 80 degrees. At outdoor barbecues and salmon feeds in the Last Frontier, Palin remained the talk du jour. The Alaska legislature was scheduled to take up Palin's veto of a small portion of the federal stimulus package on August 9, and it appeared that there were enough votes in the Republican-dominated body to override it. It would be a stinging coup de grâce to Palin's aborted governorship.

Word spread that Palin made a sudden exit from Alaska in advance of the special override session. On August 5, she was seen dining at Michael's restaurant in Manhattan—the trendy meeting place of the media elite—with her agent, Bob Barnett. She was also there with Todd, who apparently had come at the last minute, in part to dispel rumors of marital disharmony. Stapleton was also in tow. *Politico* reported that the dinner party—"which arrived without a reservation, according to Michael's manager Danny DiVella"—requested a table in the front of the restaurant so that they could all be seen together by gawkers outside. Reports indicated that Palin drank Deutz champagne and ordered lobster "off the menu." From that point on, Palin's public behavior changed drastically. No more tweets. No more Facebook rants. (Facebook would be reserved for more orderly policy statements and discussions.)

Two days after the public showing at Michael's, Palin's obsession with President Obama manifested itself again, this time with a formal Facebook posting. Gone, however, were the ungrammatical and nearly incoherent ramblings that had characterized so much of Palin's recent public expressions. In a carefully crafted commentary that would soon be picked up by media around the world, Palin was instantaneously elevated to serving as a spokesperson for the evangelical right on the issue of health care. "As more Americans delve into the disturbing details of the nationalized health care plan that the current administration is rushing through Congress," she posted, "our collective jaw is dropping, and we're saying not just no, but hell no!"

Palin credited conservative congresswoman Michele Bachmann with highlighting "the Orwellian thinking of the president's health care advisor, Dr. Ezekiel Emanuel, the brother of the White House chief of staff, in a floor speech to the House of Representatives. I commend her for being a voice for the most precious members of our society, our children and our seniors."

And then she went further overboard. She cited the laissez-faire economist Thomas Sowell, who asserted that the Democrats' health care plan would inevitably lead to health care "rationing."

> And who will suffer the most when they ration care? The sick, the elderly, and the disabled, of course. The America I know and love is not one in which my parents or my baby with Down Syndrome will have to stand in front of Obama's "death panel" so his bureaucrats can decide, based on a subjective judgment of their "level of productivity in society," whether they are worthy of health care. Such a system is downright evil.

While the writing was clearly not hers (nothing posted to her name on Facebook following her August 4 meeting with Barnett would be), the views she was expressing had also been hijacked, this time from former New York lieutenant governor and tobacco industry lobbyist Betsy McCaughey, who on July 14 had appeared on *The Fred Thompson Show* declaring that Obama's health care reform proposal was "a vicious assault on elderly people, all to do what's in society's best interest, or your family's best, and cut your life short." Ten days later, McCaughey, who like Palin was no stranger to exaggeration and deceit (the Web site *Gawker* had dubbed her a "professional liar"), wrote an opinion piece entitled "Deadly Doctors" for the *New York Post,* in which she attacked Dr. Emanuel by name and "translated" Obama's medical reform as: "Don't give much care to a grandmother with Parkinson's or a child with cerebral palsy." The fact that McCaughey's claims had been widely disputed in the ensuing weeks made no difference to Palin. They had caught fire with the GOP's right-wing fringe and would help advance her own political agenda. Palin's references to "death panels" and a proposed health care system that is "downright evil" fully embraced Palin's duplicitous and Manichaean view of the world. The personalizing of the issue with references to her parents and her son Trig gave Palin ample excuse to unleash her self-righteous rancor, no matter how untrue it was, no matter that it was all based on false assumptions. It was part of the same of old Palin brand, only this time it was dispensed with a little more polish on the prose.

Palin's charges created an instant furor. The following day economist Robert Reich, who had served as secretary of labor under Bill Clinton, responded directly to Palin. He called her remarks "odious." "It's a deliberate lie," he asserted, "that preys upon the fears of many people who are already scared as hell about loss of their jobs, health care, homes, and savings." Reich noted that the anger being ramped up in town hall meetings across the country reflected "deep-seated fears that are welling up across America" during a time of economic crisis. This was nothing new in the long history of American politics, but Reich rightfully characterized it as an insidious form of demagoguery that was being spread across the political landscape by Palin and her ilk. "The demagogues that are manipulating those fears for political gain don't give a hoot [about health care reform]," Reich lamented. "Have they no shame?"

Apparently not. Even Alaska's Republican U.S. senator Lisa Murkowski, to whom Palin had just contributed $5,000 from SarahPAC, had heard enough of Palin's deceit. "It does us no good to incite fear in people by saying that there's these end-of-life provisions, these 'death panels,'" Murkowski said during a speech in Anchorage. "Quite honestly, I'm so offended at that terminology because it absolutely isn't [in the legislation]. There is no reason to gin up fear in the American public by saying things that are not included in the bill."

Ironically, little more than a year earlier, Palin had declared April 16 in Alaska "Healthcare Decisions Day" as part of a nationwide initiative coordinated by a collective of organizations, including the Hospice Foundation of America and the American Medical Association, intended "to encourage patients to express their wishes regarding healthcare and for providers and facilities to respect those wishes, whatever they may be." Palin herself had added a passage to the resolution. "Fewer families and healthcare providers will have to struggle with making difficult healthcare decisions in the absence of guidance from the patient," she wrote in the proclamation. But neither the truth nor her own past actions ever mattered to Sarah Heath Palin—just as they had not since she was a young girl in Wasilla, just as they had not when she was mayor and governor, and just as they would not as she slogged through the wreckage of her abandoned governorship.

T HE DEATH PANEL CONTROVERSY was an orchestrated distraction used by Palin to deflect attention from the impending override of her veto at a special legislative session called for Monday, August 10, in Anchorage. On what was a glorious day in the middle of their coveted summer recess, a grumpy bunch of Alaska legislators assembled for the special legislative session (only the second to have ever been called in Anchorage), and it was costing the state a pretty penny—at least $112,000 in assorted expenses. In addition to forcing the legislature to override her veto, they also had to confirm who would succeed Alaska's lieutenant governor, Sean Parnell. In an annual protocol required by Alaska statutes, Palin had originally named her high school buddy, Department of Corrections commissioner Joe Schmidt, to be next in line to succeed Parnell. But when she announced her resignation in July, she indicated that Craig Campbell, the commissioner of the Department of Military and Veterans Affairs, would assume the position of lieutenant governor. Alaska's attorney general (and Palin appointee), Dan Sullivan, issued a ruling arguing that Campbell could only "be designated as temporary/acting lieutenant governor pursuant to Alaska statutes," which presented constitutional problems for the state. Palin's attempted last-minute switch, Sullivan argued, "raises questions about proper constitutional and statutory succession procedures." It was one more revelatory example of Palin's administrative ineptitude and recklessness. "You don't nominate someone, put them through hearings, have the legislature

confirm them and then just change your mind without offering any explanation," said Alaska legislator Les Gara. "By doing that, the governor has created
the need for a special session. This is probably the most avoidable special session in state history." Her failure to follow the simple constitutional protocols
of succession had given more cause for scheduling the special session than even
the veto override (indeed, without the former problem looming, many legislators indicated the stimulus vote might have waited until January). This aspect
of Palin's shaky transition had been largely swept under the rug, but it was in-
dicative of her incapacity to govern.

Moreover, Palin never fully explained her change of mind regarding Schmidt.
It was only after she announced Campbell as the successor to Parnell on July 3
that Schmidt was even brought into the loop. When asked about Palin's change
of mind, he said he had no idea what had taken place. Palin's designation of
Schmidt as second in line earlier in the year had provided another example of
her unbridled cronyism practiced while governor. Many in Alaska considered
him the least qualified of Palin's commissioners to assume the position. There
were rumors that Schmidt had been a "boyfriend" of Palin's when they were in
high school (they had certainly been friends) and she clearly held a cozy relationship with Schmidt at the time of the appointment. But Schmidt became another problematic Palin appointee. In 2008, the Alaska Correctional Officers
Association issued an overwhelming vote of "no confidence"—514 to 19—
against Schmidt. The association argued that Schmidt's administration had
created a "powder keg" environment inside the prisons by cutting staff and
funding. "It's reaching a crisis stage I would say," prison guard Randy
McLellan told KTUU News in Anchorage. "Incredibly dangerous." A year later
the association sued the Palin administration over its failure to negotiate a salary contract—an act that union leader Danny Colang argued was one of
"vengeance" and "retribution" against the union because of its vote of no
confidence against Schmidt.

By the time of Palin's resignation, however, Schmidt was no longer in Palin's
inner circle. He clearly had been left out of the loop in respect to Palin's decision. "She just threw poor Joe Schmidt under the bus," said Representative
Beth Kerttula. "Who knows why? But Joe Schmidt was under the bus. And it
reflected how little understanding she has of the process; but more than that,
how little respect. It was horrifyingly undemocratic. It's, you know, dictatorial.
It's everything that shouldn't happen. Where's the democracy in that?"

Schmidt later said he had no knowledge of what led Palin to change her
mind regarding succession. He claimed it was "not my business." Many in

Alaska speculated that it was Parnell who requested—or demanded—the change during his meeting in July with Palin when she informed him that she was resigning. Both men refused to respond to questioning about the selection. Schmidt later issued a simple letter, dated July 6 (written three days after Palin's resignation), thanking Palin for earlier "selecting me to succeed the Lieutenant Governor, it is truly an honor. At this time, however, I believe it is in the best interests of the Department of Corrections and subsequently the State of Alaska that I remain Commissioner of Corrections." Nothing else was ever said formally about the matter. It was another oddity of Palin's erratic governorship.

But the lieutenant governor's confirmation—for all it revealed about Palin's inability to govern and to grasp the basic details of administering the state—was the backdrop for what was at stake in Anchorage that August afternoon—not only a final rebuke of Palin, but a formal and public rejection of Palin's position on the stimulus package.

Little more than twelve hours before legislators were to meet on her override, Palin retreated to Facebook once again, this time with a short entreaty entitled "A Message to Alaskans About the Stimulus Veto and the Health Care Town Halls." It was an almost pathetic attempt to govern from behind her curtain. "Tomorrow begins an important week for Alaskans," she declared.

> On Monday, state lawmakers will meet to override my veto of stimulus funds. As Governor, I did my utmost to warn our legislators that accepting stimulus funds will further tie Alaska to the federal government and chip away at Alaska's right to chart its own course. Enforcing the federal building code requirements, which Governor Parnell and future governors will be forced to adopt in order to accept these energy funds, will eventually cost the state more than it receives. There are clear ropes attached, and Alaskans will soon find themselves tied down by codes which will dictate how we build and renovate homes and businesses. The state has hundreds of millions of dollars already budgeted for conservation, weatherization and renewable energy development. Legislators don't need to play politics as usual and accept these funds and the ropes that come with them.

In the halls of the Egan Center before the vote, Alaska legislators from both parties were joking openly about Palin's references to the strings-cum-ropes metaphor, and though none said so openly (indeed, they struggled to avoid the issue of Palin entirely), there was a feeling that Palin was about to receive her political comeuppance, that her political tab in the Last Frontier was about to come due. There was little to no loyalty left for Palin in the legislature or among the public at large. A small group of a hundred or so Palin supporters had gathered across the street, hardly an imposing presence. Some openly brandished guns in their holsters and hurled crass insults at their opponents, but, in truth, they looked very much like a ragtag mob, their spirits dampened by near certain defeat.

Inside, the atmosphere was remarkably collegial. The legislature quickly (and overwhelmingly) confirmed Campbell as Alaska's lieutenant governor, by a vote of 55–4. They then turned toward the matter of overriding Palin's veto. The discussion was polite and respectful. A handful of Palin supporters spoke in opposition to the override, but the vast majority talked about how important the federal funding was to Alaska and its people. Palin, they declared, not only misstated the significance of the funding, but she had distorted about the federal restrictions she said came attached.

The key figure in the veto override was Larry Persily, fifty-eight, a former aide to Palin who had become one of her staunchest and most visible Alaska-based critics in the aftermath of her vice presidential bid. During the override vote, Persily, a quiet and serious journalist–turned–policy wonk, was serving as a legislative specialist on oil and gas issues for House Finance Committee co-chair Mike Hawker.

Raised in Chicago and a graduate of Purdue University, Persily had arrived in Alaska in the 1970s as a young journalist, working in Juneau, Wrangell, and Anchorage in a variety of posts—he had even started a weekly in Juneau—before being named editorial page editor of the *Anchorage Daily News*. Persily had served Palin in the Office of the Governor of Alaska in Washington, D.C., assisting with energy, transportation, and tax issues. During the Knowles administration, he had served as deputy commissioner for the Department of Revenue. In spite of being a self-proclaimed "blue-collar Chicago Democrat," Persily was well liked across the political spectrum and had a hard-earned reputation as someone who forged bipartisan support for energy initiatives. In 2002, he had edited the Department of Revenue's publication *State Financial Participation in an Alaska Natural Gas Pipeline*.

Persily had given little quarter, however, when it came to Palin. During the national campaign, Persily told *The Washington Post* that "[Palin's] not known for burning the midnight oil on in-depth policy issues." On *Hardball with Chris Matthews,* he had called Palin a "small 'd' demagogue," said that she wasn't "qualified" to be vice president, and characterized her as "too immature politically." In an interview with CNN, he described Palin's incendiary rhetoric directed at Obama as "distasteful, destructive, divisive, mean, and ignorant."

In the spring after the campaign, when Palin had first indicated she intended to veto the $28.56 million portion of the stimulus package, Persily served as the point person for dealing with the senior staff for State Energy Programs at the U.S. Department of Energy. Hawker had assigned him to go over the stimulus legislation page by page. "Let's face it," Persily said, "the stimulus bill was rushed through Congress, and we needed to know what was really in there. Palin had already made statements that were factually inaccurate. . . . We needed accurate information. We weren't going to get it from the governor." Persily completed the painstaking task of combing through the legislation. He flew to Washington and met with federal bureaucrats seeking answers. Eventually, he was convinced that the supposed "strings" or "ropes" imposed by "the Feds" that Palin said existed did not. He realized it was a political ploy by Palin directed toward her national base at the expense of Alaska citizens. He thought Palin's opposition was "asinine." In March, he sent out a memorandum to legislators directly challenging Palin's position on the energy stimulus:

> The governor was incorrect to suggest or imply at last week's announcement that Alaska's eligibility for home weatherization funds ($28.56 million) and Energy Efficiency and Conservation Block Grants ($8.5 million) is dependent on adoption of a statewide building code. The state is fully eligible for both funds, regardless of any energy codes.
>
> Two points:
>
> The energy-efficiency building standards apply ONLY to State Energy Program Funds ($28.56 million). The stimulus bill requires that within eight years of the act (by February 2017) the state adopt building codes for residential and commercial structures that meet or exceed international energy-efficiency standards. The standards must apply to 90 percent of new or renovated building space; not existing structures.

> The requirement deals with energy-efficiency standards, not a complete set of building codes.
>
> The energy-efficiency standards DO NOT apply to the weatherization funds or block grants. I confirmed that point Friday with the supervisor of the weatherization program at the U.S. Department of Energy and an attorney/adviser at the department's headquarters in Washington, D.C.

Knowing that it took a 75 percent majority to override her veto, Palin no doubt felt that she had a comfortable political margin to assert her opposition to the energy component of the stimulus bill. Moreover, many Alaskans were opposed to federal interference of any kind in Alaskan politics, particularly when it came to building codes. Palin calculated that she had picked the right issue on which to take a stand. But once again, she did it imperially, without consulting legislative leaders. "She was such a jerk about it," Persily assessed. She drove some of her remaining political allies in the other direction. Persily likened it to trying to "cram it down their throats." Moreover, Palin's track record with the legislature was by then suspect. Her proclamations "did not instill confidence."

Two months after his March memo, following meetings with staff of the Department of Energy, Persily sent out an e-mail to legislators assuring them that "the Department of Energy will not measure or count square footage, nor will it demand or expect states to count square footage. The department will not require that states prove in 2017 that they achieved compliance with 90% of new and renovated square footage. They realize it would be unreasonable to require such measuring."

Finally, on Friday, August 7, at a special hearing in Kenai, Persily provided detailed testimony to the Alaska House Energy Committee further dispelling Palin's assertions that Alaska would have to adopt rigorous statewide building codes. It was a political death blow. He produced a letter from the Department of Energy confirming that "the [Alaska] Legislature . . . does not need to adopt, impose or enforce a statewide building code in order to qualify for State Energy Program funds." The state merely needed to "provide assurances to DOE . . . that the state will encourage, promote and assist municipalities that choose to adopt their own energy-efficiency codes to achieve the goals of . . . reduced energy consumption in public and private buildings." The DOE letter and Persily's careful and precise testimony sealed the deal for the final votes required to override Palin's veto. As for Palin, she had lost all traction with the legislature. "The legislators no longer trust [Palin]," Persily said the day of the stimulus vote. "They view her as an irrational, factually inaccurate, emotional, self-serving, self-aggrandizing personality."

Palin made no formal comment on the override. Those close to her in Wasilla said that she was bitter about the vote. One legislative aide who had been close to Palin during the first legislative session two years earlier said that she felt that Palin was "devastated" by it. Ironically, Palin's brother, Chuck Heath, Jr., had been working that summer as a legislative aide on mining and transportation issues for state senator Linda Menard, Palin's family friend and the mother of Curtis Menard. Heath watched his boss intently from the gallery as she cast her vote to support the veto override. There was a buzz in the chamber when Menard formally stated her vote against Palin. It turned out to be the deciding vote: 45–14. As Heath exited the chambers, he could be seen immediately ascending the stairs to the foyer while talking on his cell phone. "Who do you want to bet that call was to?" one legislative aide asked. "His father or his sister? That could not have been a pleasant conversation."

Menard later took heat for her vote back in the Mat-Su, but she held to her guns. She issued a statement—directly contradicting Palin—asserting that the "burdens" allegedly placed on Alaskans by the stimulus bill were nonexistent and "that the responsible thing to do is to accept these dollars and use them wisely for the benefit of Alaskans, as we are one of the top coldest states in the U.S."

In *Going Rogue,* Palin made it clear that she took the veto override personally. She discussed her farewell speech in Fairbanks where she brought up the stimulus funding and claimed that while her supporters gave her "a standing ovation," many legislators in the audience "remained seated." In what is another remarkable instance of Palin denial, she asserted that the "Democrat-controlled legislature overrode my veto."

"That's hilarious," said Christopher Clark, who had once worked for Palin and was then serving as a legislative aide for Republican House member John Harris from Valdez. "And absolute rubbish, of course." It would certainly be news to any member of the legislature. While the Alaska Senate was then split evenly with ten Republicans and ten Democrats, then–Senate president, Gary Stevens, is a Republican. In the lower house, Republicans held a commanding 22–18 edge—so that the entire legislative body had a Republican majority of 32–28. Palin's repeated deceptions in *Going Rogue* about the partisan composition of the Alaska legislature were clearly directed at an Outside audience unfamiliar with the basic legislative arithmetic in the Last Frontier. Indeed, her deceit reached the point of absurdity when she referred to Senator Bert Stedman, a conservative Republican from Sitka who serves as co-chair of the Senate Finance Committee, as a "Democrat lawmaker." He also voted in favor of the override.

Afterward, many legislators felt that the session had provided final closure to the Palin governorship. One likened it to an "Irish wake." Several legislators from both parties celebrated afterward at local pubs and dinner spots in Anchorage before returning home to enjoy the final days of their cherished Alaska summer.

WHILE THE SIGNIFICANCE OF THE veto override had little resonance in the Lower 48, in Alaska it had provided a bitter coda to Palin's governorship—and she found herself in desperate need of another national distraction. Two days following the override, she returned to Facebook and her claims about the "death panels." It was Palin's peculiar way of showing Alaskans that she was now bigger than the override—she was a national figure no matter what petty Alaska legislators did to her—and that she had now moved on and had put Alaska politics behind her.

In a posting entitled "Concerning the 'Death Panels,'" filed late on the evening of Wednesday, August 12, Palin launched another assault on the White House. It was quintessential Palin—opening with a lie and closing with a lie—and resplendent with eleven footnotes.

The posting opened with what was a real eye-roller. "Yesterday," she asserted, "President Obama responded to *my* statement that Democratic health care proposals would lead to rationed care." Obama had done nothing of the kind. He had not mentioned Palin by name in his statement—"The rumor that's been circulating a lot lately is this idea that somehow the House of Representatives voted for 'death panels' that will basically pull the plug on grandma because we've decided that we don't, it's too expensive to let her live anymore"—was a generic response to the chattering of the right wing about health care reform. But by claiming Obama was now responding directly to her—*personally*—it was Palin's way of asserting her faux self-importance by pretending that she was in some sort of national dialogue with the president of the United States.

The logic of Palin's posting was as flawed as it was duplicitous. She linked the legislation's intended impact of reducing "the growth in health care spending" with the provisions calling for "the continuum of end-of-life services and supports available, including palliative care and hospice." Not only did she refuse to back down on her "death panel" charges, she accused Obama of trying "to gloss over the effects of government authorized end-of-life consultations." Palin had drawn another line in the sand.

There was a national public outcry over Palin's continued "death panel" assertions, but none more passionate than Keith Olbermann, who, on his MSNBC show, responded to Palin's duplicities with equal parts furor and indignation, characterizing Palin's charges as "dangerously irresponsible" and reflecting "a terrible moment in American history."

Olbermann went right to the heart of her charge. "There is no 'death panel,'" he intoned. "There is no judgment based on societal productivity. There is no worthiness test. But there is downright evil, and Ms. Palin, you just served its cause." Olbermann didn't stop there. He identified Palin's brand of demagoguery and labeled it "a clear and present danger to the safety and security of this nation. Whether the 'death panel' is something you dreamed, or something you dreamed up, whether it is the product of a low intellect and a fevered imagination, or the product of a high intelligence and a sober ability to exploit people, you should be ashamed of yourself for having introduced it into the public discourse, and it should debar you, for all time, from any position of responsibility or trust in the governance of this nation or any of its states or municipalities."

It was classic Olbermann, ramping up the hyperbole, blistering with anger. And unlike others in the mainstream press, Olbermann had both the temerity and the long-distance vision to gaze into the dark underbelly of the American right. He did not like what he saw. "Ms. Palin, you might as well have declared that the government is being run by a coven of witches with fake Kenyan birth certificates," he intoned. "And you might as well have told the vast unthinking throng that mistakes your ability to wink for leadership, that they should start shooting at Democrats." And then Olbermann got deeply personal. He called Palin on what others had merely said under their breath, castigating her for using her son Trig as both prop and foil.

Madam, you have forfeited your right to be taken seriously the next time you claim offense at somebody mentioning your children. You have just exploited your youngest child, dangled

him in front of a mindless mob as surely as if you were Michael
Jackson. You have used this innocent infant as an excuse to pan-
der to the worst and least of us in this nation. You have used
him to create the false image of "death panels." The only "death
panels," Ms. Palin, are the figurative ones you have inspired with
such irresponsible, dangerous, facile, vile, hate speech.

Olbermann was on a roll. He charged Palin with contributing to a culture
of violence in this country, a culture of hatred. "You might very well become,
Ms. Palin," he concluded, "the very thing you have sought to create in the lurid
imaginations of those spoiling for a fight, waiting for an excuse, looking for a
rationalization of their own hatred, their own racism, their own unwillingness
to accept democracy. You, Ms. Palin, may yet become the de facto chairman of
a Death Panel . . . God forgive you, Ms. Palin."

The intensity of Olbermann's remarks was matched only by the intensity
of the brewing national debate over health care. With a pair of Facebook postings, Palin had signaled to the American public that neither her resignation nor
the indignity of the veto override would deter her from the national stage. And
just as she had whenever Chuck Heath had caught her in a lie as a little girl,
Sarah Palin would clench her fists and dig in her heels on the "death panels."
No retreat, no compromise. That her allegation would later earn her the Lie
of the Year Award from the nonpartisan news organization PolitiFact made no
matter to her. She stuck out her lower jaw and seemed to delight in her duplicity.

Ever since the time that Palin had been selected as John McCain's running
mate—ever since she had ranted around the country about Obama "pallin'
around with terrorists" and claiming that Obama was a socialist—Obama
had taken the high road and had not dignified her lies and distortions with a
rejoinder. He had played his Palin card close to his vest, had kept his response
private, a well-kept secret limited only to his closest advisers.

As the debate over health care reform ratcheted up in the weeks ahead,
however, it became clear that Barack Obama had finally had his fill of Palin's
lies and demagoguery. He would remain silent no longer. On the evening of
September 9, 2009, Obama delivered an emotional and passionate address on
health care reform to Congress and the American people. While he did not
mention the former governor by name, it was clear that he was addressing a
portion of his remarks directly at Palin. "I have no doubt that these reforms
would greatly benefit Americans from all walks of life, as well as the economy

as a whole," he declared. "Still, given all the misinformation that's been spread over the past few months"—he was interrupted by loud applause at this point—"I realize that many Americans have grown nervous about reform. So tonight I want to address some of the key controversies that are still out there."

The normally cool and unruffled Obama allowed his emotions to rise to the surface during his address. He had just lost his own beloved grandmother less than a year earlier to a prolonged battle with cancer, just as he had lost his mother a decade and a half before. The reform he was promoting was coming from a place of deep personal experience with end-of-life struggles. It was now time for him to take the gloves off.

"Some people's concerns have grown out of bogus claims spread by those whose only agenda is to kill reform at any cost," the president asserted, zeroing in on Palin and her ilk. "The best example is the claim made not just by radio and cable talk show hosts, but by prominent politicians, that we plan to set up panels of bureaucrats with the power to kill off senior citizens. Now, such a charge would be laughable if it weren't so cynical and irresponsible. It is a lie, plain and simple." There was a loud roar of applause in the House chambers, filled to capacity for the president's historic address. There was no mistaking who had been "cynical and irresponsible." There was no wiggle room in the words of the president. He had gone on record. *It is a lie, plain and simple.* The Democrats rose to their feet and issued a lengthy ovation. Finally, and in front of a national audience, Sarah Heath Palin had been publicly brought to account for her lies.

Epilogue:

Crosshairs

What a hoax she is.
—Joan Walsh, *Salon*

Behind the curtain was a small booth. In the booth was a man.
He was pulling levers and talking into a microphone. He was the
one making the head of Oz talk! Oz was not a real Wizard at all!
—M. J. Carr, Victor Fleming, and L. Frank Baum,
The Wizard of Oz: A Novelization

I think it's time as a country that we do a little soul searching.
—Clarence Dupnik, Pima County sheriff

O N A COOL, GRAY DAY in the winter of 2010, I drove nearly three hundred miles through Northern California to see a speech delivered by Sarah Palin before the Sierra Cascade Logging Conference, a congregation of corporate management and sales agents in the Pacific Northwest timber industry—an industry that has been thoroughly devastated by the sharp economic downturn in worldwide construction in recent years. It was a lovely drive through my home state—a rare period of alone time through a countryside now a lush green from winter rains. As I cruised through the confines of the San Francisco Bay Area, past the University of California at Berkeley campus and then over the Martinez-Benicia Bridge into the sprawling farmlands of the Sacramento River delta, I realized that at some point (the exact boundary is uncertain) I had crossed from decidedly liberal territory into the red-state California of the Great Central Valley. I then swung north, along Highway 5,

toward Redding, which I likened to Fairbanks—both geographically and politically—a conservative, inland community a long way from the Left Coast of
America.

At the conference, I was meeting a close friend from high school who is a
vice president of one of the biggest lumber companies in the country, widely
respected in the industry, and someone who had survived the great timber
wars with environmentalists two decades earlier. He is an avid outdoorsman—a
conservationist by both necessity and inclination—and someone whose career
in a controversial industry I both admire and respect. He had driven down to
the conference from coastal Humboldt County, once a logging stronghold in
the Golden State, but where the underground marijuana industry now challenges lumber as the driving economic engine in the region.

My friend describes himself as a "moderate" or "independent" in an industry dominated by conservative Republicans, but he is a fiscal pragmatist,
and as we greet each other at the Redding Convention Center on the outskirts
of town, it's clear that he knows many of those who will be attending Palin's
speech later that afternoon. Indeed, Palin's participation at the conference was
so widely anticipated that she sold out her first scheduled appearance in the
2,000-seat arena—with tickets selling at $50 and $75 each—in a matter of a
few hours, so that a second speech was added to accommodate the demand.
Her celebrity status had marketability even in Northern California. The second show nearly sold out as well—netting Palin a combined fee estimated at
anywhere from $100,000 to $150,000. She was raking in roughly her entire annual salary as governor of Alaska in little more than four hours. And she didn't
have to deal with a single legislator.

Nor did she have to endure any of the public scrutiny. Members of the
media were not allowed in the event, unless they were paying customers. Those
of us entering the building were frisked heavily for cameras, phones, or any
type of audio or video recording equipment. Those who had forgotten to leave
their phones back in their cars had to hike a long way back to the parking lot
and return to the end of the line. The previous September, Palin had signed
an exclusive contract with the Washington Speakers Bureau, the elite lecture
agency founded by Bernie Swain and Harry Rhoads, Jr., which features an array
of political figures, media stars, journalists, and athletes ranging from Colin
Powell to George Bush to Bill Clinton. Palin was rolling with the elites. Reports
indicated that she was requiring a minimum fee of $100,000, with a discounted
fee for West Coast appearances. It was later learned that her standard contract
required two bottles of water placed near her lecterns with "bendable straws,"

upscale hotel rooms, and that if first-class commercial flights from Anchorage were not available, then "the private aircraft MUST BE a Lear 60 or larger." Once arrived, "transportation will be by SUV(s) from a professionally licensed and insured car service"—which is precisely how she arrived at the convention center in Redding. Photo opportunities were to be considered on a "case-by-case basis," and "in order to ensure that all guests are able to have their photo taken with speaker the following are the number of clicks as appropriate for length of photo op: 45 min/75 clicks; 60 min/100 clicks; 90 min/125 clicks." Palin had become a political rock star, and she was demanding all the perks.

With a giant American flag draped behind the stage and country music blaring over the convention center's sound system (an all-white country band calling themselves the California Cowboys had opened the event), Palin—dressed in a red suit jacket, snug black skirt, and high-heeled sandals—made her way across the stage to thunderous applause. I was a bit startled by the level of enthusiasm. Sarah Palin was in California—*my* home state and where my family had lived for five generations—but this was very clearly *her* region of the country and, even more clearly, *her* crowd: almost entirely white, middle aged, middle class, and rather evenly split in terms of gender. Many of the men actually whistled their approval.

Only a few days earlier she had told Chris Wallace of Fox News that it would be "absurd" for her not to consider a run for the presidency in 2012 "if I believe that that is the right thing to do for our country and for the Palin family." She added, echoing a phrase she had used before, "I won't close the door that perhaps could be open for me in the future."

Palin's recent remarks about the possibilities of 2012 infused her appearance in Redding with an added charge—and the crowd realized it might be witnessing the latest contender for the heavyweight crown. I was struck by how Palin was trying to remold her image away from the ranting, anti-terrorist candidate hell-bent on scaring the electorate into voting for her ticket that she had unleashed little more than a year earlier. This was a tamer, more refined Palin, a more subtle and nuanced orator with an imposing mission: to reframe the narrative of the 2008 presidential election and her startling resignation from office. Her challenge was also two-fold: to reconnect with her base and reconfigure her brand. She immediately set out to undertake the former. "You're proof that the best of America is not all gathered in Washington, D.C.," she declared. Palin praised the crowd "for doing 'green jobs' before it was cool." The government, she asserted, "needs to stop playing politics with your responsible livelihoods!" She bonded with the audience by reminding them that she and her family also held "politically incorrect jobs"—as Alaska fishermen—and declared to a rousing round of applause that "government bureaucracy has broken faith with the people that they are supposed to be serving." At one point, returning to a routine that she would repeat over and over again in the months ahead, she held up the palm of her hand with the notation that claimed "Loggers rock!" The crowd went wild with approval.

I was reminded of U.S. Senator Saxby Chambliss's exuberant response in November of 2008 when Palin had spent a day on the campaign trail with him in Georgia to fire up his candidacy. He recognized the power of her celebrity and, more specifically, the way in which she was able to generate a cumulative energy in the body politic—an ability that none of the other national candidates in the Republican Party could come close to matching. It is Palin's political capital — no policy wonk she—and she knows how to market it on the stump.

Palin continued to connect with her crowd in Redding through a series of homespun platitudes. "I've always had a soft spot for you guys and gals in the industry," she said. "You built this country. You know what hard work is all about." Describing global warming as "bogus" and "a bunch of snake oil science," she exulted in the fact that President Barack Obama had failed in his efforts to secure an agreement at the United Nations Climate Change Conference in Copenhagen a month earlier. She repeatedly took swipes at "environmentalists" throughout her speech. The crowd lapped it up. "When a tree falls in the forest, and there's nobody around to hear it," Palin queried with a smirk, "what happens to environmental lawsuits?" It made absolutely no sense, but the crowd cheered her on. She delighted in the roar of approval. It was as though she were delivering a stand-up comedy routine with a series of one-liners. "I named my daughter Willow," she concluded with mock sarcasm. "Isn't that granola enough for them?"

Palin then took a series of preselected questions from Nadine Bailey, the logging conference's executive director and a widely respected legislative aide in Northern California with a long history in the logging industry. My friend knew her well and considered her a superb choice for the questioning. Indeed, it was a brilliant setup. It gave the appearance of Palin being able to respond in a seemingly impromptu "interview" format and helped to push away the memories of her interviews with Katie Couric and the other television anchors with whom she had stumbled so famously. Palin handled the conversation without the slightest miscue, was confident in her responses, and left to a rousing standing ovation. The crowd had gotten its money's worth.

Outside there was a gaggle of protestors—perhaps two dozen—carrying signs with messages: "Half-Baked Alaskan," "Beauty Fades—Stupidity is Forever," "Corporatocracy Rules U.S." There was little energy to the protestors, no chanting or catcalls, and beyond them stretched another line of two thousand waiting to enter the convention center for Palin's second speech of the evening. Several people were carrying banners proclaiming: "Palin for President 2012."

My pal and I chatted for a few moments before heading our separate ways home. Given that he knew my feelings about Palin, he held his cards close to his sleeve. "She was very good," he said. "She really connected with the crowd." He was impressed by her professionalism—the quality of her presentation and the fact that she had carefully shaped her remarks for her intended audience. She had won the crowd over, he noted, many of whom were his friends and long-time colleagues in the profession. He told me that prior to seeing her that day he had looked upon her as something of a joke, as a punch line. "I don't think that's the last we'll be seeing of her," he said. "She's probably running for president, isn't she?"

O N MY RETURN DRIVE BACK TO MY HOME in Santa Cruz, on the northern rim of Monterey Bay along the central California coast, my pace was slower and I found myself in a contemplative mood. No more rush to get there, no deadline. In Redding, my friend had asked me why I was so concerned about a Palin run for the presidency. That was before he had seen her power on the stump. He understood why I felt she wasn't going to leave the national stage anytime soon. Palin, I told him, was the first national presidential candidate with a chance of actually receiving the nomination to give both *body* and *voice* to the political zeitgeist of American right-wing talk radio. I saw what she did to the tenor of political discourse on the campaign trail in 2008. It was frightening the way she ramped up her rhetoric toward violence. To borrow a phrase from former governor Tony Knowles, who had run against Palin for governor of Alaska in 2006, I feared for my country. Moreover, as the father of a daughter with so-called special needs—and as a cancer survivor myself—I was both terrified of, and outraged by, Sarah Palin having any substantive role in American political discourse. The fact that she had even the slightest impact in the debate over health care reform was absolutely chilling.

For all her shortcomings, however, I was beginning to sense, quite accurately as it turned out, that Palin's anticipated fifteen-minutes-of-fame afforded her by John McCain was going to extend a good deal beyond the 2008 election and well into the next decade. Her appearance in Redding marked one of her first stump speeches on the road to her candidacy for president in 2012. Sarah Palin was clearly itching for a rematch with Barack Obama. And she seemed particularly resilient to a rising tide of criticism from across the political spectrum. In a prescient essay appearing in *The Huffington Post*, the Web site's founder, Arianna Huffington, noted that "it's not Palin's positions people respond to—it's her use of symbols." Invoking Carl Jung's notion of the *archetype*—the "collective unconscious" of the human psyche in which "universal images" reside—Huffington argued "that Palin's message operates on a level deeper than policy statements about the economy or financial reform or health care or the war in Afghanistan." Archetypes, Jung argued, are particularly potent during times of crisis. "There is no lunacy," Jung asserted, "that people under the domination of an archetype will not fall prey to."

Palin had, indeed, tapped into an archetypical force in American politics and culture. It was visceral, and most certainly anti-intellectual. I kept thinking of Palin's image in Redding—perched on high heels behind an elevated podium and with a massive American flag as a background—with her screechy high-pitched voice amplified over the convention center's sound system. The scene had an entirely surreal quality to it, eerie even, and it reminded me of a totemic work of cinematic fantasia in popular American culture, Victor Fleming's 1939 musical, *The Wizard of Oz*.

There is, admittedly, something of Dorothy in Palin, the young innocent from Kansas (read: Wasilla) who wakes one day to have her black-and-white life transported to the colorful land of the yellow brick road and the Emerald City. Palin's trademark red Naughty Monkey shoes that she wore throughout the campaign were directly reminiscent of Dorothy's ruby red slippers in the film. When Palin arrived for her first speech in Dayton, Ohio, it very much felt like life imitating art, as the young-Judy-Garland-as-Dorothy utters: "Toto, I have a feeling we're not in Kansas anymore." But the comparison to Dorothy is a bit too easy, and in the end, not quite accurate. The real parallel lies somewhere else.

With her Facebook posts and her brief remarks on Twitter—as well as with her canned appearances on Fox News and the staged scenarios on her "reality" show, *Sarah Palin's Alaska*—Palin has become the modern-day version of the Wizard, hiding behind a phalanx of curtains and screens with no direct accountability, pulling her levers and turning her wheels to create a fraudulent illusion of power and influence. In the end, as it has been from the very beginning in Wasilla, her political legitimacy is all smoke and mirrors, and most of all like the Wizard's, founded on deception and fueled by fear.

In Baum's original *The Wonderful Wizard of Oz*, the realization that the Wizard is a hoax comes as the main characters enter the so-called Throne Room, where Dorothy's dog, Toto, accidentally uncovers the faux wizard, "a little old man, with a bald head and a wrinkled face."

> "I thought Oz was a great Head," said Dorothy.
> "And I thought Oz was a lovely Lady," said the Scarecrow.
> "And I thought Oz was a terrible Beast," said the Tin Woodman.
> "And I thought Oz was a Ball of Fire," exclaimed the Lion.
> "No, you are all wrong," said the little man meekly. "I have been making believe."

So, too, has Palin. Her appearances before her rabid supporters are staged and controlled—she never allows the American public behind the curtains: it is all a carefully crafted construction, a fiction. Sarah Palin is our modern-day Wizard of Oz.

> "Making believe!" cried Dorothy. "Are you not a Great Wizard?"
> "Hush, my dear," he said. "Don't speak so loud, or you will be overheard—and I should be ruined. I'm supposed to be a Great Wizard."
> "And aren't you?" she asked.
> "Not a bit of it, my dear . . ."

FREE OF THE BURDENS OF ELECTED OFFICE, AND WITH the 2012 presidential campaign clearly in her sights, Palin sought attention every way she knew how—often through hyperbolic and inflammatory rhetoric on her Facebook page, her Twitter account, or Fox News. To many Americans, it seemed like little more than a daily act of desperation, a way to feed her narcissistic tendencies and her political delusions. It was all but incomprehensible for them to grasp Palin's political traction in what many deridingly referred to as "fly over" America. But Palin's poll numbers in the 2012 Republican sweep-stakes consistently put her up near the head of the pack—along with Mitt Romney, Mike Huckabee, and, occasionally Newt Gingrich—and, in the winter of 2010, even odds makers in Las Vegas listed her as the favorite to win the GOP nomination. To those paying close attention to Palin, there was an undeniable method to her madness. With rare exception, her target was Obama, her objective clearly the White House, and her calculated machinations often brought her headlines, magazine covers, or sound bites on the nightly news.

Palin delivered the keynote address at the inaugural National Tea Party Convention in Nashville, providing her not only with a national stage, but also with an opportunity to claim the movement as her own. She proclaimed that "America is ready for another revolution" and characterized the Tea Party movement as "a ground-up call to action"—apparently unaware that billionaires like the Koch Brothers were quietly funneling money into Tea Party support groups—but such details never seemed to get in the way of Palin's narrative.

Much of her speech, of course, was devoted to mocking Obama, who she described as a "charismatic guy with a teleprompter." She sarcastically asked, "How's that hopey-changey thing workin' out for you?" to roars of approval. And she charged Obama with spending the past year "reaching out to hostile regimes, writing personal letters to dangerous dictators, and apologizing for America." She said that what America needed was "commander in chief, not a professor of law"—all memes that she would pull out time and time again over the course of the following months.

Palin also hinted at what was clearly going to be her midterm election strategy as she ramped up her run down the yellow brick road to the White House. She signaled that she would take to the hustings supporting candidates who "understand free market principles" (though she never elaborated on what those were) and "personal responsibility," sneering in that braggadocio manner of hers that "I'll probably tick off some people as I get involved." And, perhaps, most important, she celebrated the concept of "contested, competitive primaries," declaring that this was "how we are going to find the cream of the crop to rise to be able to face a challenger in the general." She held herself up as an example of the process, claiming that she had "faced five guys in the party and we put our ideas and our experience out there on the table for debate." (This was, of course, the type of gross exaggeration to which Palin remained prone—there had only been two other GOP contenders on the ballot and two write-in candidates who garnered less than 1 percent of the vote combined). Once again, the details didn't matter. "That is a healthy process," she concluded. "And it gives Americans the kind of leadership that they want and they deserve. And so in 2010, I tip my hat to anyone with the courage to throw theirs in the ring, and may the best ideas and candidates win." When she was done, she left to chants of "Run, Sarah, Run!"

A MONTH LATER, PALIN WAS BACK ON THE attack against Obama again, this time targeting his health care reform package. "With the president signing this unwanted and 'transformative' government takeover of our health care system today with promises impossible to keep," Palin wrote on her Facebook page, "let's not get discouraged. Don't get demoralized. Get organized!" She launched an attack on members of Congress "who disregarded the will of the people" by supporting the legislation. "We're going to fire them and send them back to the private sector," she declared, "which has been shrinking thanks to their destructive government-growing policies." Then she noted that she was going to be "paying particular attention" to House members who voted in favor of "Obamacare," as she was wont to dub it, and represent those districts that she and McCain had carried in the 2008 election. Her Facebook page—as did her SarahPAC Web site—carried maps of the United States with twenty targeted congressional districts identified by crosshairs. The third targeted Congress member was Gabrielle Giffords of Arizona. "We'll aim for these races and many others," Palin declared. "This is just the first salvo in a fight to elect people across the nation who will bring common sense to Washington." She then urged her supporters to go to her SarahPAC Web site where they could join her "in the fight." It was a pitch for money—for contributions to Palin's political action coffers—and Palin had resorted to ballistic imagery and incendiary rhetoric to close the deal. The following day, Palin went to her Twitter account, urging her followers: "Don't Retreat, Instead—RELOAD! Pls see my Facebook page."

Pundits and political figures from across the political spectrum quickly criticized Palin for her use of martial imagery. Elizabeth Hasselbeck, the conservative co-host of *The View* who had enthusiastically joined Palin on the campaign trail in 2008, called Palin's use of the crosshairs "despicable." On the other side of the divide, MSNBC host Rachel Maddow placed the imagery in a broader perspective, noting that Palin had fed off the recent "gun fervor" and the "effort to intimidate by a show of force" leading up to the vote on the health reform bill. "The armed and dangerous theme isn't just in the streets and at the protests," she noted. "It's now the vernacular by which supposedly mainstream conservative politicians address their followers now." *Salon*'s Joan Walsh was equally condemnatory. "In a country where angry right-wingers carry guns to see the president speak, and spit on African-American congressmen, I thought it was a chilling statement," Walsh declared. "Will any Republican denounce Palin's language?"

Certainly not Palin's former running mate John McCain, who defended Palin's imagery and rhetoric as "part of the political lexicon." When pressed on the matter by NBC's *Today Show* host Ann Curry, a clearly irritated McCain stated such images "are fine" and that they were used "all the time." To say that "someone's in a 'battleground state' is 'offensive,'" McCain added with a sarcastic smirk, "simply, I'm sorry." Curry refused to back down. "I think it is the 'reload' and 'crosshairs' that's caused a lot of people to be concerned, Senator." McCain refused to concede the point.

In response to the criticism, Palin amped up her remarks. At a speech in Arizona supporting McCain's reelection bid, Palin defended the imagery and called the criticism a "ginned-up controversy." In a Facebook posting on college basketball's March Madness, Palin mocked her critics by calling on those teams in the Final Four to "use your strong weapons—your Big Guns" and warned of team leaders being caught in the "enemy's crosshairs." No matter how tough it got, she concluded, "never retreat, instead, RELOAD!"

A few months later, she was caught up in another Twitter controversy, this time over her incendiary tweets about the proposed Islamic cultural center and mosque, Park51, located two blocks from the site of the World Trade Center.

> Ground Zero Mosque supporters: doesn't it stab you in the heart, as it does ours throughout the heartland? Peaceful Muslims, pls refudiate

Palin's use of the term "refudiate" quickly drew heaps of scorn, so she pulled down her initial posting and took a second shot at the controversy:

> Peaceful New Yorkers, pls refute the Ground Zero mosque plan if you believe catastrophic pain caused @ Twin Towers site is too raw, too real.

She then pulled the second attempt down and took a third swipe at it.

> Peace-seeking Muslims pls understand. Ground Zero mosque
> is UNNECESSARY provocation; it stabs hearts. Pls reject it
> in interest of healing

Palin then quickly threw up a defense of her use of the term "refudiate," comparing herself to William Shakespeare in the process.

> "Refudiate," "misunderestimate," "wee-wee'd up." English is
> a living language. Shakespeare liked to coin new words too.
> Got to celebrate it!

Palin's manic Twitter postings ignited a national rage directed at the proposed sixteen-story facility, originally named Cordoba House. She was countered by New York City mayor Michael Bloomberg, who declared that "government should never—*never*—be in the business of telling people how they should pray, or where they can pray. We want to make sure that everybody from around the world feels comfortable coming here, living here, and praying the way they want to pray." When conservative critics echoed Palin's sentiments, Bloomberg stood firm. "We would betray our values if we were to treat Muslims differently than anyone else," he asserted. "To cave to popular sentiment would be to hand a victory to the terrorists, and we should not stand for that." The battle over the center, however, continued to flare. Imam Feisal Abdul Rauf, the leader of the proposed mosque, called Palin's opposition "disingenuous" and singled her out for the "growing Islamophobia" that was sweeping the United States. "What has happened," he declared, "is that certain politicians decided that this project would be very useful for their political ambitions."

Palin seemed to take delight in kindling political conflict wherever she could. Not only did it continue to garner her headlines and record-breaking Internet traffic, it succeeded in keeping any other conservative contenders for the 2012 Republican nomination from gaining political traction. Palin left no vacuum to fill. As the summer wore on, many of Palin's remarks began to take a strange sexualized taunting to them. In response to the controversial legislation in Arizona aimed at curbing illegal immigration, Palin declared that Arizona's Republican governor "Jan Brewer has the *cojones* that our president does not have. If our own president will not enforce a federal law, more power to Jan Brewer."

D URING THE LATE SUMMER OF 2009, SHORTLY AFTER Palin resigned her governorship, I had sent an e-mail to Fred Malek, who had served as co-chair of McCain's National Finance Committee, requesting an interview with him. Malek had been identified in many news stories as a close confidant of Palin's—he had hosted a widely publicized dinner in January of 2009 honoring both McCain and Palin, marking the first time they had seen each other since Election Day—and Malek was constantly being quoted in the press as a source for inside knowledge of Palin's political activities and ambitions. Much to my gratification, Malek provided me with two lengthy telephone interviews from his Rocky Mountain vacation retreat overlooking Aspen, Colorado.

Malek told me that he had "barely heard of Palin" when she was selected by McCain, and that he was surprised to find out that "she was on his short list." But he had grown to like her through the process of the campaign. He viewed her as "down to earth," "very easy to talk to," and possessed with "an appealing personality," and he cultivated the relationship, not only with Palin directly, but through Palin's then-close adviser, Meghan Stapleton. Malek con-firmed to me that he had remained in close contact with Stapleton via e-mail in the aftermath of the campaign.

Malek told me that he was concerned about the company that Palin kept—or didn't keep. He confirmed that in late March of 2009, an emissary from the Republican Governors Association (RGA) had traveled to Alaska to advise Palin about being more organized and structured in her dealings outside Alaska. According to a report in *The New York Times,* Palin was advised to make "a long-term schedule and stick to it, have staff members set aside ample and inviolable family time to replenish your spirits, and build a coherent home-state agenda that creates jobs and ensures reelection." She simply needed help, Malek asserted, "getting organized for the national figure she'd become." She needed some key players in place, he said, "to handle the press of national interest and to field all of the requests" coming her way in "an ex-peditious and professional manner." He had heard horror stories from those who had tried to schedule Palin appearances. There was too much incoming, he assessed. Stapleton couldn't handle it all. Moreover, Malek advised Palin to focus on her governorship, to rebuild her relationships in Alaska, and to focus on some signature legislation in the second half of her term.

Palin's response, at the time, was largely to ignore Malek's and the RGA's recommendations. "Like so much of the advice sent Ms. Palin's way by influential supporters," the *Times* noted, "it appeared to be happily received and then largely discarded." Her experience with those outside her immediate circle had led her not to trust people, and she still operated on her gut instincts when bringing outsiders into her brain trust. In a lengthy profile of Palin's cohort, entitled "The Palin Network," that appeared in *The New York Times Magazine* the following year, journalist Robert Draper, who garnered a rare interview with Palin, portrayed a figure with a bunker mentality, still cautious, if not paranoid, after her disastrous two-month experience on the national ticket in 2008 with "unprincipled" political operatives "who are in it for power, money and job titles." The experience, she said, "taught us, yes, to be on guard and be very discerning about who we can and can't trust in the political arena." If she were to expand her organization, Palin told Draper, it would have to be with "people who are trustworthy."

Palin had never understood that trust is a two-way enterprise, a dynamic. She viewed it, said one of her former staffers, as "blind loyalty, a one-way street, all or nothing." For her, trust required something akin to "devotion." Unable to maintain relationships with those in close association with her throughout her political career, Palin had gone through numerous "trusted" advisers in recent years. By the summer of 2010, none of her inner-circle from Wasilla, or from anywhere in Alaska, for that matter, was still in place. Those chief advisers from her gubernatorial campaign in 2006 —John Bitney, Frank Bailey, Paul Fuhs, Curtis Smith, and Christopher Clark—had all been tossed under Palin's bus. Her chief of staff, Mike Tibbles, and her attorney general, Talis Colberg, both resigned long before their terms expired. Indeed, as Draper noted, "It's a curious feature of Palin World that none of its charter members knew her before 2008." She was continuously shuffling the deck.

As a result, the Palin brain trust that was assembled on the verge of the 2010 midterms had the appearance of a ragtag and patchwork street gang. Malek remained somewhere on the periphery, still providing quotes about Palin and alleged insights, though it was uncertain if he still had any substantive contact with the former governor. In the immediate aftermath of her resignation, Palin's close friend Kris Perry had made a quiet exit from the Palin payroll; a year later, in February 2010, Stapleton followed suit, resigning abruptly from her nearly $100,000-per-year position at SarahPAC. Her role was largely filled by a would-be screenwriter from Los Angeles via Detroit, Rebecca Mansour, who had worked her way into Palin's confidence through the Web site she cofounded, *Conservatives4Palin,* on which she originally posted *anonymously* and for which Mansour wrote an extensive, adulatory profile of her soon-to-be boss in March of 2009, entitled "Who Is Sarah Palin?" Mansour, who described herself on Twitter as a "Lebanese Maronite Christian," was a political neophyte when she signed up with SarahPAC. Her lone, previously reported political experience was attempting to volunteer for Barack Obama's campaign in 2008.

Also a political neophyte was Palin's consigliore Van Flein, a previously unknown labor attorney from Anchorage who was best recognized in Alaska (until his association with Palin) for having survived a murder attempt by a jealous gunman in 1990. As of December 2010, both Van Flein and Mansour were earning annual stipends from SarahPac of $120,000 and $96,000 respectively; though in January 2011, Van Flein abruptly quit his law firm and his position with SarahPAC to serve as legislative director and deputy chief of staff for a conservative congressman from Arizona, Paul Gossar. Others on the SarahPAC payroll at the beginning of 2011 included: Andrew Davis, the Sacramento-based Republican consultant who was an opposition researcher for the RNC and who had worked with Palin at the end of the 2008 campaign; another McCain castoff, Tim Crawford, who serves as SarahPAC's treasurer; Scheunemann, Palin's staunch lobbyist-supporter from the McCain campaign who continues to advise her on foreign policy issues; and Pam Pryor, an evangelical Republican described by the Web site *Texans for Palin* as Palin's "kindred spirit" and "go-to girl." According to Draper, this hodgepodge of advisers engages in thrice-weekly conference calls "sans Palin."*

In addition to those on the SarahPAC payroll, Palin maintains a small coterie of confidants and advisers, like Malek, who remain in the outer Palin orbit. One of them has been the Washington, D.C.–based power attorney, Robert Barnett, who negotiated both of Palin's book deals for her with HarperCollins. Not only did Barnett serve as Obama's agent for his second blockbuster, *The Audacity of Hope,* he also represented both Bill and Hillary Clinton in seeking book deals of their own. His other recent clients have included Laura and George W. Bush, Dick Cheney, former treasury secretary Henry Paulson, and Obama's campaign manager David Plouffe.

The other odd power brokers connected to Palin have been John Coale, who had been a staunch supporter of Hillary Clinton's during the 2008 campaign, and his wife, Fox News host Greta Van Susteren, who has had unparalleled

---

* "The Palin Network," by Robert Draper, *The New York Times Magazine,* November 21, 2010.

access to both Palins since the presidential election and who has conducted a series of fawning interviews with them for Fox News.

Coale, like Barnett, a powerful Washington, D.C.–based attorney, has acknowledged to *Politico* that he advised Palin in setting up SarahPAC and was also one of the attorneys who advised her about establishing what became her ill-fated legal defense fund. Coale has described himself variously as "a pirate" and as "an ambulance chaser." Coale and Van Susteren are longtime members of the Church of Scientology.

A 1986 Scientology document, signed by Coale, entitled "How Scientologists Can Take Responsibility for and BE AT CAUSE OVER the Fourth Dynamic," is, in essence, a manifesto riddled with Scientology jargon for developing political power and influence at the national and international levels of government. "We have been advised by legislative consultants, by allies who are experienced with the government and Congress and even by congressmen themselves," the document asserted, "that the only viable way to get the attention, assistance or support of politicians is to be in a position to deliver to them either (or both) of their most sought-after needs—MONEY and VOTES." Since then, Coale has taken it upon himself to implement the tenets of his 1986 manifesto. During the 2008 campaign, the *Baltimore Sun* reported that Coale admitted to being "enamored" with Palin and jokingly referring to her as "his girlfriend." Between October and December of 2008, Coale made contributions totaling $54,700 to the coffers of "McCain Victory 2008" and the Republican National Committee.

The lone constant, of course, in Palin's inner circle has been her husband, Todd, who attorney Van Flein told Draper was always "part of the information chain." Such an assessment has been made abundantly manifest by the thousands of government e-mails released by the state of Alaska on which Todd Palin was copied, at his private e-mail address. John Ziegler, the conservative talk show host who made the film *Media Malpractice: How Obama Got Elected and Palin Was Targeted* immediately after the McCain-Palin defeat in 2008, observed on his blog site that "anyone not named Todd or Sarah who pretends to know for sure what Palin's long-term plans are is either delusional or a liar." Todd "is clearly her anchor," said one of Palin's former associates in Alaska, "both politically and personally. He has a very strong practical side to him. He's grounded in an Alaska sort of way. But he has zero understanding of the American political process. Zero."

———

THREE WEEKS BEFORE THE MIDTERM ELECTIONS in November of 2010—and a little less than a year since I had last seen her in Redding—Sarah Palin brought her political road show back to California, this time to San Jose in the heart of Silicon Valley, home of the high-tech revolution that not only gave birth to the Information Age and transformed the way we communicate with one another, but also augured the reconfiguration of global capital over the last quarter century. In purely geographical terms, the Silicon Valley is not entirely unlike the Matanuska and Susitna valleys, 1,500 miles to the north and west. Before the great economic boom of World War II, the Santa Clara Valley, as it was originally named by Spanish explorers, was an agricultural stronghold known as "The Valley of Heart's Delight," with sprawling orchards that blanketed the horizon each spring in a sea of white-and-pink blossoms. Politically, however, the valleys are on opposite sides of the spectrum, as the Northern California vale is a bastion of New Age ideology and liberal sensibilities that have made it a Democratic stronghold for several generations.

This was one of Palin's first forays into traditionally "blue" territory in California—or for that matter, anywhere in the country. Sarah Palin, for all her protestations to the contrary, doesn't like to get out of her comfort zone. Her previous appearances in California had taken place in "red" pockets of conservativism throughout the Central Valley and Southern California. As I pulled up to the San Jose Center for the Performing Arts, a postmodern 2,600-seat venue designed in the early 1970s by the Frank Lloyd Wright Foundation, I wasn't sure what to expect, though I was conjecturing some sort of protest outside (the center, after all, was only a few blocks away from San Jose State University). There were none. Unlike the last Palin event I had attended in Redding, California, where there was a modicum of protests and horribly long lines of people being frisked before being allowed inside, this one was eerily quiet, even sober, and entirely uneventful. With a fleet of television news trucks perched on the periphery and only a handful of elderly libertarian activists handing out brochures and campaign literature, ticket-holders quickly skirted through the foyer of the circular complex to escape the 90-plus-degree Indian summer heat beating down on the sidewalk.

As I found my seat, midway in the opera section, I looked back through the hall. It appeared to be roughly three-quarters full—slightly less than two thousand people—not a sellout by any means, but certainly not an empty house either. I later learned that approximately 1,400 tickets were sold, at a price range of $25 to $199. The crowd was more diverse (in respect to both age and ethnicity) and much mellower than I anticipated. There were a fair amount of college-aged students, and lots of Asian Americans of all ages, in a region noted for a large and politically active Vietnamese American community. This was not country club America—more like the dispirited *petit bourgeoisie*— many of them small business owners sick of a government bureaucracy they perceive to be taxing and regulating them at every turn. Nor was it intensely angry, right-wing America blistering with hatred at each breath. They were polite and reserved and waiting to hear the canned utterances of the Queen of the Tea Party, whom they clearly adored.

My seat was situated between a woman ("Jean") from Redwood City, on the San Francisco Peninsula, who owned a floral shop (and was the mother of grown children) and a retired mechanic from nearby Fremont ("Glenn") in his late sixties, clearly concerned that the social security system was on the verge of bankruptcy. (I didn't have the heart to tell him that Palin's candidate for the U.S. Senate in Alaska, Joe Miller, viewed social security as unconstitutional). Jean found Palin "pretty, bright, and quick on her feet," while Glenn viewed her as "tough and fearless." Both were overtly fearful of what they view as the impending collapse of the American economy and the imposition of "European socialism" (they both used the term) in the United States. Both admitted to watching a lot of Fox News. Jean was a fan of Beck; Glenn of Hannity. They both thoroughly detested Obama—and both were quite eagerly anticipating a Palin run for the White House in 2012. Jean was confident. "He doesn't stand a chance against her," she said.

As Michael Paul Gross noted in a controversial *Vanity Fair* portrait of Palin that appeared in October 2010, many of Palin's previous engagements in the year since she resigned from her governorship had been staged by what Gross characterized as shady, right-wing front organizations that seemingly "have been created for a single purpose: to pay Sarah Palin to give a speech." This included a political action committee calling itself Preserving American Liberty, out of Missouri, and the Blue Ridge Educational Resource Group, located in South Carolina. Palin's appearance in San Jose proved to be no exception. It was produced by the so-called Liberty and Freedom Foundation, headed up by a former figure skater and graduate of nearby Hillsdale High, Victor Cocchia, who first appeared on the Palin radar when he produced an event at the exclusive Petroleum Club in Midland, Texas, six months earlier. The foundation was listed in an article appearing in the *Midland Reporter* as "a New York City–based political organization."

At the time of Palin's arrival in San Jose a half-year later, the foundation's unfinished Web site listed an address in Washington, D.C., as its home base, but in its paperwork submitted to the Federal Election Commission, the foundation's address was listed as a post-office box in Midland. The latest FEC filing by the foundation recorded not a single penny going through its coffers. Another Palin event scheduled by the foundation in Miami, for which tickets were sold, was canceled, then rescheduled, then canceled in its entirety. For all her push toward the mainstream, Palin was still dealing with the fringe.

The opening remarks were handled by San Francisco Bay Area right-wing talk show host Brian Sussman, who received a rousing, standing ovation as he walked onto the stage. My guess is that a significant portion of those in attendance were devoted followers of Sussman, who promoted the event repeatedly throughout the week on his show—but still couldn't pack the house. He was irreverently glib and took plenty of predictable potshots at California politicians Nancy Pelosi, Jerry Brown, and Barbara Boxer and, then, Barack *Hussein* Obama—emphasis on the "H." Then Cocchia, affecting a Prince Valiant haircut, delivered a long-winded introductory speech (rumor had it that Palin was late). There was a pledge of allegiance to a massive American flag that stretched from top to bottom of the stage, then a rendition of "God Bless America," and then later yet, "The Star Spangled Banner," performed admirably by a quintet of young sisters calling themselves Celestial City.

But the star of the show was clearly Palin, clad in high-heeled sandals, yet another snug black skirt, and a purple suit jacket with the requisite American flag pin on her lapel. After watching far too much stump footage of Palin these past two years, I wasn't sure which Sarah Palin would show up—the angry, vicious Palin (who delivered a demagogic speech just a week earlier in San Diego); the giddy, nearly vacuous Palin (all smiles and giggles, as she appeared on Newsmax a few days before); the stunned, cross-eyed Palin (of Katie Couric fame); or "America's sweetheart," as the *Washington Post*'s Chris Cillizza generously dubbed her (following her speech at the Republican National Convention in Minneapolis). She came mostly with the A-game version of the latter in San Jose, and the audience feasted on her performance.

Palin made sure to garner headlines with remarks about Pelosi, Brown, and Boxer—saying that they "act like they're permanent residents of some unicorn ranch in Fantasy Land"—although the only one, as it turned out, living in a fantasy land was Palin, as all three of the Democrats she attacked were easily elected or reelected three weeks later. In her peculiar way of reaching out to the Bay Area crowd, she joked about there being a Mama Grizzly on the state flag and made several references to the San Francisco Giants and their 2010 National League West title, but mocked the fact that the Giants hadn't won a World Series since 1954 (which, given her history of jinxing her hometown hockey teams in recent years, almost certainly assured their ensuing victory over the Texas Rangers in the fall classic).

She also paid due homage to the patron saint of the modern-day conservative movement, Ronald Reagan, the Republican president (and former governor of California) whose presidential administration expanded federal spending and increased the national deficit by 300 percent. Such details have never mattered to Sister Sarah and her minions. What matters is the symbolism of Reagan—the *image,* the *legacy*—and as Palin borrows her manner of speaking from the cadences of the evangelical clergy (think Elmer Gantry in drag), she refers to Reagan in almost deistic tones, as if his words were taken from the Scripture. Part of her electoral strategy, of course, is simply to claim the political mantle of Reagan—and to wrestle it away from her GOP opponents Huckabee and Gingrich—but there is also something more profound at work. She is transposing the hierarchy of the pulpit to the secular lectern, with the Great Communicator serving as a divine force of both salvation and redemption as America seeks its way back from the political desert. "We're gonna get America back on the right track," Palin intoned early on, "toward that exceptionalism that Ronald Reagan used to speak of. We are ready to take our government back and put it back on our side and become that exceptional America."

A short time later, she returned to the Gipper again:

> As Ronald Reagan would put it respectfully, he'd call all of us the little guy. Well, when they're not listening to the little guy I have to ask you, are you ready to take it back and put government back on the side of *you* and I, and have government work for you?

And again:

> He came from here. He, Ronald Reagan, believed that government needed a big dose of common sense. He cut taxes,

he cut regulations, he made decisions that would bring a new prosperity to America. For the next two decades, he would . . . had put us right on the right track. He refused, rejected those who wanted to overregulate the new technology industry. Instead, he got government out of the way of the high-tech revolution that was sweeping the nation, especially here in California. And, America came back bigger and better than ever. What an example that you all have, those roots here, Ronald Reagan could stand on and grow from and bring prosperity to the rest of the nation from here.

Anyone who doesn't think that Palin still has a hand in writing her more recent speeches is fooling themselves. She brings in her respective ghostwriters to work on them, but they contain the same disjointed syntax, the same non sequiturs, the same word-salad idioms that have dominated her public comments for nearly two decades.

If Reagan is the hero of Palin's emerging narrative of the American political terrain, then the villain, of course, is none other than President Barack Obama. Palin had become virtually obsessed with him since her ticket's loss in the 2008 election. "It's like she's back in high school and someone is more popular than she is," said her former legislative liaison John Bitney. "It's unnerved her. She can't let it go." Many of her Facebook and Twitter postings were little more than ad hominem attacks on the president. The same can be said for her occasional op-ed pieces in national newspapers. And when the magazine *Runner's World* asked her offhandedly if she could beat Obama in a foot race, Palin couldn't help but affirm:

> I betcha I'd have more endurance. My one claim to fame in my own little internal running circle is a sub-four [hour] marathon. It wasn't necessarily a good running time, but it proves I have the endurance within me to at least gut it out and that is something . . . So if it were a long race that required a lot of endurance, I'd win.

When Palin brought up Obama in San Jose, her body language immediately became more animated, her facial expressions more intense. And she returned to a rendition of events that had been thoroughly discounted in Alaska, but on which she could bank on getting away with Outside, as they related to Obama's stimulus package. Her remarks provide yet another fascinating glimpse into her thought process.

> When I was governor, some of those dollars that were coming down into Alaska I vetoed those dollars because I knew that, basically, I looked at a lot of those stimulus dollars as being bribes to states where, oh, it was so tempting to take this money and legislatures—they hold the purse strings to a state budget—they wanted to take the money and for a lot of conservative governors the legislature would go around—there was language within the stimulus bill to make sure those lawmakers could be the ones to go around the governor and take the money anyway. . . . So as governor I vetoed some of those and vetoing some of those things because fat strings are attached to federal monies when they come to a state. You have to become beholden to a big centralized government in Washington, D.C., if you accept their money and they have more control over how that money is spent. So, in vetoing it, my *Republican*-led legislature overruled my veto because too many of the *Republicans* even in the machine thought that that somehow, some way it was going to be free money and nobody would have to be held accountable. So some of us still trying to do something about that, still knowing though that some of what was in that stimulus package, some of the examples that we have seen of where those dollars have gone are just atrocious and now we even have the president finally admitting, oh there's kind no such thing as a shovel ready project . . . Now we know what they were shoveling— and it wasn't asphalt.

If Palin is imbued with a political philosophy, it is the politics of snark— the quick hit, the nasty dig, the eye-rolling one-liner. Forget that she accepted more than 97.2 percent of the stimulus package; even when presented with the opportunity for prepared remarks and a canned speech, she still couldn't help but go Katie Couric on her audience. And note that this time around—only a few months after the release of *Going Rogue,* in which she blamed the "Democrat-controlled legislature" for the veto—it was now the *Republicans* in Alaska, because Republican legislators made a better foil for her current political narrative.

But for all her testaments to the wisdom and divinity of Reagan, the tenacity and fortitude of Sarah Palin, and the failures and socialistic machinations of Obama, Palin reserved her most galling—and insensitive—passages for the late Pat Tillman, the San Jose–reared football hero turned NFL star who gave up the glories of the gridiron to serve in the Army Rangers in the Middle East, and whose tragic death by fratricide in Afghanistan was shamefully covered up by several members of the Bush administration. After several tours of duty Tillman had become critical of U.S. military policy in the Middle East and opposed the war in Iraq, where he had also served. Only two months prior to Palin's arrival in San Jose, the award-winning film *The Tillman Story* (which documented the Tillman saga in painful detail) had been released nationally to sterling reviews. Palin seemed absolutely oblivious to the details of Tillman's saga and his family's ordeal, carelessly using the slain soldier's death as a billboard advertisement for American militarism. While praising the "heroes" who "fight for our rights and our values in faraway battles," Palin singled out Tillman:

> One of those heroes was from right here in San Jose. Pat Tillman, who gave up the money and the glamour of the NFL. Think what Pat has sacrificed and his family has sacrificed. Giving up a pro-football career to serve his country, and he, ultimately giving his life for our freedom. You know, remember to thank God every day for Pat, for his family, for the thousands like him who make us so proud to be Americans.

It was yet another applause line in a speech full of patriotic platitudes. Palin had apparently not gotten the message about Tillman. In a letter written to Brigadier General Gary M. Jones in the aftermath of the Army's cover-up, Tillman's father, Pat Tillman, Sr., called the Army's investigative process "shameless bullshit" and signed the letter, "In sum: Fuck you . . . and yours." At the memorial services for Tillman, none other than John McCain issued a hollow eulogy in which he directed his closing remarks to Tillman's family, promising them "that you will see him again, when a loving God reunites us all with the loved ones who preceded us in death." Tillman's younger brother, Richard, followed McCain at the services by responding, "Make no mistake—he'd want me to say this—he's not with God; he's fucking dead. Thanks for your thoughts, but he's fucking dead."

Palin—and her advance staff—were shamefully ignorant about the details surrounding Tillman's death, the corrupt military cover-up that followed and, most significant, the emotional scars and moral outrage carried by Tillman's family. Even among her faithful in San Jose that afternoon, her remarks elicited a mixed response from those who knew the full story. Then, literally, in the very same breath, Palin segued directly from Tillman into mocking some remarks made by Michelle Obama during the 2008 campaign: "You know, when I hear people say, or had said during the campaign, that they've never been proud of America," Palin spat out in her high-pitched whine, her chin stuck out in that peculiar pose of hers and with a self-satisfied grin spreading across her face. "Haven't they met anybody in uniform yet? I get tears in my eyes when I see that young man, that young woman, walking through the airport in uniform . . . you too . . . so proud to be American!"

It was a classic Palin cheap shot—distorting something that one of her opponents had said or taking it completely out of context—and the crowd roared its approval. Palin showed her willingness to stick the dagger not only into the president, but into the popular first lady as well. Palin is a figure straight out of World Wrestling Entertainment, and she loves playing the part of the political miscreant. "The success of professional wrestling," writes Chris Hedges in *Empire of Illusion,* "like most of the entertainment that envelops our culture, lies not in fooling us that these stories are real. Rather it succeeds because we ask to be fooled." Throughout American cities, Hedges argues, "night after night, packed arena after packed arena, the wrestlers play out a new, broken social narrative." And in what is an inevitable consequence of celebrity culture, "the line between public and fictional personas blurs." As Palin takes to the stump across America, she reflects the same broken narrative, the same blurred lines. Palin's political paradigm, like that of professional wrestling, is one between good and evil; there is no gray. Her attacks on her opponents—whether it be the Obamas or the Democrats or Muslims or the "good ol' boys" in the Republican Party—are all framed in black and white. Palin clearly delights in her hyperbolic attacks.

And they fire up her base. The nice lady and gentleman on both sides of me cheered her on.

Palin concluded her remarks with one more reference to the Gipper, citing his words as though they were biblical.

> Like Reagan would say, that time-tested truth, that belief that America is that shining city on a hill, and that our best days really are yet to come, if we do our part, as President Reagan said—standing on those Californian roots. What Reagan would say, was, "The great confident roar of America's progress, and growth, and optimism will resound again." So, I thank you for being here, for being part of the solution. We can take it back, let it start here in California. November 2nd is right around the corner. God bless you California and God bless America!

The crowd rose to its feet. They had come for a *spectacle*—an encounter with *celebrity*—and Palin had delivered. Like an aging rock band with a medley of number-one songs in their repertoire, Palin had delivered a greatest-hits performance, with her canned "you betcha's," her holding up the palm of her hand to show notes on it, to her attacks on Obama and the "lamestream media" and the "liberal elite."

Many of my friends in Alaska refer to Palin as the "Grifter Governor"— and that was certainly an undercurrent in San Jose. After the talk she headed off to a nearby hotel, where big-ticket supporters of Palins had the chance to take pictures with her and, then, at an even stiffer price, to partake in a sit-down dinner with her and Todd. Palin trades on her celebrity at every turn—in her Fox News contract, her million-dollar book deals, her reality television series, and in positioning herself for a run at the presidency—and she collects every step of the way.

As Bill Clinton noted in an interview with CNN, we are apparently entering into a "fact-free" period in American politics, "where experience in government is a negative." Palin's only political commodity remains her celebrity—nothing more, and certainly nothing less. She's parlayed it into an international brand; she's getting her shtick down and has tapped into a troubling American zeitgeist. As I headed back to my car I couldn't help but think of what a very wise man once said: buyer beware. Sarah Palin was still peddling a bridge to nowhere.

A S THE CLOCK TICKED DOWN TO ELECTION DAY, Palin found herself embattled on several fronts, and her organization—or lack thereof—was often at the root of the conflict. By far the biggest skirmish was with the news organization *Politico,* which on the Sunday before the election published a piece entitled "Next for GOP Leaders: Stopping Palin," by two of the Web site's top reporters, Mike Allen and Jim VandeHei (who was also one of its founders). Citing several "unnamed sources," Allen and VandeHei reported what many mainstream Republican political operatives had been saying for months: "that an urgent party task after the midterm elections will be to discredit Sarah Palin and halt what they see as her march toward a GOP nomination for president in 2012." It was clear to anyone paying close attention that Palin was positioning herself for a run at the White House; the question was no longer "if" but "when."

Two of John McCain's once trusted strategists—Steve Schmidt and John Weaver—had separately gone on the record during the past year and given voice to their strong concerns about a Palin candidacy. At the First Draft of History Conference, held in Washington, D.C., Schmidt took a direct dig at the talking heads at Fox News and Rush Limbaugh declaring, "The leadership of the party cannot be outsourced to the conservative-entertainment complex." In respect to Palin specifically, his remarks were equally direct. "In the year since the election has ended, she has done nothing to expand her appeal beyond the base. The independent vote is going to be up for grabs in 2012. That middle of the electorate is going to be determinative of the outcome of the elections. I just don't see that if you look at the things she has done over the year . . . that she is going to expand that base in the middle."

When moderator John King pressed him with a follow-up question about Palin, Schmidt declared, "I think that she has talents, but my honest view is that she would not be a winning candidate for the Republican Party in 2012, and in fact, were she to be the nominee, we would have a *catastrophic* election result." John Weaver, another chief strategist on the Straight Talk Express, followed up on Schmidt's comments in an interview with Chris Cillizza of *The Washington Post.* If Palin won the GOP nomination, Weaver declared, "it would surely mean a political apocalypse is upon us."

Catastrophic and *apocalyptic.* As the tensions surrounding the 2010 midterms ramped up and potential presidential contenders (and their strategists) elbowed their way into position for 2012, Karl Rove, the dean of GOP political strategists and the architect of George W. Bush's successful runs for the White House in 2000 and 2004, told the conservative-leaning British newspaper *The Daily Telegraph* that he did not think Palin was up to the task of being president. In what was clearly a dig at Palin's upcoming television show, *Sarah Palin's Alaska,* Rove said, "with all due candor, appearing on your own reality show on the Discovery Channel, I am not certain how that fits in the American calculus of 'that helps me see you in the Oval Office.'" Rove did not pull any punches. "There are high standards that the American people have for it [the presidency] and they require a certain level of gravitas," Rove declared, "and they want to look at the candidate and say 'that candidate is doing things that gives me confidence that they are up to the most demanding job in the world.'"

That the Republican Party establishment was preparing to ambush Palin should have been obvious to anyone paying attention. It was Republicans, not "liberals" or "the left" or Democrats, as Palin would always like to claim—both in Alaska and in the Lower 48—taking the swipes at her. In another biting *Politico* piece, senior writer Jonathan Martin painted a devastating portrait of Palin as a slipshod inside player in the national game:

> According to multiple Republican campaign sources, the former Alaska governor wreaks havoc on campaign logistics and planning. She offers little notice about her availability, refuses to do certain events, is obsessive about press coverage, and sometimes backs out with as little lead time as she gave in the first place.
>
> In short, her seat-of-the-pants operation can be a nightmare to deal with, which, in part, explains why Palin doesn't often do individual events for GOP hopefuls.

The article went on to describe a series of specific Republican Party events in which her inability to execute simple matters of scheduling and to make firm commitments to the campaigns of Republican candidates had proved utterly frustrating to GOP field operations throughout the country.

Palin was clearly outraged by the two *Politico* pieces. She attacked Martin on Glenn Beck's radio show. "Hey, you can lie about me *Politico,* Jonathan Martin, ya punk," she declared. "You guys can lie about me, but you're takin' on the big guns, you're takin' on Beck. You know, you're an idiot if you take 'em on!" In an interview with her colleague Greta Van Susteren of Fox News, she called Allen and VandeHei "jokes" for using anonymous sourcing, saying of those who hide behind the cloak of anonymity: "If they would man up and if they would, you know, make these claims against me then I can debate them, I can talk about it, but to me they're making stuff up again." She took it a step further in an e-mail to the Web site *Daily Caller,* declaring: "I suppose I could play their immature, unprofessional, waste-of-time game, too, by claiming these reporters and politicos are homophobe, child molesting, tax evading, anti-dentite, [*sic*] puppy-kicking, chain smoking porn producers . . . really, they are." Just as she had her entire political career—even dating back to her junior high school days in Wasilla—Palin needed to make it personal and to turn herself into the victim. Indeed, Palin had transformed victimhood into a political platform. It was the antithesis of feminism. But it was the only reaction she could count on to bring her continued media attention.

Indeed, Palin's response to such exposés has always been to attack the messenger—and that is how she continued to play it in the final hours leading up to the 2010 midterm elections. Having worn out her cliché of the "lamestream media," she now referred to the mainstream media as "this yellow journalism world." She said of *Politico,* "It's not worth even wrapping my king salmon in. I'll just ignore this crap," but then, curiously, she admitted "I haven't read the article yet"— the very article on which her entire interview with Van Susteren was based. *Politico's* Martin didn't back down. The following day he went on MSNBC's *Morning Joe* and placed Palin's response in a larger context that many in the media were expressing quietly but few were willing to state publicly. "There is something broader going on here," he noted. "If Sarah Palin can call a journalist 'yellow' and try to denounce every story written about her, it's an effort to try to make the mainstream media not legitimate. If they're not legitimate, she doesn't have to deal with us and can stay in the Fox News world, conservative talk radio world. If we're not real and legit, there's no point to deal with us, which means she doesn't have to face scrutiny and accountability." It was another way of saying that Palin had retreated back into the Land of Oz, behind the curtains and the smoke screens, into her fantasy world of make-believe.

Palin delighted in the throwing of elbows. When she responded to Rove's comments about her reality television show, she glibly declared to Chris Wallace of Fox News, "Wasn't Ronald Reagan an actor? Wasn't he in 'Bedtime for Bonzo,' Bozo, something? Ronald Reagan *was an actor.*" It was a shocking diminishment of Reagan's biography by someone who allegedly held him in absolute esteem. The smart answer would have been to compare her show,

Sarah Palin's Alaska, to Reagan's role in *Death Valley Days*—the television series celebrating the history of the American West, which he hosted before he was first elected governor of California—but Palin had clearly grown to prefer wise-ass and glib over smart and considered. Her response infuriated many Reagan loyalists—"flipped their lids" as Reagan's former speechwriter Peggy Noonan put it—and it offered Noonan the opportunity to craft another blistering critique of Palin for *The Wall Street Journal.* She described Palin as a "nimcompoop" and then summarized Reagan's remarkable career not merely as an "actor," but as a seven-time president of the Screen Actors Guild; his two terms as governor of California; and, most significant, his forging, as Noonan put it, of a "modern conservative political philosophy without the help of a conservative infrastructure." Only then was he elected president. "He brought his fully mature, fully seasoned self into politics with him," Noonan concluded, her words clearly directed at Palin. "He wasn't in search of a life when he ran for office, and he wasn't in search of fame; he'd already lived a life, he was already well known, he'd accomplished things in the world."

It was a stinging rebuke from someone who had, literally, sat at the Great Communicator's feet, and it foreshadowed, if not framed, the assessment of Palin's influence on the 2010 midterms. Palin would boast of victory—she trumpeted on Twitter: "Remember months ago 'bullseye' icon used 2 target the 20 Obamacare-lovin' incumbent seats? We won 18 out of 20 (90% success rate; T'aint bad)"—and 53 out of her 81 endorsees claimed victory on election night, including John McCain in his reelection bid for his U.S. Senate seat in Arizona and Nikki Haley for governor in South Carolina. But the fact was that several of Palin's more prominent candidates had lost in key races, and there were those who blamed her specifically for costing the Republican Party critical seats in the U.S. Senate. Her most controversial protégée, Christine O'Donnell of Delaware, had been crushed by Democratic incumbent Chris Coons, 57 to 40 percent; and Sharron Angle, for whom Palin had campaigned in Nevada in an effort to defeat Senate Majority Leader Harry Reid in the U.S. Senate, was also defeated soundly, 50 to 45 percent.

Palin's biggest loss, however, came in Alaska, where her hand-picked candidate, Joe Miller, was soundly trounced by the historic write-in candidacy of incumbent Lisa Murkowski. After edging Murkowski in a close, hotly contested Republican primary, Miller had gloated on Twitter: "What's the moose hunting like in the Beltway?" Later he boasted about picking up "some office furniture" and "a name plaque for the door" and referenced his "future colleagues in D.C." But Miller also got caught up in a widely publicized e-mail feud with Todd Palin and his campaign seemed to sour from that point on. Less than two months before the election, Todd Palin, who had heard a secondhand remark Miller had allegedly made about his wife's presidential qualifications, sent off an angry e-mail to Miller and copied two of his wife's paid advisers, Tim Crawford and Thomas Van Flein, who were also working on the Miller campaign.

> Joe and Tim,
>
> Hold off on any letter for Joe. Sarah put her ass on the line for Joe and yet he can't answer a simple question "is Sarah Palin Qualified to be President." I DON'T KNOW IF SHE IS.
>
> Joe, please explain how this endorsement stuff works, is it to be completely one sided.
>
> Sarah spent all morning working on a Face book post for Joe, she won't use it, not now. Put yourself in her shoes Joe for one day.
>
> Todd

It was a revelatory e-mail on many fronts, not the least that it appeared to reflect Sarah Palin's intentions to run for the presidency and an expected quid pro quo from Miller regarding an endorsement. Three days later, an obviously disgruntled Miller forwarded the e-mail to a trio of his campaign advisers, Randy DeSoto, Robert Campbell, and Walter Campbell, and then misaddressed a copy to himself, that eventually wound up in the hands of AKMuckraker (Jeanne Devon) of the progressive Alaska Web site, *The Mudflats*. "Just found this in my inbox," Miller wrote. "This is what we're dealing with. Note the date and the complete misconstruction of what I said. Holy cow."

Holy cow, indeed. Miller had said no such thing—Todd Palin admitted as much later—but in the general election, Miller wound up receiving a dismal 34 percent of the vote. Many Alaskan pundits privately viewed as a central factor in his loss the fact that he had been too closely associated with (if not beholden to) Palin—a fact that had been underscored by the e-mail kerfuffle. A poll conducted by Public Policy Polling (PPP) and released in December 2010 revealed that Palin's popularity rating in Alaska had dropped to 33 percent—approximately the same level of support that Miller received in the regular election. In nine of the ten swing states polled by PPP, Palin had less than a 40 percent favorability rating. Her lowest was in Massachusetts, where merely 27 percent of the electorate had a favorable disposition toward her. A private poll conducted by Lake Research Partners for Democratic candidate Scott McAdams in September found Palin's favorability rating in Alaska at 37 percent and, perhaps most astonishingly, revealed that Palin's favorability rating among Alaskan women with a college education stood at just 24 percent.

The GOP attack on Palin and her polarizing impact on the American electorate did not diminish in the aftermath of the election. In December, Palin's nemesis from the 2008 campaign, Nicolle Wallace, who had just released a novel about the first woman president entitled *Eighteen Acres,* intuitively assessed what the polls had exposed about Palin's image on the hustings:

> I believe that if she were on the cusp of becoming the nominee for the Republican party a whole lot of people would talk about some of her more troubling deficiencies—her incredible cynicism, her bitterness, her aggressive attempts to claw anyone that points out an area for her to work on. I think these things will continue to reveal themselves about her, and the people that love her will continue to love her, but the people who are not so sure about her will, I think, formulate harder opinions and more clarity about her.

As was the case in Alaska, the more people came to know Palin, the more unfavorably they viewed her. The numbers didn't lie.

IF PALIN'S STAR HAD FALLEN IN ALASKA, one certainly wouldn't have known from the media attention she commanded Outside. Her second book, *America by Heart,* although not nearly as successful as *Going Rogue,* quickly found its way onto the *New York Times* bestseller list. Only days after the midterms—and while her daughter Bristol was engaged in a controversial run on ABC's *Dancing With the Stars*—Palin launched an eight-part reality television show on The Learning Channel (TLC) entitled *Sarah Palin's Alaska.* The series premiered to the largest launch in TLC's history, with nearly five million viewers, though by the second episode the show's audience had plummeted by 40 percent.

The critics were not kind. "Those of us [Alaskans] who've actually lived off the land are less than impressed by Palin's televised exploits and, more important, by what they tell us about her," wrote award-winning Alaska outdoor writer Nick Jans in a scathing review in *USA Today*. "Tentative, physically inept, and betraying an even more awkward unfamiliarity with the land and lifestyle that's supposedly her birthright, Palin deconstructs her own myth before our eyes." As Jans rightfully pointed out, most of the "adventures" on which Palin and her family embarked throughout the series were "aimed at mass-market tourists. You won't find many Alaskans on those theme park rides, which require no skills beyond a pulse and the ability to open your wallet." *Anchorage Daily News* columnist Julia O'Malley was more subtle in her critique, though equally biting. She noted that Palin wanted to spend "some quality time" with her family. "And soon a floatplane, 'Alaska's taxi,' pulls up to their private dock and whisks them into the wild," O'Malley wrote, the irony dripping from her laptop. "This is where *Sarah Palin's Alaska* veers away from ours. . . . The idea is that they do these kinds of things all the time. We all do."

The series was riddled with gun imagery and killing. No fewer than four of the eight episodes featured Palin with her finger on the trigger. The most controversial episode (entitled "She's a Great Shot") was the one in which Palin went on a hunting expedition to the Arctic tundra—just west of the Arctic National Wildlife Refuge, in which Palin supports drilling for oil—with her father and a family friend, Steve Becker. While many condemned Palin for killing a young female caribou in graphic fashion for what were purely commercial purposes and publicity, the episode also provided a troubling insight into the Chuck Heath and Sarah Palin father-daughter dynamic. In one instance, Heath oddly referred to his daughter with both her first and last name, saying "whether it's hunting or fishing or politics, anything Sarah Palin does, she does with all four feet, let me tell you that"—though it was unclear whose four feet he was referring to.

The episode also revealed that for all her banter about hunting moose, Palin, as Levi Johnston had pointed out in his 2009 *Vanity Fair* profile of Palin, didn't own a hunting rifle of her own and wasn't knowledgeable about firearms. "She says she goes hunting and lives off animal meat," Johnston wrote. "I've never seen it." The episode was certainly intended as a counter to Johnston's narrative that "the only thing [Palin] knows now is Gucci and Prada." When it came to the shooting sequence, however, Chuck Heath actually had to load his daughter's "varmint gun," as he described it—working the bolt action for her—following each occasion that she missed her target.

And miss her target she did. As the trio stalked a caribou for Palin to shoot—Becker had already killed a large bull the day earlier—they huddled together on the tundra while Becker spotted a young female caribou on the ridge. Palin—originally using the small-caliber weapon carried for her by her father—missed a total of *five* shots, before she borrowed Becker's carbine. When Palin, wearing a stylish "Girls With Guns" bucket hat, rose with her new rifle to take her prey, Palin's father addressed her as though she were a teenager, his finger wagging, anxiously admonishing her to "get settled down, Sarah. . . . Sarah . . ." Palin eventually squeezes off her *sixth* shot, killing the caribou. The final image before she squeezes the trigger is a full-frame view, *through the crosshairs,* of her rifle scope. When it's clear that his daughter has, at last, killed the caribou, her father became curiously manic. *"There you go, baby!"* he gloated excitedly. *"There you go, baby! There you go!"* Heath then glanced over at one of the off-camera producers (whose presence is otherwise never acknowledged) and pumped his fist in triumph. He was back coaching track again—and his daughter had pleased him.

"That's my girl," he said afterward, his chest full. "That's the way I raised her, and I'm proud I raised her that way."

When they go to take a photo of Palin with her dead trophy, he asks her, "Do you feel better now?"

"I feel *a lot* better now," she responds gleefully.

"See, Dad," she says when the cameras are focused on her in interview mode. "I did it. I listened to what you said and I learned!" Later on she expanded on her jubilation. "When you're shooting, everything seems to be happening very, very quickly. It starts just flyin' at you, you're shootin' and the gun's kickin' and then, when you see that you have a successful hit, it's a great feeling of accomplishment."

The killing unleashed a storm of criticism, the most richly textured coming from Hollywood screenwriter Aaron Sorkin who called Palin "deranged" and a "phony pioneer girl," and accused Palin of killing the caribou for "political gain." At least one Hollywood-based entertainment Web site calculated that such a hunting expedition—involving several chartered small planes—would have cost an estimated $42,400, or $141.33 per pound of caribou meat netted by the hunt. It was hardly a way to fill one's freezer.

Many, however, missed the telling details in the denouement to the episode. When Palin says good-bye to her friend, teary-eyed Susan Aikens, at Kavik River

Camp, Palin refuses to match her emotions, saying in reference to her family, "I know, we don't like feelings either." And as Palin is boarding a single-passenger plane on the return flight home, her father waves and says, "Hey, Sarah, thanks for coming with me—it was good getting to know you again."

O N SATURDAY, JANUARY 8, 2011, THE NEWS COMING out of Tucson, Arizona, regarding the assassination attempt on Democratic congresswoman Gabrielle Giffords—and the killing of six and wounding of thirteen other innocent bystanders attending a Congress on the Corner event in a shopping center—provided a wake-up call about the nature of incendiary rhetoric and imagery by the radical right in American political discourse. And while it was clear that the young man charged with the shooting, Jared Lee Loughner, was a severely disturbed individual, there were many in the country who immediately recalled the crosshairs images over Giffords's eighth congressional district appearing on the Web site of Palin's political action committee and her Facebook page.

The first major media figure to make the connection was Nobel Prize–winning economist Paul Krugman, whose *New York Times* blog simply noted that Giffords had been on "Palin's infamous 'crosshairs' list." Soon, the blogosphere and Twitter were afire with references to Palin's list and imagery.

In a tense, emotional press conference the day of the shooting, Pima County sheriff Clarence Dupnik—a fifty-year veteran of law enforcement in southwest Arizona—made reference to the incendiary nature of the political climate not only in Arizona, but in the entire country, as he discussed the attack on Giffords. He declared "that people who are unbalanced are especially susceptible to vitriol." But Dupnik pushed the indictment further:

> I think that the vitriolic rhetoric that we hear day in and day out from the people in the radio business, and some people in the TV business, and what we see on TV and how our youngsters are being raised. It may be free speech but it does not come without consequences.

Pro-Palin Web sites quickly came to her defense. In March 2010, Palin rather delighted in the metaphorical violence of her political rhetoric and paid little heed to the consequences. Her paid political consultant Rebecca Mansour went on her friend Tammy Bruce's podcast and declared "Where I come from, the person that is actually shooting is the one who is culpable. You know, we had nothing whatsoever to do with this." She further contended that "we never imagined, it never occurred to us that anybody would consider [the graphic] violent." That was hard for many to reconcile, especially since Palin had tweeted "Don't Retreat, Instead—RELOAD!" immediately afterward.

One person who hadn't been dissuaded by Palin's explanation was Gabrielle Giffords herself. Following her office being targeted by an act of violence in the aftermath of her vote on health care reform, Giffords pointed to the climate of rhetorical violence in the United States and called out Sarah Palin by name for contributing to it. "Sarah Palin has the crosshairs of a gun sight over our district and when people do that," Giffords observed in an interview on MSNBC, "they've got to realize there are consequences to that action." When asked by MSNBC political analyst Chuck Todd if Giffords "really thinks that's what [Palin] intended," Giffords held her position:

> You know, I can't say. I'm not Sarah Palin. But what I can say
> is that in the years that some of my colleagues have served—
> twenty, thirty years—they've never seen it like this. We have to
> work out our problems by negotiating, working together. . . .
> Leaders—community leaders, not just political leaders—need
> to stand back when things get too fired up and say, "Whoa,
> let's take a step back here."

Palin's embrace of gun imagery and gun rhetoric had not been limited to her crosshairs graphic. Palin had actively endorsed Tea Party Senate candidate Sharron Angle who, during her ill-fated run for the U.S. Senate seat in Nevada, had declared that "if this Congress keeps going the way it is, people are really looking toward those *Second Amendment remedies*." Palin also endorsed Giffords's opponent in the bitterly contested congressional seat—Jesse Kelley—who distinguished himself by holding a campaign event with the following enticement: "Get on Target for Victory in November. Help remove Gabrielle Giffords from office. Shoot a fully automatic M16 with Jesse Kelly." The invitation to the event contained a picture of Kelly in military regalia holding what appeared to be an assault rifle.

The night of the Tucson shootings, Keith Olbermann issued an impassioned plea on his MSNBC show, calling for an end to "gun rhetoric" and "the ever-escalating, borderline-ecstatic invocation of violence in fact or in fantasy in our political discourse." While acknowledging his own misdeeds in such respects during his career, he directed a specific challenge to Palin:

> If Sarah Palin, whose Web site put and, today, scrubbed bull's-eye targets on twenty Representatives including Gabby Giffords, does not repudiate her own part in amplifying violence and violent imagery in politics, she must be dismissed from politics—she must be repudiated by the members of her own party, and if they fail to do so, each one of them must be judged to have silently defended this tactic that today proved so awfully foretelling, and they must in turn be dismissed by the responsible members of their own party.

There was no such repudiation by Palin in the days and weeks ahead. She offered an embarrassingly shallow and disengaged statement of condolences on the day of the shooting, claiming that "we all pray for the victims and their families, and for peace and justice." Palin's paid consultant, Mansour, issued an odd, nearly manic series of Twitter postings and a politically motivated radio interview. With families of the victims suffering, people wounded in hospitals, and Congresswomen Giffords fighting for her life, Mansour re-tweeted an observation that it's "more logical to say Robert De Niro spawned the Reagan assassination attempt than to say Sarah Palin caused today's tragic events." She also felt somehow compelled to send Amanda Coyne of the *Alaska Dispatch* a correction demand: "I am not Palin's 'spokeswoman.' She speaks for herself. I was speaking for myself. Correct your story."

Almost unfathomably, Mansour spent more than a half hour on the day of the killings on a special podcast produced by Palin's ally, Bruce, for the sole purpose of defending Palin against the mounting attacks and counterspinning what Bruce characterized as the "orgy of blame" coming from "liberals," "the Left," "Zombies," the "lamestream media," "Democrats," and even "Republicans." Mansour angrily denounced "the weird politicizing of this tragedy—it's so disgusting . . . It's appalling." She declared further that "I'm gonna resist the temptation—I'm gonna try to resist—getting anything more than just disgusted with the people who are accusing Governor Palin of something, people who are going to politicize this." In the end, Mansour's comments revealed the depths of the sense of remorse and accountability of Palin's world.

"We cannot ban words like 'targeted district' from the English language. We did nothing wrong here . . . There was nothing irresponsible about our graphic."

Palin did her best to distance herself from the events in Tucson, despite the centrifugal force of the liberal blogosphere and the media. The two-hour finale of her reality show, *Sarah Palin's Alaska*, which had frequently celebrated Palin's gun use, was scheduled for the night after the shootings, and Palin gleefully tweeted about her family's pursuit of gold in the Last Frontier. On Palin's Facebook page, her supporters expressed remarkably little concern for the victims of the shootings and the nature of the violence in Tucson. Their concern, mimicking Mansour, was largely limited to the political impact on Palin and the media fallout from the event. "No one should blame Sarah for this crime," wrote one typical respondent. "I know that the left progressives will exploit this to advance their sick agenda of defying free speech and the infringement of the second amendment." Yet another brought it back to the language linking Palin's religious beliefs with gun use:

> Just know that Sarah belongs to God. If God is for you who can be against you? Read the Bible and you'll no longer live in darkness. Jesus is the light and the life. Don't forget, Jesus sent out his 12 fishermen with swords. We have the right to protect ourselves. No, you cannot and will not get my gun.

PALIN'S SUPPORTERS—AND THEY WERE VOCAL—USED THE assassination and the attempt on Giffords's life as an opportunity to attack anyone who made any connection between Palin's rhetoric and the violence in Tucson. Rush Limbaugh accused liberals of "making fools of themselves to take an incident like this and to try to turn it into a political advantage by accusing people that have nothing whatsoever to do with this sordid, unfortunate event, as accomplices to murder. It's silly on its face." It was the type of crude, insensitive remark that one came to expect from Limbaugh at a time of grief and tragedy. "Don't kid yourself," he continued. "What this was all about is shutting down any and all political opposition and eventually criminalizing it. Criminalizing policy differences, at least when they differ from the Democrat Party agenda."

Palin herself laid low throughout the first days of the controversy. She issued statements through others, through Facebook, and perhaps most strangely, through an e-mail exchange with Glenn Beck, which he then read on his morning radio show:

> I hate violence. I hate war. Our children will not have peace if politicos just capitalize on this to succeed in portraying anyone as inciting terror and violence. Thanks for all you do to send the message of truth and love. And God has the answer.
>
> —Sarah

Her response echoed the meme put out by Palin's inner circle in the immediate aftermath of the shootings. The object of her concern was neither the victims nor their families—nor even the country—but on the "politicos" who she viewed were trying to "capitalize" on the ungodly events in the Arizona dessert. There was no sense of remorse, no apology, no accountability. There was also none of the bravado usually associated with Palin; for once, Sarah Palin was in retreat, if not hiding, back in her Throne Room, behind the curtains and the screens.

Beck's response to the tragedy was also to turn Palin into a victim. He urged her to seek "protection for your family," and offered that "an attempt on you could bring the republic down." Beck then made what should have been a telling distinction for anyone associated with Palin, though the irony of his remarks was clearly lost on him.

> There is a difference between a hard-fought political battle and violence. That's why they are two separate terms. The press and politicians know this. It's time for politics to stop and sanity to begin.

What Beck did not note about Palin in his response was that she and her supporters often had a hard time discerning between the two. From her ramped-up rhetoric on the campaign trail in 2008 to the guns and violence-riddled metaphors and imagery leading up to—and after—the 2010 midterm elections, Palin continually pushed across the line, refusing to separate the terminology and the imagery. She did so willingly, even mockingly. She spurned any suggestion to rein it in. When called on it—and she was repeatedly chastised for it long before the crazed shooting spree in Arizona, by everyone from Congressman John Lewis to media figures ranging from Maddow to Hasselbeck—she consistently disrespected and dismissed her critics and urged her supporters to "reload." It was all a "ginned-up controversy" and "B.S. coming from the lamestream media." Palin didn't have a recalcitrant bone in her body. When push came to shove—and it often did in Palin's world—her response was to up the ante.

The distinction between politics and combat has always been difficult, if not impossible, for Palin to grasp. When you see the world in such stark black-and-white terms, as she does, politics is a zero-sum game, all or nothing. Once again, it was not a *liberal* critic of Palin making the argument, but a *conservative* pundit, David Frum—a former special assistant to George W. Bush—who placed the discussion in proper perspective. Frum accurately assessed that Palin's rhetoric and imagery did not "cause" the carnage in Tucson. But the violence, he argued, should "summon us to some reflection on this talk. Better: This crime should summon us to a quiet collective resolution to cease this kind of talk and to cease to indulge those who engage in it."

From Sarah Palin, there would be no reflection, no resolution. Five days following the massacre—on the same day that a moving, bipartisan memorial was held in Tucson honoring the victims of the violence—Palin decided to go to her Facebook page again and deliver a recorded, carefully scripted response to the killings and the national discourse that had ensued in their wake. The timing of her remarks, which she astonishingly titled "America's Enduring Strength," was shocking and decidedly ill-advised. Many of the funerals for the victims had yet to be held. It was as though she were trying to upstage the memorial—and particularly the eulogy to be delivered by President Obama—to focus the national spotlight back on her and her self-perceived victimhood. It was an act of political narcissism in the extreme. She had once again returned to the fantasy Land of Oz, to some strange world of make-believe sustained only by her delusions and relentless ambition. Both the tone and the substance of her remarks were unabashedly shameless. It appeared as though Palin thought she was delivering a presidential address—she had featured a large American flag behind her, in a staged formal setting—and in one passage shaped her comments as if she viewed herself on an equal leadership plane with Obama. "You know, Sarah Palin just can't seem to get it, on any front," Assistant House Minority Leader James Clyburn observed in a radio interview. "I think intellectually, she seems not to be able to understand what's going on here."

Palin claimed to have spent "the past few days reflecting on what happened and praying for guidance"—though not about the monstrous act of violence that had stained and shocked the nation, but about the complicity being ascribed to her in its aftermath. "After this shocking tragedy," she declared, her lower jaw protruding, "I listened at first puzzled, then with concern, and now with sadness, to the irresponsible statements from people attempting to apportion blame for this terrible event." Palin was defiantly defensive. She never once mentioned the crosshair imagery targeting Giffords on her SarahPAC Web site, or her exhortation on Twitter to "reload." Nor did she reference Giffords's warnings about Palin's ballistic rhetoric and imagery. It was all one grand orgy of omission and denial.

Making an obligatory reference to "President Reagan"—Palin cited his oft-repeated passage "that each individual is accountable for his actions"—she also exhorted America's "foundational freedoms," without noting what they were, and returned to her cliché of American exceptionalism, an issue over which she had frequently taunted Obama during the past year. Palin was, in essence, delivering a coded manifesto for her most ardent supporters when her political career was clearly on the line. Instead of expressing even the slightest degree of remorse or regret about her actions, Palin doubled-down on her audacity.

Palin attacked "journalists and pundits" for manufacturing what she labeled "a blood libel that serves only to incite the very hatred and violence they purport to condemn." Her use of "blood libel"—a term rooted in the false anti-Semitic accusation of Jews murdering Christian children to use their blood in religious rituals—was even more startling and heinously inappropriate. Palin seemed to be utterly oblivious once again to the historic nuances of her discourse. "We wish that Palin had used another phrase, instead of one so fraught with pain in Jewish history," declared the national director of the Anti-Defamation League, Abraham Foxman. Other Jewish leaders were less temperate in their criticism. "The term 'blood-libel' is not a synonym for false accusation," said Simon Greer, head of the Jewish Fund for Justice. "Unless someone has been accusing Ms. Palin of killing Christian babies and making matzo from their blood, her use of the term is totally out of line."

Palin's comments and the cloistered setting in which they were delivered contrasted vividly with those delivered by President Obama at the McKale

Center at the University of Arizona, in Tucson, where more than thirteen thousand were in attendance, including Palin's former running mate, Arizona senator John McCain. "At a time when our discourse has become so sharply polarized," Obama declared, "at a time when we are far too eager to lay the blame for all that ails the world at the feet of those who happen to think differently than we do, it's important for us to pause for a moment and make sure that we're talking with each other in a way that heals, not in a way that wounds."

"President Obama and I may not agree on everything," Palin had declared from her studio in Wasilla, "but I know he would join me in affirming the health of our democratic process." He had done nothing of the sort in Tucson. Nor had he made the slightest reference to Palin. Instead, he framed his remarks in direct contrast to hers, their moral antithesis. He called upon Americans to renovate the democratic process. "We should be willing to challenge old assumptions in order to lessen the prospects of such violence in the future," he asserted. "Let's use this occasion to expand our moral imaginations, to listen to each other more carefully, to sharpen our instincts for empathy and remind ourselves of all the ways that our hopes and dreams are bound together." The moral foundation of the two speeches—one a moving eulogy, the other a tone-deaf invective—could not have been more disparate.

Palin shamed herself and, most significant, disrespected the victims of the tragedy with the utter heedlessness of her remarks. "She could have used the opportunity to try to elevate the discourse," wrote Ruth Marcus in *The Washington Post*. "Instead, she further coarsened it. At a time when the country is looking for words that heal, Palin chose to do what she does best: attack and provoke." Critics ranged from across the political spectrum. "Sarah Palin seems trapped in a world that is all about confrontation and bravado," declared Matthew Dowd, the longtime Republican political consultant who had condemned McCain's choice of Palin in the fall of 2008. "When the country seeks comforting and consensus, she offers conflict and confrontation."

Palin was given a second chance at redemption shortly after the rampage. She squandered the opportunity. In an "exclusive interview" with Sean Hannity on her home network, Fox News (it was uncertain if she was paid for her appearance or not), Palin again refused to acknowledge accountability for her incendiary rhetoric and imagery. On Martin Luther King, Jr., Day, little more than a week after the bloodshed, there was still no backing down. She defended her use of "blood libel" and proclaimed that "we should not use an event like that in Arizona to stifle debate." It would be "futile," she asserted, to "censor everyone's speech and everyone's icons."

What was even more revelatory about the interview—and what stood in direct contradiction to her apologist Mansour—was her acknowledgment that the images on her Web site were, indeed, "crosshairs" and "targets." For all her bravado, however, Palin seemed strangely stilted and one-dimensional, as if she were being forced to hold back a deep-seated rage. She seemed utterly absent of either a moral or an emotional center, as if she were nothing more than a mannequin made of plastic. She couldn't help making a dig at Obama's eulogy in Tucson, calling the setting of the memorial "a bit bizarre" and characterizing it as a "pep rally" or "campaign stop." It was another troubling moment in the Palin video archive. Once again, it was all about her. "They're not going to shut me up," she assured Hannity, referring to her enemies. With six dead and fourteen wounded, she remarkably still managed to frame herself as the victim. "Those on the left," she declared, "if they didn't have double standards, they'd have no standards at all." She kept repeating her recent memes of "time-tested truths" and "common-sense conservativism," though she still couldn't come to name any of the victims in Tucson, including Gabrielle Giffords. Once again, neither she nor Hannity would acknowledge that Giffords *herself* had warned about the use of such imagery.

B ACK IN THE LAST FRONTIER, THE darkness of winter had settled in, with sunlight a rare commodity, and Alaskans from all walks of life were hunkering down for the inevitable cold that would blanket their lives until well into spring. Many of those who had opposed Palin during her political career watched the events in Arizona—and Palin's self-indulgent response to it— unfold in horror and with no small amount of anxiety. Several had predicted privately to me over the past two years that Palin's "toxic language," as John Lewis described it when Palin first went "rogue" during the 2008 campaign, would somehow lead to violence. They viewed it as an inevitability of Palin's angry, hyperbolic, and often duplicitous rhetoric that fueled her political discourse.

In particular, I couldn't help but recall the concerns expressed to me in the weeks leading up to the fall 2010 elections by Laura Chase, who had served as Palin's campaign manager during her first run for mayor of Wasilla. Palin, she told me, was a "dangerous person." It was to Chase, who still resided in Wasilla, that Palin had first divulged her presidential ambitions a decade and a half earlier. As Chase watched Palin's career unfold over the years, she recognized all too well the terrifying dynamics of Palin's political celebrity. "I think she's inspiring hatred among people, and I think that's really putting this country in danger," Chase asserted. "And I think we're really at high risk right now. We're in a really bad position as a country in respect to violence. And for [Palin] to inspire people to hatred—to the point where somebody's gonna end up getting killed some day—because, well, hatred is hatred. To me, she's scary. She's good at what she does and she's very dangerous."

ACKNOWLEDGMENTS

This book begins and ends with my late father, Frank Dunn, an itinerant cowboy, jack-of-all-trades, and master saddle repairman who never quite grasped the intricacies of fatherhood. He first introduced me to the Alaska wilderness in 1974, and whatever it took for me to write this book, he instilled in me during the first two decades of my life.

My late friend, the writer James D. Houston, who first introduced me to the concept of the Pacific Rim (on which Alaska resides quite prominently), said that you put your whole life into every book you write. This project provided no exception. Like all books, this one is the product of an endless stream of relationships and life journeys, one that stretches back to my familial roots in the Italian fishing community on the Santa Cruz Municipal Wharf in California.

I envisioned this book in October of 2008 during the historic presidential campaign in which Sarah Palin appeared in the final act. I thank my friends Mark Schwartz and Debra Joy for encouraging me to write for The Huffington Post. My friends Roz Spafford and Conn Hallinan made the requisite connections. I thank Arianna Huffington for making it possible along with my editors there, including Stuart Whatley, Colin Sterling, Rob Fishman, David Flumenbaum, Lila Shapiro, Amy Hertz, and Jessie Kunhardt; and HuffPo reporters Sam Stein and Jason Linkins, who have been of such great assistance during my tenure there. Editors Milton Allimadi, Greg Archer, Sita Bridgemohan, Royal Calkins, Michael S. Gant, Deborah John, Lois Kazakoff, and Don Miller all guided early articles of mine on Palin to print.

I owe a great deal of debt to my two inimitable undergraduate professors at the University of California, Santa Cruz, the late Grant McConnell and Jack Schaar, who first inspired my love of American political history and theory. David Traxel, friend and mentor, first introduced me to the genre of American-wilderness literature following my first trip to Alaska three and a half decades ago. My graduate school professor, G. William ("Bill") Domhoff, encouraged this project as an exploration of American political power. His son, my dear friend Joel Domhoff, served as a loyal assistant on this book. Giovana Galvao Lemes-Silveira, Amy McGeever, Cody-Leigh Mullin, Katie Wheeler-Dubin, and Laura Pinkerton all provided early background research for this project. I thank both Mike Rotkin and Craig Reinarman for helping to facilitate that research.

During my stay in Alaska during the summer of 2009 I was welcomed by a grand community of bloggers in the Last Frontier that included Jeanne Devon (AKMuckraker) and Shannyn Moore, both of whom have been generous of their time, insights, and resources throughout. I am also particularly grateful to Dennis Zaki, who made his marvelous Alaska photographs and videos available to me, Phil Munger, Jesse Griffin, Andrew Halcro, Linda Kellen Biegel, Sherry Whitstine, and Paul Jenkins. Many journalists in Alaska have been helpful, most notably Yereth Rosen, Gregg and Judy Erickson, Rebecca Braun and Steve Quinn. My attorney in Alaska, Jeffrey Feldman of Feldman Orlansky & Sanders, was consistently supportive and brilliant.

Dozens of Alaskans from across the political spectrum gave willingly of their time and insight: Jeanne Ashcraft, Rex Butler, Howard Bess, John Bitney, Nick and Kay Carney, Stephanie Carper, Laura Chase, Mark Chryson, Christopher Clark, John Cyr, Ron Devon, Charles A. Dunngan, Dan Fagan, Paul Fuhs, Les Gara, George Gee, Patty Ginsburg, Lyda Green, Andrew Halcro, Zane Henning, William L. Iggiagruk Hensley, Scott Heyworth, Ermalee Hickel, the late Walter J. Hickel, Beth Kerttula, Anne Kilkenny, Susan and Tony Knowles, Steve Lindbeck, Rhonda McBride, J. C, McCavit, Andreé McLeod, Terry Monegan, Walt Monegan, Rynnieva Moss, Larry Persily, Hawk Pierce, Steve Quinn, Jay Ramras, Leslie Ridle, Cindy and Malcolm Roberts, Deb Seaton, Irl Stambaugh, John Stein, the late Ted Stevens, Mary Van Treeck, Nicholas Tucker, Kelley Walters, Corky and Gary Wheeler, Diane Woodruff, and Michael Wooten. Many Alaskans spoke to me on the condition that I not use their names for fear of reprisal. I thank them all as well.

Several outside sources also contributed in various ways to this book: Jim Barnett, Linda Bergthold, Max Blumenthal, Alan Butterfield, Donnie Fowler, Yvonne Bashelier, Maxwell Copello, Steve Duprey, Mike Gherke, Victor Davis Hanson, Leslie Goodman-Malamuth, Fred Malek, Special Agent Jim Margolin, Terry Nelson, Steve Schmidt, Matthew Scully, John Weaver, Cheryl Welch, and "Kathleen" and "Patrick" at Politicalgates.com. I recognize that many people who participated in this project may not agree with either my perspective or my thesis, and I thank them for participating in spite of those differences.

My pal Joe McGinnis, who is also writing a book on Palin and was her famous neighbor for a spell in Wasilla, has been a prince. My friend Kathy Jackson has been irreplaceable in transcribing long hours of interviews into print.

My agent, Deborah Grosvenor, of Grosvenor Literary Agency believed in me—and this book—from the very beginning, and she has helped me to navigate through some difficult waters. She is the consummate professional. I can never thank her enough. She led me to my editor at St. Martin's, Phil Revzin, a Chicago Cubs fan, who also believed in the book and stuck with the project even when I went rogue on him. Like a good Cubs fan, he brought it home the hard way. Ellis Levine of Cowan, DeBaets, Abrahams & Sheppard LLP was absolutely wonderful in providing legal counsel, and I am eternally grateful. My thanks to Sally Richardson and George Witte at St. Martin's Press who supported this project through publication.

I am grateful to Ryan Coonerty, Zach Friend, and Chris Reyes for their support and continued political discussion. Ed Penniman and Anna May Guagnini loaned me a copy of *Into the Wild* at a critical time in this process. I am grateful to Neal and Casey Coonerty of Bookshop Santa Cruz for their support. I want to thank Townes Van Zandt and my Z-Boyz, Turtle, Vince, E and Drama, for the inspiration. Ditto to Willie Mays, Vincent Van Gogh, Joan Didion, *Blood on the Tracks*, Keith Olbermann, and the 2010 San Francisco Giants. I also need to thank my medical team for keeping me on this earth in recent years, in particular Robert Allen, Michael Alexander, Joseph Poen, Benjamin Potkin, Don Davies, and the late Ron Wickum, among many others, and all the nurses and assistants, most notably René Curtis. And to all my brothers and sisters who sat with me in the chemo room: may the angels of the universe bless you.

I thank my friends Pete Newell, George Ow and Gail Maichaelis-Ow, Pete Pappas, Norman Schwartz, Stu Walters, Johnny "No-No" Wilson, and Tommy Wilson for their encouragement and friendship throughout the writing of this book, and to the rest of the extended Santa Cruz posse: Nane Alejandrez, Luis Alejo, Wallace Baine, Al Barabas, Hillary Bryant, Gerry Christiansen, Neal Ewald, Richard "Rip" Harris, George Homer, Scott Kennedy, Thorton Kontz, Don Lane, Mike Marini, Paul Meltzer, Cori Houston, Jeanne Wakatsuki Houston, Mike Mason, Cynthia Mathews, Bill Monning, Ed Morrison, Michelle Poen, Lee Quarnstrom, Lynn Robinson, John Sandidge, Kim Stoner, David Terrazas, Bubba Towne, Jeff Traugott, Mark Wagner, Matt and Ron Walters, Bill Welch, and the Santa Cruz Little League Orioles and Angels.

I lost two exceptional friends in recent years, Tony Hill and Chris Matthews, along with my loving aunt, Gilda Stagnaro. I thank my extended family—Peggy Dunn Heil, Joseph Heil, Cullyn Vaeth and Michael Russell, Patrice Vaeth Caetano and Raul Caetano, and my beautiful nieces and nephews—for tolerating so much talk about Alaska these past two years. My cousin Kenneth Lamb encouraged me to stay on the national beat throughout the duration, particularly when the going got tough. To my immediate family—my mother Lindy, my children Tess and Dylan, and my wife Siri, who has been there every step of the way—I express my profound gratitude and eternal love.

SELECTED BIBLIOGRAPHY

BOOKS

Abrams, Jeremiah, and Connie Zweig, eds. *Meeting the Shadow: The Hidden Power of the Dark Side of Human Nature*. Los Angeles: Jeremy P. Tarcher, Inc., 1991.

Benet, Lorenzo. *Trailblazer: An Intimate Biography of Sarah Palin*. New York: Threshold Editions, 2009.

Benson, Kristina. *God, Prayer, and Sarah Palin*. Villanova, PA: Equity Press, 2008.

Bergman, Gregory, and Paula Munier. *101 Things You (and John McCain) Didn't Know about Sarah Palin*. Avon, MA: Adams Media, an F + W Media Company, 2008.

Bernstein, Carl. *A Woman In Charge: The Life of Hillary Rodham Clinton*. New York: Alfred A. Knopf, 2007.

Boehlert, Eric. *Bloggers on the Bus: How the Internet Changed Politics and the Press*. New York: Free Press, 2009.

————. *Lapdogs: How the Press Rolled Over for Bush*. New York: Free Press, 2006.

Blumenthal, Max. *Republican Gomorrah: Inside the Movement that Shattered the Party*. New York: Nation Books, 2009.

Branchflower, Stephen. *Stephen Branchflower Report to the Legislative Council: Public Report*. Alaska Legislative Council, October 10, 2008.

Brock, David, and Paul Waldman. *Free Ride: John McCain and the Media*. New York: Anchor Books, 2008.

Burton, Leah L. *TheoPalinism: The Face of Failed Extremism*. Huntington Beach, CA: Vervanté, 2008.

Carney, Domonic. *Our Home Is Wasilla*. Raleigh, NC: Lulu, 2009.

————. *We're Going to Alaska*. Raleigh, NC: Lulu, 2005.

Cashman, Kay, and Kristen Nelson. *Sarah Takes On Big Oil: The Compelling Story of*

Governor Sarah Palin's Battle with Alaska's "Big 3" Oil Companies, as Told by the State's Top Oil and Gas Editors. Anchorage: PNA Publishing, 2008.

Coakley, Jay. *Sports in Society: Issues and Controversies, Eighth Edition*. New York: McGraw-Hill, 2004.

Conroy, Scott, and Shushannah Walshe. *Sarah from Alaska: The Sudden Rise and Brutal Education of a New Conservative Superstar*. New York: PublicAffairs, 2009.

Continetti, Matthew. *The Persecution of Sarah Palin: How the Elite Media Tried to Bring Down a Rising Star*. New York: Penguin Group, 2009.

Didion, Joan. *Political Fictions*. New York: Alfred A. Knopf, 2001.

Domhoff, G. William. *The Higher Circles: Governing Class in America*. New York: Vintage Books, 1971.

Drew, Elizabeth. *Citizen McCain*. New York: Simon & Schuster, 2002.

Durbin, Kathie. *Tongass: Pulp Politics and the Fight for the Alaska Rain Forest*. Corvallis, OR: Oregon State University Press, 1999.

Editors of the *Wasilla Iron Dog Gazette*. *Terminatrix: The Sarah Palin Chronicles*. New York: Collins, 2008.

Filiquarian Publishing. *Sarah Palin: The Alaskan Barracuda*. Minneapolis: Filiquarian Publishing, LLC, 2008.

Frank, Thomas. *What's the Matter with Kansas? How Conservatives Won the Heart of America*. New York: Henry Holt and Company, LLC, 2004.

Gottehrer, Dean M., ed. *The Associated Press Stylebook for Alaska*. Fairbanks: Epicenter Press, 2000.

Haycox, Stephen. *Alaska: An American Colony*. Seattle: University of Washington Press, 2002.

———. *Frigid Embrace: Politics, Economics and Environment in Alaska*. Corvallis, OR: Oregon State University Press, 2002.

Hayes, Ernestine. *Blonde Indian: An Alaska Native Memoir*. Tucson: University of Arizona Press, 2006.

Hedges, Chris. *American Fascists: The Christian Right and the War on America*. New York: Free Press, 2008.

———. *Empire of Illusion: The End of Literacy and the Triumph of Spectacle*. New York: Nation Books, 2009.

Heilemann, John, and Mark Halperin. *Game Change: Obama and the Clintons, McCain and Palin, and the Race of a Lifetime*. New York: HarperCollins, 2010.

Hensley, William L. Iggiagruk. *Fifty Miles from Tomorrow: A Memoir of Alaska and the Real People*. New York: Sarah Crichton Books/Farrar, Straus and Giroux, 2008.

Hickel, Walter J. *Crisis in the Commons: The Alaska Solution*. Oakland: ICS Press, 2002.

Hilley, Joe. *Sarah Palin: A New Kind of Leader*. Grand Rapids, MI: Zondervan, 2008.

Hofstadter. Richard. *Anti-Intellectualism in American Life*. New York: Vintage Books, 1966.

———. *The Paranoid Style in American Politics and Other Essays*. New York: Vintage Books, 1967.

Homes, Su, and Sean Redmond, eds. *Framing Celebrity: New Directions in Celebrity Culture*. New York: Routledge, 2006.

Indiana, Gary. *Schwarzenegger Syndrome: Politics and Celebrity in the Age of Contempt*. New York: The New Press, 2005.

The Institute of Politics, John F. Kennedy School of Government, Harvard University. *Campaign for President: The Managers Look at 2008*. Lanham, MD: Rowman & Littlefield Publishers, Inc., 2009.

James, G. Robert. *Sarah Palin: The Real Deal*. Lakeland, FL: White Stone Books, 2008.

Johnson, Kaylene. *Sarah: How a Hockey Mom Turned the Political Establishment Upside Down*. Kenmore, WA: Epicenter Press, 2008.

Joseph, Mark. *Sarah Barracuda: The Rise of Sarah Palin*. Los Angeles: Bully! Pulpit Books, 2008.

Kazlowski, Steven. *The Last Polar Bear: Facing the Truth of a Warming World*. Seattle: Braided River Books, 2008.

Kent, Rockwell. *Wilderness: A Journey of Quiet Adventure in Alaska*. New York: Putnam, 1920.

Kim, Richard, and Betsy Reed, eds. *Going Rouge: Sarah Palin, An American Nightmare*. New York: OR Books, 2009.

Kollin, Susan. *Nature's State: Imagining Alaska as the Last Frontier*. Chapel Hill: University of North Carolina Press, 2001.

Kornblut, Anne E. *Notes from the Cracked Ceiling: Hillary Clinton, Sarah Palin, and What It Will Take for a Woman to Win*. New York: Crown Publishers, 2009.

Krakauer, Jon. *Into the Wild*. New York: Random House, 1996.

Leahy, Michael Patrick. *What Does Sarah Palin Believe? Post Denominational Christianity in Today's Public Arena*. Nashville: Harpeth River Press, 2008.

Litman, Malia. *Rebuttal to the Rogue*. San Ramon, CA: Falcon Books, 2009.

London, Jack. *The Best Short Stories of Jack London*. Garden City, NY: Doubleday & Company, Inc., 1945.

———. *The Call of the Wild*. New York: Macmillan, 1903.

———. *Lost Face*. New York: Macmillan, 1910.

———. *White Fang*. New York: Macmillan, 1906.

Long, Huey P. *Every Man a King: The Autobiography of Huey P. Long.* Cambridge, MA: Da Capo Press, 1996.

Manchester, William. *The Death of a President: November 1963.* New York: Harper & Row, 1967.

Matanuska Maid Dairy. *Matanuska Maid: A Colony, A Legacy, A Future.* Anchorage: Matanuska Maid Dairy, 2006.

McBeath, Gerald A., and Thomas A. Morehouse. *Alaska Politics and Government.* Lincoln: University of Nebraska Press, 1994.

McCain, John, with Mark Salter. *Faith of My Fathers: A Family Memoir.* New York: Perennial, 2000.

———. *Worth the Fighting For.* New York: Random House Trade Paperbacks, 2003.

McCain, Meghan. *Dirty Sexy Politics.* New York: Hyperion, 2010.

McGinniss, Joe. *Going to Extremes.* New York: Alfred A. Knopf, 1980.

———. *The Selling of the President 1968.* New York: Trident Press, 1969.

McPhee, John. *Coming into the Country.* New York: Bantam, 1982.

Michener, James A. *Alaska.* New York: Fawcett Crest, 1988.

Muir, John. *Travels in Alaska.* Boston: Houghton Mifflin Company, 1979.

Obama, Barack. *The Audacity of Hope: Thoughts on Reclaiming the American Dream.* New York: Crown, 2006.

———. *Dreams from My Father: A Story of Race and Inheritance.* New York: Three Rivers Press, 2004.

Ochoa, Recaldo. *Sarah Palin: Poised to Become America's First Female President.* North Charleston, SC: BookSurge Publishing, 2009.

Office of the Governor, State of Alaska. *Governor Sarah Palin's Official Daily Schedule, 2007–2009.*

O'Neill, Dan. *A Land Gone Lonesome: An Inland Voyage Along the Yukon River.* New York: Basic Books, 2007.

Palin, Sarah. *America By Heart: Reflections on Family, Faith, and Flag.* New York: HarperCollins, 2010.

———. *Going Rogue: An American Life.* New York: HarperCollins Publishers, 2009.

Parr, Susan Sherwood. *Sarah Palin: Faith, Family, Country.* Alachua, FL: Bridge-Logos, 2008.

Pawlenty, Tim. *Courage to Stand: An American Story.* Carol Stream, IL: Tyndale House, 2011.

Plouffe, David. *The Audacity to Win: The Inside Story and Lessons of Barack Obama's Historic Victory.* New York: Viking, 2009.

Potter, Louise. *Early Days in Wasilla*. Wasilla, AK: Alaskana Books, 2002.

Raban, Jonathan. *Passage to Juneau: A Sea and Its Meanings*. New York: Pantheon, 1999.

Remnick, David. *The Bridge: The Life and Rise of Barack Obama*. New York: Alfred A. Knopf, 2010.

Roberts, Cindy. *Cracking the Code: A Citizen's Guide to the Alaska Natural Gas Pipeline Discussion and the Alaska Gasline Inducement Act (AGIA)*. Anchorage: Alaska Business Monthly, 2008.

Roderick, Jack. *Crude Dreams: A Personal History of Oil and Politics in Alaska*. Fairbanks: Epicenter Press, 1997.

Rosen, Fred. *Deadly Angel: The Bizarre True Story of Alaska's Killer Stripper*. New York: Harper, 2009.

Scully, Matthew. *Dominion: The Power of Man, the Suffering of Animals, and the Call to Mercy*. New York: St. Martin's Press, 2002.

Shirley, Craig. *Rendezvous with Destiny: Ronald Reagan and the Campaign That Changed America*. Wilmington, DE: ISI Books, 2009.

Signer, Michael. *Demagogue: The Fight to Save Democracy from Its Worst Enemies*. New York: Palgrave Macmillan, 2009.

Sitka, Warren. *Sourdough Journalist*. Anchorage: Parsnackle Press, 1981.

Strohmeyer, John. *Extreme Conditions: Big Oil and the Transformation of Alaska*. New York: Simon & Schuster, 1993.

Timberg, Robert. *John McCain: An American Odyssey*. New York: Touchstone, 1999.

Touré. *Never Drank the Kool-Aid*. New York: Picador, 2006.

Thomas, Clive S., ed. *Alaska Public Policy Issues: Background and Perspectives*. Juneau: The Denali Press, 1999.

Thomas, Evan. *"A Long Time Coming": The Inspiring, Combative 2008 Campaign and the Historic Election of Barack Obama*. New York: PublicAffairs, 2009.

Traister, Rebecca. *Big Girls Don't Cry: The Election That Changed Everything for American Women*. New York: Free Press, 2010.

Twain, Mark. *The Adventures of Huckleberry Finn*. New York: Harper & Brothers Publishers, 1896.

Warren, Robert Penn. *All the King's Men*. New York: Bantam Books, 1959.

Washut, Henry Jack. *Henry's War: The World War II Diaries of a Supply Sergeant for the 741st Tank Battalion*. Edited by Domonic L. Carney. Raleigh, NC: Lulu, 2006.

Welch, Matt. *McCain: The Myth of a Maverick*. New York: Palgrave Macmillan, 2007.

West, Darrell M., and John Orman. *Celebrity Politics*. Upper Saddle River, NJ: Prentice Hall, 2003.

Williams, T. Harry. *Huey Long: A Biography.* New York: Alfred A. Knopf, 1969.

Wohlforth, Charles. *Alaska For Dummies: A Travel Guide for the Rest of Us!* New York: Wiley Publishing, Inc., 2003.

———. *The Whale and the Supercomputer: On the Northern Front of Climate Change.* New York: North Point Press, 2004.

Wolff, Michael. *The Man Who Owns the News: Inside the Secret World of Rupert Murdoch.* New York: Broadway Books, 2008.

Wolffe, Richard. *Renegade: The Making of a President.* New York: Crown Publishers, 2009.

Woodward, Kesler E. *Spirit of the North: The Art of Eustace Paul Ziegler.* Augusta, GA: Morris Communications Corporation, 1998.

Wright, Lawrence. *The Looming Tower: Al-Qaeda and the Road to 9/11.* New York: Alfred A. Knopf, 2006.

FILMS

The Gold Rush. Directed by Charlie Chaplin. United Artists, 1925.

Grizzly Man. Directed by Werner Herzog. Lions Gate Films and Discovery Docs, 2005.

Insomnia. Directed by Christopher Nolan. Warner Bros. Studios, 2002.

Into the Wild. Directed by Sean Penn. Paramount Vantage and River Road Entertainment, 2007.

ARTICLES

In addition to those specific articles cited below, the author made use of material from the following newspapers, blogs, and publications in Alaska: *Alaska Budget Report; Alaska Dispatch; Alaska Real; Anchorage Daily News; Anchorage Daily Planet; AndrewHalcro .com; Celtic Diva's Blue Oasis; Fairbanks Daily News-Miner; Juneau Empire; Just a Girl from Homer; Ketchikan Daily News; Mat-Su Valley Frontiersman; The Alaska Report; The Alaska Standard; The Mudflats; The Immoral Minority; Progressive Alaska;* and *Syrin from Wasilla*

Allen, Mike and VandeHei, Jim. "Next for GOP leaders: Stopping Sarah Palin." *Politico* (October 31, 2010).

Arendt, Hannah. "Reflections: Truth and Politics" *New Yorker* (February 25, 1967).

Armstrong, Ken, and Hal Bernton. "Sarah Palin Had Turbulent First Year As Mayor of Alaska Town." *Seattle Times* (September 7, 2008).

The Associated Press. "Fact Check: Palin's Book Goes Rogue on Some Facts." *New York Times* (November 13, 2009).

Auletta, Ken. "Non-Stop News." *New Yorker* (January 25, 2010).

Bai, Matt. "Alaska May Offer a View to Future Elections." *New York Times* (November 10, 2010).

———. "Palin Finds Comfort as a Crowd-Sourced Candidate." *New York Times* (November 15, 2010).

Baird, Julia. "Too Hot to Handle: Stop Ogling Republican Women." *Newsweek* (July 3, 2010).

Balz, Dan "Aides Say Team Interviewed Palin Late in the Process." *Washington Post* (September 3, 2008).

Balz, Dan, and Perry Bacon Jr. "The Sarah Palin Chronicles Mask Deeper GOP Troubles." *Washington Post* (July 2, 2009).

Balz, Dan, and Haynes Johnson. "High Risk, High Reward." *Washington Post* (August 3, 2009).

Barnes, Fred. "Sarah Palin's Future." *Weekly Standard* (October 27, 2008).

Barr, Andy. "Palin Rips 'Impotent' Reporters." *Politico.com* (September 2, 2010).

Barr, Andy and Jonathan Martin. "McCain Camp: Palin Account 'All Fiction'". *Politico* (November 13, 2009).

Barrett, Wayne. "The Book of Sarah (Palin)." *Village Voice* (October 8, 2008).

Bartiromo, Maria. "Bartiromo Talks with Sarah Palin." *Bloomberg Businessweek* (August 29, 2008).

Bateman, Christopher. "Meet Andree McLeod, Sarah Palin's Worst Nightmare." *Vanity Fair.com* (July 20, 2009).

Becker, Jo, and Peter S. Goodman and Michael Powell. "Once Elected, Palin Hired Friends and Lashed Foes." *New York Times* (September 13, 2008).

Benjamin, Mark. and "Did McCain's Foreign-Policy Advisor Profit from the Iraq War?" *Salon.com* (August 1, 2008).

Birnbaum, Jeffry H. and John Solomon. "Aide Helped Controversial Russian Meet McCain." *Washington Post* (January 25, 2008).

Blumenthal, Max. "Palin Goes Rogue on the Facts." *MediaMatters for America* (November 17, 2009).

———. "Palin's Final Insult." *Daily Beast* (July 12, 2009).

Blumenthal, Max, David Neiwert. "Meet Sarah Palin's Radical Right-Wing Pals." *Salon.com* (October 10, 2008).

Boraas, Alan. "Kopp Hiring Proved Palin's Fundamentalist Street Cred." *Anchorage Daily News* (September 20, 2008).

Boxer, Barbara, and John F. Kerry. "What Palin Got Wrong About Energy." *Washington Post* (July 24, 2009).

Breslau, Karen. "Now This Is Woman's Work." *Newsweek* (October 9, 2007).

Brooks, David. "The Class War Before Palin." *New York Times* (October 10, 2008).

———. "Why Experience Matters." *The New York Times* (September 16, 2008).

Bruck, Connie. "Right Fight: California Joins the Battle for the Republican Soul." *New Yorker* (June 7, 2010).

Bumiller, Elisabeth. "Internal Battles Divided McCain and Palin Camps." *New York Times* (November 6, 2008).

———. "Palin Disclosures Raise Questions on Vetting." *New York Times* (September 2, 2008).

Bumiller, Elisabeth, and Michael Cooper. "Conservative Ire Pushed McCain From Lieberman." *New York Times* (August 31, 2008).

Bumiller, Elisabeth, and Larry Rohter. "2 Camps Trying to Influence McCain on Foreign Policy." *New York Times* (April 10, 2008).

Calmes, Jackie. "McCain Campaign Is Dealt New Blow as Media Team Resigns." *Wall Street Journal* (July 26, 2007).

———. "McCain Manager Roils Campaign." *Wall Street Journal* (July 23, 2007).

Calmes, Jackie, and David D. Kirkpatrick. "McCain Aide's Firm Was Paid by Freddie Mac." *New York Times* (September 24, 2008).

Canby, Peter. "The Specter Haunting Alaska." *New York Review of Books* (November 17, 2005).

Carr, David. "How Sarah Palin Became a Brand." *New York Times* (April 4, 2010).

Cavett, Dick. "The Wild Wordsmith of Wasilla." *New York Times* (November 14, 2008).

Cillizza, Chris. "Fred Malek, Sarah Palin and the Case for Loyalty." *Washington Post* (July 8, 2009).

Cockerham, Sean. "Palin Staff Pushed to Have Trooper Fired." *ADN.com—Anchorage Daily News* (August 14, 2008).

———. "Portrayal in Palin Book Irritates Former Aide." *Anchorage Daily News* (November 23, 2009).

Cockerham, Sean, and Loy Wesley. "Choice Stuns State Politicians" *Anchorage Daily News* (August 29, 2008).

Cohen, Richard. "Ruedrich Faces Ouster Attempt." *Washington Post* (March 9, 2008).

Collins, Gail. "The Grizzly Manifesto." *New York Times* (November 5, 2010).

Conason, Joe. "The Losers Who Gave Us Sarah Palin." *Salon.com* (July 10, 2009).

Conroy, Scott. "Palin's 'Mad as Hell' Speech." *CBSNews.com* (July 26, 2009).

———. "GOP Presidential Race Likely to be a 'Competence Primary.'" *Real Clear Politics* (December 2, 2010).

Continetti, Matthew. "The Palin Persuasion." *Weekly Standard* (November 16, 2009).

Cooper, Michael. "McCain Abandons His Efforts to Win Michigan." *New York Times* (October 3, 2008).

Darman, Jonathan. "The Palin Problem." *Newsweek* (November 3, 2008).

Demer, Lisa. "New Chief: Mayor Taps 27-Year Police Department Veteran." *Anchorage Daily News* (January 31, 2001).

DeVaughn, Melissa. "The Constitution—50 Years Later." *Alaska Magazine* (November 2008).

———. "Palin's Way." *Alaska Magazine* (February 2008).

Dickinson, Tim. "Make-Believe Maverick." *Rolling Stone* (October 16, 2008).

Ditzler, Joseph. "Palin Is Ready for Return to the Public Arena and Service." *Anchorage Daily News* (June 8, 2005).

D'Oro, Rachel. "North Slope Oil Estimates Cut By 90 Percent." *Santa Cruz Sentinel* (October 27, 2010).

Dowd, Maureen. "Sarah's Secret Diary." *New York Times* (July 8, 2009).

Draper, Robert. "The Making (and Remaking) of McCain." *New York Times* (October 26, 2008).

———. "The Palin Network." *New York Times* (November 17, 2010).

———. "The Rogue Room." *New York Times Magazine* (November 21, 2010).

Drew, Elizabeth. "Why the Greg Craig Debacle Matters." *Politico* (November 19, 2009).

Editor, Voice of the Times. "Candidate Palin, Alaskans Are Waiting, Where's the Dirt?" *Anchorage Daily News* (July 14, 2006).

Editors, The New Republic. "The Case Against Sarah Palin." *New Republic* (September 2008).

Egan, Timothy. "Building a Nation of Know-Nothings." *New York Times* (August 25, 2010).

Eilperin, Juliet, and Robert Barnes. "Before Speech, Running Mate Gets Some Coaching." *Washington Post* (September 3, 2008).

Elis, Roy, and D. Sunshine Hillygus and Norman Nie. "The Dynamics of Candidate Evaluations and Vote Choice in 2008: Looking to the Past or Future?" *Electoral Studies* (2010).

English, Deirdre, and Gail Sheehy. "The Word From Wasilla: Sarah Palin's Pentacostal Supporters in Alaska Hail Her Debate Performance and Her Rise to the National Stage as the Work of God." *Salon.com* (October 3, 2008).

Erickson, Gregg. "Candidate Palin Has Character Problem." *Anchorage Daily News* (June 27, 2009).

Fabian, Jordan. "Key Republican: Palin Cost Us the Senate." *Hill* (November 8, 2010).

Fagan, Dan. "Sarah Palin has Become Mentally Unstable." *Alaska Standard* (July 9, 2009).

Fitzpatrick, Laura. "How Did Sarah Palin Write Her Memoir So Fast?" *Time* (October 7, 2009).

Foer, Franklin. "Welfare State." *New Republic* (May 6, 2002).

Forgey, Pat. "Legislators Blame Palin for Deteriorating Relationship." *Juneau Empire* (April 12, 2009).

Frank, Thomas. "Poor, Persecuted Sarah Palin." *Wall Street Journal* (July 15, 2009).

Fryer, Jane. "Sarah Palin, the 'Dragon Slayer of Political Correctness' and her Riotously Non-PC Supporters." *Daily Mail* (July 23, 2010).

Gawande, Atul. "Letting Go: What Should Medicine Do When It Can't Save Your Life?" *New Yorker* (August 2, 2010).

Gay, Timothy M. "Echoes of Fillmore and the GOP Know-Nothings." *Boston Globe* (November 10, 2008).

Gerson, Michael. "The GOP's Sarah Palin Problem." *Washington Post* (November 5, 2010).

———. "Why the Tea Party is Toxic for the GOP." *Washington Post* (August 25, 2010).

Gingrich, Newt, and Craig Shirley. "Republicans Need to Relearn Lessons of the Reagan Revolution." *Union Leader* (November 1, 2005).

Goldberg, Michelle. "Flirting Her Way to Victory." *Guardian* (October 3, 2008).

Goldenberg, Suzanne. "Sarah Palin Drops 2012 Presidency Hint with Staff Visit to Iowa." *Guardian.co.uk* (November 21, 2010).

Goode, Jo C. "Knowles Signs Sexual Assault Bill." *Frontiersman* (May 23, 2000).

Grann, David. "The Fall; John McCain's choices." *New Yorker* (November 17, 2008).

Grimaldi, James V., and Karl Vick. "Palin Billed State for Nights Spent at Home." *Washington Post* (September 9, 2008).

Gross, Michael Joseph. "Is Palin's Rise Part of God's Plan?" *Vanity Fair* (September 17, 2010).

———. "Sarah Palin the Sound and the Fury." *Vanity Fair* (October 2010).

———. "Sarah Palin's Shopping Spree: Yes, There's More . . ." *Vanity Fair* (September 1, 2010).

Hagan, Joe. "What Would a Maverick Do?" *New York Magazine* (July 11, 2010).

Halcro, Andrew. "A Costly Personal, Vindictive Palin Vendetta? You Betcha." *Anchorage Daily News* (October 18, 2008).

———. "The Frank Bailey Hangover: Is He Moving Out?" *AndrewHalcro.com* (November 30, 2008).

———. "Frank Bailey's Paid Vacation: The Cover Up." *AndrewHalcro.com* (August 20, 2008).

Halperin, Mark. "The Palin Pick: Bold or Disastrous?" *Time* (August 29, 2008).

———. "Attn. Media and Politicians: It's All About Palin." *Time.com* (September 20, 2010).

Hanson, Victor Davis. "Why the Elitist Hatred Toward Palin?" *Real Clear Politics* (July 10, 2009).

Harris, Lynn. "Sarah Palin and the Victims-Pay-for-Rape-Kits Story; One Way in which Wasilla, Alaska, is not Unique." *Salon.com* (September 10, 2008).

Haycox, Steve. "Palin's Anti-intellectualism Dangerous." *Anchorage Daily News* (November 27, 2009).

Heilemann, John. "The Sixty-Day War." *New York Magazine* (September 5, 2008).

———. "2012: How Sarah Barracuda Becomes President." *New York Magazine* (October 24, 2010).

———. "2012? You Betcha." *New York Magazine* (November 2, 2008).

Hendler, Clint. "Shades of Lipstick: Vintage Palin Press Umbrage from the Last Frontier." *Columbia Journalism Review* (September 22, 2008).

Hensley, William L. Iggiagruk. "In Alaska, Qiviters Never Win." *New York Times* (July 25, 2009).

Hess, Pamela. "The Secret Trials of Greta Van Susteren." *George* (November 2009).

Hickel, Wally. "Alaskans Can Rise Above Petty Politics, Hateful Acts." *Anchorage Daily News* (September 26, 2009).

———. "Note to Our Governors: Alaskans Come First." *Anchorage Daily News* (July 25, 2009).

Hillyer, Quin. "The Problem With Palin." *American Spectator* (April, 2010).

Hitt, Jack. "Is Sarah Palin Porn?" *Harper's Magazine Notebook* (June 30, 2010).

Holmes, Anna, and Rebecca Traister. "A Palin of Our Own." *New York Times* (August 28, 2010).

Hopkins, Kyle. "Governor: Knowles and Halcro Raise Doubts About Palin's Readiness." *Anchorage Daily News* (October 17, 2006).

Hoste, Richard. "The Goddess of Implicit Whiteness: A Review of *Going Rogue*." *Occidental Observer*. (November 25, 2009).

Huffington, Arianna. "Sarah Palin, "Mama Grizzlies," Carl Jung, and the Power of Archetypes." *Huffingtonpost.com* (August 1, 2010).

Isikoff, Michael. "Can He Stop 'Troopergate'?" *Newsweek* (September 16, 2008).

Jacobson, Mark. "Sarah Palin's Heaven." *New York Magazine* (October 12, 2008).

Jenkins, Paul. "Palin E-mails Still a Secret; What Are They Trying to Hide?" *Anchorage Daily News* (November 14, 2009).

Johnson, Rebecca. "An Alaskan Straight Shooter Is Determined to Fight Corruption." *Vogue* (February 2008).

Johnston, Levi. "Me and Mrs. Palin." *Vanity Fair* (October 2009).

Jonnson, Patrik. "Sarah Palin's Gun Imagery Takes Aim at Political Targets." *Christian Science Monitor* (March 27, 2010).

Kakutani, Michiko. "Playing Basketball, Playing Politics: Lessons From the Top Game Changer." *The New York Times* (June 2, 2009).

Kamiya, Gary. "The Poison of Celebrity." *Salon.com* (July 9, 2009).

Kilgore, Ed. "Gingrich v. Palin." *New Republic* (July 20, 2010).

Klein, Joe. "The American Myth: Sarah Palin appeals to nostalgia for a country that no longer exists. This year, it might be enough to win." *Time* (September 22, 2008).

Kranich, Nancy. "What's 'Daddy's Roommate' Doing in Wasilla?" *Nation* (September 18, 2008).

Kristol, William. "Fire the Campaign." *New York Times* (October 13, 2008).

———. "How to Pick a V.P." *New York Times* (August 4, 2008).

Kroll, Andy, and Daniel Schulman. "Sarah Palin's Mystery Research Firm." *Mother Jones* (November 22, 2010).

Kurtz, Rod. "What Do You Think of the Sarah Palin Brand?" *AOL Original* (October 4, 2010).

Labash, Matt. "R U Lovin' Sarah's Alaska: From Governor to TV Star." *Weekly Standard* (November 29, 2010).

Lauesen, Elstun. "Palin Enthusiastically Practices Socialism, Alaska-style." *Anchorage Daily News* (November 7, 2008).

Leahy, Michael. "Back Home in Alaska, Palin Finds Cold Comfort." *Washington Post* (February 18, 2009).

Lelyveld, Joseph. "John & Sarah in St. Paul." *New York Review of Books* (October 9, 2008).

Levin, Yuval. "The Meaning of Sarah Palin." *Commentary* (February 2009).

Levy, Ariel. "The Lonesome Trail." *New Yorker* (September 15, 2008).

Lilla, Mark. "The Tea Party Jacobins." *New York Review of Books* (May 27, 2010).

Lithwick, Dahlia. "Lost in Translation: Why Sarah Palin Really Quit Us." *Slate.com* (July 8, 2009).

Lizza, Ryan. "On The Bus." *New Yorker* (February 25, 2008).

Lucier, James P., Jr. "What Palin Really Did to the Oil Industry." *Wall Street Journal* (September 5, 2008).

Luo, Michael, "G.O.P. Paid Almost $55,000 for Palin Fashion Stylist." *New York Times* (December 5, 2008).

———. "Top Salary in McCain Camp? Palin's Makeup Stylist." *New York Times* (October 24, 2008).

MacGillis, Alec. "As Mayor of Wasilla, Palin Cut Own Duties, Left Trail of Bad Blood." *Washington Post* (September 14, 2008).

Mansour, R. A. "Who Is Sarah Palin?" *Conservatives4Palin.com* (March 14, 2009).

Martin, Jonathan. "Hurricane Sarah." *Politico* (October 21, 2010).

———. "Palin Camp Eyed Clinton Alliance." *Politico* (May 18, 2009).

———. "Palin Story Sparks GOP Family Feud." *Politico* (June 30, 2009).

Matthiessen, Peter. "Alaska: Big Oil and the Inupiat-Americans." *New York Review of Books* (November 22, 2007).

———. "Inside the Endangered Arctic Refuge." *New York Review of Books* (October 19, 2006).

Mauer, Richard. "Palin Explains Her Actions in Ruedrich Case." *Anchorage Daily News* (September 19, 2004).

Mauer, Richard, et al., "Questions Surround Palin's Background Check." *Anchorage Daily News* (September 2, 2008).

Mayer, Jane. "The Insiders: How John McCain Came to Pick Sarah Palin." *New Yorker* (October 27, 2008).

McGinniss, Joe. "Palin's Bus Hoax." *Daily Beast* (November 29, 2009).

———. "Pipe Dreams." *Condé Nast Portfolio* (April, 2009).

McGrath, Ben. "The Movement: The Rise of Tea Party Activism." *New Yorker* (February 1, 2010).

Mead, Rebecca. "Rage Machine: Andrew Breitbart's Empire of Bluster." *New Yorker* (May 24, 2010).

Medred, Craig. "Palin: Hunting Devils in the Details." *Outpost: AlaskaDispatch* (November 25, 2009).

————. "The 49th State gives Birth to a Cultural Warrior." *Outpost: AlaskaDispatch* (November 13, 2009).

Miller, Lisa. "Saint Sarah: What Palin's Appeal to Conservative Christian Women Says About Feminism and the Future of the Religious Right." *Newsweek* (June 21, 2010).

Murphy, Mike. "To Go Forward, GOP Must Snap Out of Its Sarah Palin Spell." *New York Daily News* (July 9, 2009).

Newton-Small, Jay. "Palin in Progress: What Does She Want?" *Time.com* (December 9, 2010).

Nichols, Capper. "Literature of the Last Frontier." *Utne Reader* (May/June 2006).

Noonan, Peggy. "A Farewell to Harms: Palin Was Bad for the Republicans—and the Republic." *Wall Street Journal* (July 10, 2009).

————. "Americans Vote For Maturity." *Wall Street Journal* (November 5, 2010).

————. "The Special Assistant for Reality: Obama Needs to Hear a Voice from Outside the Presidential Bubble." *Wall Street Journal* (November 26, 2010).

Palin, Sarah. "Commentary." *Anchorage Daily News* (December 17, 2004).

Parker, Kathleen. "Palin Problem: She's Out of Her League." *Washington Post* (September 26, 2008).

————. "Sarah Palin, From Pit Bull to Mama Grizzly." *Washington Post* (July 14, 2010).

Pollitt, Katha. "Sarah Palin, Affirmative Action Babe." *Nation* (September 24, 2008).

————. "Sayonara, Sarah." *Nation* (November 6, 2008).

Purdum, Todd S. "Prisoner of Conscience" *Vanity Fair* (February, 2007).

Purnell, Thomas, et al., "Defining Dialect, Perceiving Dialect, and New Dialect Formation: Sarah.

Sage. "Palin's Speech." *Sage* (November, 2009).

Quinn, Sally. "Palin's Peculiar Family Values." *Washington Post* (July 8, 2009).

Quinn, Steve. "New Stuyahok: The Governor Hopes to Address Alcoholism in the Yup'ik Village." *Anchorage Daily News* (December 30, 2006).

Raban, Jonathan. "Cut, Kill, Dig, Drill." *London Review of Books* (October 2008).

————. "Sarah and Her Tribe." *New York Review of Books* (January 14, 2010).

Reich, Robert. "Sour Economy Could Put Sarah Palin in the White House." *Christian Science Monitor—CSMonitor.com* (December 1, 2010).

Rich, Frank. "Could She Reach the Top in 2012? You Betcha." *New York Times* (November 29, 2010).

————. "She Broke the G.O.P. and Now She Owns It." *New York Times* (July 12, 2009).

———. "The Very Useful Idiocy of Christine O'Donnell." *New York Times* (October 2, 2010).

Robinson, Eugene. "A Starter, Not a Finisher." *Washington Post* (July 7, 2009).

Romano, Andrew. "McCain's Right-Hand Men." *Newsweek* (July 2, 2008).

Romano, Lois. "The Silver Bullet." *Washington Post* (August 21, 2008).

Rosen, Yereth. "Alaska Should Cut Risk of Natgas Pipeline—Sponsor." *Reuters* (November 19, 2009).

———. "In Alaska, Many Pine for the Old Palin." *Christian Science Monitor* (July 2, 2009).

Rosin, Hanna. "Is the Tea Party a Feminist Movement?" *Slate* (May 12, 2010).

Rubin, Jennifer. "Why Jews Hate Palin." *Commentary* (January, 2010).

Rutenberg, Jim, and Jackie Calmes. "False 'Death Panel' Rumor Has Some Familiar Roots." *The New York Times* (August 14, 2009).

Rutenberg, Jim, and Serge F. Kovaleski. "For Palin, a Long March to a Short-Notice Resignation." *The New York Times* (July 13, 2009).

Salam, Reihan. "Sarah, You Blew It." *Daily Beast* (April 16, 2009).

Scarborough, Joe. "GOP Should Take on Palin." *Politico* (November 30, 2010).

Schaller, Thomas. "How the Conservative Media Duped McCain." *Salon.com* (September 2, 2008).

Scheiber, Noam. "Barracuda: The Resentments of Sarah Palin." *New Republic* (October 22, 2008).

———. "How Cindy Hensley Invented John McCain . . ." *New Republic* (September 10, 2008).

Scherer, Michael. "Decoding the New, New John McCain." *Time.com* (July 12, 2010).

Scoblic, Peter. "An Astonishingly Arrogant V.P. Selection." *CBSNews.com* (August 29, 2008).

Shear, Michael D., et al., "Rivalries Split McCain's Team: After Months of Staff Fights, Rick Davis Emerges as the Leader of a Diminished Campaign." *Washington Post* (July 14, 2007).

Sherman, Gabriel. "The Revolution Will Be Commercialized." *New York* (May 3, 2010).

Simmons, Dan. "I'm a Runner: Sarah Palin." *Runner's World* (July 2009).

Spillius, Alex. "John McCain's 'Bullet' Leads the Assault on Barack Obama." *Telegraph* (August 1, 2008).

———. "Karl Rove Questions Sarah Palin's Suitability for President." *Telegraph.co.UK.* (October 27, 2010).

Suderman, Alan. "Palin Keeps Tight Grip on Records." *Juneau Empire* (November 17, 2008).

Sullivan, Andrew. "Beware the Powerful Fantasy World of Sarah Palin, Warrior Princess." *Sunday Times* (November 22, 2009).

———. "The Daily Dish: Sarah Palin and Magical Thinking." *andrewsullivan.theatlantic .com* (September 18, 2008).

———. "The Daily Dish.; The Odd Lies of Sarah Palin: A Round Up." *andrewsullivan .theatlantic.com* (July 7, 2009).

Taibbi, Matt. "The Lies of Sarah Palin." *Rolling Stone* (October 2, 2009).

Talbot, David. "I Fear for My Country." *Salon.com* (September 12, 2008).

———. "Mean Girl; Sarah Palin Has a Way of Using "Old Boys"—Then Dumping Them When They Become Inconvenient." *Salon.com* (September 23, 2008).

———. "The Pastor Who Clashed With Palin." *Salon.com* (September 15, 2008).

———. "Sarah Palin's Wasteful Ways." *Salon.com* (September 17, 2008).

Tanenhaus, Sam. "North Star: Populism, Politics, and the Power of Sarah Palin." *New Yorker* (December 7, 2009).

Toomey, Christine. "The Ice Queen." *Sunday Times Magazine* (October 26, 2008).

Townsend, Kathleen Kennedy. "Sarah Palin Is Wrong About John F. Kennedy, Religion and Politics." *Washington Post* (December 3, 2010).

Traister, Rebecca. "Sarah Palin's Feminist Revolution." *Salon.com* (September 13, 2010).

———. "Sarah Palin's Grab for Feminism." *Salon.com* (June 1, 2010).

———. "Sarah Palin: 'The Time for Choosin's Comin' Real Soon.'" *Salon.com* (October 31, 2008).

———. "Sarah Palin's Pity Party." *Salon.com* (September 30, 2008).

———. "Palin, Pregnancy and the Presidency." *Salon.com* (September 1, 2008).

———. "A Scary Halloween with Sarah Palin." *Salon.com* (November 1, 2008).

———. "Zombic Feminists of the RNC." *Salon.com* (September 11, 2008).

Turner, Frederick Jackson. "The Significance of the Frontier in American History 1893." Paper read at the Meeting of the American Historical Association; Chicago, Illinois; July 12, 1893.

Valenti, Jessica. "The Fake Feminism of Sarah Palin." *Washington Post* (May 30, 2010).

Vidal, Gore. "The Wizard of the 'Wizard.'" *New York Review of Books* (September 29, 1977).

Vogel, Kenneth P. "Palin's Cold Shoulder." *Politico* (September 5, 2008).

Walsh, Joan. "If Sarah Palin Falls in a Forest?" *salon.com* (October 16, 2010).

———. "When Elites Bash Elitism." *salon.com* (February 12, 2010).

————. "Why Is Palin Lying About State Ethics Probe?" *Salon.com* (July 10, 2009).

Walshe, Shushannah. "The Mama Grizzly Scorecard." *The Daily Beast* (November 3, 2010).

————. "Palin's Katie Couric Myths." *The Daily Beast* (November 18, 2009).

Weisberg, Jacob. "McCain's Burden: He Bears the Shame of Picking Sarah Palin." *Newsweek* (July 10, 2010).

Weisskopf, Michael, and Nathan Thornburgh. "Palin's *Pipeline* to Nowhere?" *Time* (October 2, 2008).

Wills, Garry. "A Country Ruled by Faith." *New York Review* (November 16, 2006).

Wills, Garry, et al. "A Fateful Election." *New York Review of Books* (November 6, 2006).

Winell, Marlene, PhD. "Sarah Palin, Warrior Princess for God." *Marlenewinell.net* (August 2008).

Wolf, Naomi. "Palin Biography Makes Waves." *New York Times* (November 21, 2009).

Wood, Daniel B. "'Toxic' Touch? Why Carly Fiorina and Meg Whitman Shy from Sarah Palin." *Christian Science Monitor* (October 8, 2010).

Wood, James. "Tocqueville in America: The Grand Journey, Retraced and Reimagined." *The New Yorker* (May 17, 2010).

WTVM News Leader 9. "Blackburn Qualifies for Georgia House of Representatives." *WTVM.com* (April 29, 2010).

Yardley, William. "For Alaska, a Remarkably Tumultuous Year." *New York Times* (July 19, 2009).

Yardley, William, and Michael Cooper. "Palin Calls Criticism by McCain Aides 'Cruel and Mean Spirited.'" *The New York Times* (November 8, 2008).

Zakaria, Fareed. "Palin Is Ready? Please." *Newsweek* (October 6, 2008).

INDEX